# THE CHANGING FACE OF FORM CRITICISM
*for the*
## TWENTY-FIRST CENTURY

# The Changing Face of Form Criticism for the Twenty-First Century

*Edited by*

Marvin A. Sweeney & Ehud Ben Zvi

WILLIAM B. EERDMANS PUBLISHING COMPANY
GRAND RAPIDS, MICHIGAN / CAMBRIDGE, U.K.

Wm. B. Eerdmans Publishing Co.
255 Jefferson Ave. S.E., Grand Rapids, Michigan 49503 /
P.O. Box 163, Cambridge CB3 9PU U.K.

Printed in the United States of America

08  07  06  05  04  03      7  6  5  4  3  2  1


**Library of Congress Cataloging-in-Publication Data**

The changing face of form criticism for the twenty-first century /
edited by Marvin A. Sweeney & Ehud Ben Zvi.
p.        cm.
Includes bibliographical references and index.
ISBN  0-8028-6067-2 (pbk.: alk. paper)
1. Bible — Criticism, Form.
I. Sweeney, Marvin A. (Marvin Alan), 1953-
II. Ben Zvi, Ehud, 1951-


BS521.5.C48    2003
220.6′63′01 — dc21

2003044890

www.eerdmans.com

# Contents

# CONTENTS

# Contents

# Introduction

## MARVIN A. SWEENEY AND EHUD BEN ZVI

From its inception over a century ago, form criticism (*Formgeschichte* or *Gattungsgeschichte*) has functioned as one of the fundamental exegetical methods in the field of biblical studies.[1] Throughout most of the twentieth century, it has been conceived as an inherently historical or diachronic discipline that focuses on the identification and analysis of typical patterns of language that appear and function within and give shape and expression to the overall form of a text. Standard aspects of form-critical exegesis include an analysis of the individual form or structure of a text, the identification of its genres or typical features of expression, the societal function or setting of both the form and the genre of the text, and the application of these aspects to the overall reading and interpretation of the text in question.

---

1. For overviews of the development of form-critical method, see Klaus Koch, *The Growth of the Biblical Tradition: The Form-Critical Method* (trans. S. M. Cupitt; New York: Scribner's Sons, 1969); idem, *Was ist Formgeschichte? Methoden der Bibelexegese* (3d ed.; Neukirchen-Vluyn: Neukirchener Verlag, 1974); Gene M. Tucker, *Form Criticism of the Old Testament* (GBS; Philadelphia: Fortress, 1971); Wolfgang Richter, *Exegese als Literaturwissenschaft: Entwurf einer alttestamentlichen Literaturtheorie und Methodologie* (Göttingen: Vandenhoeck & Ruprecht, 1971); Rolf Knierim, "Old Testament Form Criticism Reconsidered," *Int* 27 (1973): 435-68; idem, "Criticism of Literary Features, Form, Tradition, and Redaction," in *The Hebrew Bible and Its Modern Interpreters* (ed. D. A. Knight and G. M. Tucker; Chico, Calif.: Scholars Press, 1985), 123-65; John H. Hayes, ed., *Old Testament Form Criticism* (TUMSR 2; San Antonio: Trinity Univ. Press, 1974); Harald Schweizer, *Metaphorische Grammatik: Wege zur Integration von Grammatik und Textinterpretation in der Exegese* (ATSAT 15; St. Ottilien: EOS, 1981); Martin Buss, *Biblical Form Criticism in Its Context* (JSOTSup 274; Sheffield: Sheffield Academic Press, 1999); Marvin A. Sweeney, "Form Criticism," in *To Each Its Own Meaning: Biblical Criticisms and Their Application* (ed. S. L. McKenzie and S. R. Haynes; Louisville: Westminster John Knox, 1999), 58-89.

Form-critical exegesis has evolved substantially throughout the past century. It started, at least in part, as a reaction to the "literary" approach best exemplified by the work of Julius Wellhausen, which was at the time prevalent in academic circles. At the outset, form-critical exegesis was also influenced by romanticism and the related lionization of oral texts. Hermann Gunkel, the founder of form-critical methodology, focused especially on the analysis of short, self-contained literary units, including historical legends, prophetic oracular speeches, and individual psalm types, as the basis for the reconstruction of the originally oral speech forms that were employed in various settings in ancient Israelite society.[2] Second-generation form critics, such as his students Albrecht Alt and Sigmund Mowinckel, continued their mentor's work with, respectively, analyses of the forms, settings, and functions of legal language that pointed to the evolution of Israelite law from its Canaanite antecedents, and comprehensive studies of the hymnic literature that pointed to the cultic matrix in which individual psalms and prophetic texts developed and functioned.[3] Third-generation form critics, such as Gerhard von Rad and Martin Noth, began to examine larger literary units, such as the Hexateuch and the Deuteronomistic History, in an effort to trace the later growth of earlier traditions and theological reflection on them.[4] Claus Westermann has emphasized the identification of the typical forms of prophetic speech and cultic poetry, particularly the prophetic judgment speech and the lament, in an effort to gain insight concerning the social roles of the prophets and cultic singers in Israelite society and thought.[5]

These early stages in the development of form-critical theory were heavily influenced by diachronic considerations, particularly the questions of the relationship of the text to the sociohistorical setting in which it was

---

2. See esp. Gunkel, *Das Märchen im Alten Testament* (Tübingen: Mohr, 1917); idem, "Israelite Prophecy from the Time of Amos," in *Twentieth Century Theology in the Making*, vol. 1, *Themes of Biblical Theology* (ed. J. Pelikan; New York: Harper & Row, 1969), 48-75; idem with J. Begrich, *Einleitung in die Psalmen* (Göttingen: Vandenhoeck & Ruprecht, 1933).

3. Albrecht Alt, "The Origins of Israelite Law," in *Essays on Old Testament History and Religion* (trans. R. A. Wilson; Garden City, N.Y.: Doubleday, 1967), 1-100; Sigmund Mowinckel, *Psalmenstudien I-VI* (Kristiana: Dybwad, 1921-24); idem, *The Psalms in Israel's Worship* (trans. D. R. Ap-Thomas; 2 vols.; Nashville: Abingdon, 1962).

4. Gerhard von Rad, "The Form-Critical Problem of the Hextateuch," in *The Problem of the Hexateuch and Other Essays* (trans. E. W. Trueman Dicken; 1966; repr. London: SCM, 1984), 1-78; Martin Noth, *The Deuteronomistic History* (JSOTSup 15: Sheffield: JSOT Press, 1981).

5. *Basic Forms of Prophetic Speech* (trans. H. C. White; 1967; repr. Louisville: Westminster John Knox, 1991); idem, *Praise and Lament in the Psalms* (trans. K. Crim and R. N. Soulen; Atlanta: John Knox, 1981).

produced and the subsequent growth and development of a text in both its oral and written forms. But from the mid-1960s on form criticism has been heavily influenced by the emergence of newer critical methodologies that have pointed increasingly to synchronic literary concerns. James Muilenburg's call for rhetorical criticism has prompted much greater attention to larger literary units and the interrelationship between texts, whether oral or written, and their audiences.[6] The emergence of text linguistics and semiotics has prompted form critics, such as Wolfgang Richter and Klaus Koch, to examine the roles of syntax and semantic meaning in the overall form of a text and to consider a text in relation to both its societal setting *(Sitz im Leben)* and its literary setting *(Sitz in der Literatur)*.[7] The study of structural anthropology has prompted Rolf Knierim to examine the impact of cultural and linguistic presuppositions in the formulation of a text and its underlying concepts.[8] New studies of oral poetry and its influence in textual formation have prompted the research of George Coats and Michael Floyd.[9] Intertextual studies have caused scholars to reconsider the role of the written text and its interaction with other biblical traditions as indicated in the work of Michael Fishbane, Patricia Tull Willey, and Hyun Chul Paul Kim.[10] In the work of Roy Melugin, reader-response criticism has emphasized the reception and interpretation of a text by its reading audiences.[11] Ehud Ben Zvi in particular has emphasized the character of prophetic books as literature that

6. James Muilenburg, "Form Criticism and Beyond," *JBL* 88 (1969): 1-18; see also Phyllis Trible, *Rhetorical Criticism: Context, Method, and the Book of Jonah* (Minneapolis: Fortress, 1994); Patricia K. Tull, "Rhetorical Criticism," in *To Each Its Own Meaning*, ed. McKenzie and Haynes, 156-80.

7. Richter, *Exegese als Literaturwissenschaft*; Koch, *Was ist Formgeschichte?* esp. 289-342. See also Schweizer, *Metaphorische Grammatik*.

8. See esp. "Old Testament Form Criticism Reconsidered"; idem, *Text and Concept in Leviticus 1:1-9* (FAT 2; Tübingen: Mohr [Siebeck], 1992).

9. George W. Coats, *Genesis, with an Introduction to Narrative Literature* (FOTL 1; Grand Rapids: Eerdmans, 1983); idem, *Saga, Legend, Tale, Novella, Fable: Narrative Forms in Old Testament Literature* (JSOTSup 35; Sheffield: JSOT Press, 1986); Michael H. Floyd, "Oral Tradition as a Problematic Factor in the Historical Interpretation of Poems in the Law and the Prophets" (Ph.D. diss.; Claremont Graduate School, 1980).

10. Michael Fishbane, *Biblical Interpretation in Ancient Israel* (Oxford: Oxford Univ. Press, 1985); Tull, "Rhetorical Criticism"; Patricia Tull Willey, *Remember the Former Things: The Recollection of Previous Texts in Second Isaiah* (SBLDS 161; Atlanta: Scholars Press, 1997); Hyun Chul Paul Kim, "An Intertextual Reading of 'A Crushed Reed' and 'A Dim Wick' in Isaiah 42.3," *JSOT* 83 (1999): 113-24.

11. Roy Melugin, "The Book of Isaiah and the Construction of Meaning," in *Reading and Writing the Scroll of Isaiah: Studies of an Interpretive Tradition* (ed. C. C. Broyles and C. A. Evans; 2 vols.; VTSup 70; Leiden: Brill, 1997), 1:39-55.

is read and reread by its primary readership and over the course of many centuries in changing sociohistorical contexts.[12] The interrelationship between synchronic literary structure and diachronic models of redactional composition is a fundamental concern in the work of Marvin Sweeney on both the Deuteronomistic History and the prophetic literature.[13] Indeed, the interaction of diachronic and synchronic considerations in the interpretation of the present form of biblical compositions has taken more and more a central place in contemporary research. It informs, among others, recent work on the Pentateuch by Erhard Blum, Sue Boorer, Antony Campbell, Won Lee, and Rolf Rendtorff;[14] the Deuteronomistic History by Bob Becking, Antony Campbell, Mark O'Brien, and Thomas Römer;[15] the prophetic books by Bob Becking, Martin Buss, Roy Melugin, Martti Nissinen, Margaret Odell, and David Petersen;[16] the wisdom literature by Tremper

---

12. *Signs of Jonah: Reading and Rereading in Ancient Yehud* (JSOTSup 367; Sheffield: Sheffield Academic Press/Continuum, forthcoming 2003); idem, *Micah* (FOTL 21B; Grand Rapids: Eerdmans, 2000); idem, *A Historical-Critical Study of the Book of Obadiah* (BZAW 242; Berlin and New York: de Gruyter, 1996); idem, *A Historical-Critical Study of the Book of Zephaniah* (BZAW 198; Berlin and New York: de Gruyter, 1991).

13. *King Josiah of Judah: The Lost Messiah of Israel* (New York: Oxford Univ. Press, 2001); idem, *The Twelve Prophets* (Berit Olam; Collegeville, Minn.: Liturgical Press, 2000); idem, *Isaiah 1–39, with an Introduction to Prophetic Literature* (FOTL 16; Grand Rapids: Eerdmans, 1996); idem, "Formation and Form in Prophetic Literature," in *Old Testament Interpretation: Past, Present, and Future* (ed. J. L. Mays et al.; Nashville: Abingdon, 1995), 113-43.

14. Erhard Blum, *Die Komposition der Vätergeschichte* (WMANT 57; Neukirchen-Vluyn: Neukirchener Verlag, 1984); idem, *Studien zur Komposition des Pentateuch* (BZAW 189; Berlin and New York: de Gruyter, 1990); Suzanne Boorer, *The Promise of the Land as Oath: A Key to the Formation of the Pentateuch* (BZAW 205; Berlin and New York: de Gruyter, 1992); Antony Campbell and Mark O'Brien, *Sources of the Pentateuch: Texts, Introduction, Annotations* (Minneapolis: Fortress, 1993); Won W. Lee, "Punishment and Forgiveness in Israel's Migratory Campaign: The Macrostructure of Numbers 10:11–36:13" (Ph.D. diss.; Claremont Graduate University, 1998); Rolf Rendtorff, *The Problem of the Process of Transmission in the Pentateuch* (JSOTSup 89; Sheffield: JSOT Press, 1990).

15. Bob Becking, "No More Grapes from the Vineyard? A Plea for a Historical Critical Approach in the Study of the Old Testament," *Congress Volume: Oslo 1998* (VTSup 80; ed. A. Lemaire and M. Sæbø; Leiden: Brill, 2000), 123-41; idem, *The Fall of Samaria: An Historical and Archaeological Study* (SHANE 2; Leiden: Brill, 1992); Antony Campbell and Mark O'Brien, *Unfolding the Deuteronomistic History: Origins, Upgrades, Present Text* (Minneapolis: Fortress, 2000); Mark O'Brien, *The Deuteronomistic History Hypothesis: A Reassessment* (OBO 92; Freiburg: Universitätsverlag; Göttingen: Vandenhoeck & Ruprecht, 1989); Thomas Römer, *Untersuchungen zur Väterthematik im Deuteronomium und in der deuteronomistischen Tradition* (OBO 99; Freiburg: Universitätsverlag; Göttingen: Vandenhoeck & Ruprecht, 1990).

16. Bob Becking, "The Times They Are A Changing: An Interpretation of Jeremiah

Longman and Raymond Van Leeuwen;[17] and even the Septuagint by Martin Rösel.[18]

At the end of the twentieth century, form criticism has changed markedly. Its tent now includes a variety of approaches that are seen at times as complementary, and at times as incompatible with one another. Form-critical approaches are concerned at present with the analysis of large and small literary units, the interrelationship between text and audience (both ancient and modern), the oral and written character of texts, the impact of cultural setting in relation to both the formulation of texts and their reception, and texts as an expression of language systems. They advance synchronic and diachronic literary analyses as well as studies of the interrelationships between text and language, text and society (and social structures), text and culture, text and audience, and texts and other texts. This is a time bubbling with activity in form-critical studies, of emerging patterns of substantial methodological change and conceptual reshaping of what form criticism either is or should be about. It is therefore an opportune time to reexamine form-critical methodology and to consider its conceptualization and potential for future research.

It was with this end in mind that the editors of the present volume organized a special two-part session at the 2000 Annual Meeting of the Society of Biblical Literature held November 18-21 in Nashville, Tennessee, on "The Changing Face of Form Criticism in Hebrew Bible Studies." One of the sessions was a joint session of three SBL program units, the Pentateuch Section, the Deuteronomistic History Section, and the Consultation on Prophetic Texts and Their Ancient Contexts (hereafter, PTAC). The other one was a PTAC session cosponsored by the other program units. Eleven papers were originally presented at the Nashville sessions. From the discussion generated by the papers presented at the sessions, the editors concluded that publication

---

30:12-17," *SJOT* 12 (1998): 3-25; idem, "Divine Wrath and the Conceptual Coherence of the Book of Nahum," *SJOT* 9 (1995): 277-96; Martin Buss, *The Prophetic Word of Hosea* (BZAW 111; Berlin: Töpelmann, 1969); Martti Nissinen, *Prophetie, Redaktion und Fortschreibung im Hoseabuch* (AOAT 231; Kevelaer: Butzon und Bercker; Neukirchen-Vluyn: Neukirchener Verlag, 1991); Roy F. Melugin, *The Formation of Isaiah 40–55* (BZAW 141; Berlin and New York: de Gruyter, 1976); Margaret Odell, "You Are What You Eat: Ezekiel and the Scroll," *JBL* 117 (1998): 229-48; David L. Petersen, *The Prophetic Literature: An Introduction* (Louisville: Westminster John Knox, 2002).

17. Tremper Longman III, *The Book of Ecclesiastes* (NICOT; Grand Rapids and Cambridge: Eerdmans, 1998); Raymond Van Leeuwen, *Context and Meaning in Proverbs 25–27* (SBLDS 96; Atlanta: Scholars Press, 1988).

18. Martin Rösel, *Übersetzung als Vollendung der Auslegung: Studien zur Genesis-Septuaginta* (BZAW 223; Berlin and New York: de Gruyter, 1994).

of a volume of essays, based on the papers presented at the session and others that were subsequently invited, would facilitate even more discussion and methodological reflection that would contribute to the field of biblical studies as a whole. The result is the present volume of essays that take up various dimensions of form-critical theory in relation to the current methodological ferment.

The first section includes five papers devoted to general theoretical reflection on form-critical method. Antony F. Campbell, S.J., "Form Criticism's Future," analyzes the past of form-critical theory, its essential insights, and its potential for the future. He maintains that, in contrast to past scholarship's aversion to the present text, form criticism is essentially concerned with assessing the nature of a literary work as a whole and the means by which its parts function together within the whole to communicate its message. Form criticism has a future — if its past is allowed a decent burial. Erhard Blum, "*Formgeschichte* — A Misleading Category? Some Critical Remarks," observes the problematic nature of form criticism in that some very distinct questions are subsumed under the concept, such as the definition of genres, the compositional history of a text, its content, and its esthetics. The resulting lack of methodological clarity raises the question whether one can speak of a form-critical method at all. Roy F. Melugin, "Recent Form Criticism Revisited," employs insights from rhetorical criticism, esthetics, and reader-response theory to call for greater attention to the interrelationship between the typical and the unique in the form-critical assessment of language and to raise questions concerning form criticism's role in the reconstruction of sociohistorical settings. Raymond C. Van Leeuwen, "Form Criticism, Wisdom, and Psalms 111–112," raises questions concerning the identification of wisdom as a discrete genre in biblical literature, insofar as its forms and settings of expression vary so widely. He argues instead that wisdom should be recognized as a worldview or culturally specific way of thinking about and acting within reality that transcends class and professional distinctions. Hyun Chul (Paul) Kim, "Form Criticism in Dialogue with Other Criticisms: Building the Multidimensional Structures of Texts and Concepts," places form criticism in dialogue with other critical methodologies, such as text criticism, rhetorical criticism, redaction criticism, canonical criticism, literary criticism, sociology, reader-response criticism, intertextuality, archeology, and comparative studies in an effort to point to the multiplicity of understandings inherent in study of the structure, genre, and setting of Joel 2.

The second section includes four papers that address form-critical questions on the interrelationship between biblical and ancient Near Eastern texts. Martin Rösel, "Inscriptional Evidence and the Question of Genre," attempts to demonstrate the results that may be gained from the application of form-critical theory to the study of inscriptional material from ancient Israel and its surrounding cultures. Most notably, he demonstrates that inscriptional texts exhibit far greater fluidity in the use of generic elements known from the Bible, which raises questions concerning the long-held form-critical assumption that originally oral forms of texts were incorporated without substantive change into the present forms of biblical literature. Martti Nissinen, "Fear Not: A Study on an Ancient Near Eastern Phrase," examines the use of the formula "fear not!" in Mesopotamian texts in an effort to demonstrate that it functions in relation to a variety of social settings that include private, royal, and divine discourse. The formula cannot therefore be restricted to the setting of oracular speech. Margaret Odell, "Ezekiel Saw What He Said He Saw: Genres, Forms, and the Vision of Ezekiel 1," reexamines the narrative concerning Ezekiel's inaugural visions in Ezekiel 1 in relation to Assyrian royal building inscriptions and their associated reliefs. She thereby points to the need to consider the imagery of the Assyrian throne room as the matrix that informs Ezekiel's depiction of divine glory. Tremper Longman III, "Israelite Genres in Their Ancient Near Eastern Context," employs comparative Near Eastern literature in an effort to develop a communicative-semiotic approach to genre that points to the communicative functions of genre, the expectations of its readers, and the coercion of authors to conform to genre expectations. He illustrates these insights with a comparative treatment of Akkadian autobiography in relation to Qohelet's character as fictional autobiography.

The third major section includes four papers on the narrative literature of the Hebrew Bible. Sue Boorer, "Kaleidoscope Patterns and the Shaping of Experience," examines the interrelationship between form criticism and reader-response criticism in an effort to demonstrate that form criticism operates within reader-response criticism. On the basis of her study of narratives concerning the failure of the Mosaic generation to enter the promised land (Numbers 13–14; 32:7-15; Deut 1:22–2:1), she argues that the text's relationship to life setting and function are transformed insofar as the interaction between text and reader calls for the reader to interpret the perceived world of the text rather than an original life setting or experience. Won Lee, "The Exclusion of Moses from the Promised Land: A Conceptual Approach," emphasizes a conceptual form-critical approach that treats texts in their individuality. His study of texts in Numbers and Deuteronomy pertaining to Moses' (and Aaron's) exclusion from the promised land challenges past attempts to read these texts monolithically by pointing to their individual concerns; that is, the Priestly traditions in Numbers emphasize Moses' and Aaron's role as representatives of God to the people, and the Deuteronomic texts emphasize their role in guiding the people. Thomas Römer, "The Form-Critical Problem of the So-Called Deuteronomistic History," questions the long-standing form-critical assumption that identification of a literary form provides a key for the recovery of the social setting from which it comes, as part of a larger effort to question the identification of a unified Deuteronomistic History, which comprises many distinct and diverse forms. Bob Becking, "Nehemiah 9 and the Problematic Concept of Context *(Sitz im Leben),*" reconsiders the so-called penitential prayer in Nehemiah in an effort to reexamine Gunkel's link between form and context, that is, *Gattung,* "genre," and *Sitz im Leben,* "life setting," and the corresponding assumption that form reflects the socio-historical realities of ancient Israel.

The fourth section includes six papers on various aspects of the prophetic literature. David L. Petersen, "The Basic Forms of Prophetic Literature," revisits Claus Westermann's classic *Basic Forms of Prophetic Speech,* in an effort to challenge the prevailing assumption of his time that the prophets were fundamentally orators and that their literature reflected the oral character of their speeches. Instead, his examination of typical prophetic roles and activities points to the production of prophetic literature as a fundamental form of prophetic expression. Ehud Ben Zvi, "The Prophetic Book: A Key Form of Prophetic Literature," advances the study of prophetic texts with an attempt to define the prophetic book as the fundamental genre of prophetic literature, which includes typical elements of structure, setting, and intention. Michael H. Floyd, "Basic Trends in the Form-Critical Study of Prophetic Texts," likewise focuses on the form-critical study of the genre of prophetic book as a necessary consequence of the recognition that prophetic literature appears not in the form of transcribed original oral speech acts, but in the form of a specific type of narrative literature, which displays its own rhetorical patterns and presupposes the settings and concerns of their much later redactors. Martin J. Buss, "Toward Form Criticism as an Explication of Human Life: Divine Speech as a Form of Self-Transcendence," challenges interpreters to step outside their normal contexts within Judaism and Christianity and their preoccupation with fixed or particularist assumptions concerning the reality and constancy of God and the self so that they might consider alternative dynamics in the prophetic perception and articulation of the divine. A comparison with the dynamics of self-transcendence in Buddhism, for example, demonstrates an alternative understanding of human experience of the divine that might profitably inform form-critical assessment of prophecy. Patricia K. Tull, "Rhetorical Criticism and Beyond in Second Isaiah," addresses the interrelationship between form criticism and rhetorical criticism with a study of Isa 51:9-10 that points to the necessity to consider both its typical and its unique elements of expression. Marvin A. Sweeney, "Zechariah's Debate with Isaiah," employs a combination of synchronic structural analysis of the present form of the book of Zechariah, intertextual references within Zechariah to Isaiah, and readings of Zechariah in rabbinic literature and the medieval interpreters to argue that the book of Zechariah is constructed as a means to challenge Isaiah's premise that Jews must accept Persian rule as part of YHWH's new world order.

Altogether, the essays in the present volume point to the continuing dynamism and vitality of form-critical theory or theories as critical tools for the interpretation of biblical and cognate texts. At the same time, they demonstrate that form-critical methodology must continue to evolve as a result of its conversation with other critical methodologies that are employed in biblical exegesis. Form-critical studies build on the advances of past theoreticians, but by necessity they incorporate and will continue to incorporate the advances of present and future methodological reflection. Thus form-critical methodologies will remain for any foreseen future as "work in progress."

Although no one can predict the evolution of form criticism in the next century, on the basis of the present situation some basic trends seem clear. Form-critical studies will no longer limit themselves to the presumed originally short, self-contained oral forms of expression that were presupposed throughout much of the twentieth century. Form-critical scholars will continue to study the role of smaller literary units. They will approach them either (a) in a more or less traditional way, namely as reflections of older texts and sources; or (b) as interwoven and partially fluid textual units within the book that are created through the interaction of (ancient and modern) readers and texts and at least in part influenced by textually inscribed markers; or (c) in a way that combines both (i.e., synchronically and diachronically).

Many, if not most, form-critical scholars will engage fully the literary dimensions of texts. These dimensions include the larger literary patterns that unite the smaller units that comprise larger literary compositions, such as historical works or prophetic books; their interrelationships with other literary works, whether by citation, imitation, or debate; and their aesthetics or artistic dimensions that contribute to the expression of ideas.

Form-critical studies will no longer concern themselves only or mainly with the typical features of language and text. Rhetorical criticism and communication theory have amply demonstrated that the communicative and persuasive functions of texts depend on the unique as well as the typical. Moreover, in considering the rhetorical or communicative aspects of texts, form-critical scholars will no longer presume that genres are static or ideal entities that never change. Rather, they will recognize the inherent fluidity of genres, the fact that they are historically, culturally, and discursively dependent, and they will study the means by which genres are transformed to meet the needs of the particular communicative situation of the text. Studies on genre will include more and more the study of defamiliarizations of genre.

Many, if not most, form-critical scholars will no longer restrict themselves to the presumed authors of texts or the reconstructions of their presumed sociohistorical settings and intentions. Texts are indeed composed by authors, whose outlooks and techniques are influenced by their respective sociohistorical contexts. Nevertheless, the hypothetical nature of such reconstructions has undermined confidence in the ability of modern scholars to carry out such work with precision. Despite these difficulties, many form-critical researchers will continue their efforts at reconstruction, but there will be a more candid recognition of the tentative nature of such argumentation; that is, they will realize that they put forward theories, not assured facts.

Form-critical scholars will come to terms with the perspectives of reader-response criticism, which demonstrates the fundamental role of the reader and the reader's or readers' own sociohistorical or literary contexts in the construction of the text that is read and reread. There will be an increase in the number of form-critical scholars who focus on the readership (or more precisely, rereaderships) of the ancient texts. These scholars will maintain a clearly methodological distinction between the speakers and addressees in the world of the text — which may be fluid and may create a multiplicity of interactions on rapidly shifting "social settings" created by and within the world of the text — on the one hand, and the readerships and the implied authors/communicators that they created through their historically and socially dependent rereadings of the text. They will point at the multiplicity of potential readings (not only at the purely semantic, but also at the structural, level) of a single text even within the particular sociohistorical location and discourse, and the way in which these different readings may interact with one another. The more historically oriented among these scholars will continue to study the possible relation among intended, ideal, and actual readerships of texts, as they aim at reconstructing the social circumstances within which texts were written, edited, copied, read, reread, and read to those who were unable to read, that is, the vast majority of the population.

Finally, studies of literature in other religious or cultural contexts and historical periods have much to offer, both in terms of comparative examples and in terms of supplying hermeneutical models for interpretation, even though such literature and its contexts have barely been tapped. The world of the Bible and the ancient Near East or the later worlds of Judaism and Christianity will not be the only realities that must be considered.

To a certain extent, the old, traditional form criticism is making and will continue to make way for the new form-critical approaches, as the older conceptualizations of the method accommodate the newer insights. Such a model hardly means the death of the form-critical method. Instead, it points to its vitality and the transformations that a "living" methodology has to endure to remain alive and to continue to develop. The old "face" of form criticism is disappearing; in its place a number of related "faces" are beginning to take shape. It is our hope that the essays in this volume will provide some sense of the shape these faces may take.

PART I

# THEORETICAL REFLECTION

# Form Criticism's Future

## ANTONY F. CAMPBELL, S.J.

Form criticism had a meteoric rise in the early part of the twentieth century and fell from favor toward its end. For some the future of form criticism is not an issue: it has none. But if form criticism embodies an essential insight, it will continue. If it is to continue in the reflective and thinking world of academic scholarship, the attraction that triggered its rise, the flaws that caused its fall, and the aspects that assure its future all need to be analyzed. Thus this essay has three parts: the past — the rise and fall of form criticism; the essentials — form criticism's insight; the future — form criticism's changing face.

To read the pioneers of form criticism is to be left with little doubt that their enthusiasm for the new approach was fueled in part by their aversion to the excesses of source-critical (in those days, literary-critical) research and in part, too, by a less explicit resistance to claims for the historicity of the Bible's earlier traditions.[1] There is both an irony and a rightness in the recognition that it has been the excesses of both source-critical and form-critical claims

---

1. See Hugo Gressmann's comment on *Literarkritik:* "In our field we need not more but less literary-critical research. Literary criticism *(Literarkritik)* has generally exhausted the tasks that it had to and was able to do" ("Die Aufgaben der alttestamentlichen Forschung," *ZAW* 42 [1924]: 8).

Both concerns come together in Klaus Koch's comment in the context of historicity. The study of the transmission of a tradition "is of particular significance for the early history of Israel, i.e. before 1000 B.C. It was naive of the literary critics . . . to translate as they did the accounts of the early history of Israel . . . directly into events. First of all it is essential to make a form-critical assessment of the changes which the pre-literary traditions will have undergone" (*The Growth of the Biblical Tradition: The Form-Critical Method* [trans. S. M. Cupitt; New York: Scribner's Sons, 1969], 54).

coupled with the demands of interests in other areas that relegated so-called historical criticism to the backburner of biblical publication.

Highly competent and intelligent scholars, at the top of their field, do not usually embrace the new solely out of aversion to the old. An insight and a value are seen in the new that lead to its embrace. If form criticism, which once was new, is to regain a place in the panoply of the interpretive arts, it needs to be refocused on the lasting insight and value that once contributed to firing enthusiasm for it. Two concerns embody this insight and give it its value: concern for the nature of a text and concern for its shape or structure. If the incrustations can be scraped away, the good stuff may still be there. A couple of the areas of incrustation are certainly the passion for the preliterary past of stories and the condescension — at times almost contempt — felt on occasion for the storytellers, audiences, and even the later writers of ancient Israel.

In this present time we seem to have two options: either to go back or to go beyond. The move beyond has been well under way for some time. A fresh grasp of form criticism may help it find its place in that move. We cannot go back. It would be as if scientists decided quantum mechanics was just too complicated and uncertain and it would be surer to go back to Newtonian physics or, better still, to flat-earth theory. After all, flat-earth theory is quite accurate within a radius of ten to fifteen miles. The only difficulty with flat-earth theory is that it is wrong — shown so by observation, such as global travel. An uncertain literalist could go back to the biblical text as a unity with a single author; it works all right for a while. The only difficulty is that it is wrong — shown so by observation, such as a couple of centuries of scholarship or any close reading today.

Thus insight has to go forward. It will help to recognize that much twentieth-century biblical research was burdened with holdovers from the nineteenth century: an obsession with the recovery and reconstruction of history, a conviction about progressive stages of development, and an often constipated view of religion. Form criticism contributed its share to this malaise. The literary forms would reveal origins and show progressive stages of development. The settings in life of the forms would be of value in the historical reconstruction of ancient Israel's institutions and literature. An understanding of form would give genuine insight into the religious feeling and life of Israel.

## The Past: The Rise and Fall of Form Criticism

The beginnings of the modern phenomenon of biblical form criticism go back to the figure of Hermann Gunkel and a relatively small group of those stimulated by him. For the Newer Testament, the names and dates are Martin Dibelius (1919), Karl Ludwig Schmidt (1919), and Rudolf Bultmann (1921) — all three sat at Gunkel's feet in Berlin (1894-1907); but that is another story and it will not be told here. For the Older Testament, Gunkel's form-critical insights began with his commentary on Genesis (1901), were developed in his commentary on the Psalms (1929), and culminated in his introduction to the Psalms (published posthumously in 1933).[2] Work on the Psalms was taken further by his pupil, Sigmund Mowinckel;[3] the implications for law, prophecy, and wisdom followed in due course. For narrative text, Gunkel's close friend Hugo Gressmann moved beyond Genesis, first with a commentary on most of Samuel–Kings (also Amos and Hosea) and then with his study on the figure of Moses (reflecting Exodus and Numbers).[4]

The early pages of Gunkel's introduction to Genesis witness to a need for freedom from the oppressive weight of the concern for history. For example: "The evangelical church . . . would do well not to oppose — as has so often happened — this recognition that Genesis contains stories."[5] From the

---

2. Hermann Gunkel, *Genesis* (8th ed.; Göttingen: Vandenhoeck & Ruprecht, 1969; 1st ed., 1901); idem, *Die Psalmen* (5th ed.; Göttingen: Vandenhoeck & Ruprecht, 1968; 1st ed., 1929); idem, *Einleitung in die Psalmen* (completed by J. Begrich; 2d ed.; Göttingen: Vandenhoeck & Ruprecht, 1966; 1st ed., 1933). The mention of these three books is, of course, far from exhaustive of Gunkel's output.

3. Sigmund Mowinckel, *The Psalms in Israel's Worship* (trans. D. R. Ap-Thomas; 2 vols.; Oxford: Blackwell; Nashville: Abingdon, 1962; Norwegian original, 1951). Mowinckel acknowledges his debt to Gunkel, his teacher in Giessen; his own move beyond Gunkel began with the *Psalmenstudien I-VI* (Oslo: Dybwad, 1921-24). For a summary overview of OT form criticism, see John Barton, *ABD* 2:838-41; for form criticism and narrative, see Jay A. Wilcoxen, "Narrative," in *Old Testament Form Criticism* (ed. J. H. Hayes; TUMSR 2; San Antonio: Trinity Univ. Press, 1974), 57-98. For background to Gunkel's life and scholarship, see the tribute by Walter Baumgartner, "Zum 100. Geburtstag von Hermann Gunkel," in *Congress Volume: Bonn 1962* (VTSup 9; Leiden: Brill, 1963), 1-18 (repr. in Gunkel's *Genesis* [6th and later editions]); as well as Werner Klatt, *Hermann Gunkel: Zu seiner Theologie der Religionsgeschichte und zur Entstehung der formgeschichtlichen Methode* (FRLANT 100; Göttingen: Vandenhoeck & Ruprecht, 1969).

4. Hugo Gressmann, *Die Schriften des Alten Testaments in Auswahl neu übersetzt und für die Gegenwart erklärt von Hermann Gunkel, W. Staerk, Paul Volz, Hugo Gressmann, Hans Schmidt und M. Haller,* part 2, vol. 1: *Die älteste Geschichtschreibung und Prophetie Israels (von Samuel bis Amos und Hosea)* (2d rev. ed.; Göttingen: Vandenhoeck & Ruprecht, 1921; 1st ed., 1910), XII-XVII, 1-220, 240-323 (for 1 Sam 1–2 Kgs 14); idem, *Mose und seine Zeit* (Göttingen: Vandenhoeck & Ruprecht, 1913).

5. "Die evangelische Kirche und ihre berufenen Vertreter würden gut tun, gegen diese Erkenntnis, dass die Genesis Sagen enthält, sich nicht — wie es bisher so vielfach geschehen ist — zu sperren" (*Genesis,* XII-XIII). Gunkel goes on: unless this is recognized, a historical understanding of Genesis is impossible.

outset, the establishment was uneasy about him; senior figures at Göttingen had not wanted his habilitation.[6] He would hardly have been unaware.[7] Also significant for form criticism's later demise is the recognition that Gunkel's focus of attention was on the original story in its oral transmission phase.[8] The tyranny of history was probably lurking in the surroundings.[9] For Gunkel the stories were not history; yet they were surely understood as history by those who told them.[10] Stories were oral; history was written.[11] History deals with major public events; story treats the personal and private.[12] History has to be susceptible of being traced back to eyewitnesses; not so with story.[13] The clearest indication that we are dealing with story, however, is the presence of things we find unworthy of belief.[14] Of its nature, history is prose; of its nature, story is poetry.[15]

There are signs of the times. Gressmann was sometimes rather more publicly venturesome than Gunkel. In approaching his work on Samuel–Kings, what he took for granted today has heads shaking with surprise, sadness, or outrage. For example: (1) story is easily distinguished from history (story: distant past and out of touch with reality — its heroes, the leading figures of the distant past; history: the present or the recent past and in touch

6. Cf. Klatt, *Hermann Gunkel*, 16-17.

7. To be noted, in this context, is his 1891 move from Göttingen to Halle and with it from NT to OT, as well as the subsequent goings-on in Berlin (cf. Klatt, *Hermann Gunkel*, 40-45).

8. *Genesis*, XXXII-III.

9. A phrase like "the tyranny of history" must be understood with exactitude when speaking of a scholar as passionately concerned for history as was Gunkel (cf. Klatt, *Hermann Gunkel*, 24-27). "Historical" is a descriptor that goes hand in hand with modern scholarship; "historical" may describe a state of intellectual awareness required in most modern scholarship. But as every modern knows, meaning is more than history; the interest of the historical is not restricted to its history alone. When the search for history denies value to whatever does not contribute to historical reconstruction of events, the obsession with history has denied worth and meaning to all that does not serve this purpose — and is rightly called tyranny. Too frequently in biblical study, the often blithely unquestioned assumption that traditions have meaning insofar as they provide access to the events that happened is a subtle mask for the denial of worth to whatever is not of value for such reconstruction. This I call "the tyranny of history." Stories have value; faith has worth.

10. Gunkel goes to considerable length in arguing against the historicality of these Genesis stories (cf. *Genesis*, VIII-XIII). Note also *Genesis*, XXX.

11. *Genesis*, VIII.

12. *Genesis*, IX.

13. *Genesis*, X-XI.

14. *Genesis*, X-XI.

15. *Genesis*, XII-XIII.

with reality — its heroes, the leading figures in the state); (2) competent scholars will eliminate "clumsy" additions *(ungeschickte Zusätze)* and recognize the "mutilation" *(Verstümmelung)* of traditions; (3) story claims belief but does not earn it; history presents what actually was *(was wirklich gewesen ist)*.[16] The literary types — story, idyll, history, legend, märchen, and so on — are not described with appropriate precision by Gressmann; to today's practiced eye, his discussion seems highly subjective.

"After Gunkel's death there was a period of relative inactivity in the field of form criticism."[17] For Gunkel, the move to the distant and mostly non-Israelite oral past may have been liberating, despite its highly hypothetical quality and deep uncertainty; it offered an opening to literary appreciation that the cold precision of contemporary literary-critical analysis did not allow for. But added to the fragmentary activity of the analysts and Gunkel's frequent comparison of the naivete of ancient Israel with that of his generation's children, the focus away from the present text into a surmised past accessible to a sensitive few did not generate enough value to find favor with those focused on the present reality of what was possessed in the final text.[18]

Both Gunkel and Gressmann exhibit what is, for me, a disturbing focus on history as the primary value within their texts. It may be ironic, but I believe it accurate to situate their emphasis on historical value within the need they felt to devalue the historical aspect of early story traditions. The need to differentiate meant that, in their introductory material at least, the attention given to a text that was believed to be of historical worth appears to distract from the value of the earlier "story" traditions, whose focus is quite different. Thought and faith go unmentioned. It may not be an exaggeration to say that both scholars felt the need to loosen the grip (the stranglehold?) of history on the earlier traditions of the Bible. Intrinsic to form criticism is a focus on text before event.

For the Older Testament, form criticism's second wave is typified by the publications of Martin Noth and Gerhard von Rad. Both had been associated with Albrecht Alt at Leipzig, who was not one of the circle personally associated with Gunkel. For Alt, however, Gunkel was the "founder of form-critical research in OT scholarship," and Alt's famous essay on the origins of Israelite

16. Gressmann, *Schriften,* II/1, XII-XIV.

17. Koch, *Growth,* 72n2.

18. The "sensitive few" reflects Gunkel's comments on *Formensprache* (the appropriateness of language to form) as demanding aesthetic study *(ästhetische Betrachtung)* on the part of the researcher and his appeal to Goethe's dictum that raw material or subject matter *(Stoff)* was available to all, that artistic worth or substance *(Gehalt)* was accessible only to the initiated, and that shape or pattern or form *(Form)* was a mystery to most — "die Form ist ein Geheimnis den meisten" *(Einleitung,* 23).

law was seen by him as filling out an aspect of Gunkel's program.[19] Alt's interests were transmitted to Noth and von Rad; clearly, these scholars were attracted by something of lasting value they saw in Gunkel's perception of Israelite literature. Von Rad's form-critical interest is best evidenced in his concern with the forces shaping the Hexateuch.[20] Noth was led particularly to his study of the remote origins of the Pentateuch.[21]

Von Rad credited the shape and structure of the present Hexateuch (Genesis through Joshua) to remote origins in the short historical credo and the themes of Israel's early worship (cf. Deut 6:20-25; 26:5-9; Josh 24:2-13). Initially well received, this understanding was doomed to dissatisfaction once it could be shown that the short credos came late in the process, more as summaries than the original core from which the process began. For Gressmann and von Rad source criticism's work *(Literarkritik)* was largely done; for Noth it was a lively and continuing debate into which he sought to introduce a new view or two. Nevertheless, in the context of his traditio-historical study, the source-critical results for the Pentateuch are relegated to "Prolegomena."[22] From von Rad's form-critical work, Noth presumed the originating role of the "basic themes" in the ritual confessions of Israel's worship. He was aware that it would frequently "be impossible to go beyond probabilities or even possibilities . . . [when moving] . . . into the dark and impenetrable area of the preliterary oral tradition"; the "creative stage" of the history of the Pentateuch was "the *pre*literary history of the formation and the growth of the tradition."[23] The abandonment of von Rad's proposal and the murky uncertainty of Noth's deterred the bulk of scholarship from following in their footsteps.

The task of systematizing OT form criticism was taken up by two of von Rad's former students, operating in different directions. Klaus Koch, asked by von Rad to write "a small guide to form criticism for our students," ended up with "a full-length book," intended "as a guide for students, as an introduc-

---

19. "Der Begründer der gattungsgeschichtlichen Forschung in der alttestamentlichen Wissenschaft" (Alt, "Die Ursprünge des israelitischen Rechts," *Kleine Schriften,* vol. I [Munich: Beck, 1959], 285n1).

20. "Das formgeschichtliche Problem des Hexateuch," *Gesammelte Studien zum Alten Testament* (TB 8; Munich: Kaiser, 1965; original, 1938], 9-86). ET: pp. 1-78 in *The Problem of the Hexateuch and Other Essays* (trans. E. W. Trueman Dicken; 1966; repr. London: SCM, 1984).

21. *Überlieferungsgeschichte des Pentateuch* (Stuttgart: Kohlhammer, 1948); ET: *A History of Pentateuchal Traditions* (trans. B. W. Anderson; Englewood Cliff, N.J.: Prentice-Hall, 1972).

22. *History of Pentateuchal Traditions,* 5-41 (cf. esp. 5-7).

23. Ibid., 3 and 44 (German: pp. 4 and 47).

tion to form-critical research."[24] Rolf Knierim set out, with coeditor Gene Tucker and a team of colleagues, to gather together the results of form-critical study of the OT in a single volume.[25]

Instead of providing a springboard into future form-critical activity, Koch's book in hindsight has had the function rather of being its gravestone. The claims on the future were too big for the present to bear. For a book that was to be a guide for students, there are far-reaching claims — "A form-critical approach permits us to discover afresh the vitality of God's Word" (p. 13); "The study of literary types . . . is the groundwork without which nothing can be maintained with certainty" (p. 66) — and there are serious lacunae. An "Index of Biblical Literary Types and Their Elements" is provided (pp. 231-33), but it is no more than an index of references to these. Few literary types are described with any degree of precision; guidelines for the identification and description of such types are not given. The troubling aspects of early form-critical research are not addressed. The major advantages of a form-critical approach are claimed rather than articulated. There is little differentiation offered between studies giving helpful evaluation and those moving instead toward unhelpful fragmentation and overly hypothetical outcomes. Such silences suggest that learning was from apprenticeship to a master and not from the guidance of a handbook. The book is a valuable pointer to the possibilities of the form-critical approach; it is not, as one might expect from an introduction intended to benefit students, the summary of a mature field of study. Harsh reality set bounds to the book. As Koch notes in his introduction, on many points convincing results were far from being achieved; many parts of the Bible had not yet been studied from a form-critical point of view. Of necessity, he was limited to "a few examples, choosing only the focal points."[26] The limits suggest an approach to research that had an early flowering and stunted subsequent growth. In other words, there was much work to be done; in the decades ahead, few were interested in doing it.

The concern of Gunkel and Gressmann for a story's growth from an ancient oral past to its incorporation into the biblical text is systematized by Koch as "the history of the transmission of tradition." Research is needed "because many biblical passages have been passed down either orally or in writing over a long period of time and have therefore been much modified

24. Koch, *Growth*, ix. The title of the original German is revealing: *Was ist Formgeschichte? Neue Wege der Bibelexegese* (What is form criticism? New paths in biblical exegesis). The title and even the subtitle of the English translation are more muted.

25. Known as the Old Testament Form Criticism project and headquartered at the Institute for Antiquity and Christianity, at what was then Claremont Graduate School.

26. Koch, *Growth*, ix.

before reaching their final shape."[27] At the least, a caution against subjectivity is needed here; it is not given.

The Knierim-Tucker project ran into the dual problem of the inadequacy of the form-critical coverage of the OT and the inadequacy of some of the form-critical work done.[28] A new focus was needed. The project was reorganized, but across the discipline of OT studies the form-critical impulse was running into the sand.

Multiple factors were involved in form criticism's fall from favor. The remove to the distant and mostly non-Israelite oral past may have been liberating in certain areas; for many later, it failed to satisfy. Furthermore, the hopes raised produced too little in the way of secure results, or the approach itself produced too much in the way of festivals and liturgies.[29] Above all, as noted, the focus away from the present text into a surmised past accessible to a scholarly few was too burdened with subjectivity to survive in a generation focused on the present reality of what was possessed in the final text.

I had considered this article to be basically finished when I came across a passage of Gunkel's that I think of as the "smoking gun." It goes a long way to explaining his attraction to form criticism and, I believe, it also sheds light on form criticism's later fall from favor. In 1910, in a letter to his publisher, Gunkel wrote: "[For the nonspecialist] the way to the substance *(Inhalt)* lies through pleasure in the aesthetic form. It is quite different with source criticism *(Literarkritik)*. . . . Now it is my particular gift to have a feeling for the

---

27. Ibid., 39.

28. "The original plan of the project was to record critically all the relevant results of previous form-critical studies concerning the texts in question" (Rolf Knierim and Gene M. Tucker, eds., in Roland E. Murphy, *Wisdom Literature: Job, Proverbs, Ruth, Canticles, Ecclesiastes, and Esther* [FOTL 13; Grand Rapids: Eerdmans, 1981], x — and subsequent forewords). The plan had to be expanded.

29. "Apparently, once the search for a cultic 'situation in life' of Old Testament narrative had got under way, there was no portion of the literature which could escape such an interpretation" (Herbert F. Hahn, *The Old Testament in Modern Research* [expanded ed.; Philadelphia: Fortress, 1966; original, 1954], 142-43). Note Hahn's later comment on the repeated discovery of cultic liturgies in the prophetic books: "Frequently, these studies showed greater zeal than judgment" (ibid., 146). On the fragility of the concept of setting, see Burke O. Long, "Recent Field Studies in Oral Literature and the Question of *Sitz im Leben*," *Semeia* 5 (1976): 35-49. Long writes: "The attempt to suggest settings or setting for a biblical genre on the basis of written texts should be made. Without this, the link between literature and life is lost. But such recontructions ought to be treated with much more than usual reserve and joined with a good deal more serious sociological research. . . . I cannot conceive of an anthropologist reconstructing the typical occasion for a literary piece on the basis of its *literary* features alone. If he were to do so, he would be more often wrong, totally wrong, than right" (p. 44).

aesthetic and to bring it to the fore."[30] Gunkel turned to form criticism because, for him, the current source criticism lacked any meaningful attraction. A later generation turned away from form criticism because, for many, it had been refined to the point of losing all meaningful attraction.

If my judgment is right, the source criticism of Gunkel's day denied worth to the present text because it was thought to be all too often a mechanical composite without the possibility of literary merit. So Gunkel was forced to retreat to the preliterary oral stage. The discovery some modern scholars have yet to appropriate fully is that the composers responsible for the present text were knowledgeable, skillful, and presumably aesthetically aware. So today we can contemplate the present text and, without scholarly embarrassment, find it aesthetically pleasing.

In the language of recent psychology and spirituality, the approach to the text needs to appeal to the whole person, not just to the head or intellect. Gunkel experienced the intellectual analysis of source criticism *(Literarkritik)* as cold and alienating. He looked for something more attractive in a form-critical approach to the whole. As the form-critical approach became fragmented into analytical demands that could not be met and hypothetical claims that could not be substantiated, later scholarship found it unappealing and in turn became alienated from it. Central to the attraction of the original impulse was the focus on the whole. This focus on the whole remains at the core of form-critical insight.

## The Essentials: Form Criticism's Insight

The essential insight of form criticism, the attraction that led to its wide acceptance by first-rate scholars, can be summed up in these terms: whatever is regarded as an individual text, whether shorter or longer, needs to be treated as a whole, and each individual whole will be affected by the influence of the typical. Two issues are thus central to the task of interpreting literature. One is ascertaining the nature of the particular work of literature under interpretation. The other is coming to grips with the particular work as a whole in order to see how its parts relate to the whole and communicate its message.

The first of these relates to the typical, the second to the individual. The first asks the question: What is typical of this text that situates it within a par-

---

30. "Der Weg zum Inhalt geht ihm [the layperson] durch die Freude an der ästhetischen Form. Ganz anders ist es mit der Literar*kritik*. . . . Nun ist es meine besondere Art, das Äesthetische nachzuempfinden u. darzustellen" (from Klatt, *Hermann Gunkel,* 118).

ticular class of texts? The second asks the question: What is it about the way this text is shaped and structured that communicates its meaning?

It is important to eliminate two misunderstandings. First, the decision about the literary type (genre) is not an understanding imposed on the text; it is a decision that emerges out of the understanding of the text. Second, the question of the shape and structure of the text is to be asked of the passage in the present biblical text; it is not asked of some remote, uncertain original form putatively assumed from the past.

The meaning of a text emerges from the text as a whole, not substantively from the fragments that can be found in it. If biblical interpretation is to find meaning, it must focus on a text as an entity: what we believe a text said and says. It is of the nature of form criticism to name the whole; that is what it means to declare the literary genre of a text. It is of the nature of form criticism to study how the parts of a text interrelate to form a whole and to give it meaning. The more advanced and specialized academic biblical study becomes, the greater the need at the right times to pull back and view the whole. The enormous contribution of form criticism to future biblical studies may be in requiring and legitimating this view of the whole.

## Literary Genre or Type (= the Typical, a Matrix for the Text [German: Gattung])

Naming something is of the essence of knowledge. Form criticism, in its concern for literary genre, is all about naming.

It may help to say what a literary genre — or literary type, if a monosyllable is preferred — is not, before moving on to what it is.

1. It is not a license to launch out into uncertain surmises about a distant past.
2. It is not an invitation to indulge in subjective speculation about how a text might have come to be what it is.
3. It is not a key to unlock the secrets of a text's understanding.

A literary genre, or literary type, is:

1. A tag that an interpreter can put on a text after its secrets have been explored.
2. A name that helps situate a text within a general class so that it can be more easily understood.

24

3. A summary of observations about a given text validating an initial intuition as to its nature.

It may be important, for example, to be able to name stirring legends as such, or well-loved stories, or the report of treasured memories; it may be important to be able to say with good reason that certain texts are not to be mistaken for history or for reflective theological pieces.

### Literary Form or Structure (= the Text Itself, in All Its Individuality [German: Form])

The term "literary form" should not be an optional alternative for those who find "literary genre" rather too difficult to pronounce; often used interchangeably, "genre" and "form" are not the same. "Form" is a good English word for the shape or structure of something. To avoid confusion in this context, the German *Form* can be best rendered by the English "structure."[31]

The meaning of a text can emerge only from the study of its shape or structure. There are many ways in which the results of such study can be reported. What is important is that the reporting renders accessible to the reader the decisions about the text on which its interpretation is based. Whether the structure is represented diagrammatically (e.g., a tabular structure analysis) with comment or whether it is expressed in an undiagrammed discussion of the text is unimportant. What matters is that the decisions about the text taken by the interpreter and the reasons for them are accessible to the reader. The shape or structure is, of course, that of an individual text. It is this constellation of its components that allows each text to make its own individual communication.

In order to regain its usefulness, modern form criticism had to shuck off the attention given to earliest origins and focus on the actual rather than the hypothetical.[32] The refocusing of form criticism, after some seven decades on the biblical scene, can be typified by the statement of purpose in the editors' foreword to the first volume published in the FOTL series. "If the results of

31. So, e.g., John Barton in his dictionary article on "Form Criticism: Old Testament": the German *Form* properly so-called "is the structure or shape of an individual passage or unit"; the German *Gattung* is used for "a general class or genre" (*ABD* 2:839). See also G. M. Tucker, "Form Criticism, OT," *IDBSup* 342.

32. The past is not easily dispensed with. Barton, while claiming form criticism as "an indispensable tool for the historical study of the OT," asserts that its focus is "on preliterary stages of the text's growth" (*ABD* 2:839). Once upon a time, it was; it should no longer be.

form criticism are to be verifiable and generally intelligible, then the determination of typical forms and genres, their settings and functions, has to take place through the analysis of the forms in and of the texts themselves. . . . In contrast to most traditional form-critical work, the interpretation of the texts accepts the fundamental premise that we possess all texts basically at their latest written stages."[33] Appropriately stripped down, devoid of the folly and pretension of some of the aspects that attended its beginnings, form criticism must take its place as an essential element in the art of interpretation.

## The Future: Form Criticism's Changing Face

Two questions, then, are central to what needs to flourish again as form criticism redivivus, embodying the direction of the changing face of form criticism.[34] The first: What is the nature of this text, its literary genre or type? The second: What is the shape or structure of this text, its basic components and their relationship to each other? Both questions are in the service of the fundamental task of textual interpretation: the expression of a text's meaning.

### Literary Genre or Type (= the Typical, a Matrix for the Text)

At one level, form criticism is as automatic as breathing, and anxieties about air quality should not keep us from breathing. Sometimes form criticism is simplistically easy; sometimes it is not. When it is not easy is precisely when it is usually important.

Martin Buss has compared form criticism with learning the rules of a language, bringing into awareness considerations that are known subconsciously.[35] It is always important that we are able to name what we observe. In many cases it is probably not necessary to go much beyond the list of genres

---

33. Knierim and Tucker, "Editors' Foreword," in Murphy, *Wisdom Literature*, x. This concern with the present text can be overlooked if it is not realized that the move from "larger literary corpora" to "any prior discernible stages" is a move that remains at the level of the present text. It is not a move from the text to its past; it is a move from larger units (e.g., an entire biblical book) to the smaller constitutive units.

34. It may be symbolized by the renewed and expanded FOTL project; it should not be restricted to it. For some of the complexities that can beset OT form-critical theory, see Rolf Knierim, "Old Testament Form Criticism Reconsidered," *Int* 27 (1973): 435-67.

35. Martin J. Buss, "The Study of Forms," in *Old Testament Form Criticism*, ed. Hayes, 1-56, esp. 2-3.

noted below. Specialists in particular areas will know where the need is for further work. My own area is narrative, and there is a potential misunderstanding that makes the naming of literary genres a major concern. Without adequate reflection, it is frequently taken for granted that the focus of OT narrative traditions is history. The naming of the matrix is essential. It brings to full awareness what may be only latent. It situates the individual text within the broader horizon of expression arising out of human experience.

Historicity is often a complex and delicate matter; it is only muddled by those who insist on treating it as simple. It is certainly not an exclusively form-critical issue. For example, reports can be accurate or erroneous; stories can be factual or fictional; and so on. A variety of elements comes into play. Form-critical clarity might contribute to the greater clarity needed amid complexity.

A variety of literary genres or types have been identified in biblical texts over the years. It is unlikely — perhaps even undesirable — that a manual of stylistic diagnosis will be produced listing and describing achieved results for all the biblical genres. Room needs to be left for individual assessment of texts and recognition given to the reality that individual interpreters will understand the same genres in different ways, no matter how carefully they are defined. Interpretation is an art, not a science. In key areas, I believe basic agreement already exists about the understanding of certain genres.

1. In narrative, story is distinguished from account, report, or notice, as well as from legend and märchen and the like. Story moves from tension to its resolution, via plot; account, report, and notice do not. Legend, märchen, and so on have their own specific characteristics and are rare enough not to worry most of us much.

2. In prophecy, judgment is distinguished from salvation, Israel from the nations, and the nation from the individual. Since Westermann's *Basic Forms*, a prophetic judgment speech is associated with the combination of an accusation and an announcement, often linked by the messenger formula or equivalent.[36]

3. In psalms, lament and complaint are distinguished from thanksgiving or praise, individual from communal, and we are aware of royal psalms and others.

4. In law, apodictic is distinguished from casuistic and most of us are aware that there are priestly genres such as ritual and instruction.

36. Cf. Claus Westermann, *Grundformen prophetischer Rede* (Munich: Kaiser, 1960); ET: *Basic Forms of Prophetic Speech* (trans. H. C. White; Philadelphia: Westminster, 1967).

5. In wisdom literature, there are certain literary genres that are accepted, and it is probably unhelpful to look at those more closely here.

Something like this may be enough for the form criticism we must do.

Gunkel took for granted that the storytellers of ancient Israel regarded their traditions as historical; for Gunkel himself, it was obvious that the early ones were not.[37] The passion for history in biblical study does not die easily. No less a figure than Claus Westermann claimed recently (1970s/1994) that in a work of history (such as the Deuteronomistic History) the primary function is expected to be the presentation of history as it unfolded (*so wie sie verlaufen ist*). Westermann complains that the portrayal of the Deuteronomistic Historian as an interpreter of the past does not preserve posterity's access to what happened in Israel's history (*was in der Geschichte Israels geschehen ist*).[38] Gunkel may write off ancient Israel's early storytellers; the poor things just were not advanced enough to distinguish clearly between fiction and fact (*Dichtung und Wirklichkeit*).[39] Westermann may yearn for posterity to know just what happened in ancient Israel. There is a genuine need to know how we tell when we are dealing with imaginative storytelling and when with historical reporting.

No modern observer, aware of "historical" novels and "historical" films, should fail to see the difficulty. A report is easily enough distinguished from a story in terms of literary type; in a nutshell, story has plot and report does not. Whether a particular piece of biblical narrative has been composed as report or story is often not at all easy to distinguish. A good example of the importance of the issue at stake is 1 Samuel 4 on the loss of the ark. Israel's elders are said to have asked: "Why has the Lord put us to rout today before the Philistines?" (4:3). If the text is a report of what happened, then the question is in the text because the elders asked it. The probable answer to it can be implied from their proposal: "Let us bring the ark . . . from Shiloh" (4:4). It does not matter that the reporter knows what is going to happen soon; the reporter is retailing what occurred on the day of the first defeat — the question was asked. If the text is a story about what happened, then the question is in the text because the storyteller wanted it there. On the other hand, because the storyteller knew the second battle would result in a disas-

---

37. *Genesis*, XXX; see above, n. 10.

38. Claus Westermann, *Die Geschichtsbücher des Alten Testaments: Gab es ein Deuteronomistisches Geschichtswerk?* (Gütersloh: Kaiser, 1994), 28-29.

39. "Die Sage stammt aus Zeiten und Kreisen, die noch nicht die geistige Kraft haben, Dichtung und Wirklichkeit deutlich zu unterschieden" (*Genesis*, XXX).

trous defeat and the ark would be lost, it becomes legitimate to ask why the elders' question was told in the story. If this is a story, the answer can no longer be simply that the elders asked it. The storyteller knows that the absence of the ark was not the cause of the first defeat. The question, then, is fraught with much deeper meaning. A preliminary answer is offered in a dying mother's naming of her son: "the glory has departed from Israel" (4:21-22). The following narrative will resolve the ambiguity of 4:22, with its active and passive verbs. The active voice gets the nod; God has chosen to go — and later to return.

It is important to recognize that what is reported provides the raw material for interpretation. In the telling of a story, interpretation has often been begun.

Interpretive comments such as "God tested Abraham" (Gen 22:1) or "the Lord raised up a deliverer for the Israelites" (Judg 3:9) do not establish the distinction between report and story. Test and deliverance can be reported. The comments do hint at how the text could be used to rehearse the tradition as story. The tension of the plot is given. What sort of a test will it be and will Abraham pass it? How will deliverance be brought about in Israel after so many years' oppression? The Bible's framing of the deliverer stories in Judges 3–8 (Ehud, Deborah/Barak/Jael, Gideon) is an example of how Israel's experience articulated in tradition can be transformed into a theology.

Form-critical assessments need to be made for every text we deal with. When the literary genre or type is obvious, the task is easy. When the literary type is far from obvious, and the task is far from easy, responsible interpreters will need to identify as explicitly as possible the elements that bear on any decision. Honesty should keep form criticism in business.

### Literary Form or Structure (= the Text Itself, in All Its Individuality)

Matrixes are all very well, but the biblical texts are the only certain realities we have. It may be important to know the class or type to which a text belongs. It is equally or more important to know what the communication is that this text, of this particular class or type, is articulating. Texts do not fall into types according to the whims of authors or classifiers. Texts adopt types because there is something typical in what the text is to communicate. The communication of a particular text may be typical (e.g., history, report, prophecy of judgment, song of praise), but as a particular text it will have its own particular communication to make (e.g., this history, this report, this prophecy of judgment, this song of praise). Discussion of the shape or structure of a text is a sure route to its particular communication.

That most biblical texts will have had some sort of oral past is nowadays largely taken for granted, as is the recognition that any precision in reconstructing aspects of that past is usually out of reach.

To use "method" as a noun with reference to the art of interpretation comes close to a crime — at least if "method" is understood as a systematic procedure following prescribed steps to achieve a preordained end. The aspects of biblical study that precede the interpretation of a text — text criticism, source criticism, form criticism, tradition history, editing history, and so on — are best described as approaches. They begin with insight and intuition that have to be tested and validated or verified methodically, and for that careful, reflective, and systematic study is needed. Not all approaches apply to every text. Not all interpreters assess various approaches in the same way. Woodenly understood, method can muzzle. Texts control; they do not muzzle.

Nevertheless, it can be helpful to have some principles of guidance when approaching a text. In my practice, awareness of certain steps is often helpful in beginning to unpack the approach to a text. The steps in interpretation will vary from text to text and from interpreter to interpreter, but the following is a useful initial checklist.

1. Boundaries: What is the extent of the passage, its beginning and end?
2. Blocks: What are the component elements of the passage and their relationships?
3. Relationships: How are the blocks structured within a passage, so that the parts form a whole?
4. External elements: if required by a particular text, assess the nature and extent of any imported components (earlier tradition or later editing).
5. Explore the possibilities of the passage for meaning, in its time and now.

The boundaries accepted for a text can often determine its meaning. Beyond simple measures, such as not having pronouns or suffixes referring across boundaries and not having verbs dependent on a subject beyond a boundary, much has to be left to the interpreter's intuition. Interpreters and readers need to be aware of the issues; often, not much more can be asked. Blocks are important. How do texts begin and end? How much is contained between beginning and end? Relationships are even more important. Is there development? Is there contrast? Are there thematic moves? Imported components, whether earlier elements that have been incorporated or additions made later, can often be identified by aspects of language or ideology, or by the fact that they do not quite fit, and so on. The point is not to dismiss what has been identified as external, but to see what meaning is given by its use or insertion. The issue of meaning is where text and reader need to be rubbed together until fire is generated. Texts often do not yield up meaning easily. All the issues of extent, components, relationships, everything that is part of shape and structure go into the making of meaning. Few texts worth interpreting will be restricted to a single meaning. Few attempts at articulating meaning will be convincing if they do not pay appropriate attention to the signals of the text. It is in seeking to grasp the shape and structure of a text that these signals are best noticed.[40]

Interpretation needs to know what sort of a text is being interpreted. Interpretation needs to know the shape and structure of the text being interpreted. Modern form criticism is concerned with precisely these two areas of knowledge. It has a future — if its past is allowed a decent burial.

40. It is appropriate that the last question should be left to the last footnote. The question: Where is the diachronic dimension in all this? If, out of the shape and structure of the text, diachronic or growth issues force themselves on an interpreter, they need to be investigated with all the insights available to scholarship. Such investigation is part of the task of interpretation. I would be slow to see it is as intrinsic to form criticism.

# Formgeschichte — A Misleading Category?
## Some Critical Remarks

### ERHARD BLUM

Scholarly investigation exists on clear distinctions. The term *Formgeschichte* (form criticism), as it is coined in biblical scholarship, is not only ambiguous itself, but is used for such varied questions and variables that it has been called an "unclear collective concept."[1] Attempts have already been made to put definitional limits on its meaning in one direction or another. One may also ask more fundamentally, however, how it relates to the necessity of this terminus at all. In other words, whether there truly are questions belonging properly to exegetical research that cannot be suitably addressed except with *Formgeschichte* (form criticism). If such genuine "form-critical" approaches cannot be clearly defined, one should consider whether it is advisable to dispense with this term completely in the future.

I pursue these elementary questions in the following sketch under several aspects that thus far have been implied or discussed under the label "form criticism." They concern the oppositions, or assignments, of form and genre, form and history, form and content, as well as form and aesthetics.

### Form and Genre

Hermann Gunkel, who is purported to be the founder of "form criticism," did not coin or use this term himself. For him the issue was not about "forms"

---

1. K. Berger, *Einführung in die Formgeschichte* (UTB 1444; Tübingen: Francke, 1987), 27.

This essay was translated from the German by Petronella Verwijs, Ph.D. candidate, Claremont Graduate University, and Scott Haslett, translator.

32

and their history, but about the program of a "history of literature," which "arranges the material according to 'genres.'"[2] In establishing a methodical genre research in biblical exegesis, Gunkel then also made a lasting contribution to the discipline.

It is not simply a matter of terminological preferences that is debatable with regard to the question of "form or genre." If that were so, the dispute could easily be settled by a synonymous use of these terms. While at first glance this is a convenient solution, such an equivocation would, however, needlessly complicate relevant categorical differentiations or even make them altogether impossible. This means that a synonymous use of "form" and "genre" is, for this reason alone, surely not advisable, as genres (as Gunkel himself already emphasized)[3] cannot be defined exclusively, and not even primarily, by characteristics of *form* — unless "form" is then defined in a rather broad sense (see the section "Form and Content"). Moreover, there is a threat of losing a simple elementary distinction: the distinction between the concrete, individual, particular text and the abstract, transindividual pattern of text formation, that is, the "genre."

Even if the difference between (the typical "form" of a) genre and (the individual "form" of a) particular text may in the end always have been obvious, it has still frequently been leveled out through terminology and methodological practice. It is therefore to W. Richter's merit that in 1971 he insisted on this distinction in his large-scale methodological investigation. He differentiates between "form criticism," based on the description of the particular text in its individual form, and "genre criticism," which attempts to establish the formative "structural pattern" in an analytical comparison of independent particular texts.[4] In 1978 C. Hardmeier presented an extended and up until now probably the soundest and most precise definition of the concept

---

2. According to Gunkel in a letter to A. Jülicher (1925); see H. Rollmann, "Zwei Briefe Hermann Gunkels an Adolf Jülicher zur religionsgeschichtlichen und formgeschichtlichen Methode," *ZTK* 78 (1981): 284. In this letter he distances himself expressly from the language and formulation of the question of his NT "students" such as M. Dibelius: "The word '*form* critically' is especially uncomfortable for me" (283).

3. Ibid., 284: "*This* [i.e., the investigation of genres] is therefore not predominantly, let alone exclusively, about *forms.*"

4. W. Richter, *Exegese als Literaturwissenschaft: Entwurf einer alttestamentlichen Literaturtheorie und Methodologie* (Göttingen: Vandenhoeck & Ruprecht, 1971). Here Richter was concerned with a conscious correction of the firmly established "methodology"; cf. ibid., 46: "The blending of the particular text (form) and the type of text (genre) and the equivalent variables of content has produced disastrous consequences in the history of research, which until now have not been cleared up."

of genre in the field of exegesis.[5] According to this definition, genres can be defined as transindividual patterns of text formation. Such "patterns" are specified as a (consciously or subconsciously acquired) part of a culturally determined communicative competence of the individual author — in a certain analogy with the general language competence. On the other hand, in analogy to rules of grammar, these structural patterns can be developed only in analytical abstractions from the comparison of particular actual texts.[6] A large part of the genre pattern can be defined in detail as the semantically and/or pragmatically coined "deep structure of the text."[7] However, genres, especially poetical ones, may also be partly or completely defined by patterns of the text's surface structures.[8]

To the extent that elements of the text's surface structure make up the genre structure, one can speak of a certain "genre style." The individual stylization of the actual example of genre must in turn be distinguished from the genre-typical stylistic elements as rhetorical, aesthetic (etc.) creative means. These means could also include, among others, the "improper" metaphorical or rhetorical application of "foreign" genre characteristics. OT examples would include the stylization of the prophecies of doom with elements of lamentation,[9] or the formation of the judgment oracle in Isa 5:1-7 with elements of a love song and the presentation of a legal case, respectively

---

5. C. Hardmeier, *Texttheorie und biblische Exegese: Zur rhetorischen Funktion der Trauermetaphorik in der Prophetie* (BEvT 79; Munich: Kaiser, 1978). Here Hardmeier consistently takes up newer approaches of literary scholarship, among others K. W. Hempfer, *Gattungstheorie: Information und Synthese* (UTB 133; Munich: W. Fink, 1973). Hardmeier's fundamental work has certainly, even in German-language exegesis, only been partially adopted until now.

6. In this respect Hempfer notes "that the 'genres' indeed represent visible phenomena of language communication, but that they are not given in the same manner, for example, as specific historical events. As more or less internalized rules that have an essential function in the actual realization of texts, 'genres' are for the analyst always only tangible in these individual text manifestations" (*Gattungstheorie*, 128; cited by Hardmeier, *Texttheorie*, 261). Completely in this sense also Richter, *Exegese*, 132: "'Genre' is furthermore a concept for an 'ideal' and 'typical' form, which does not exist in reality; it is obtained through the process of selection (abstraction), which holds several features of a form to be characteristic, though it disregards others. 'Genre' is therefore a theoretical result of scholarship; in actual literature only the forms exist. It is, however, not pure theory. For if related forms existed independent of each other, one must conclude that a certain structural pattern has preceded the individual form, which consists of a certain number of structural rules."

7. Hardmeier, *Texttheorie*, 260.

8. One thinks for example of the sonnet with its specific structure of verse and rhyme. Hardmeier (ibid.) appears, by the way, not to have thought of this possibility.

9. See again ibid., passim.

— evidently as aspects of a deliberate rhetorical strategy.[10] In Richter's reasoning the distinction between form and genre is brought to bear. Only when this discrimination is consistently observed can the question of genre unfold its important potential for an outlined interpretation of the individual text.

Research on genre should, however, by no means be limited to the horizon of exegesis of the particular text. On the contrary, the broadest possible development of the spectrum of genres appears essential where the investigation of the disclosure of the world as conveyed through language is concerned. Biblical exegesis shares all these respective lines of questioning with other literature or textual scholarship; it does not require its peculiar "form criticism."

Now as far as he is concerned, Gunkel certainly introduced what is probably an original, at any rate an eminently important, question with his looking for the *Sitz im Leben* of genres.[11] When formulated in more recent categories, it is a matter of the textually pragmatic dimensions of genres. More specifically, it concerns their character as patterns of linguistic actions *(Sprachhandlungsmuster)*, which are connected with typical interactions. Conceptually the elementary distinction between the actual particular text and the abstract pattern of text formation must also be maintained in this regard. As the term for typical communication situations of genres, *Sitz im Leben* should not be used for individual communication or reception situations of particular texts (against a widespread but thoughtless use of language).[12] In addition to these, however, there is something like a third category, namely typical communication situations of certain specific texts, which are used *recurrently* in typical interactions. This includes the formulalike use, for example, of actual Psalm texts in specific ritual or other contexts. It may appear justified to also speak of *Sitz im Leben* (in a derived sense) in this case.

---

10. A confusion of the stylization of an individual text (with the help of "borrowed" genre elements) and its genre affiliation is put forward when J. Barton names Isa 5 as an example "that one genre is often embedded in another": "In the example from Isaiah, a poem in the form of a love song is set within the larger context of a collection of oracles" ("Form Criticism [OT]," *ABD* 2:839).

11. In general textual scholarship, Gunkel's *Sitz im Leben* is from time to time accepted as a technical term.

12. See the explanation by M. J. Buss, *Biblical Form Criticism in Context* (JSOTSup 274; Sheffield: Sheffield Academic Press, 1999), 234: "The term *Sitz im Leben*, as it was employed by Gunkel, refers to the home . . . of a genre, not the context of a particular text." In the same note Buss refers to prominent examples of a divergent use of language in exegetical literature, including K. Koch, *Was ist Formgeschichte? Neue Wege der Bibelexeges* (2d ed.; Neukirchen-Vluyn: Neukirchener Verlag, 1967).

## Form and History

The rapid and complete acceptance of the term "form criticism" or "form-critical method" in post-Gunkel research may appear almost phenomenal. It can probably be explained, however, by the fact that the term promoted a fundamental factual and methodological shift relative to Gunkel's line of inquiry. The special attraction in this shift lay in its appearing to open up what had been inaccessible aspects of the world of ancient Israel. Both parts of the term *Formgeschichte,* namely "form" and "history," proved to be equally relevant. The main players were, at least in the beginning, still thoroughly aware of this shift. This becomes clear, for example, in the programmatic formulations of R. Bultmann: "I completely agree with M. Dibelius that form-critical work consists neither of an aesthetic consideration nor of a descriptive and classifying process, that is, it does not consist of simply describing the individual pieces of the written tradition according to aesthetic or other characteristics and classifying them in certain genres. On the contrary, it is the task 'of reconstructing the origin and history of the individual pieces in order to illuminate the history of the preliterary tradition.'"[13]

Here it is clearly stated that the ancestors of "form criticism" were less concerned about genres than about the individual texts whose form-typical analysis is intended to illuminate their prehistory in the oral origins. *Formgeschichte* thereby becomes almost synonymous with "oral tradition history"![14] For the time being, the connection to Gunkel's work was made by the fact that with his genre research, and in particular with his concept of *Sitz im Leben,* Gunkel seemed to have opened up a methodological access to the tradition history of the preliterary stage of *Kleinliteratur* (minor literature). On closer examination the program of Gunkel's students tends to concern itself with a narrowing instrumentalization of the genre-critical approach for specific diachronic lines of questioning, and this is exactly what the label "form

---

13. R. Bultmann, *Die Geschichte der synoptischen Tradition* (2d ed.; Göttingen: Vandenhoeck & Ruprecht, 1931), 4. The source Bultmann gives for his quote from Dibelius: *TRu* 1 (1929): 187. K. Berger points out correctly that Bultmann otherwise largely avoids the term "form-critical" and completely avoids "form criticism." Instead he speaks of "tradition criticism" (lit. "history of tradition"). "M. Dibelius, on the other hand, refers exactly to what Bultmann calls 'tradition criticism' as 'form criticism'" (Berger, *Einführung,* 20).

14. For a reflection on this also see the observation by Barton (*ABD* 2:839), "Form criticism is no longer in the center of interest in OT studies, as REDACTION CRITICISM and literary approaches (. . .) have focused on the finished form of the text, rather than on preliterary stages of the text's growth."

criticism" stands for.[15] This narrowing, which was to mark the disciplinary discourse for generations, affects several methodologically quite different levels. First, it shows itself in the factually unfounded focus on "*small* units" of the *oral* tradition.[16] Second, and more fundamentally, the narrowing shows itself in a reductionist assignment of form/genre analysis and the diachronic explanation of particular texts.[17] This occurs in a twofold, complementary respect: (a) On the one hand, genre-critical and genre-historical questioning is subordinated in an instrumentalizing way to transmission history.[18] This is to some degree understandable, as both lines of questioning *can* be interrelated in a close heuristic and methodological interdependence. At the same time this interdependence should not hide the fact that genre analysis has its own realm of perception and is not directed per se at problems of text formation. (b) On the other hand, it reduces the methodological complexity of the diachronic reconstruction in as much as genre observations *can* play an important role in it. If so, however, these genre observations generally do not stand alone but in an entire package of compositional data and historical considerations.

Ultimately, a further narrowing is apparent where reference to "*form* criticism" is partially the consequence and partially the condition for a concentration on aspects of the expression side *(Ausdrucksseite)* of the texts (the "surface structure of the text") as a supposedly reliable key to its prehistory (for more about this, see the next section).

If the concept of "form criticism" ever had a proprietary sense, then it is

15. Gunkel himself had apparently seen this μετάβασις εἰς ἄλλο γένος clearly when he rejected the term "form-critical" for his own work. At the same time he tentatively recommended to NT scholars the development of *Formgesetze* (laws of form) of the authentic words of Jesus (therefore not of transindividual genres) in distinction from those that "are more or less determined by Hellenistic taste." "But such observations would certainly start a new, substantially 'form-critical method'" (according to Rollmann, "Zwei Briefe," 285).

16. See for this, e.g., also the general exposition by F. Hahn, *Die Formgeschichte des Evangeliums* (WdF 81; Darmstadt: Wissenschaftliche Buchgesellschaft, 1985), VII-XI. Bultmann was already further along at the beginning of the 1930s when, with reference to J. Burckhardt's *Weltgeschichtliche Betrachtungen*, he remarks: "It appears that this approach is not in any way only valid for so-called *Kleinliteratur*" (*Geschichte*, 5n1).

17. For the critical discussion of some axioms that play a role here, see Buss, *Biblical Form Criticism*, 358ff., even if Buss's analysis here (e.g., in contemporary inferences) is not convincing in every respect.

18. About this, again pointedly, see ibid., 308: "The term referred to an attempt to treat formal observations as means to answer diachronic questions." On the necessity of distinguishing among genre criticism, tradition criticism, and composition criticism, cf. Berger, *Einführung*, 19-27.

probably in the outlined understanding that can be paraphrased as "a method for reconstructing the preliterary transmission of small units based on the observations of forms."[19] Such a "method" may have appeared promising to biblical exegesis, supposedly offering methodological solutions to the fundamental problem of the discipline, that is, the nasty hiatus between the demanding claim to explanation and the defective data, in this case when illuminating the difficult to access, but ever so tempting, oral prehistory of the texts. In truth, the "method" developed in this way is based on an *abridging* amalgam of elements of independent lines of questioning. Practiced with common sense, it may actually produce sound results, but then against the self-dynamic of a "method," which was constructed inadequately from the beginning.

## Form and Content

Even with the assumption of a conceptual differentiation between "form" and "genre" (see the first section above), the concept "form," as it is used by "form critics," presents considerable problems of definition. In this context the pertinent use of language cannot be pursued through the history of scholarship. However, the position of W. Richter may, to some extent, be representative in this context. His exposition of the theme also has the outstanding advantage that it (a) attempts to develop clear definitions and (b) is formulated in the concepts of linguistic scholarship. We shall therefore discuss the factual problem in the context of an analysis of Richter's position.

Richter defines "form" as a term opposite to "content."[20] More precisely, he appears to understand "form" as the "linguistic side of expression" of a literary unit.[21] Fundamental to Richter's exegetical methodology is above all the distinction between "outer form" and "inner form."[22] Of these, "outer form"

19. At least for German-speaking Protestant scholars around the mid-20th century, this probably expresses the dominant understanding.

20. Richter, *Exegese*, 75ff. Almost simultaneously to Richter's work, in the linguistic classic by J. Lyons, *Introduction to Theoretical Linguistics* (Cambridge: Cambridge Univ. Press, 1969), the opposition "form :: meaning" dominates; but he speaks (summarizing de Saussure) of "expression :: content" as well.

21. Cf. Richter, *Exegese*, 78. My formulation with *potentialis* is rooted in the fact that Richter speaks here first of "the language" and its expression side and then transfers the categories connected to it to the textual units. However, it remains unclear, for example, whether "form" is to be considered synonymous to *Ausdrucksseite*, or is to be equated with its shaping.

22. For our context I skip Richter's category "ornamental form," which is distin-

appears indeed largely confined to the linguistic expression of the texts, provided this comprises phenomena like syntactical configurations at the sentence level, as well as semantically defined categories of word classes.[23]

In contrast, Richter's description of the "inner form" implies a de facto suspension of the definition of "form" as opposite to content. According to the program, only the linguistically ascertained aspect of meaning from lexemes, word classes, and so on, is to be evaluated in addition to the aspect of expression on the levels of word, sentence, and text, without "already considering the content."[24] But in the different examples of implementation this is exactly what happens. For example, Richter lists twenty possibilities of the functions of direct speech or certain word classes within a unit as an illustration of aspects of the "inner form."[25] On closer inspection, however, most of these possibilities imply an understanding of content of the respective text (with the possible exception of the examples no. 2, 9, and 19). Indeed, the description is largely abstracted from the individual aspects of the story or the stated circumstances, and refers to fundamental structural and time references between speech and action. Yet it is decisive that such structural references also cannot be derived from the expression side of the texts alone, but instead have the interpretation of the content of the individual text *as their condition*.

This is true, for example, for Richter's case no. 3, "The speech adds past accessory lines"; no. 4, "The speech is located at the end as the justification for an action or an occurrence"; no. 8, "Action verbs dissolve the single line through recourse to what lies in the past"; no. 12, "Personal names play only an indirect role or are missing completely"; no. 16, "Yahweh/Elohim is interwoven in action and speech"; or no. 18, "Names of places unfold a movement within the unit."

The chosen text sections, which demonstrate "examples of forms," are no less informative:[26] the presumed definition of "form" matches sections of

---

guished from "structural form." "Ornamental form" in turn is differentiated from "outer and inner form."

23. However, the description of the inner-textual references through nominal and pronominal assumptions, etc., assigned to the outer form already appears problematical to me in this context (see the paradigm, Richter, *Exegese*, 85ff.), as the realization of such connections is essentially determined by the understanding of content. We need only think of Exod 4:24-27 as an extreme example.

24. Ibid., 92.

25. Ibid., 92ff.

26. Ibid., 104ff. Nine textual examples are presented, including Judg 3:15-28; Exod 3:1ab, 2b-4ab, 5, 6cd; 1 Sam 9:1-10, 16*; Judg 6:11c-17; Prov 23:10f; 1 Kgs 4:2-6.

the presented structural patterns, though certainly not such important distinctions as "exposition — corpus — closing" or the division into different scenes. For neither the one nor the other can be determined alone, or even primarily, with a description of the linguistic expression of the unit. This applies all the more to Richter's explicit descriptions of the "inner form," which is substantially content-related.[27] Moreover, it must be doubted that any outlined text profile would even be possible without the descriptions based on an understanding of the content. In other words the evidence has yet to be produced that an analysis strictly limited to the shape of the linguistic expression (*Ausdrucksgestalt*) (without taking the semantics of the text into account) can develop "the goal, namely the statement or intention of the unit," or a diachronically significant structure. Genre-specific structures would probably also be confined to a few special cases with this line of questioning (for the same reason).[28]

On closer inspection, the great majority of Richter's examples of his "inner form" offer descriptions of the "content structures" of certain text units. From this the following alternative emerges for the terminological question of interest to us. Either the definitional limitation of "form" based on the aspects of expression is maintained; then a form analysis will, however, be restricted to aspects of the so-called outer form. Or "form" also includes the content structure of a text; then, however, the opposition "form :: content" is discarded.

If general language usage and the possible exegetical yield are used as a basis, a more broadly conceived conception of "form" presents itself, which can refer both to the *Ausdrucksgestalt* of a text and to its content structure. "Form" then constitutes a synonym for "design" or "structure."[29] "Form analysis" becomes an alternate term for "structure analysis" without implying an opposition to "content analysis."

Further insights into the problems of a definition of "form" as opposite to "content" are provided by the debates on the criteria for genre determinations.

27. The presentation of the first example (Judg 3:15-18) deals with content already from the second sentence on: "The exposition is determined by an introductory nominal sentence, which introduces Ehud in a formula. It contains in circumstantial sentences two special characteristics of the main characters, which come together in the acme" (ibid., 104).

28. Cf. also n. 6; enumerating genres, such as lists, etc., should possibly also be mentioned in this context.

29. Thus also (though under purported screening of the content) Richter, according to whom "the analysis of the 'outer' and 'inner' form . . . provides a glimpse into the structure of the unit" (ibid., 114).

It is well known that Gunkel himself advocated a differentiated and — as will be shown — pioneering approach, even if his terms were rather loose according to today's standards. Thus he can formulate, "I determine 'Genres,' (a) according to the common wealth of thoughts and moods, (b) according to the same *Sitz im Leben,* (c) according to unchanging forms of expression. These considerations apply to *all* areas of the OT, not just to narrative, and are applied very differently in individual cases, depending on the nature of the genres. This means *here* it is not primarily, let alone only, a matter of 'Forms.' . . ."[30] Of course, the mainstream after Gunkel moved exactly in the direction against which the author argued in this quotation. Two main tendencies can be distinguished here. In the one the weights are merely shifted, that is, the formal criteria for genres are strengthened and a downright "mandatory" relationship between "form or genre" and "content" is postulated (this is represented in particular by A. Alt and his school). As a result, the form-critical approach according to Alt is based "on the insight that in every single literary genre, as long as it has a life of its own, certain content is firmly tied to certain forms of expression. Furthermore, these characteristic connections were substantially connected all along, that is also at the dawn of popular oral formation and passing on of all literature, as they corresponded to the special, regularly recurring events and necessities of life out of which each of the genres arose of itself."[31] As, however, the "forms of expression" as aspects of the text's surface appeared so to speak primarily given and controllable, it is only all too understandable that exactly these aspects of form were increasingly granted primacy from a heuristic-methodological perspective.

Richter separates himself more pointedly from such positions, which incorporate features of content[32] or even assume them,[33] and postulates "the form, and therefore a structured unit as the only reliable point of departure."[34] This is fully in line with his definition of "genre" as a "variable that shapes the individual forms," with which the "relationship of forms in spite of literary independence" can be explained.[35] However, if my critique holds

30. According to Rollmann, "Zwei Briefe," 284. See also the quotations by Hardmeier, *Texttheorie,* 259n5.

31. A. Alt, "Die Ursprünge israelitischen Rechts," *Kleine Schriften,* vol. 1 (repr. Munich: Beck, 1984), 284, (approvingly) quoted by Koch, *Was ist Formgeschichte,* 34. Regarding the implied theory of "form constraint" (see, e.g., Koch, 5-6), reference can be made here to the detailed text-theoretical critique of Hardmeier, *Texttheorie,* 258ff. and passim.

32. Cf. Richter, *Exegese,* 75, together with n. 7 above.

33. Ibid., 127ff. with notes.

34. Ibid., 125ff.; the quotation appears on p. 131.

35. Ibid., 132.

true, according to which Richter not only takes aspects of expression into account in his "formal" structure but describes *content* structures (with certain peculiarities of expression), then this must also apply to his genre structures. This can, in fact, be observed in most of his examples of genre descriptions — completely independent of their individual factual plausibility.[36] Even with those minor genres, which at first glance are purely defined by the syntactical structure (such as the "casuistic lawsuit"), the sentence structure, verb forms, and so on, are not sufficient as characteristics.[37]

A brief look at common OT genres "capable of consensus" in scholarship may illustrate this: (a) The "aetiological narrative": How can it be defined other than based on content and "pragmatically" ("a narrative aimed at explaining one or more conditions in the time of the narrator and intended recipients with one or more occurrences in the past")? Formal elements such as "until this day . . ." can be used, but are not obligatory. The same is probably true for most of the narrative genres, in any case for "basic categories" such as "saga," "fairy tale," and "parable." (b) The "bipartite doom-oracle": The different designations for both main parts ("Drohwort — Scheltwort," "accusation

---

36. Ibid., 141ff., with attempts to define the genres "narrative" or "constructed narrative." The characteristics for one of the subgenres are quoted here as representative: "'Prophetic narratives' have the structure of narratives, only with the distinction that the first speech gives impetus to the action with a request, while the following action reports its execution (1 Sam 9:1-10, 16)" (143) — in several respects a peculiar definition!

An equivalent outcome results with regard to Berger, who follows the basic concepts of Richter's definitions (cf. *Einführung*, 28-29, 36). Thus Berger assigns the genre "Epideixis/ Demonstration/Epiphany Announcement" texts with the following characteristics: "(1) It is about narratives, in which God or (usually) a representative of God is important. (2) An amazing singular deed or a chain of similar deeds is related. (3) The story is told from the perspective of the later reader, as beside the act, the reaction in the form of astonishment, fear, horror, or praise is also reported. This reaction follows the divine intervention in each case." As Berger points out, this group of characteristics is gained from the actual single texts through abstractions. But such — indeed unavoidable — "abstractions" do not yet change the cited features into characteristics of the text's expression side. On the contrary, it is consistently a question of (partially abstracted) specifications of content or of an aspect of text pragmatics (with regard to "the later reader").

37. Richter's "formal" definition (*Einführung*, 144): "The structural pattern consists of a certain conditional sentence structure. It is always kept in the third person singular. The protasis with *kî* or *'im* in a certain order shows prefix conjugation (. . .), the apodosis (usually without the addition wa=) has *qatal-x* or *x-yiqtol;* in the latter case *x* = infinitive absolute." Also apart from the fact that the latter characteristic is apparently not obligatory (cf. Exod 21:3, 4, 19, 29), sentence structures, as in Gen 32:9 and 1 Kgs 12:27 (cf. also 1 Kgs 1:52), would then be classified as casuistic laws according to this, which, due to content and context, they certainly are not.

— announcement of judgment," "Lagehinweis-Unheilsweissagung," etc.) already prove that the structural description includes interpretations of content. This surely also applies to the generally accepted logic of reasoning between parts one and two. In addition, the typical sender-speaker-addressee constellations lead here to specific text-pragmatic configurations. (c) Even apparently strictly structured "genres" such as the so-called salvation oracle in Deutero-Isaiah, whose structure has been based, among other things, also on syntactical characteristics by Begrich and Westermann, are substantially determined by content in their structural elements. In addition, one should ask in this case whether the relatively high congruity of the structure really represents a genre characteristic, or if it is not instead specific to the author.[38] Genres that purely, or primarily, are characterized by form of expression remain a marginal phenomenon in OT literature; possibly, one might think of acrostic Psalms or refrain poems in prophetic literature.[39]

In critical retrospective it therefore becomes clear that it is Gunkel's criteria for genre definitions that in their breadth (and vagueness) at least may provide something like the "raw material" for an appropriate genre analysis. Here his criterion of "thoughts and dispositions" would have to be transferred to the categories "content structure" and "purpose of communication"; the *Sitz im Leben* would, beyond Gunkel, apply not just to the sociological setting but also to the typical communication situation embedded in it.[40] Unvarying expressions or genre style remains a third possible criterion.

## Form and Aesthetics

On the basis of a broadly conceived concept of "form" (in the sense of "structure," "design," etc.), one could ask whether "form criticism" in a wider sense could not (also) encompass those approaches that seek to describe and interpret the aesthetic-formal structure of the text. However, in a *forschungs-geschichtliche* perspective this would at least be a new definition, if not to say a "redefinition" of "form criticism." But as diverse as the "form-critical" lines of inquiry may be, they are generally more interested in typical characteristics, not in special ones; in "coined" elements of language and text, not in individ-

---

38. This question presents itself especially in comparison with the Neo-Assyrian "prophetic salvation oracles"; see, e.g., the material in M. Weippert, "Assyrische Prophetien in der Zeit Asarhaddons und Assurbanipals," in *Assyrian Royal Inscriptions: New Horizons* (ed. F. M. Fales; Rome: Istituto per l'Oriente, 1981), 71-111.

39. Cf. also n. 28.

40. See Hardmeier's critique of Gunkel, *Texttheorie*.

ual ones; in institutional orientations, not in specific ones; and so on. More-over, the at times explicit disdain for the individual, aesthetic arrangement of the texts by "the form-critical scholars" was already considered deficient by scholars such as M. Weiss and L. Alonso Schökel as early as the 1960s.[41] They wrote against the current of dominant form criticism in those days, promot-ing a holistic interpretation that pays attention to the individuality and the often artistic structure of biblical texts. With similar intent, J. Muilenburg (to mention just one more outstanding example) saw the need in his celebrated presidential address in the late 1960s to bring questions of a "rhetorical criti-cism" into play that went "beyond form criticism(!)."[42] An expansion of the concept of form criticism based on just such approaches would, however, not only have been problematical in the light of the *Forschungsgeschichte*, but also unnecessary, as suitable designations (with different nuances) for this have al-ready been established ("rhetorical criticism, holistic reading, literary criti-cism," etc.).

## Summary

Our considerations started with the quest for a significant and pregnant defi-nition of the diversely used term "form criticism." The significance of any definition had to be measured by asking whether the defined term denotes a truly specific methodological approach within exegetical research or — alter-natively — is to be given preference over other established terms due to its ex-

41. M. Weiss, "Wege der neuen Dichtungswissenschaft in ihrer Anwendung auf die Psalmenforschung," *Bib* 42 (1961): 255-302; idem, "Einiges über die Bauformen des Erzählens," *VT* 13 (1963): 456-75; idem, "Die Methode der 'Total Interpretation' — von der Notwendigkeit der Struktur-Analyse für das Verständnis biblischer Dichtung," in *Congress Volume: Uppsala 1971* (VTSup 22; Leiden: Brill, 1972), 88-112; idem, *The Bible from Within: The Method of Total Interpretation* (Jerusalem: Magnes, 1984 [Hebrew 1967]); L. Alonso Schökel, "Erzählkunst im Buche der Richter," *Bib* 48 (1961): 143-72; idem, *Hermeneutical Problems of a Literary Study of the Bible* (VTSup 28; Leiden: Brill, 1975), 1-15.

42. J. Muilenburg, "Form Criticism and Beyond," *JBL* 88 (1969): 1-18, presented as the presidential address at the annual meeting of the SBL in Berkeley, California, 1968. In this ad-dress Muilenburg explicitly professed his belief in "form criticism" — understood as "genre criticism." At the same time, however, he asked that it be supplemented with other questions: "What I am interested in, above all, is in understanding the nature of Hebrew literary com-position, in exhibiting the structural patterns that are employed for the fashioning of a liter-ary unit, whether in poetry or in prose, and in discerning the many and various devices by which the predictions are formulated and ordered into a unified whole. Such an enterprise I should describe as rhetoric and the methodology as rhetorical criticism" (ibid., 8).

actness. The result was negative. In addition, it became apparent that, due to its vagueness resulting from its use in scholarship, the conventional term is given a virtually misleading potential. However, this finding in no way implies a questioning of the different lines of inquiry which thus far have — also — been discussed under the label "form criticism." On the contrary!

Thus the investigation of genres and their *Sitz im Leben* forms an indisputable task of exegetical investigation. "Form criticism" as an additional designation of genre research is, however, not only unnecessary, but in scholarship to date has been linked to portentous shortcomings — due to the insufficient differentiation of individual text and genre, on the one hand (see the first section above), and to problematical uses of the category "form" on the other hand (see the previous section above).

In the same way, the question of the written or oral prehistory of biblical texts will remain an essential one (even if the methodological possibilities are, for example, remarkably limited in view of the oral tradition). Here the insights of genre investigation often also have, among others things, eminent significance. However, the linking of "tradition history" and "genre analysis" introduced in the course of research after Gunkel into the now so-called form criticism reduces the complexity of such diachronic hypotheses along the road of "form analyses," which are supposedly more easily objectified. Moreover, in this simplifying reduction ultimately lies the (unconscious) raison d'être of this type of "form criticism."

In short: OT exegesis asking for the historical, intended meaning of the texts will always be dependent on "genre investigation" in Gunkel's sense. It will be dependent on the question of the form and meaning of the individual texts in their intended reception, which is pursued with literary-critical methods. It will also be dependent on the reconstruction of the history of transmission and tradition history — not to mention the reconstruction of the historical environment to which the text tradition belongs. None of these lines of questioning can be practically pursued in a methodological manner without including all others. However, no specific "form-critical method" exists in between. Do we really need the label of "form criticism" or *Formgeschichte*?

# Recent Form Criticism Revisited in an Age of Reader Response

## ROY F. MELUGIN

As we enter the twenty-first century, form criticism remains an invaluable tool in the study of biblical literature. Perhaps one of its most striking continuing contributions is its ability to help us determine what *kinds* of utterances we encounter in the text. In Amos 3, for example, analysis of genre makes it possible to distinguish between genre units and thus to guide us in our ability to understand better the significant shifts that manifest themselves in our reading of the text. Verses 1 and 2 are modeled on the genre of the prophetic oracle of judgment. First there is a call to hear: "Hear this word that YHWH has spoken against you. . . ." Next comes a reason for judgment: "You only have I known of all the families of the earth," followed by an announcement of judgment: "Therefore I will visit upon you all your iniquities."

In vv. 3-8 a shift from YHWH speech to human speech takes place, and we are confronted with a disputation[1] instead of the genre of the prophetic oracle of judgment: "Do two walk together unless they have met by appointment? Does a lion roar in the forest if it has no prey? . . . The lion has roared; who would not fear? The Lord YHWH has spoken; who would not prophesy?" In vv. 9-11 still another shift takes place. It begins with what appears to be an instruction to messengers[2] — instruction to go to foreign nations to summon them to journey to Samaria and observe what goes on there, perhaps as witnesses in figuratively formulated legal proceedings against Sa-

---

1. J. L. Mays, *Amos: A Commentary* (OTL; Philadelphia: Westminster, 1969), 59; H. W. Wolff, *Dodekapropheton 2: Joel und Amos* (BKAT XIV/2; Neukirchen-Vluyn: Neukirchener Verlag, 1969), 218-21; ET: *Joel and Amos* (trans. W. Janzen, S. D. McBride Jr., and C. A. Muenchow; Hermeneia; Philadelphia: Fortress, 1977), 181-84.

2. See Wolff, *Dodekapropheton,* 229 = *Joel and Amos,* 191.

maria: "Proclaim to the fortresses in Ashdod and to the fortresses in the land of Egypt and say, 'Gather yourselves on the mountains of Samaria and see the great tumults within her, and the oppressions in her midst.'" The instruction to messengers is molded into a prophetic judgment oracle with a reason for judgment ("they don't know how to do right . . . who treasure up violence and robbery in their fortresses" [v. 10]) and an announcement of judgment that proclaims the coming of an enemy who will invade and destroy Samaria's fortresses (v. 11).[3]

Despite the continuing value of form criticism, there is need for fundamental reappraisal of certain practices commonly undertaken by form critics. At the very outset two issues come immediately to mind: (1) the relationships between what is typical and what is unique in the use of language, and (2) the problem of highly speculative reconstructions of settings.

## Relations between the Typical and the Unique

In 1968 a major development occurred with the SBL presidential address of James Muilenburg, entitled "Form Criticism and Beyond."[4] In his essay Muilenburg argues that form criticism, despite its important contribution in biblical studies, suffers from placing too much emphasis on what is typical about language in texts and paying insufficient attention to what is particular and unique in texts' use of language. Without doubt, typicalities of speech often play an important role in the shaping of texts; thus form criticism is important. Yet form criticism "does not focus sufficient attention upon what is unique and unrepeatable, upon the particularity of the formulation."[5] In Jer 2:1–4:4* there is "an impressive sequence of literary units of essentially the same *Gattung*, i.e., the *rîb* or lawsuit or legal proceeding, and the *Sitz im Leben* is the court of law."[6] Yet there is also considerable variety in the literary formulation of the various pericopes in this text. Indeed, Muilenburg contends that much of this Jeremiah text consists of "excerpts or extracts, each complete in itself, to be sure, but refashioned into the conventional structures of metrical verse and animated by profuse images." Only Jer 2:1-13 at the beginning and 3:1–4:4* at the end represent genres "preserved with any degree of completeness." Yet he indicates that Jer 2:1–4:4* represents imitations of a

---

3. Wolff, *Dodekapropheton*, 230 = *Joel and Amos*, 192.
4. Muilenburg, "Form Criticism and Beyond," *JBL* 88 (1969): 1-18.
5. Ibid., 5.
6. Ibid.

conventional genre. According to Muilenburg, many texts have been influenced by conventional genres (and presumably by other kinds of typicalities of language), but it is essential that biblical scholars also recognize the ways in which particular texts betray considerable uniqueness and literary artistry in their formulation.

Muilenburg's insights are of utmost importance for the practice of form criticism. Analysis of typicalities in the form and usage of language cannot adequately be formulated without also taking into account the unique features of individual texts. Indeed, Muilenburg's title, "Form Criticism and Beyond," seems to imply that what takes place "beyond" form criticism would be seriously engaged with form criticism itself. But Muilenburg actually does very little in that regard. Concerning Jer 2:1–4:4, for example, he does not say much beyond a few general statements about how typicalities of speech have shaped that text; he does little actual comparison of how typicalities and unique reformulations of typicalities interact with one another. In the rest of the essay (esp. pp. 9-18) he focuses almost entirely on how the rhetoric of individual texts shapes their particular artistry and structure, all the while largely failing to pay serious attention to the *interaction* between the typical and the unique in their formulation. I consider it of utmost importance to do both. Indeed, much of my own scholarly writing has attempted to explore the relationships between the typical and the unique in the formulation of texts.[7]

As we enter a new century, I consider it still to be of great importance that interrelationships between typicalities of language and unique *artistic* creativity be given greater emphasis, especially from the side of form criticism. Let me illustrate by means of an abbreviated discussion of Isa 1:2-20 — a text that I have discussed in more detail elsewhere.[8] Verses 2-3 open with a call to hear directed to heaven and earth: "Hear, O heavens; give ear, O earth, for YHWH has spoken." Then YHWH begins to speak: "Children [lit. 'sons'] I have reared and brought up, but they have rebelled against me." It appears that heaven and earth are here summoned as witnesses in a lawsuit of YHWH the parent against YHWH's children Israel. There are indeed linguistic con-

---

7. Melugin, "The Typical Versus the Unique among the Hebrew Prophets," *SBLSP* (2 vols.; 1972), 2:331-41; "The Conventional and the Creative in Isaiah's Judgment Oracles," *CBQ* 36 (1974): 301-11; *The Formation of Isaiah 40–55* (BZAW 141; Berlin and New York: de Gruyter, 1976); "Muilenburg, Form Criticism, and Theological Exegesis," in *Encounter with the Text: Form and History in the Hebrew Bible* (ed. M. J. Buss; Philadelphia: Fortress; Missoula, Mont.: Scholars Press, 1979), 91-100; "Figurative Speech and the Reading of Isaiah 1 as Scripture," in *New Visions of Isaiah* (ed. R. F. Melugin and M. A. Sweeney; JSOTSup 214; Sheffield: Sheffield Academic Press, 1996), 282-305.

8. Melugin, "Figurative Speech," 282-91.

ventions for summoning natural phenomena such as heaven and earth to participate in a legal controversy against Israel.[9] Moreover, Deut 21:18-21 exhibits a social convention of a parental lawsuit against a stubborn and rebellious son — a convention that surely lies behind YHWH's speech in Isa 1:2b.[10] Yet the text is shaped with artistic imagination. Heaven and earth are summoned to hear the accusatory speech, a speech that contrasts YHWH's guidance as parent ("children I have reared and brought up") and the children's rebellion ("and they rebelled against me"). Then comes parable-like language: "The ox knows its owner and the ass its master's crib; but Israel does not know, my people do not understand."[11] It is indeed fruitful to understand how typicalities of language have contributed to the formulation of vv. 2-3, but it is also crucial to comprehend the artistic freedom that can also be seen in the formulation of the text.

Verses 4-9 continue to emphasize the rebellious behavior of YHWH's children, but the speech is no longer in the mouth of God. Instead it is in large measure a conventional human woe speech *about* God with regard to God's disobedient children: "Woe, sinful nation, people heavy with iniquity, seed of evildoers, destroying sons" (v. 4).[12] Moreover, they have forsaken YHWH, despised the Holy One of Israel, and turned backward. Then a question is posed to the rebellious children: "Why will you still be smitten, continue to turn aside?" (v. 5). Questions are not uncommon in woe speeches,[13] but here the question has a particular function. Given the fact that God's children are wounded from the bottom of the foot to the top of the head, that their wounds are open sores without benefit of healing, and that their land lies desolate with cities destroyed by fire and daughter Zion left alone "like a booth in a vineyard, like a lodge in a cucumber field" (vv. 5-8), why do they keep coming back for more blows?

Verses 4-9 exhibit much of the typical language of prophetic woe speeches, even with the question style (v. 5a) as part of the depiction of the woeful behavior of YHWH's rebellious children. For the question, "why will you still be smitten?" poetically describes the ongoing stupidity of disobedient children who keep coming back for further blows upon their already bruised bodies. The poet uses a conventional speech form as a vehicle for quite unique imagery. Moreover, at the end of the speech, after the foolish

9. Mic 6:1-2; Jer 2:12; see also Ps 50:4.

10. See J. W. Whedbee, *Isaiah and Wisdom* (Nashville: Abingdon, 1971), 21.

11. Ibid., 39-43.

12. For the woe speeches of the prophets, see, e.g., E. Gerstenberger, "The Woe-Oracles of the Prophets," *JBL* 81 (1962): 249-64; Whedbee, *Isaiah and Wisdom*, 80-110.

13. See, e.g., Isa 1:5; 10:3; 45:9-10, 11; Amos 6:2.

and rebellious children have been told that their country is desolate, their cities burned with fire, and their land "eaten" by aliens (v. 7), they hear not a conventional announcement of punishment but rather: "If YHWH of hosts had not left us a few survivors, we would have been like Sodom and become like Gomorrah," that is, totally destroyed (v. 9).[14] That vv. 4-9 end with "if YHWH of hosts had not left us a few survivors . . ." rather than with a more typical announcement of judgment shows the capacity of a poet to formulate a creative and unique utterance by making use of well-known typicalities of speech and artfully reshaping them.

The combining of a trial speech in the mouth of YHWH (vv. 2-3) and a woe utterance as human voice (vv. 4-9) shows how artistically reshaped conventional speech forms can be juxtaposed for creative purposes. Both "genre units" portray God's children as both rebellious and foolish: in the first unit they are compared unfavorably with animals who "know" who provides them with food to eat. In the second they foolishly keep coming back for further beatings, even though their entire bodies are completely covered with still-festering wounds and their land (*all* of it?) is being eaten by aliens. Two different linguistic conventions are artfully juxtaposed by creatively combining similar themes and by the skillful poetic use of imagery.

Limitation of space prevents a discussion of vv. 2-20 as a whole, but my concern for showing the interrelationships of typicalities of speech and individual artistic creativity should by now be clear. Indeed, form criticism in a new century can profitably pay more careful attention to the relationships between typical and unique elements in texts, especially when texts are formulated with consummate literary artistry. Muilenburg suggested the need for such a midcourse correction, but sophisticated literary analyses of the artistic interrelationships between the two have not yet been undertaken with the frequency for which one might hope. Form criticism and studies of creative poetic artistry still tend not to appear together. A task for form criticism in a new century indeed!

Rolf Knierim's essay, "Old Testament Form Criticism Reconsidered,"[15] has also had a major influence on the ways in which some form critics have conceptualized relationships between typical and unique aspects of texts. Interrelationships between the typical and the unique are only part of Knierim's

---

14. B. S. Childs argues that the usual "invective-threat" (or "announcement of judgment" and its accompanying "reason for judgment") has undergone modification by the announcement's having been replaced by a lament. See Childs, *Isaiah and the Assyrian Crisis* (SBT 2/3; Naperville, Ill.: Allenson, 1967), 20-22.

15. Knierim, "Old Testament Form Criticism Reconsidered," *Int* 27 (1973): 435-68.

concerns, for he argues in this essay that much of what was commonly assumed about form criticism needs considerable rethinking. For instance, he contends that form criticism should not be limited to orality but should be extended to written speech as well. Furthermore, what a genre *is* needs reconsideration. It is mistaken, he says, to believe that genres are always governed primarily by linguistic form. Although that is often the case, they can be governed by other kinds of typicalities, for example, the setting.[16]

The tendency to limit "setting" to social setting also needs reconsideration, Knierim argues. There can be variety in kinds of settings.[17] There can indeed be "institutional" settings, but the style of a particular epoch or age can sometimes account for certain typicalities. Or particular typicalities could perhaps be governed by prerational structures of the mind,[18] or by a certain kind of mental orientation or "occupation of mind" *(Geistes-beschäftigung),* says Knierim.[19] There are of course other possibilities as well.

The totality of Knierim's arguments can scarcely be presented in the space available here, but anyone who reads Knierim's essay will recognize that perhaps its greatest significance has to do (1) with his understanding of the immense variety of ways in which typicalities may be expressed, and (2) with his awareness of the necessity for taking into account both what is typical and what is unique in individual texts. Indeed, he makes explicit reference to the work of Muilenburg in this regard.[20] Furthermore, he argues the necessity of *beginning* with the structure of individual texts as they presently appear before us. Structural analysis of the particular form of individual texts must precede investigation of how those texts are governed by typicalities.[21]

A perusal of various volumes in the Forms of the Old Testament Literature (FOTL) series shows the influence of Knierim in recent form-critical study, especially in North America. In the FOTL volumes on 1 and 2 Kings, for example, Burke Long begins with the structure of the entire written text in its present form.[22] Moreover, in his discussion of various smaller units, he constantly considers their role in the book as a whole to be of primary importance for his commentary. A few examples must suffice. Although Long acknowledges that the narrative of the killing of Joab (1 Kgs 2:28-35) may have

16. Ibid., 456.
17. Ibid., 464ff.
18. Ibid., 438-41.
19. Ibid., 441-42.
20. Ibid., 458.
21. Ibid., 461.
22. Burke O. Long, *1 Kings, with an Introduction to Historical Literature* (FOTL 9; Grand Rapids: Eerdmans, 1984), 13-30.

originated among Solomonic partisans, the story's "most important setting" is now the literary context of the book of 1 Kings.[23] The account of Solomon's wisdom as reported in a dream epiphany (3:16-28) might have originated in the royal court "among courtesans who supported Solomon," but "more to the point, however, is to reflect on the present literary setting given the unit."[24] The story about the "care and provisioning of Elijah" (17:2-16) is a prophetic legend that may have originally been preserved in prophetic circles, but it now has an important setting in its present *literary* context.[25]

Marvin Sweeney's FOTL commentary on Isaiah 1–39 also begins with the structure of Isaiah 1–66 as as whole. As Sweeney understands the entirety of the book, it has two major concerns: (1) YHWH's plans for worldwide sovereignty at Zion (Isa 1–33), and (2) realization of YHWH's plans for worldwide sovereignty at Zion (Isa 34–66).[26] Although many of the smaller units arose in a variety of settings, each of the smaller units presently in the book of Isaiah contributes to the larger purpose represented by the two-part macrostructure of Isaiah 1-66. Indeed, Sweeney argues in some detail that various smaller structural units support the purposes of the book as a whole.[27] Though Sweeney sees the book as a composite work that was formed by four major stages of redaction (in the 8th century, the late 7th century, the 6th century, and the 5th century), its present form "was designed to support the reforms of Ezra and Nehemiah."[28] Thus the most fundamental intent of Sweeney's commentary is to show how each of its smaller parts contributes to the structure and intention of the book of Isaiah as a whole, even though he also tries to reconstruct the composition history of the book as well.

## The Problem of Setting

Another common practice of form critics that needs evaluation is the tendency to put forth highly speculative reconstruction of *settings,* especially reconstructed historical settings in which texts supposedly originated. One might think, for example, of Hans Walter Wolff's speculative proposals about the redaction history of the book of Amos or of Micah, or those of James Lu-

23. Ibid., 55.
24. Ibid., 66.
25. Ibid., 181-83.
26. Marvin A. Sweeney, *Isaiah 1–39, with an Introduction to Prophetic Literature* (FOTL 16; Grand Rapids and Cambridge, U.K.: Eerdmans, 1996), 39-41.
27. Ibid., 39-51.
28. Ibid., 51-60.

ther Mays on those same prophetic books. Or one might think of Marvin
Sweeney's hypotheses regarding the growth of the book of Isaiah.

The tendency among the form-critical commentaries in the FOTL series to de-emphasize redaction-historical questions to some degree in favor of
more attention to books in their final form takes a more radical turn in the
recent form-critical commentary on Micah by Ehud Ben Zvi.[29] Ben Zvi intentionally centers almost all of his discussion on the written book of Micah
in its presently completed form. He steadfastly refuses to deal with form and
setting of traditions used in the book of Micah prior to the time of the written *book* of Micah. Indeed, he criticizes scholars who try to reconstruct earlier
stages in the formation of the book.

> They tend to agree that the references or allusions made by the textually in-
> scribed speaker to events such as the destruction of a city or town were di-
> rectly and unequivocally related, at least in the original text, to actual, par-
> ticular, historical events that happened either shortly before or soon after
> the composition of the text. Moreover, the temporal references conveyed by
> the speaker to the addressees in the world of the text tend to be interpreted
> mimetically. To illustrate, if the speaker's words in the text are understood
> to describe the fall of Samaria as standing in the future from the perspective
> of the utterance in the text, then the claim is often made that these words of
> this text were actually composed or uttered before the historical event, in
> this case, the fall of Samaria.
>
> One may notice, in short, that these approaches tend to focus their at-
> tention on a set of possible, but still speculative, reconstructions of the
> words of the historical Micah; these reconstructions are in the main
> achieved by selective deletions from the present text on the grounds of
> (1) perceived rules of stylistic, thematic consistency, and (2) an approach to
> the text that presupposes that its original version must have been consistent
> with an assumed high degree of direct correspondence between the world
> in the text and that of monarchic Judah in the 8th century.[30]

Indeed, argues Ben Zvi, there is not necessarily a strong correspondence
between what is depicted in a text and the empirically experienced realities of
an actual historical situation. Let me illustrate from his discussion of Mic 2:1-5.
Woe is pronounced upon persons who "devise wickedness and work evil upon
their beds" (v. 1a). They make evil plans at night when they are on their beds;

---

29. Ehud Ben Zvi, *Micah* (FOTL 21B; Grand Rapids and Cambridge, U.K.: Eerdmans,
2000).

30. Ibid., 25.

and when morning comes, they carry out their evil plans because they have the power to carry out their evil intent (see v. 1b). They "covet fields and seize them, and houses and take them away" (v. 2a). We can readily comprehend the *kind* of circumstance that the text depicts: the evildoers described in the text oppress those who are economically vulnerable, and they are able to deprive persons of their inheritance.[31] But, as Ben Zvi says, "the most significant feature of this particular characterization of the evildoers is that in itself it is devoid of unequivocal markers pointing to a specific historical situation."[32] Indeed, this kind of activity could have taken place at almost any time and therefore cannot be shown to have come from the eighth-century Micah.

If one reads Mic 2:1-5 as a word spoken by Micah about events in the eighth century, one does so not because the language within 2:1-5 demands it, but because the superscription in 1:1 provides a context for reading 2:1-5 as the "word of YHWH that came to Micah of Moresheth in the days of Jotham, Ahaz, and Hezekiah, kings of Judah." In 2:1-5, taken by itself, "these wrongdoers are presented as a timeless type of 'land-grabber,' one that could be taken up by different referents depending on the world of the rereaders."[33]

If the *language* of 2:1-5 (and many other texts in Micah) cannot tell us the historical setting of the text's origin, the reconstruction of the history of the growth of the book is placed in considerable jeopardy. Indeed, Ben Zvi forces us to ask whether redaction-historical reconstruction as a correlative of form criticism can be used persuasively with great success.

I am convinced that Ben Zvi has recognized something quite significant. I have argued that many texts use language figuratively — that they portray a "fictive" picture of reality, a picture that cannot be directly correlated with historical reality.[34]

> Most of what the book of Isaiah portrays . . . is difficult to correlate precisely with actual historical events. We read about "daughters of Zion" whose stylish glitter will be replaced by the worst ready-to-wear imaginable (3.16–4.1), but we know almost nothing about the particular historical events which might have occasioned this utterance. We hear a song about Israelites and Judahites who judge Yahweh's vineyard because of the failure to produce justice (5.1-7), but we know virtually nothing of the specific cir-

---

31. Ibid., 43-44.

32. Ibid., 44.

33. Ibid., 44.

34. Melugin, "Prophetic Books and the Problem of Historical Reconstruction," in *Prophets and Paradigms: Essays in Honor of Gene M. Tucker* (ed. S. B. Reid; JSOTSup 229; Sheffield: Sheffield Academic Press, 1996), 63-78 (esp. 70-74).

cumstances which may have occasioned this song. Because these portrayals are metaphorical, we do not know whether specific events generated them or whether they are metaphorically formulated descriptions of *characteristic* behavior. The very language of the text is indeed a barrier to precise resolution of such uncertainties.[35]

If Ben Zvi has seen correctly that the language of texts is often not mimetic, and if my own view is right that texts — especially poetic texts — frequently depict a "fictive" picture of reality, many attempts to reconstruct the history of the growth process of texts may be unreliable. For the purpose of testing this assertion, I turn to the sophisticated reconstruction of the redaction history of the book of Isaiah by Marvin Sweeney.[36] Lamentably, given the limitations of space, I must give less than full justice to the complexity of his arguments, but I hope that my critique will nonetheless prove useful.

Even though Sweeney understands that Isaiah 1–66 in its present completed form is a unified literary work, he sees it as a redactional composition of the mid- to late-fifth century BCE — a work designed to support the reforms of Ezra and Nehemiah.[37] The fifth-century redactors themselves created 1:1, 19-20, 27-28; 2:1; 4:3-6; 33; 34; 56–59; and 63–66.

The fifth-century redactional composition built its edifice upon a late-sixth-century redaction. These sixth-century redactors shaped the basic form of several major blocks of text (2:2–4:2; 24–27; 35; 60–62), as well as the oracle against Babylon at the beginning of the body of oracles against the nations. And, in Isaiah 36–39, they added and reworked materials from 2 Kings 18–20. In addition, the late-sixth-century redactors actually composed a number of texts, including 2:2-4, 5; 4:2; 13:2-22; 14:1-2, 3-4a, 22-23; 24–26; 35; and 60–62. Sweeney believes that this redactional layer was connected with the completion of the second Jerusalem temple.[38]

A late-seventh-century redactional layer reworked earlier material and contributed significantly to the shape of chaps. 5–12; 14–23*; 27; 28–32; and 36–37 for the sake of supporting Josiah's "national and religious restoration in Jerusalem."[39] Indeed, several texts were composed especially for this redaction: a reconfigured form of chap. 7 (vv. 1-4, 10, 18-19, 21-25); 15:2b; 16:13-14; 20; 23:1a, 15-18; 27; 30:19-33; 32:1-8, 15-20; and a "reworked form of 2 Kings 18–19 in Isaiah 36–37" (along with 19:18-25 also).

35. Ibid., 72.
36. Sweeney, *Isaiah 1–39*, 51-60.
37. Ibid., 51-55.
38. Ibid., 55-57.
39. Ibid., 57-59.

The eighth-century Isaiah contributed materials from various periods of his career, according to Sweeney: from the period of the Syro-Ephraimite war (1:21-26, 27-31; 5:1-24; 6:1-11 [12-13]; 7:2-17*, 20; 8:1-15; 8:16–9:6; 15:1b-16:12; and 29:15-24), the fall of Samaria and early rule of Sargon II (5:25-30; 9:7–10:4; 10:5-34; 14:24-27; 17-18; 19:1-17; 29:1-14), Hezekiah's revolt against Assyria (1:2-9, 10-18; 2:6-19; 3:1-9, 12-15; 3:6–4:1; 14:4b-21, 28-32; 22:1b-14, 15-25; 23:1b-14; 28; 30:1-18; 31; 32:9-14), and Sennacherib's attacks against the Chaldean Merodach-baladan (21:1-10, 11-12, 13-17).[40]

Almost no one doubts that the book underwent growth over a period of several centuries, but there is reason to question whether the growth process can be reconstructed with the precision claimed by Sweeney. For example, I would raise serious questions about the construction of the supposed "Josiah redaction." Although some of the material that Sweeney assigns to this hypothetical layer of redaction is surely later than the eighth century, the connection with Josiah seems extremely tenuous. For instance, the claim that a "small boy leading them" in 11:6b is "an allusion to the boy-king Josiah" seems far-fetched.[41] The little child who leads is not designated in the text as a king; what we have here is a depiction of a state of paradise during the new king's rule — a paradise so complete that animals who are usually enemies will dwell together so peacefully that even a small child will be able to lead them. Furthermore, Sweeney's assertion that the new "shoot" or "sprout" of Isaiah 11 is clearly a reference to Josiah because his father was assassinated, whereas Hezekiah's father was not, appears to be a prosaic overliteralizing of poetic imagery — exactly the kind of mimetic understanding of poetry that Ben Zvi criticizes. At least as tenuous is the supposed tie between the justice and wisdom of the king in Isaiah 11 and the newly found lawbook as a basis for Josiah's reform,[42] as well as the hypothesized connection between the exodus traditions in 11:11-16 + 12:1-6 and Josiah's concern with Passover.[43] The alleged similarity between the nations mentioned in 11:11-16 and Josiah's attempt to rebuild the Davidic empire involves an assumption that the poetry in this part of Isaiah mimetically represents political reality.[44]

This kind of mimetic interpretation of poetic language is characteris-

---

40. Ibid., 59.
41. Ibid., 204.
42. Ibid., 204.
43. Ibid., 117, 205.
44. Ibid., 116, 205. Sweeney's arguments supporting his reconstruction of a redactional layer associated with Josiah's reform is of course more complex than I have had space to discuss, but I have questions about some of the remainder of his arguments supporting a "Josiah redaction."

tic of other passages in Sweeney's hypothesized layers of redaction as well. Indeed, such interpretation of poetic texts is not at all unusual among redaction historians. This approach to poetry is, however, not nearly so prevalent among literary critics outside the guild of biblical studies. Redaction historians such as Sweeney are indeed learned and extremely sophisticated, but wider reading in literary criticism, I strongly suspect, might result in a significant lowering of confidence in the kinds of redaction-historical analysis currently in vogue among many biblical scholars. I must not be understood as recommending that redaction history disappear altogether as we enter a new century. It can continue to be useful, but only in a more limited and less speculative mode. We must learn to let poetry function with its own kind of referentiality, no longer artificially the servant of historical reference exclusively.

There are good reasons for attempting to recover the *conventional* (as opposed to the historically particular) settings in which typical kinds of speech were habitually employed. One thinks of conventional settings for various kinds of psalms, or of priestly torah, or of prophecies of judgment addressed to individuals, all of which have certain conventional settings that we can identify with a relatively high degree of probability. Conventional settings for many typicalities of speech, however, cannot be so easily identified. Are the "fear not" oracles of Deutero-Isaiah priestly salvation oracles (Begrich), oracles used by prophets in the cult (von Waldow), or war oracles (Conrad)?[45] Similar doubts exist about setting for many other typicalities of speech.

That we cannot recover settings for some typicalities of speech need not necessarily undermine confidence in the enterprise of attempting such reconstructions. But if we do not have enough information to recover settings for a large percentage of typicalities of speech (and I fear that this may be quite often the case), we should not proceed into the new century by continuing almost always to place high priority on something that is in practice frequently incapable of successful realization.

Because we often lack information regarding historical settings or the conventional settings in which certain speeches, together with their typicalities, were employed, we might do well to place less emphasis on reconstructions of settings outside the text and focus more on how the *text itself* depicts

---

45. Joachim Begrich, "Das priesterliche Heilsorakel," *ZAW* 52 (1934): 81-92; Hans-Eberhard von Waldow, *Anlass und Hintergrund der Verkundigung des Deuterojesajas* (diss., Bonn, 1953); Edgar W. Conrad, *Fear Not Warrior: A Study of 'al tira' Pericopes in the Hebrew Scriptures* (BJS 75; Chico, Calif.: Scholars Press, 1985).

the "reality" with which it is concerned. In Mic 2:1-5, for example, we are told nothing definite about the particular historical setting in which the text originated, nor have we hard information about the conventional settings in which woe oracles against groups of persons were used.

What we are almost always able to identify is what might be called a *textually portrayed* setting. For example, Mic 2:1-5 portrays calculated planning that evildoers undertake when they lie on their beds. Isaiah 41:21-29 depicts an imaginary trial between YHWH and the gods. Or Isa 40:1-11 portrays an imaginary scene in the heavenly council — probably an act of commissioning. Such depictions of reality — often imaginary — represent what is actually given to us in the text. When we focus on these aspects of the text, we are not forced into speculative reconstructions about realities that lie behind the text. Moreover, I would argue, such textual portrayals are of immense value in the enterprise of interpretation. Indeed, they often provide more insight for interpretation than do dubious reconstructions of hypothetical extratextual realities. Such textually portrayed settings are of course not extratextual realities, and perhaps the term "setting" as a technical term should not be used for these purely literary phenomena. Yet these textual portrayals of reality are of utmost importance in the activity of interpretation. Moreover, they sometimes represent typicalities in textual depiction of "reality." In any event, whatever terminology we use, should we not learn to pay more attention to such important kinds of "settings"?

We should also pay increased attention to the ways in which smaller units of text relate synchronically to larger literary texts, up to and including entire biblical books. As one can see from my discussion of Rolf Knierim earlier in this essay, such a concern is clearly implied in his reconceptualization of form criticism. Further examples in my discussion above may be found in Long's discussions of setting, in Sweeney's presentations of structure, and in my own analysis of Isa 1:2ff. Ben Zvi's analyses of how smaller literary units fit into the book of Micah as a whole are also examples of what I have in mind.

## Form Criticism in an Ethos of Reading and Rereading

In this essay thus far I have tended to place more confidence in the literary (especially "literary-artistic") side of form criticism and in a focus on the completed written text than in an ability on our part to reconstruct historical or conventional societal settings. Indeed, in so doing, I am following in some respects the holistic literary-artistic approaches that have been present in our discipline for some time (see the work, e.g., of Robert Alter, James Ackerman, and Cheryl Exum).[46]

I have been especially interested in Ben Zvi's new FOTL commentary on Micah because he, as a form critic, is concerned with the written book of Micah as a text to be read holistically. He is furthermore concerned with the activities of readers as they engage in reading and rereading an entire written book. Readers of the book of Micah, Ben Zvi argues, were reading the book as a postmonarchic text written for readers in the postexilic period. Even though the world *within* the text (i.e., the world that the text presents) is portrayed within the text as a monarchic world, especially because of the superscription (Mic 1:1), the actual readers of the book lived in a postexilic situation. Indeed, because they lived in a historical setting different from the world portrayed within the text, they would not have read the text mimetically, but rather as a text that they used to speak to their own situation — a situation that was markedly different from the monarchic world presented *within* the text. And because these postmonarchic readers possessed a written book, they could (and surely did) read and reread the book. What must have resulted, Ben Zvi argues, was a multiplicity of readings. Multiple readings occurred because the text itself is not monovalent but polyvalent. Moreover, a first reading would undoubtedly differ from a second reading, and a third reading, and a fourth reading, and so on.[47]

It is noteworthy that Ben Zvi has moved from focusing primarily on authorial intent to what readers do. Indeed, in recent years an entire movement in literary criticism has centered on the role of readers in the setting forth of meaning (see, e.g., Wolfgang Iser, Umberto Eco, Stanley Fish).[48] While "reader-response" critics do not all agree as to the nature and extent of the reader's role in the making of meaning, they do concur that what readers

---

46. Robert Alter, *The Art of Biblical Narrative* (New York: Basic Books, 1981); James S. Ackerman, "The Literary Context of the Moses Birth Story (Exodus 1–2)," in *Literary Interpretations of Biblical Narratives* (ed. K. R. R. Gros Louis, with J. S. Ackerman and T. S. Warshaw; Nashville and New York: Abingdon, 1974), 74-119; J. Cheryl Exum, "'Whom will he teach knowledge?': A Literary Approach to Isaiah 28," in *Art and Meaning: Rhetoric in Biblical Literature* (ed. D. J. A. Clines, D. M. Gunn, and A. J. Hauser; JSOTSup 19; Sheffield: JSOT Press, 1982), 108-39.

47. Ben Zvi, *Micah*, 5-10.

48. Wolfgang Iser, *The Act of Reading: A Theory of Aesthetic Response* (Baltimore and London: Johns Hopkins Univ. Press, 1978); Umberto Eco, *The Role of the Reader: Explorations on the Semiotics of Texts* (London: Hutchinson, 1981); Stanley Fish, *Is There a Text in This Class? The Authority of Interpretive Communities* (Cambridge, Mass., and London: Harvard Univ. Press, 1980).

bring to the activity of interpretation affects to no small degree how a text will be understood.[49]

Ben Zvi is not attempting to be hermeneutically postmodern, as far as I can see; he simply intends to reconstruct what readers did in a particular historical period, that is, the situation of Israelites in the Persian II period (ca. 450-332 BCE).[50] But his emphasis on the polyvalence of the text and on the activity of rereading complicates the recovery of what these Persian-period readers actually did. The most Ben Zvi can do is to imagine the meanings they *might* have produced as they read and reread and came up with everdifferent meanings as the various rereadings were undertaken. To be sure, Ben Zvi sometimes speaks of textual intent, implied audience, and signals that the text itself gives.[51] But if later interpretations of rabbis or early Christian writers suggest any analogies at all for how ancient readers reread texts, one wonders whether Persian-period readers would have focused as intently on the text's linguistic signals as Ben Zvi seems to imagine. My hunch is that Persian-period rereadings also would have characteristically involved reading *into* texts many things that are scarcely prompted by the text itself. I wonder, therefore, if Ben Zvi, with his emphasis on *textual* signals and *textual* polyvalence, isn't prompting us to imagine kinds of readings more like present-day literary rereadings than like the kinds of rereadings that Persianperiod Israelites would probably have practiced.[52] Indeed, it appears to me that Ben Zvi may unintentionally be "postmodern" in the sense that he imaginatively *constructs* his proposed readers of Micah — fictive rereaders who are halfway ancient and halfway modern because they seem to follow the signals of the text in ways that seem characteristic of trained readers of our own age.

49. If this is so, we can no longer uncritically assume that meaning resides solely, or perhaps even primarily, in author or text.

50. Ben Zvi, *Micah,* 10.

51. Even though Ben Zvi speaks of what readers might do, especially when the text itself gives ambiguous signals, he still focuses on how the *text* leads the reader (see, e.g., ibid., 23-27) and the understanding that the "intended" reader was supposed to manifest (see, e.g., 34). Even though Ben Zvi talks about what readers do, his way of describing what readers would be led to do seems strongly influenced by formalistic impulses.

52. If Persian-period readers would, as I suspect, have rather freely read *into* texts much that was generated by the experiences of the social situation of their time, they surely would not have approached the text with a singleminded focus on the signals given by the text. Ben Zvi's supposed readers appear to me, at least as I can best understand, to be readers much like trained modern readers — readers who are disciplined to follow the signals of the text in ways analogous to our modern critical focus on the text and its signals. Obviously, Persian-period readers would have paid attention to the text and its signals, but surely not the ways we moderns do it.

My purpose here is to argue that, as we enter a new century, form criticism cannot avoid recognizing the immensity of the interpreter's role in the making of meaning. It is patently obvious that any of our interpretations of a text will undoubtedly be influenced considerably by what *we* bring to the text. A form critic, for example, will ask questions a non–form critic would not formulate. Moreover, different kinds of form critics will read the text somewhat differently.

Furthermore, as we move into an age that values holistic readings more than was the case a quarter of a century ago, we must recognize that the shift from the earlier searching for the *smallest* units to looking for patterns that constitute the whole is not the result of a change in the text itself but rather a marked difference in how scholars ask questions of the text. And as we engage increasingly in holistic approaches, it will become more and more obvious that different interpreters will construe the meaning of the whole in different ways. For example, H. G. M. Williamson emphasizes verbal similarity in his argument that "Second Isaiah" was constructed by building upon older "First Isaiah" texts. Isaiah 52:13 and 57:15 were influenced by Isaiah 6 and its vision of the Lord as "high and lifted up" (6:1), to cite but one example from his impressive set of arguments.[53] Yet if Williamson had decided to concentrate on ways in which imagery is used rather than on verbal repetition, he would have undoubtedly developed a different interpretation of the interrelationships of various texts within the book of Isaiah. Or if Sweeney, instead of constructing a structural outline for the book of Isaiah that is fundamentally hierarchical and sequential in character, had proposed a significantly less hierarchical and less sequential conceptualization of structure, we would have undoubtedly been given a rather different, but perhaps equally viable, understanding of the meaning of the book.[54]

While I would certainly not want to argue that any construal is necessarily as adequate as any other construal, I would contend that there can sometimes be different interpretations for which an equally good case can be made.[55] We are indeed living in an age in which such possibilities are increasingly recognized in the community of interpreters of literature. For form crit-

---

53. H. G. M. Williamson, *The Book Called Isaiah: Deutero-Isaiah's Role in Composition and Redaction* (Oxford: Clarendon, 1994), 30-56, esp. 38-39. See also the discussion of Williamson in Melugin, "The Book of Isaiah and the Construction of Meaning," in *Writing and Reading the Scroll of Isaiah: Studies of an Interpretive Tradition* (ed. C. C. Broyles and C. A. Evans; 2 vols.; Leiden, New York, and Cologne: Brill, 1997), 1:39-55, esp. 44-45.

54. See the discussion by Melugin in "Book of Isaiah," 47-48.

55. Ibid., 48, 50-51.

ics to continue on without recognition of the interpreters' role in the making of meaning would indeed be to hide our heads in the sand.

Since form criticism has generally seen itself in large measure as a discipline strongly committed to historical criticism, it will become increasingly important for form critics to take into account the arguments of those who contend that historians themselves do not simply *describe* the past but, in some significant degree, play roles as *creators* of particular portrayals of the past. There are reasons why this is so. First of all, our resources for historical reconstruction are often verbal resources, whether oral or written. Moreover, these resources come already packaged, framed often, for example, as "memoirs, reports, published writings, archives, monuments," that is, as packages in which the past is already given particular interpretations.[56] Thus we cannot claim to have unbiased resources.

Second, we cannot claim that our own historical reconstructions are utterly neutral. As Hayden White teaches us, the totality of resources available to us for our historical research is often so large that we have to choose what is relevant for our historical inquiry and what is not.[57] *We* do the choosing; and our choices are by no means unaffected by *our* particular worldviews, *our* views of human nature, and much else from our own culture and our culture's interpretive communities. Then, White tells us, our resources are too small: we must *decide* how to connect what we have found in the various parts of the body of resources from which we have chosen what seems to be relevant. *We* must create a story; *we* must "emplot," that is, create a plot or story, which is in some sense *our* reconstruction of history.[58] Again, how our own culture has shaped us is a significant factor — though by no means the only factor — in the ways we emplot the past. What is in our resources will have significantly affected our historical reconstruction; but who *we* are, as persons shaped by particular interpretive communities, will also dramatically influence the form of the story that *we* play a major role in creating.

Obviously there is no reconstruction of the past that is completely neutral and objective. Does this mean that we can make no valid evaluations between historical claims? Yes and no. No in the sense that no claim is without

56. See L. S. Kramer, "Literature, Criticism, and Historical Imagination: The Literary Challenge of Hayden White and Dominick LaCapra," in *The New Cultural History* (ed. L. Hunt; Los Angeles: Univ. of California Press, 1989), 114-15. See also the discussion by E. Conrad, "Prophet, Redactor, and Audience: Reforming the Notion of Isaiah's Formation," in *New Visions of Isaiah*, ed. Melugin and Sweeney, 306-26, esp. 311-17.

57. Hayden White, *Tropics of Discourse: Essays in Cultural Criticism* (Baltimore and London: Johns Hopkins Univ. Press, 1978), 51.

58. Ibid., 61-75.

any bias at all. But yes, if by that we mean that we can often make reliable judgments. We can quite reliably show, for example, that fundamentalists have judged unreliably when they "familiarize Genesis 1 and read it as science."[59] We can indeed make a good case for arguing that the paradigms responsible for shaping Genesis 1 were quite different from those that gave rise to a modern paradigm of biblical inerrancy and its perceived need for the Bible and science to be compatible. Nevertheless, even our own reliable evaluative arguments will still be shaped in some ways by *our* culture and its ways of thinking.

To what extent form criticism will continue to require the activity of historical reconstruction remains to be seen. The proposals I have made in this essay downplay to a considerable extent the necessity of historical reconstruction. But I would still be among the first to argue that historical inquiry can profitably continue to play important roles in the study of the Bible. Yet when historical reconstruction does take place, the resulting historical picture will be in some significant degree the creative product of the historian and the historian's own cultural setting.

## Conclusion

To sum up: I have argued here the need for greater emphasis on the *interrelationships* between the typical and the unique (with particular concern for poetic artistry) and for greater focus on the study of texts in their completed written form. Moreover, I have argued for a significant de-emphasis in attempts to reconstruct historical and conventional societal settings, not because such reconstructions would inherently be of little value but because such reconstructions are often highly speculative. Furthermore, I have proposed that form critics develop greater awareness of the creative and imaginative role played by interpreters in both their literary and historical research.

What I have proposed here has been based to a large extent on my understanding of what we can and cannot do well. To try to do more would transcend the limits of this essay. Yet further discussion about method ultimately needs to be undertaken. In the end I would want to argue that exegetical method is task-oriented. Attempts to understand the history of the religion of Israel and endeavors to interpret biblical texts for the sake of aiding present-day communities of faith to use the text for imaginatively constructing a symbolic world for transformation of identity and behavior are

59. See Conrad, "Prophet, Redactor, and Audience," 315.

significantly different undertakings, and they might well require different kinds of exegetical strategies.[60] They also might need to employ form criticism differently. Such questions cannot be answered here, but correlations between particular interpretive purposes and appropriate exegetical methods are ultimately issues of great importance. May the discussion continue!

60. Attempts to reconstruct Israelite religion might conceivably have an interest in reconstructing the redaction history of a text (at least if such an enterprise could be done successfully). For a recent argument as to why a redaction-historical approach ought not be primary for *theologically* oriented interpretation, see Brevard S. Childs's most recent commentary, *Isaiah: A Commentary* (OTL; Louisville: Westminster John Knox, 2001). While not all theologically oriented commentators would necessarily agree with Childs about this, his entire commentary attempts to show why an approach that is primarily redaction-historical is not productive for interpreting biblical texts for the shaping of the life of communities of faith.

# Form Criticism, Wisdom, and Psalms 111–112

## RAYMOND C. VAN LEEUWEN

*Form ever follows function.*

LOUIS HENRY SULLIVAN

The questions, What is wisdom? How is it to be recognized? Where is it to be found? remain unresolved in biblical studies.[1] The questions are basic and seem to entail a vicious hermeneutical circle, for *how* one understands wisdom determines where one finds wisdom, while the (interpreted) texts are in turn presented as evidence for one's account of wisdom. Researchers inevitably bring to their exegetical work a variety of unstated theoretical and methodological assumptions. The textual data themselves are complex and diverse, and the HB/OT labels a wide range of things "wisdom" or "wise" (root *ḥkm* and terms in semantic relation to it).[2] One is tempted to say with Clifford

---

1. Cf. R. N. Whybray, "The Wisdom Psalms," in *Wisdom in Ancient Israel: Essays in Honour of J. A. Emerton* (ed. J. Day, R. P. Gordon, and H. G. M. Williamson; Cambridge: Cambridge Univ. Press, 1995), 152.

2. Many biblical "word studies" still ignore the basic linguistic tools for semantic analysis. For crucial conceptual tools such as "paradigmatic and syntagmatic relations," see J. Lyons, *Introduction to Theoretical Linguistics* (London: Cambridge Univ. Press, 1979), 70-81; or M. Silva, *Biblical Words and Their Meaning: An Introduction to Lexical Semantics* (Grand Rapids: Zondervan, 1994). For linguisticly informed studies of wisdom terms, see M. V. Fox, "Words for Wisdom," *ZAH* 6 (1993): 149-69; idem, "Words for Folly," *ZAH* 10 (1997): 1-10; idem, *Proverbs 1–9* (AB 18A; New York: Doubleday, 2000), 28-43. For problems of definition

---

I am indebted to my colleague, Kent L. Sparks, for insightful criticism on an earlier draft of this paper and for an unpublished chapter on "Generic Comparison" in a book on form criticism still in progress.

Geertz that these are "questions which seem . . . to turn so completely on defi-nitions as to reduce without residue to matters of intellectual policy and rhe-torical taste."[3] While conflicting definitions do play a role in the debate on wisdom in the Psalter, the temptation is to be resisted.

Natural kinds[4] and human artifacts (like a monarchy or minuet) em-body a richness of features and functions "out there" in reality to which our analytical acts of comparison, contrast, and classification respond more or less adequately, and according to our various epistemological or practical purposes. Some differences in classification arise simply because different features in the object are highlighted as significant. Thus a tree may belong to the classes of objects combustible, economic, aesthetic, and sacred. The real properties of the tree make possible its various functions in human use, in-cluding epistemological use. It is not simply one or another "kind" of thing, as we arbitrarily choose to name it, but potentially many things, if we rightly name the one tree in its diverse aspects. This does not mean that the tree is unreal or unknowable, just that its reality is functionally rich and complex, and that analysis may legitimately take many approaches to that reality. Nor does it mean that the tree is a dog or a rock — such use of language abuses the requirements of truth. The present paper revisits the problem of form criti-cism and wisdom in the Psalms, with primary reference to the "twin" Psalms 111–112.[5] Epistemologically, I reject a positivist or objectivist approach, which assumes object and definition or name wholly correspond, but I do assume that a careful, critical-realist approach may produce a hermeneutical "spiral" that advances our understanding of the ancient texts and wisdom.[6]

---

and concept formation, see F. Ungerer and H. J. Schmid, *An Introduction to Cognitive Linguis-tics* (New York: Longman, 1996). R. B. Y. Scott's well-known list of terms he thought charac-teristic of the wisdom literature is merely statistical and has no foundation in scientific lin-guistics and lexicography (*The Way of Wisdom in the Old Testament* [New York: Macmillan, 1971], 121-22).

3. C. Geertz, *Local Knowledge: Further Essays in Interpretive Anthropology* (New York: Basic Books, 1983), 75. Cf. R. Wellek, "Concepts of Form and Structure in Twentieth-Century Criticism," in *Concepts of Criticism* (ed. S. G. Nichols Jr.; New Haven: Yale Univ. Press, 1963), 54.

4. I use the phrase in a nonphilosophical, ordinary language sense to mean things given in nature such as stones, plants, animals, and stars.

5. E. Gerstenberger, "Psalms," in *Old Testament Form Criticism* (ed. J. H. Hayes; TUMSR 2; San Antonio: Trinity Univ. Press, 1974), 179-223, provides a convenient history of form-critical research that came to dominate psalm studies in the twentieth century.

6. For the (non-Platonic) sense of "critical realism" intended, see N. T. Wright, *The New Testament and the People of God* (Christian Origins and the Question of God; Minneap-olis: Fortress, 1992), 31-46. For evaluation of Wright's epistemology and method, see T. Moritz, "Critical but Real: Reflecting on N. T. Wright's *Tools for the Task*," in *Renewing Bib-*

In the last century or so, the biblical books designated "wisdom litera-ture" (Proverbs, Job, Ecclesiastes; secondarily Sirach and Wisdom of Solo-mon) have in one way or another functioned as the touchstone by which "wisdom" was recognized in the Bible or the ancient Near East.[7] Yet these books, for all that links them, are themselves diverse in genres and topics, many of which appear elsewhere in the Bible or ancient Near East. Scholars are not agreed about their generic unity or function, except perhaps that they inculcate wisdom![8] Recently, even such a leading wisdom scholar as J. L. Crenshaw could say of them only: "They retain *a mysterious ingredient* that links them together *in a special way.*"[9] Given the present diversity of ap-proaches, assumptions, and methods, it is not surprising that the search for wisdom has produced diverse opinion rather than settled results. Some seemed to find wisdom almost everywhere, while others found only minimal instances of wisdom outside the wisdom books.

In the scholarly quest for wisdom, form criticism has played an impor-tant but troubled role, especially in the Psalms.[10] Unlike most of Gunkel's *Gattungen* ("royal psalms" excepted), *Weisheitsdichtung* was vaguely defined,

---

*lical Interpretation* (ed. C. Bartholomew, C. Greene, and K. Möller; Carlisle: Paternoster, 2000), 172-97, with bibliography.

7. Explicitly Whybray, "Wisdom Psalms," 158. R. Smend, "The Interpretation of Wis-dom in Nineteenth-Century Scholarship," in *Wisdom in Ancient Israel,* ed. Day, Gordon, and Williamson, 257-68, provides a helpful overview of the nineteenth-century and early-twentieth-century background to this development.

8. R. N. Whybray, "The Social World of the Wisdom Writers," in *The World of Ancient Israel: Sociological, Anthropological and Political Perspectives* (ed. R. E. Clements; Cambridge: Cambridge Univ. Press, 1989), 229; cf. Whybray, "Wisdom Psalms," 158. J. L. Crenshaw be-lieves that "The goal of all wisdom was the formation of character." Thus for him Job's ethical testament in Job 31, "the most problematic in the wisdom literary corpus . . . is a good text to use in identifying wisdom" (*Old Testament Wisdom: An Introduction* [rev. ed.; Louisville: Westminster John Knox, 1998], 3, 7).

9. Crenshaw, *OT Wisdom,* 9.

10. Among others, see Gerstenberger, "Psalms"; D. M. Howard Jr., "Recent Trends in Psalms Studies," in *The Face of Old Testament Studies: A Survey of Contemporary Approaches* (ed. D. W. Baker and B. T. Arnold; Grand Rapids: Baker, 1999), 360-65; R. E. Murphy, "A Con-sideration of the Classification 'Wisdom Psalms,'" in *Congress Volume: Bonn 1962* (VTSup 9; Leiden: Brill, 1963), 156-67; L. G. Perdue, *Wisdom and Cult: A Critical Analysis of the Views of Cult in the Wisdom Literatures of Israel and the Ancient Near East* (SBLDS 30; Missoula, Mont.: Scholars Press, 1977), 261-343; J. Trublet, "Le Corpus Sapientiel et le Psautier," in *La Sagesse Biblique de l'Ancien au Nouveau Testament: Actes du XVᵉ Congrès de L'ACFEB (Paris, 1993)* (ed. J. Trublet; LD 10; Paris: Cerf, 1995), 139-74; Whybray, "Wisdom Psalms"; P. W. Ferris Jr., *The Genre of Communal Lament in the Bible and the Ancient Near East* (SBLDS 127; At-lanta: Scholars Press, 1992), 1-16.

being mostly based on content. In this connection, a recent essay by Crenshaw is worth discussing in some detail because of his stature in wisdom studies, because of the issues it raises, and because his article also appears virtually unchanged in his new textbook on the Psalter, where it is likely to exert wide influence.[11] He declares that he has come "to question the very category of wisdom psalms."[12] Referring to a seminal article by R. E. Murphy, Crenshaw argues that most of Murphy's content-related criteria for wisdom in the Psalter appear also in Amos and other prophets. Such shared ideas are not peculiarly sapiential. "These ideas belong rather to *a common ideology* in the ancient world."[13] Similarly, Crenshaw dismisses J. K. Kuntz's attempt to specify "rhetorical elements" of wisdom in the Psalms by showing that such elements were "shared rhetorical features in ancient Israel."[14] So also with vocabulary: "The linguistic basis for attempts to separate sapiential vocabulary from prophetic, priestly, and everyday discourse appears dubious to me, for *all social groups use language in pretty much the same way,* although minor differences in vocabulary and rhetoric may occur here and there. That reality explains the failure of all efforts to locate vocabulary peculiar to sages."[15]

Crenshaw reaches similar negative conclusions with regard to "thematic elements" presumed characteristic of wisdom. He rightly considers "the fear of YHWH" as a common Israelite term for "religion" or "piety," not specific to the sages (though the wisdom literature does use the idea frequently and foundationally).[16] Crenshaw considers "the fear of Yahweh" as wisdom only

---

11. J. L. Crenshaw, "Wisdom Psalms?" *CurBS* 8 (2000): 9-17; idem, *The Psalms: An Introduction* (Grand Rapids: Eerdmans, 2001).

12. Crenshaw, "Wisdom Psalms?" 15.

13. Ibid., 11 (my emphasis), discussing Murphy, "Classification."

14. Crenshaw, "Wisdom Psalms?" 11, citing J. K. Kuntz, "The Canonical Wisdom Psalms of Ancient Israel — Their Rhetorical, Thematic, and Formal Dimensions," in *Rhetorical Criticism: Essays in Honor of James Muilenburg* (ed. J. J. Jackson and M. Kessler; PTMS 1; Pittsburgh: Pickwick, 1974), 186-222.

15. Crenshaw, "Wisdom Psalms?" 12, my emphasis. The emphasized clause is either false or too general to be analytically useful. For example, all social groups use their mouths to speak, they all use Hebrew words. On p. 14, however, he cites A. Hurvitz, "Wisdom Vocabulary in the Hebrew Psalter: A Contribution to the Study of 'Wisdom Psalms,'" *VT* 38 (1988): 41-51, with approval. But Hurvitz's argument, based on unique vocabulary, is precarious, partly because so little of the classical Hebrew literature survives. Quite different methodologically is A. Hurvitz, "צדיק = 'Wise' in Biblical Hebrew and the Wisdom Connections of Psalm 37," in *"Sha'Arei Talmon": Studies in the Bible, Qumran, and the Ancient Near East Presented to Shemaryahu Talmon* (ed. M. Fishbane and E. Tov; Winona Lake, Ind.: Eisenbrauns, 1992), 131*-35* (Hebrew). I cannot agree with Hurvitz's semantic assumptions in this article.

16. Crenshaw's statement that "fear of the Lord" (*yir'at yhwh*, a bound phrase) appears

when it is coupled with "the beginning or fundamental principle of knowledge or learning" (Ps 111:10; cf. Prov 1:7; 9:10; Job 28:28).[17] Even though Ps 111:10 meets this strict criterion, Crenshaw feels vindicated in rejecting Psalm 111 as a "wisdom psalm," since it is not accepted as a wisdom psalm by Kuntz and many others. This, however, is a non sequitur, since the prevalence of a view does not make it right. Moreover, the conclusion appears based on a confusion of categories. Obviously the use of a wisdom genre, the saying, in a letter, historical account, or hymn does not make the latter three into wisdom *genres*. But the saying itself *is* a wisdom genre, perhaps the most fundamental of wisdom genres. So there is "wisdom," even by Crenshaw's standards, in Psalm 111. The question is, what does this mean for our understanding of Israelite wisdom and for the psalm as a whole? Crenshaw's reply is significant: "Many of the proverbial glosses [*sic*] may easily have entered the Psalter as prayers of the same people who instructed their children through ancestral tradition."[18] While most of the proverbial sayings in the Psalter are not "glosses" but integral to the poems they appear in,[19] it is true that such say-

---

only three times in the Psalter is factually correct, but profoundly misleading. The closely related participial phrase "who fear/s the Lord" (*yĕrē' yhwh* or *yir'ê yhwh*) appears 9 times in the Psalter, as do a multitude of related phrases like "who fear him" (i.e., YHWH), "who fear God" (esp. in the Elohistic psalms), or the simple declaration that YHWH is to be feared (*nôrā'*; cf. the niphal imperfect in Ps 130:4). Simply incorrect is his declaration that "the admonitory address to sons (34:12) has no parallel in biblical wisdom, which always has the singular 'my son'" ("Wisdom Psalms?" 11-12). The plural admonitory address appears in Prov 4:1a; 5:7a; 7:24a; 8:32a. Ironically, Ps 34:12a is a virtual duplicate of the last three Proverbs texts.

17. Crenshaw, "Wisdom Psalms?" 12-13. The profoundest treatment of the fear of YHWH as the beginning of knowledge or wisdom remains G. von Rad, *Weisheit in Israel* (Neukirchen-Vluyn: Neukirchener Verlag, 1970), 75-101, the chapter on "Gottesfurcht und Erkenntnis." The English translation of von Rad (*Wisdom in Israel* [trans. J. D. Martin; Nashville: Abingdon, 1972]) is too often unreliable, even on fundamental concepts like *Eigengesetz(lich/keit)*, mistranslated often as "inherent determinism" and the like (e.g., Eng. 59, 60, 61, 90, 106 = Ger. 83, 84, 85, 122, 143, respectively).

18. Crenshaw, "Wisdom Psalms?" 15. Ps 111:10a cannot be a "gloss" because it is the required *Resh* line in the alphabetic acrostic, corresponding in theme to the "fearful is his name" in 111:9c. Nor is this a "prayer" but a declarative statement.

19. As is shown convincingly in Perdue's discussion of "Proverb Poems" (Pss 1, 34, 37, 73, 112, 119B, 127), in which "the structure and content of the poem are developed around a simple proverbial saying" (*Wisdom and Cult*, 269-99). Somewhat oddly, Perdue lists "'Ashrê Poems" (Pss 32, 119) as a separate category (pp. 299-312), even though *'ashrê* sayings appear in Psalms previously designated "Proverb Poems" (Pss 1:1; 112:1; 127:5; cf. 128:1, 2) and frequently elsewhere, and though Ps 119 is an "individual lament" in genre (that *uses* the *'ashrê* saying), as convincingly shown by W. Soll, *Psalm 119: Matrix, Form, and Setting* (CBQMS 23; Washington, D.C.: Catholic Biblical Association of America, 1991).

ings are the common property of a whole culture, as is the very nature of proverbs. Those who collect, compile, edit, and compose wisdom literature may simply be called experts in what "everybody knows," literary specialists in the wisdom of ordinary life, as orators are specialists ("wise"!) in speech.

Some of my own presuppositions need to be stated at this point. The cultural fundamentals of a society — what may be called its worldview — are something deeper and broader than the intellectual, theological, or socio-political debates or conflicts *within* a society.[20] Thus both capitalism and communism, for all their differences, share a common set of post-Enlightenment industrial practices and assumptions about the use of the natural world and about economic power as the motor of civilization and the essence of culture.[21] Most of a society's quarrels are merely internecine, no matter how vicious, and do not touch cultural basics. A society's *wisdom* is then the oral or written, culturally specific, commonly accepted "truth" about reality and how to live in terms of that truth. Such wisdom has its roots in traditional insights, continuously adapted to meet new circumstances. Wisdom articulates worldview, and comes to utterance especially in parcels like sayings and admonitions (which fit a situation into the cosmic whole) or in more extended genres like instructions that instruct concerning aspects of life (farming, for example)[22] or about the world as a whole.[23] Thus scholars have tended to identify wisdom with certain genres. But as the anthropologist A. Dundes has shown, a worldview and the wisdom peculiar to it are not genre specific.[24] Yet fundamental aspects of a worldview (such as Israel's "salvation history," covenant, laws, election traditions, cultic practices) may be entirely absent from this or that genre, simply because the genre has a different *function*. Thus the

20. For worldview as an analytical category in biblical studies, see Wright, *New Testament and the People of God.*

21. N. M. Wildiers, *The Theologian and His Universe: Theology and Cosmology from the Middle Ages to the Present* (trans. P. Dunphy; New York: Seabury, 1982), brilliantly shows that a common, underlying worldview is what makes vigorous debate and cultural difference possible. Where worldviews are too different, no argument is possible. Thus most Western persons cannot entertain the question whether a certain death was due to witchcraft, a question that the Azande automatically ask. See E. E. Evans-Pritchard, *Witchcraft, Oracles and Magic Among the Azande* (Oxford: Clarendon, 1937).

22. As in Hesiod's *Works and Days,* or the "Sumerian Farmer's Manual," now available in a new, critical edition: M. Civil, *The Farmer's Instructions: A Sumerian Agricultural Manual* (Barcelona: Editorial AUSA, 1994).

23. R. C. Van Leeuwen, "Liminality and Worldview in Proverbs 1–9," *Semeia* 50 (1990): 111-44; Geertz, *Local Knowledge,* 73-93, "Common Sense as a Cultural System."

24. A. Dundes, "Folklore Ideas as Units of Worldview," *Journal of American Folklore* 84 (1971): 93-103.

general silence of Proverbs on the cult and so forth is a function of its over-arching genre (an "ethical testament" or parenesis in which a parent instructs his son, incorporating traditional sayings and admonitions),[25] and not an in-dicator of a different worldview or religious vision. The almost exclusive use of YHWH as designator of God in Proverbs is an indicator of the book's claim to be in the mainstream of Israelite religion as presented in the HB/OT.

Such an approach develops the research program implicit in Murphy's helpful statement of the problem:

> The problem of the relationship between wisdom literature and other por-tions of the Old Testament needs to be reformulated in terms of a shared approach to reality. . . . It is not a question of the direct influence of the sages or of the widom literature, but rather of an approach to reality which was shared by all Israelites in varying degrees. The teachers were of course the experts. . . . But the existence of experts even presupposes that the aver-age Israelite shared to some extent in the sapiential understanding of reality (which was, without doubt, not alien to Yahwism for them). Such an un-derstanding was not a mode of thinking cultivated exclusively by one class; it was shared at all levels of society that interpreted daily experience. It came to be crystallized in a recognizable body of "wisdom literature."[26]

It is instructive to take a form-critical approach (as developed in Psalm stud-ies) and apply it instead to texts taken from Proverbs, Israel's premier "wis-dom" book. In a definitive essay, A. Wolters has shown that the genre of Prov 31:10-31 is "heroic hymn," which is in this passage uniquely (to our limited knowledge) applied to the deeds of the "valiant woman."[27] For our purposes, it is important to note that this "wisdom" poem (in hymnic genre) is an al-phabetic acrostic whose nearest acrostic parallel, especially with regard to

---

25. Fox (*Proverbs 1–9*, 17-19) calls such teachings of father to son simply "Didactic Wis-dom," but understands the overarching genre of the book much as I do. See K. A. Kitchen, "Proverbs and Wisdom Books of the Ancient Near East: The Factual History of a Literary Form," *TynBul* 28 (1977): 69-114; K. A. Kitchen, "The Basic Literary Forms and Formulations of Ancient Instructional Writings in Egypt and Western Asia," *Studien zu Altägyptischen Lebenslehren* (ed. E. Hornung and O. Keel; OBO 28; Freiburg: Universitätsverlag; Göttingen: Vandenhoeck & Ruprecht, 1979), 235-82. Kitchen's work is useful mostly for its presentation of data, rather than its conclusions.

26. R. E. Murphy, "Wisdom — Theses and Hypotheses," in *Israelite Wisdom: Theologi-cal and Literary Essays in Honor of Samuel Terrien* (ed. J. G. Gammie, et al.; Missoula, Mont.: Scholars Press, 1978), 39-40.

27. A. Wolters, "Proverbs XXXI 10-31 as Heroic Hymn: A Form-Critical Analysis," *VT* 38 (1988): 446-57. Cf. R. J. Clifford, *Proverbs* (OTL; Louisville: Westminster John Knox, 1999), 272-74.

content and function, is Psalm 112. Each poem describes a virtuous man or woman who is praised for one's character as expressed in what one does. The terms of praise in Proverbs 31 are the verbs *hll* (31:30-31) but also *'šr*, for the valiant woman's sons declare her "blessed" (*'šr* parallel *hll*, 31:28; cf. 31:30). *'šry* in Psalm 112 (and elsewhere) functions as a form of indirect praise, for it is predicated of one who is virtuous and godly. The "man" of Psalm 112 and the "woman" of Proverbs 31 both "fear the Lord" (Ps 112:1; Prov 31:30) and show it by their deeds. Both give generously to the poor (Ps 112:4-5, 9; Prov 31:20), and the houses of both are filled with wealth (Ps 112:3; Prov 31:11, 15, 21-22, 27). If the same criteria that lead Crenshaw to reject the category "wisdom psalm" are applied to Prov 31:10-31, we would be compelled to conclude that this "hymn" also is not "wisdom," even though it appears in Proverbs.

We may take another example from Proverbs. Prov 30:7-9 is generically a sparse, second-person "prayer"[28] of an individual to God, though one hesitates to call it a lament or some other genre found in the Psalter. Generically, this prayer does not seem to be "wisdom," though it appears in the wisdom literature. Yet this prayer for "neither poverty nor riches" reveals a subtle discernment of the ambiguity of things, even of very good things, that can only be called "wisdom." Perhaps "wisdom," whatever it is, is not a matter of genre, even if we accept that "instruction," "proverb" (including "sayings" and short "admonitions"), and perhaps "dialogue" are the genres most at home in the wisdom literature.[29]

In the Psalms, as in the wisdom literature itself, and often in the Bible generally, the further question of the relation of genres to putative *Sitze im Leben* has proven especially intractable, largely because we lack the data needed to settle such questions reliably.[30] Modern form criticism's initial sim-

---

28. So R. E. Murphy, *Wisdom Literature: Job, Proverbs, Ruth, Canticles, Ecclesiastes, Esther* (FOTL 13; Grand Rapids: Eerdmans, 1981), 80.

29. Crenshaw divides wisdom literature into two main types: "experiential" and "theoretical." He links "experiential wisdom" tightly to genre, for it exists "chiefly in the form of brief proverbial sayings and longer instructions" (Crenshaw, *OT Wisdom*, 5). One may ask if the writers would have recognized the modern categories used by Crenshaw.

30. See J. L. Crenshaw, "Wisdom," in John H. Hayes, ed., *Old Testament Form Criticism* (San Antonio: Trinity University Press, 1974), 228-29; R. E. Murphy, *The Tree of Life: An Exploration of Biblical Wisdom Literature* (Grand Rapids: Eerdmans, 2002 [3rd edition]), 192. The problem afflicts form-critical studies generally, though it is especially acute in the wisdom literature and Psalms. Cf R. K. Knierim, "Criticism of Literary Features, Form, Tradition and Redaction," in *The Hebrew Bible and Its Modern Interpreters* (ed. D. A. Knight and G. M. Tucker; Chico, Calif.: Scholars Press, 1985), 144. Knierim's acknowledgment that we generally do not have the sociological knowledge of ancient Israel that traditional form criticism requires is a decisive blow to such an understanding of form criticism and its possibilities.

plistic assumptions about a direct correspondence between genre and (institutional) life setting frequently led to a vicious circle of deducing life settings
from literary evidence and then interpreting the literary evidence in terms of
the hypothetical *Sitz*.[31] As M. Sneed has observed, one may ironically call
such sociological reasoning a form of "vulgar Marxism."[32] This speculative
practice (a substitute for knowledge) has contributed to a decline in form
criticism among some strands of HB/OT study. Moreover, from Gunkel to
the present, unstated philosophical, historical, and sociological presuppositions have been problematic companions to form-critical work. Without
clarification of such underlying presuppositions, the theory and practice of
an indispensable scholarly tool is subject to changing intellectual fashions
and even disrepute.[33]

Some type of form criticism, explicit or implicit, is however inevitable,
because meaningful texts do have generic dimensions, which communicate
on the basis of normative conventions shared by writer and reader.[34] "Genre
is an essential ingredient in communication because it establishes the ground
rules shared by author and readers."[35] Generic conventions are embedded in
a text and exist as a heuristic set of expectations in the mind of writers and
readers. For example, the vocabulary, *realia,* and practice of cooking and eating must be in the mind of a reader of cookbooks to understand or realize a
recipe. As generic, such norms and conventions exist in the "real" world and
embody a linguistic and social matrix of meaning that can be learned and
discerned. Readers produce a hypothesis, usually triggered by the initial lines

31. Recent Gospel studies provide a dramatic example, with a hypothetically reconstructed Q document analyzed diachronically in terms of development from a Cynic or
quasi-gnostic wisdom (closest to "the historical Jesus") to a later, apocalyptic worldview.
Such analysis is claimed to produce historical knowledge of the "Q Community." On the
form-critical and historical issues, see Wright's methodological critique in *New Testament
and the People of God,* 418-43, esp. 435-43.

32. M. Sneed, "Wisdom and Class: A Review and Critique," *JAAR* 62 (1994): 651.

33. For these issues see the important work of Martin J. Buss, "The Study of Forms," in
*Old Testament Form Criticism,* ed. Hayes, 1-56; idem, *Biblical Form Criticism in Context*
(JSOTSup 274; Sheffield: JSOT Press, 1999); idem, "Form Criticism, Hebrew Bible," in *Dictio-
nary of Biblical Interpretation* (ed. J. H. Hayes; Nashville: Abingdon, 1999), 406-13.

34. On the necessary relation of normativity and morphology, with a historical demonstration of their interaction in the history of architectural criticism, see E. H. Gombrich,
"Norm and Form: The Stylistic Categories of Art History and Their Origins in Renaissance
Ideals," in *Gombrich on the Renaissance,* vol. 1, *Norm and Form* (London: Phaidon, 1966), 81-
98.

35. Sparks, "Generic Comparison," 5, citing P. Ricouer, "The Hermeneutical Function
of Distanciation," *Philosophy Today* 17 (1973): 129-41.

of a work, concerning its meaning as a dialectic of (implied) whole and parts. Such implicit hypotheses function heuristically as a set of generic expectations that are confirmed or modified in the process of reading.[36]

Speaking broadly, each instance ("individual") of a "genre" as kind or class is unique or particular. There is only one Socrates, with his peculiar nose and fingerprints, yet Socrates is an instance or individual of the "genre" human. Such natural genres (kinds) are relatively stable and usually straightforward. We know a domestic cat from a dog. We recognize both "family resemblances" and differences: mammalian, carnivore, quadruped are resemblances, but cats climb trees and dogs don't (to make a perhaps "unscientific" distinction).[37] Yet there are borderline cases that may puzzle us, as does the Australian platypus.[38] We name something but have difficulty classifying it, because it bears characteristics of more than one kind or class. In this or that respect it does not "fit" what we "know" about, say, mammals, reptiles, or birds. The platypus has fur and lactates like a mammal, but lays eggs like a bird and some reptiles. It is warm-blooded like birds and mammals, but unlike cold-blooded reptiles. Should we ask, Which is it? or perhaps, Which is it most like? or should we conclude it is none of the above?

Artistic or communicative genres can be even more mixed and resistant to classification than are natural kinds, because they are human artifacts. Yet the same principle seems to hold. We classify new or anomalous individuals in terms of those aspects, characteristics, and functions found in genres we already know. We re-cognize the new in terms of the old and familiar.[39] This is not to say that we impose old patterns on new realities, thus falsifying our cognition of the new. Rather, nothing that communicates is absolutely new,

36. For a fuller presentation of this specific argument, see E. D. Hirsch Jr., *Validity in Interpretation* (New Haven: Yale Univ. Press, 1967), 68-126. For a description of the heuristic process of reading, see T. Munro, *Form and Style in the Arts: An Introduction to Aesthetic Morphology* (Cleveland: Case Western Reserve Univ. Press, 1970), 71.

37. I am obviously working with ordinary language modes of reference to species. The fascinating (meta)problems concerning Aristotelian, Linnaean, and evolutionary schemes of classification need not detain us.

38. For purposes of this essay, I consider artistic and literary genres to be defined by a "family resemblance" (a term derived from Wittgenstein). Thus even in mixed genres or "new" genres enough of previous generic patterns must remain so that a "family resemblance" can be recognized. Without a shared genre (like a shared language), communication is impossible and artworks do not signify. See Ungerer and Schmid, *Introduction*.

39. Note Gunkel's language concerning wisdom poems in the Psalter: "Es ist bedeutsam, dass man dabei die Hauptstufen, die wir ausserhalb des Psalters beobachtet haben, *wieder erkennen kann*" (*Einleitung in die Psalmen: Die Gattungen der Religiösen Lyrik Israels* [Göttingen: Vandenhoeck & Ruprecht, 1933], 384, my emphasis).

bearing no similarity to existing genres. The absolutely new is literally unrecognizable.[40] Moreover, we encounter individuals as *wholes* in which each subaspect, characteristic, or function finds its contributory place. Knowledge of individuals and of genres requires a grasp of comparable wholes, parts, and function(s), within which relatively independent (sub)genres may well also be found. We make sense of composite or complex forms in terms of those genres and individuals that are similar, in spite of differences. Individual artistic works are made in response to knowledge of similar works; thus they grow out of modification, combination, or rejection of previous generic conventions. When individual texts or utterances perform basic human functions that are repeatable (and most human functions are not unique), we recognize a common genre. The many individuals of a genre all attempt to do one (main) thing. When that one communicative thing or function is performed optimally, its features, patterns, and order seem "natural." They are repeated. They become common, traditional. They make it possible for subsequent artists and communicators to work efficiently. "By and large, great writers are rarely inventors of genres."[41] It makes no sense to reinvent the wheel each time land travel is required. Hence genres of artifacts (especially in traditional societies with little regard for "originality") bear a discernible "family resemblance" to one another.

Thus Hammurabi's Law Code is a "form" of law code (as genre) comparable to the "Covenant Code" in Exodus. Each form of a genre resembles other forms of the genre, more or less closely. Both genres and particular forms are subject to analysis, as are individual creatures and their kinds. We get to know keyboard sonatas as a genre only as we learn particular sonatas like Haydn's "Genzinger," and we do not really know the "Genzinger" unless we know its genre.[42] The process is similar with our coming to know natural kinds and representative individuals within a kind. There are humans with only one leg (not a "biped"). The mere enumeration of "generic" features does not establish membership in a kind or genre.[43] The ability to recognize a

40. Much of this analysis is indebted to O. O'Donovan, *Resurrection and Moral Order: An Outline for Evangelical Ethics* (Grand Rapids: Eerdmans, 1986), chap. 2.

41. R. Wellek and A. Warren, *Theory of Literature* (3d ed.; New York: Harcourt, Brace and World, Harvest, 1957), 235.

42. Generic knowledge is necessarily synchronic knowledge, for it puts comparable things side by side, whatever their historical origin. This is not to deny the diachronic dimension of text(s) or its importance.

43. This error has been common in Psalm studies. Cf. Ferris, *Genre;* W. Bouzard Jr., *We Have Heard with Our Ears, O God: Sources of the Communal Laments in the Psalms* (SBLDS 127; Atlanta: Scholars Press, 1992), 201.

kind or genre requires a certain insight or wisdom as to what, of all its possible features and functions — or rather the peculiar configuration of features and functions — actually are definitive of a kind. Without flesh we would not be human beings, yet the fact that humans are edible is not what makes us human as opposed to sheep or kine.

Generic comparisons and contrasts may also include formal features, like an alphabetic acrostic or the rhyme schemes that are characteristic of the subtypes of sonnet. The sum of structural patterns (from phonological to semantic)[44] that give order to a text or utterance *helps* define its genre and function, even if most generic classifications are not solely based on form or structure. Structure informs genre, since a text's artistic order and form build on generic features and functions that are shared cultural knowledge. Thus the alphabetic acrostics that contribute to the order of Psalms 111–112; 119; and Prov 31:10-31 are a feature of their genre because they function to express order and totality in the poem. Even though they are properly subject to different form-critical classification, they share this feature and function in common.

To anchor our reflections on form criticism and wisdom in the Psalter in textual reality, let us turn to Psalms 111–112, two psalms that form a sharply etched diptych, composed as a pair, if not by one verbal Mondrian, then certainly by a Mondrian and a pupil in his workshop. W. Zimmerli famously called them "Zwillingspsalmen."[45] Each is a twenty-two-member alphabetic acrostic, in which the anthropological "blessing" of Psalm 112 mirrors the theological thanksgiving in Psalm 111. The tight relationship of the two psalms is reinforced by verbatim repetitions: the *Vav* lines are identical, while the *Ṣadeh* line in Psalm 112 differs from the *Vav* lines only by lacking an introductory *Vav*, and the *Ḥet* lines are close variants of one another, as are *Ṣadeh* and *Tav:*

ו And his righteousness  stands forever (111:3b = 112:3b)
צ His righteousness stands forever (112:9b)
ת His praise  stands forever (111:10b)
ח Merciful and compassionate is YHWH (111:4b)//
ח Merciful and compassionate and righteous (112:4b)[46]

---

44. This does not exclude the phenomena of random "noise" or of redundancy in communication.

45. Cf. S. K. Sherwood, "Psalm 112 — A Royal Wisdom Psalm?" *CBQ* 51 (1989): 57.

46. D. Pardee has shown that verbatim repetition is the strongest form of "distant parallelism" and functions to unite larger poetic structures (*Ugaritic and Hebrew Poetic Parallelism: A Trial Cut ['Nt I and Proverbs 2]* [VTSup 39; Leiden: Brill, 1988], 168-92).

That Psalms 111 and 112 are a diptych is already suggested by their symmetrical juxtaposition, their parallel acrostic structure, and their repetition of lines. More fundamentally they are a diptych because their parallels combine with generic differences to create an interactive whole whose theological function is greater than the sum of its parts. Psalms 111 and 112 form a conceptual whole, the idea that humanity is image and imitator of God. Psalm 111 describes Israel's God from A to Z while its companion describes the righteous, God-fearing human from A to Z, after the pattern and works of God. S. K. Sherwood's syntactical reading of Psalm 112 is no doubt correct in dividing it into two halves of eleven lines (vv. 1-6a with "man" as subject, and vv. 6b-10 with "righteous" and "wicked" as antithetical subjects — as in Ps 1 and Prov 10–15 passim).[47] In all the HB/OT, only Psalm 112 ascribes the first attributes of the divine name to a human being, who like God is "merciful and compassionate" as well as righteous (cf. Exod 34:6-7 and parallels).[48]

The form-critical problem arises, however, in that Psalm 112 has usually been classified as a "wisdom psalm," while its literary and theological twin, Psalm 111, has not. They do not share the same genre, even though they share the same alphabetic acrostic structure, vocabulary, theology, and much of their "form" or individuality is composed of identical elements. On the face of it, the generic difference is obvious, for in terms of traditional form criticism, Psalm 111 is a hymn of thanksgiving, while Psalm 112 is an extended 'šry or "blessing,"[49] a common genre found in Prov 3:13-18; Psalm 1; and Matthew's

---

47. Sherwood, "Psalm 112," 52-55.

48. Ibid., 52, 57-58, 64.

49. 'šry differs from brwk in several respects: the latter "may describe either God or a human being, but [the former] a human being only" (J. P. Brown, *Israel and Hellas III* [BZAW 299; Berlin and New York: de Gruyter, 2001], 39); cf. M. Saebo, *THAT*, 1:258. The related verbs can appear in parallelism, as in Ps 72:15, 17. However, according to Sherwood, "Psalm 112," 60, *brk* is used to describe the *goods* petitioned or wished for on behalf of a person or persons, while 'šry is used to describe the *person* who prospers. The 'šry tells us *who* prospers; the *brwk* tells us *what* sort of gifts or goods are involved, usually fertility and well-being. This distinction is crucial, for it determines the syntagmatic relation of each term to what follows it. According to B. Levine, *brk* connotes a "gift" (cf. Gen 33:11) that is given, whether of material or words. 'šry, on the other hand, connotes forward mobility as in "getting ahead" and prospering (personal communication, New York, April 26, 2001). While I reserve judgment on *brk*, Levine's suggested sense of 'šry seems correct. J. Barr's criticism of Snaith's similar view (*Semantics of Biblical Language* [Oxford: Oxford Univ. Press, 1961], 116) makes valid points (e.g., that the relative pronoun is irrelevant), but paints too broadly. Barr ignores the verb 'šr and its relevant uses. This not quite dead metaphorical nuance fits in perfectly with the predominant "two ways" imagery of Ps 1 and Prov 1–9 (cf. Prov 3:13, 18). The one who advances on the way of life is like this. Cf. Van Leeuwen, "Liminality and Worldview."

"Sermon on the Mount" (Matt 5:3-12).[50] While one may argue whether the 'šry is a sign of "wisdom," it is clearly an indicator of a genre that is used in the wisdom literature.[51]

The 'šry blessing is at heart a two-part proverbial form consisting of the *pronouncement of prosperity* (in the sense of "advancement" or "progress" along the road of life — the 'šry itself) followed by a *descriptor of those who prosper* (Prov 3:13 [cf. 3:18]; 8:32, 34; 14:21 [cf. Ps 112:5a];[52] 20:7; 28:14; 29:18b [cf. Ps 119:2]; Job 5:17). Ps 1:1 with its theme of "the way" nicely plays with the "progress" nuance of 'šry. This form may be expanded by various means, such as an extended account (sometimes introduced by *ky*) explaining why the described person prospers (e.g., Prov 3:14-18a). As is widely acknowledged, the inclusio of 'šry in Ps 1:1 and 2:12 marks off the end redactor's double preface to the Psalter and its themes. As Jerome Creech has shown, however, the 'šry in Ps 2:12 ("Blessed are all those who take refuge in him") exerts a powerful thematic influence throughout the Psalter, not so much in the twenty-four other occurrences of 'šry (though see Ps 34:9), as in the *descriptor* of the blessed persons, "those who take refuge in him."[53]

In Psalm 112 a good part of the expansion of the 'šry consists of an elaboration of the prosperity interspersed with further descriptions of the good person. But the 'šry form itself is terse and best described as a type of proverbial "saying" *(Aussage)*. Like any proverb, the short saying can serve within a larger composition of different genre. In Psalm 119 the initial double 'šry (119:1-3), which Gunkel considered "a blessing-saying from wisdom poetry," gives way to a complex, extended individual lament whose petitions are grounded in the pious petitioner's adherence to Torah.[54] The "blessing" is a statement of

---

50. K. Koch, *The Growth of the Biblical Tradition: The Form-Critical Method* (trans. S. M. Cupitt; New York: Scribner's Sons, 1969), passim, gives an extensive treatment of the "apocalyptic blessing" of Matt 5. He distinguishes another type of blessing, to which Ps 112 belongs, which "first appears in Old Testament wisdom sayings" (7, referring to Prov 3:13; 8:32-33; Ps 1). More basically, one must distinguish 'šry from expressions like *brwk*.

51. The Beatitudes in Matt 5 and the Sermon as a whole have been classified as wisdom at least since Herman N. Ridderbos's work on Matt 5–7 (*De Komst van het Koninkrijk* [Kampen: J. H. Kok], 1950, 249-85). More recently, John S. Kloppenborg has understood "Q" as a wisdom document, inclusive of the Sermon (*The Formation of Q: Trajectories in Ancient Wisdom* [Philadelphia: Fortress, 1987]).

52. *ṭwb-'yš* is a very near semantic parallel to *'šry-'yš*, which opens Ps 112. The NJPS translation renders 112:5a, "All goes well with the man. . . ."

53. Jerome F. D. Creech, *YHWH as Refuge and the Editing of the Hebrew Psalter* (Sheffield: Sheffield Academic, 1996). Cf. Prov 30:5b and 5a (parallel to Ps 18:31; 2 Sam 22:31; cf. Ps 119:140), which takes us close to the piety of the Psalter.

54. For the form-critical analysis of the psalm as individual lament, see Soll, *Psalm 119*,

faith, which is tested by the struggles of the psalmist in his life and lament. An *'šry* tells something about a person of a certain character, qualities, or actions. Thus the *'šry* is an evaluative predication about people, a discernment of reality that is proper to wisdom, as opposed to a blessing proper (root *brk*), which has a *performative* function as an implicit prayer to God that brings about what the blesser wishes to "give" the subject of his blessing.

The statement of blessing in Psalm 112 is followed by themes and issues that many have considered typical of wisdom literature: righteous versus wicked. But as noted above, Crenshaw has shown that such features are in fact common in a variety of Israelite genres; they belong to the general worldview of biblical Israel. Moreover, if K. Seybold is correct in arguing that Psalm 111 schematically represents key events in Israel's *Heilsgeschichte* — a concern that the wisdom literature notoriously lacks (though so does the usual *Danklied* of the individual), this would confirm the common view that Psalm 111 is not wisdom.[55]

If we accept the conclusion that Psalms 111 and 112 constitute two distinct genres, a *Danklied* and a *Weisheitsdichtung* or "proverb poem" (L. Perdue), the form-critical problem becomes yet sharper: What shall we do with the presupposition that genre reflects a *Sitz im Leben?* This presupposition is both the genius and Achilles' heel of form criticism: genius because it takes seriously the relation of speech and writing to life; Achilles' heel because it has engendered a host of questions that may be inappropriate and are often unanswerable. Certain forms of these questions have for decades bedeviled wisdom scholarship: Who are the wise and what is their social location, status, and role in Israel? Who are the wise and what is their ideological relationship to other segments of Israelite society and their traditions? Who are the wise and what of the Hebrew canon have they written? Did the wise exert "literary influence" in ancient Israel? To this last question, Crenshaw's seminal essay answered with a resounding no.[56] Ac-

---

59-86, followed by D. N. Freedman, J. C. Geoghegan, and A. Welch, *Psalm 119: The Exaltation of Torah* (Winona Lake, Ind.: Eisenbrauns, 1999), 93.

55. Cf. R. E. Murphy on "Wisdom Psalms." Recently, Seybold considers Pss 111 and 112 *Weisheitspsalmen* but then ascribes to Ps 111 the "Gattungsmuster des individuellen Danklieds" (*Psalmen* [HAT 1/15; Tübingen: Mohr [Siebeck], 1996], 9, 441). Yet the Psalm lacks one basic characteristic of a *Danklied*: recall of personal rescue. Indeed, it alludes instead to salvation history, including, according to Seybold, liberation in the form of exodus (111:9), covenant and law (111:5, 7-9; cf. 105:8-10), manna and quails in the wilderness (111:5; cf. Exod 16; Num 11), name revelation (Ps 111:4b, 9b; cf. Exod 34:6), and conquest of the land (Seybold, *Psalmen*, 441-42). Unfortunately for form criticism, these are all themes virtually absent in the wisdom literature. Thus most scholars reject Ps 111 as a wisdom psalm, in spite of its association with Ps 112.

56. J. L. Crenshaw, "Method in Determining Wisdom Influence upon Historical Literature," *JBL* 88 (1969): 129-42.

cording to the form-critical ideas with which wisdom studies have generally operated, these two psalms should not stem from the same persons, social (institutional) setting, or conceptual world. And yet they do.

Let's consider the first, most basic question in relation to Psalms 111 and 112: What of the presupposition that genre reflects *Sitz im Leben*? To ask this question is to destroy the putative link between genre and life setting as traditionally understood. The twin psalms are of different genres, but they form a conceptual whole *(imago et imitatio dei)*, and their literary art stems from one hand, or at most, from one workshop with a common purpose.[57] Evidently, we have two genres, but one *Sitz*. From this follow two simple but fundamental points whose importance is regularly ignored in the biblical guild. First, the relationships of writing to life are manifold, complex, and often indirect. Second, *anyone of sufficient literary competence can employ any genre*, unless a genre is *defined* as written by a specific class of persons or in a specific type of situation (the "genre" of letters by death-row inmates, for example).[58] In these two crucial respects, literary activity basically differs from oral activity. The scribe can write a funeral lament, a love lyric, or a hymn of praise, though only the bereaved truly mourn, only lovers praise the beloved, and only worshipers truly praise God.

Yet analysis of oral activity was the theoretical matrix of early-twentieth-century form criticism: genres were thought to arise from the oral interactions of daily life, from cult to agriculture.[59] The situation is more complex, however. Intermediate between oral and free literary compositions, we may place inscriptions of various types, which have a literal *Sitz* in a palace or tomb, on a statue, or in a more fleeting instance of human business captured in a letter. Such inscriptional genres have evident functions that are attached to and arise from their placement in monumental artifacts or specific social transactions.[60] But literary production permits the adaptation of pri-

---

57. See L. C. Allen's careful attempt to distinguish between the art of the two psalms in *Psalms 101–150* (WBC 21; Waco: Word, 1983), 88-98.

58. I owe the example to Kent Sparks. Gunkel wrote, "Segnen wie auch fluchen kann jederman" *(Einleitung,* 294). He meant that blessing and cursing were not institutionally bound or determined. Yet the dictum is true far more broadly than Gunkel thought, not only in oral speech but especially in writing.

59. Here the development of "relevance theory" in linguistics is especially important. See Dan Sperber and Dierdre Wilson, *Relevance: Communication and Cognition* (2d ed.; Oxford: Blackwell, 1995); see also Andrew Goatly, *The Language of Metaphors* (London: Routledge, 1997), which gives an overview of the rudiments of relevance theory.

60. See M. Rösel's essay in this volume. Consider also how meaning is conveyed by the placement of inscriptions and artworks in Sennacherib's "Palace Without a Rival." A starting point is John Malcolm Russell, *Sennacherib's Palace Without a Rival at Nineveh* (Chicago and London: Univ. of Chicago Press, 1991).

mary genres to new contexts, functions, and the creation of new genres based on the *extension* and *combination* of primary oral or inscriptional genres, or of previous literary genres.[61] This generic fecundity is rampant in Scripture, both on the micro- and macrolevels.

This means that while all human utterances and writings employ genres and possess social location and function, it does not follow that writings always reveal their social or historical settings. Genres can be adapted for a variety of purposes outside their original contexts, whether oral, inscriptional, or literary. Specifically, genres and their subunits can be adapted in a literary culture into larger works, for purposes different from their original, situational ends. The power of genres is that even when modified and adapted, their original, primal force is evoked.[62] Indeed, larger literary works — such as *War and Peace* and also composite ones like the Bible — often serve not a specific life setting but many, and try to address human existence comprehensively, by creating a literary *world* that implicitly encompasses all human situations. One must distinguish life setting as a generative *source* of genre (via the author) from the implicit life setting that is *intrinsic* to a genre's meaning (as when a poet who is not in love writes a love poem). Both of these types of "life setting" must be further distinguished from life setting as communicative *target,* that is, of those to whom the literary wishes to speak. The last is initially local, but may ultimately be universal in its intended audience. The target must be initially local, because an audience is required that shares language and generic expectations. Yet Thucydides claims to write his "local" history of the Peloponnesian War for all ages and peoples: "My work is not a piece of writing designed to meet the taste of an immediate public, but was done to last for ever."[63] The point is not negligible. Some writers, some literary works, seek to articulate *existence,* the human condition, the nature of reality, even when they speak of and out of a local life setting. For example, the common interpretive practice of "explaining" the meaning of Genesis 1 in terms of a Priestly response to the postexilic historical situation seems to me not so much mistaken (though it is by no means certain) as a failure to grapple with what Gadamer called the text's *Wahrheitsanspruch.* What more-than-local truth claims are being made about reality in forms and language alien to us?

61. Thus, correctly, H. D. Hirsch, *Validity in Interpretation* (New Haven: Yale Univ. Press, 1967), 102-11, on "The Historicity of Genres."

62. S. Talmon, "The 'Desert Motif' in the Bible and in Qumran Literature," in *Biblical Motifs* (ed. A. Altmann; Cambridge: Harvard Univ. Press, 1966), 39.

63. Thucydides 1.22 in Rex Warner, trans., *Thucydides: The Peloponnesian War* (London: Penguin, 1972), 48.

As M. Buss has pointed out, OT/HB form criticism has run into some dead ends by insisting on an *institutional* setting for literary and oral genres.[64] More helpful is to ask concerning the human functions and problems that a genre seeks to address. First, for example, problems of relating to God are not simply "institutional," a matter of the temple, cult, synagogue, or shrine. Matters of religion are *human* functions, and while certain institutions may specialize in those functions, prayer, adoration, celebration, sacrifice, piety, and religious instruction are not per se institutional functions. One must ask of genres, What recurring human *problem*, general or particular, is this piece of communication seeking to address or solve? *Genres attach to life settings or existence in terms of a common human problem or function, broad or narrow, as the case may be.* Second, genres possess common features, such as (but not limited to) subject matter, ordering devices, patterns, tone, illocutionary stance, style, and rhetoric as a result of the rules of parsimony and tradition. Humans find and repeatedly use those patterns of speech that do a particular communicative job best, both on the macrolevel, and on the microlevel of generic subunits or elements, because some situations are complex and multifaceted. A successful instance of a genre will relate all of its language elements to one another and to a human problem so that the whole and its parts work harmoniously and parsimoniously to accomplish the genre's main function (and subfunctions) well. Thus to recognize a specific "kind" or genre of communication requires, among other things, that we understand its purpose or "end" in addressing the broad world of human functions and concerns.[65]

A final theoretical word about the existence and recognition of genres is necessary, for much confusion exists here. Perennially, in scientific and scholarly discourse, ontic and noetic categories are fused and confused. Specifically, epistemological problems of knowledge are read back into reality. In dealing with verbal artifacts such as genres, problems of identity and diversity "out there" in the real world of texts and speech acts naturally create the epistemological problem of recognizing this or that literary genre. Again, an approach based on function can be helpful. To accomplish a certain function, an artifact must have a certain "shape" and certain features of content (a "chair" needs a horizontal surface and "legs," etc.). Recent cognitive linguists, borrowing a phrase from Wittgenstein, rightly say that human artifacts bear a

---

64. I owe much of the stimulus for my discussion of genre to Prof. Buss, who forthrightly responded to an earlier version of this paper (SBL annual meeting, Nashville, November, 2000) with the necessary question: "What do you mean by genre?"

65. For the ontological and conceptual basis of my argument on genres and their purposive functions, I am indebted to O'Donovan, *Resurrection*, 31-52.

"family resemblance" to one another. A "chair" may or may not have a back, and a "table" may serve as a "kind of chair," though only as a borderline instance.[66] At the *cognitive* boundaries of things there may appear a certain fuzziness (is this thing a chair or table, perhaps a terrible, useless chair?), but in most cases no one has difficulty in recognizing a *typical* chair and its (primary) function. So it is with literary genres: their common function creates a recognizable group of features. Genres have a certain gestalt, with functions and features that appertain thereto. Writers and readers can re-cognize these things, and this recognition forms the basis for their specific literary and human transaction. One instance of a genre has a "family resemblance" to other instances of the transaction, and this resemblance makes communication *possible* in the face of individual differences.

I would like to posit some theses on the basis of this all too brief glance at wisdom in the Psalter.

1. What distinguishes the wisdom literature of the HB/OT from nonwisdom writings is not necessarily a difference in general worldview or theology.[67] What distinguishes these books (Proverbs, Ecclesiastes, Job) is a set of related genres and themes, defined primarily by a common educative function of fostering discernment, reflection, and action concerning life in general ("existence" or the human condition) and for a wide spectrum of specific situations.

2. In a literary community, gifted writers or redactors are free to employ or modify any genre for their own purposes. Genres always bear a relation either to the human condition in general or to specific life settings, but those life settings should be defined in terms of human functions, rather than primarily in terms of institutions, as has usually been the case in HB/OT studies. Prayer, for example, takes place both in and outside the cult.

3. While Israel no doubt had a professionally trained group of scribes, it is methodologically mistaken to assume, based on differences of literary genre, that these literary "wise men" had an ideology or theology that was radically different from other groups or classes portrayed in the Bible, or worse, imagined by modern biblical scholarship. Professional groups, whether priests, courtiers, scribes, or temple builders, do not necessarily occupy *fundamentally* opposed or different ideological locations. They may share a common, deep worldview, what von Rad called *Wirklichkeitsverständnis*.

4. Consequently, the problem of "wisdom influence" needs to be fundamentally restated. If wisdom is a culturally specific way of thinking about and

---

66. Ungerer and Schmid, *Cognitive Linguistics,* 1-113.
67. See Alan Dundes, "Folk Ideas as Units of Worldview."

acting within reality (a worldview), then it is something that transcends class and professional distinctions. It is an all-encompassing cultural set of presuppositions and assumptions, *within which various groups are able to articulate their differences, interrelationships, and conflicts,* precisely because they share the same basic assumptions. As noted above, Wildiers's portrayal of cultural diversity amid basic unity in the Middle Ages ought to give us pause. Our contemporary culture and society has an unprecedented degree of worldview and ideological fragmentation. Ancient Near Eastern and biblical scholarship should be wary of reading our own late-modern ideologies and fragmentation into ancient texts. Not every biblical text is a "wisdom" text generically. But as a fundamental, all-encompassing cultural virtue, wisdom thought and action, with or without the typical vocabulary and forms, may be an element in any biblical text.

The ancients believed that all wisdom came primevally from the bringers of culture, whether Apkallu, Prometheus, or Lady Wisdom. All cultural activities are thus gifts of "wisdom."[68] Israel believed that the entire world had order and coherence, so that being wise is to live in tune with that cosmic coherence and order, both in general and in the historical particulars of existence. In this sense Psalms 111 and 112 together are a profound instance of wisdom, based on the notion of *imitatio dei.* Moreover, Psalm 111 employs a wisdom genre (the saying in 111:10a), and both psalms show many features and themes at home in the wisdom literature. To use form criticism to separate Psalm 111 from 112 and both from wisdom literature proper may obscure more than it reveals.

---

68. Clifford, *Proverbs,* 8-9, 24-27; C. Wilcke, "Göttliche und Menschliche Weisheit im Alten Orient: Magie und Wissenschaft, Mythos und Geschichte," in *Weisheit* (ed. A. Assmann; Munich: Fink, 1991), 259-70. For Prometheus see Aeschylus, *Prometheus Bound,* 447-71; cf. Wis 7:15-22.

# Form Criticism in Dialogue with Other Criticisms: Building the Multidimensional Structures of Texts and Concepts

HYUN CHUL PAUL KIM

## Introduction

When I first learned about the discipline of "form criticism" or *Form-geschichte,* my initial reaction was, "What does 'form' mean?" To me, "form" denoted that which is of the surface, something like a shell, package, or building. Then I learned that it also denotes some kind of type or pattern, especially in the notion of genre, *Gattung.* In the Platonic definition, "Form" can also be differentiated from "Idea": that which is concrete, tangible, and changeable (Form) and that which is abstract, invisible, and unchanging (Idea). Then, in the study of the Hebrew Bible, I came in contact with the four subcategories of this discipline: structure, setting, genre, and intent.[1] As this illustration shows, form criticism can imply various orientations and methods. Furthermore, as this discipline evolved through the twentieth century, it seems natural that its branches grew tremendously, extending in many directions, some of which may even be distinct from, or contrary to, others. The root may be still there, yet the branches may have made the tree look quite different. Indeed, the face of form criticism has been changed.[2]

In the following study, I investigate this changing face of form criticism by comparing some of its key features with those of other biblical criticisms. I

---

1. These subcategories are followed in the commentaries of FOTL, edited by Rolf P. Knierim, Gene M. Tucker, and Marvin A. Sweeney.

2. Rolf Knierim, "Old Testament Form Criticism Reconsidered," *Int* 27 (1973): 468: "By being subservient to those factors that dominate texts rather than by dominating the texts through its own methodological system, form criticism will, *probably with some kind of new face,* continue to have its unique role in the concert of exegetical disciplines" (emphasis added).

give special attention to the overlap between form criticism and other criticisms, with regard to orientation, method, and contributions. I attempt to (re)define structure, setting, and concept in light of their correlations with other criticisms. I argue that each of these terms needs to be reconceptualized both for a dialogue with various other criticisms and toward building the multidimensional structures of biblical texts and concepts. To do so, I use a study of Joel 2 as an example of these reconceptualizations. I also argue that these overlaps are essentially positive signs of the healthy growth of form criticism and that a more cognizant interaction with these various criticisms can further deepen the goals of form criticism and thereby enrich our exegesis of the Bible. The present study concludes with a modest outlook toward form criticism's continuous reshaping.

## Structure

Hermann Gunkel's pioneering definitions of the various types of the Psalms made a lasting impact on the discipline of form criticism. Each text contains its own inherent type or genre. Each genre defines not only its compositional identity but also its probable setting. In other words, a text has a type but also a history. Likewise, a text also has its own concept. One of the purposes of form criticism, therefore, has to be correlating the form with these other features of a text. Form, in this sense, should encompass its genre, setting, and concept. What ties these seemingly independent components together? What is it that cohesively connects the various departments of a building? It is structure.

A text has its structure that is built for a certain form.[3] It is this structure that helps readers identify what genre, setting, and concept the text may signify. Certainly, structure is not genre, setting, or concept. Then how are they related? On the one hand, they are mutually interdependent. The essential elements of genre, setting, and concept reside as key factors within a structure. For instance, an individual lament psalm has a certain type that contains its basic structure of, for example, "address to God," "complaint," "confession of trust," "petition," "words of assurance," "vow of praise."[4] Thus

3. See ibid., 461: "Not only must the structural analysis of the individuality of texts be included into the form-critical method, it must, in fact, precede the analysis of the typical structure if the claim that such a typicality inherently determines an individual text is to be substantiated."

4. Bernhard W. Anderson, *Out of the Depths: The Psalms Speak for Us Today* (rev. and expanded ed.; Philadelphia: Westminster, 1983), 76-77. Note, likewise, how Knierim groups

a structure cannot exist without the ingredients such as genre, setting, and concept. It would be like a tree without any fruit or leaves. Yet, on the other hand, structure is foundational to genre, setting, and concept. Structure shares common denominators with genre, setting, and concept, whereas these three elements may be independent from the other two. A prophetic call for repentance in Hos 6:1-3, for example, may allude to a quite different concept when read in its larger context of 5:15–6:6 (cf. Zeph 2:1-3). A certain set of setting and genre may likewise be irrelevant, once isolated from a text. Rather, it is the structure of a text that holds these together. Structure of a text in this sense has a connotation of a building structure that functions as a skeleton or framework. Thus studying the structure of a text is an essential step for a form-critical study.

What then is the relationship between a text and a structure? A text may have a variety of forms. Similarly, a text may also have more than one structure. Here we need to take a look at other criticisms for their contributions to form criticism: textual criticism and rhetorical criticism. First, textual criticism has unleashed many discoveries as well as debates, just like form criticism. At least two important schools have made their own significant contributions. Here what we focus on in a text-critical study is the very existence of textual variants. These variants range from word difference to addition or omission of one or more paragraph(s). Some of them may be scribal facilitations at a later stage. Others, however, may be true variants, representative of different textual traditions or communities.[5] When there are variants of significant difference, we may have more than one text or tradition available to us. In the cases of textual variants, for example, in the structure of the book of Jeremiah (cf. also Esther), the MT and LXX texts have different structures. Comparing the structures of those different texts can help the reader better understand the legitimacy and implication of each text, tradition, and community.

Moreover, the different structures of different texts can indicate that a text may signal more than one form. Strictly speaking, there may be no "final form" of a text, just as there may be no *Urtext*. The final form we are talking

---

the components "structure" and "genre" in a closely linked category: "The components which comprise a text's typicality (structure/scheme/genre — setting — content/mood/function/intention) are not always unified in the same way" ("Reconsidered," 458).

5. James A. Sanders, "The Task of Text Criticism," in *Problems in Biblical Theology: Essays in Honor of Rolf Knierim* (ed. H. T. C. Sun and K. L. Eades; Grand Rapids: Eerdmans, 1997), 315-27: "The task of text criticism can be formulated succinctly as the quest for true variants. . . . What should be done with true variants once located? Here is where the proposal of a truly pluriform Bible is pertinent."

about may be the "given form" of a masoretic text, whereas the "given form" of a Septuagint or Qumran text may be substantially different. A single text we are talking about may allude to not one final form but several, displayed by the divergent structures of the text traditions.

Second, rhetorical criticism, in response to literary criticism, made a significant call to the importance of the given form of a text, especially with regard to its "consummate skill and artistry" within "the modes of Hebrew literary composition."[6] In response to this call, form criticism was reoriented to start with the final or given form of a text.[7] This has led to a crucial revitalization of form criticism. For example, this reorientation has helped a redaction-critical reading become more systematic and tangible. Now its method can further be enriched by utilizing some of the features of rhetorical criticism.[8] Form criticism in this way benefits from and contributes to redaction criticism and rhetorical criticism. Rhetorical criticism has helped readers pay closer attention to the art of biblical poetry. It has discovered more ways to see the structure of a text. Hence we can study the structure of a text in light of form-critical and rhetorical-critical tools. Put another way, we can study at least two structures of a single text.

Let us look at an example with a biblical text. Joel 2:21-27 is a unit within the larger unit of 2:21–4:21 (Eng. 2:21–3:21).[9] In this pericope, on one dimension, we can find an explicit structure that moves in a nice monolithic pattern. We will call this structure a "parallel" structure:

I. Threefold call to fear not/rejoice (YHWH in the third person)   21-24
  A. Ground (the addressee)   21
    1. Command: fear not, be glad, and rejoice   21a
    2. Reason: YHWH's deeds   21b
  B. Animals of the field (the addressee)   22
    1. Command: fear not   22a
    2. Reason: nature's reactions ("for" occurs twice)   22b
  C. Children (lit. "sons") of Zion (the addressee)   23-24

6. James Muilenburg, "Form Criticism and Beyond," *JBL* 88 (1969): 18.

7. Rolf Knierim, "Criticism of Literary Features, Form, Tradition, and Redaction," in *The Hebrew Bible and Its Modern Interpreters* (ed. D. A. Knight and G. M. Tucker; Chico, Calif.: Scholars Press, 1985), 156.

8. In retrospect, Knierim had already signaled the possibility, and thereby necessity, of the interdependence among structuralism, rhetorical criticism, and form criticism with regard to the study of structure; see Knierim, "Reconsidered," 459-62.

9. Marvin A. Sweeney, *The Twelve Prophets* (Berit Olam; 2 vols.; Collegeville, Minn.: Liturgical Press, 2000), 1:152.

1. Command: be glad and rejoice — 23a
2. Reason: YHWH's deeds and nature's reactions — 23b-24
II. Promise of salvation (YHWH in the first person) — 2:25-27
  A. YHWH's deeds: I will repay (שׁלם) — 25
  B. Consequences on YHWH's people — 26-27
    1. Description of physicality — 26
      a. Positively described: you will eat, praise — 26a
      b. Negatively described: never be ashamed — 26b
    2. Description of spirituality (or cognition) — 27
      a. Positively described: you will know — 27a
      b. Negatively described: never be ashamed — 27b[10]

This unit can be nicely divided into two subunits, vv. 21-24 and 25-27. The first subunit depicts YHWH in the third-person form, whereas the second subunit delivers YHWH's speech in the first-person form. At the same time, however, both of these subunits share many similarities. For example, the "sons of Zion" are addressed in the second-person plural form throughout. Moreover, vv. 23-24 function as "double-duty verses."[11] Thus their addressee, "sons of Zion," connects to the preceding verses (vv. 21-22) as a third component of the addressees, alongside "ground" and "animals." At the same time, it also connects to the following verses (vv. 25-27) for an introductory statement of YHWH's restoration of the people of Zion. Within this skillfully concatenated structure, we can find further patterns. Within vv. 21-24, "ground," "animals," and "sons of Zion" are all offered an admonition of encouragement.[12] Even the reasons for the promises with the כי clauses occur in all three places (vv. 21b, 22b, 23b). Whereas it is Jacob/Israel who is proclaimed to "fear not" in other parts of the prophetic literature (e.g., Isa 35:4; 41:10; Jer 30:10; 46:27; cf. Isa 40:9; Zeph 3:16), here both the ground and animals are admonished to "fear not" (Joel 2:21, 22). In a sequential development, the children of Zion are encouraged similarly but with more extensive explications of the encouragement after the admonition, "be glad and rejoice" (2:23; cf. 2:21). Read in this structural sequence, it denotes that the promise of restoration in vv. 21-22 is a significant prerequisite for the promise of restoration in vv. 23-24. Therefore, on the one hand, YHWH's restoration of nature is a condition for YHWH's

---

10. Many specific terms for various sections in this structural analysis are borrowed from the one on Zech 9:9-10 by Michael H. Floyd, *Minor Prophets, Part 2* (FOTL 22; Grand Rapids: Eerdmans, 2000), 464-65.

11. Cf. Ehud Ben Zvi, *Micah* (FOTL 21B; Grand Rapids: Eerdmans, 2000), 7.

12. Sweeney, *Twelve Prophets*, 1:172: "Once again, this demonstrates Joel's perspective that the natural and the human worlds are inextricably intertwined."

restoration of the people of Zion. Without the former, the latter cannot be made. Not only does this subunit start with the call to the "ground" (v. 21), with which both the animals and human beings have their root of conformity (vv. 22-23), but also it is with the "ground" that both the phrase to "fear not" (also to the animals) and the phrase to "be glad and rejoice" (also to the humans) are associated. On the other hand, YHWH's promise of restoration culminates at the very restoration of YHWH's own people. YHWH's healing of the resources of the soil, crops, and cattle has a direct relationship — or rather purpose — toward YHWH's covenant promise to heal YHWH's own people (vv. 25-27).

Now, on another dimension, this text can disclose yet another structure that is formed with a chiastic correlation. This is a "chiastic" structure:

a   Ground                                                        21
   b   Animals and fruit                                          22
      c   Human beings: fourfold definitions of rain      23-24
      c'  Restoration: fourfold definitions of locust     25
   b'  Eating                                                     26
a'  Land: "in the midst of Israel"                                 27

This chiastic structure certainly shares many similarities with the parallel structure above. However, other subtle implications can become apparent when we look at the text through a chiastic lens. For instance, this unit starting with a call to the "ground" (v. 21) makes a nice inclusio — inverted parallelism — with the notion of the land, "in the midst of Israel" (v. 27). The "animals" are associated with the abundance of fruit (v. 22), which correlates with the notion of YHWH's provision for the people of Israel to "eat" (v. 26). In its chiastic center, we find the notion of YHWH providing the rain to restore what was destroyed (vv. 23-25). These components of a chiastic correlation can have several implications. First, the correlations of these key terms and ideas echo the portraits of the garden of Eden in Genesis 1–3.[13] The soil, out of which human beings were made, will yield green vegetation and fruit for human beings to "eat" and be satiated. The paradise regained will return in such an awesome manner that Israel will "know" that not the forbidden tree but YHWH will be "in the midst of Israel." Second, YHWH's faithfulness shown to be fulfilled in this covenant promise indicates the notion of YHWH as the creator. YHWH, the creator of all (Gen 1), will be assuredly capable of doing all these things, as YHWH declares, "I YHWH am your God, and there

---

13. Cf. James L. Crenshaw, *Joel* (AB 24C; New York: Doubleday, 1995), 153-54.

is no other" (Joel 2:27). Third, this God, who is in control of the rain, pastures, and beasts, is certainly in control of the courses of history. This YHWH who promises to restore the years lost to the forces of nature (locusts) and empires (army) is the same YHWH who has kept the divine promises already made in ancient times (cf. Lev 26:1-13).

In summary, the text of Joel 2 displays at least two dimensions of structures. Its parallel structure signifies the notions that the restoration will encompass all of nature as well as human beings, that all components are precious and essential, and that the restoration anticipates its culmination with the children of Zion, the people of YHWH. Its chiastic structure signifies yet another notion that YHWH is the only God, who is the creator of all creation and thus solely capable of controlling, destroying, and restoring any course of history. A form-critical study of the structure can thus be enriched by rhetorical-critical study of the structure, enabling readers to look at the text from various angles and with various compositional and conceptual implications.

Because other scholars in this volume deal specifically with the aspects of genre within form criticism, here it suffices to make a brief remark on genre vis-à-vis structure. Most importantly, structure can be an important factor for genre or genre studies. For example, in this volume Margaret Odell utilizes the genre of Babylonian royal inscriptions for understanding Ezekiel. Martin Rösel engages in the similar genre studies of various inscriptions along with the studies of *Sitz im Leben*. Therefore, genre studies, especially in comparison with the ancient Near Eastern texts, should continue to be important in the study of prophetic literature. What other areas should then remain also important? Comparing the ancient Near Eastern legal texts with the biblical legal texts should also be a worthwhile effort. Since the dawn of the age of archeological discovery in Mesopotamia, scholars have discovered, translated, and interpreted many legal texts. Now, comparing the structures — along with genres — of those texts can offer further insights in terms of similarities and differences.[14] Furthermore, it would be equally fruitful to compare the biblical texts with other ancient sagas, folklore, and the like, such as African, Asian, and other cultures.[15] Comparing the types, formation processes, and especially structures of each would be essential components for further research.

14. For a case study of analyzing the conceptual structure of the Laws of Eshnunna, primarily based on the extant written form, see H. C. P. Kim, "The Conceptual Structure of the Laws of Eshnunna," *Journal of the Association of Graduates in Near Eastern Studies* 6 (1995): 15-25.

15. Martin J. Buss, "Toward Form Criticism as an Explication of Human Life: Divine Speech as a Form of Self-Transcendence," in this book makes a succinct point on this aspect.

## Setting

If form for a text implies its various literary elements such as structure and genre, then setting depicts elements of history. A text has a historical dimension as well as a literary dimension. A text is not only a literature but also a portrait of life: setting in life *(Sitz im Leben)*. Discoveries (or lack thereof) and studies of the many resources of the ancient Near Eastern history have provided ample evidence for both relevance and gap between literature and history. Not only archeology but also sociology and anthropology have offered increasing amounts of data to reconstruct the life of ancient Israel and neighboring regions. Consequently, form criticism has a lot to do with ancient history.

The problem is how to define the twenty-first-century reader's understanding of "setting" in the reconstruction of the "setting(s)" of the ancient biblical text. Is it the setting of the very event (e.g., the specific date, hour, and locale of a prophet's preaching), or that of the author, transmitter, redactor, or manuscript copyist that should be the target? How can we retrieve facts out of a form?

Going back to Gunkel may help shed some light in this fluid space. It is Gunkel's view of oral tradition in form criticism that has directed biblical scholarship to a deeper level. By this we have come to appreciate the setting in life beyond the setting in text. In a way Gunkel's form criticism was a reaction to the old literary criticism, such as Wellhausen's source criticism.[16] Instead of looking at the sources of the text only, Gunkel called for the validity of imagining and finding the events and settings of the text. Sigmund Mowinckel's reconstruction of the settings of the Psalms is a prime example of this method.[17]

Ironically, it is also the new literary studies, which arose in reaction to the historical-critical methods, that have challenged Gunkel's form-critical approach. For instance, Gunkel's view of oral tradition has shaped a somewhat narrow perspective on the composers, transmitters, and compilers of the biblical texts; he believed that the shortest forms are the purest.[18] This

---

16. David L. Petersen, "The Formation of the Pentateuch," in *Old Testament Interpretation: Past, Present, and Future: Essays in Honor of Gene M. Tucker* (ed. J. L. Mays, D. L. Petersen, and K. H. Richards; Nashville: Abingdon, 1995), 37: "Earlier, scholars used the term literary criticism as simply another way of describing source criticism."

17. Sigmund Mowinckel, *The Psalms in Israel's Worship* (trans. D. R. Ap-Thomas; 2 vols.; Nashville: Abingdon, 1962).

18. Marvin A. Sweeney, "Formation and Form in Prophetic Literature," in *Old Testament Interpretation*, ed. Mays, Petersen, and Richards, 113-14.

view suffers a serious problem. A case can be made that the ancient people were capable of reciting far lengthier stories, poetry, and texts than many of us are able. Literate people do not necessarily have a memory capability superior to that of illiterate people. Literary criticism, along with rhetorical criticism, has thus challenged and contributed to focus attention on the final written form of a given text. Likewise, thanks to Martin Noth, redaction criticism also pointed to the importance of the setting in life of the (final) redactor rather than the setting in life of the narrated event. Hence we are talking about not only the remotely possible setting in life of the people involved, such as the prophet who walked barefoot and naked (e.g., Isa 20:2; Mic 1:8), but also the very setting in life of the redactor(s) who retold the stories in their own context, theology, and ideology. Therefore, just like structure and genre, we start with the final written form of a given text for the reconstruction of its setting. For this, Rolf P. Knierim has already laid a firm foundation to shift the direction of form criticism.

What then is the issue? It is the delicate difference of methodological orientation between "final form only" and "final form and more." To put it another way, we seem to be in a dilemma between "*final* form criticism" and "back to Gunkel." The present study intends to highlight a third possibility, which cautiously synthesizes the disconnection of these two poles. This possibility in the reconstruction of setting must take into account the following aspects. First, Roy F. Melugin succinctly delineates the inherent difficulty in reconstructing specific dates or identifying additions by means of syntactical evidence. Not only is distinguishing source A from source B a difficult task, but also matching a conjecturally cut-out segment with a specific ancient setting is a tantamount endeavor.[19] Thus Melugin offers another idea of setting, "*textually portrayed* setting," in distinction from the setting of "extratextual realities."[20] It is one thing to reconstruct and talk about the setting of the completed given form of a text. It is another, and more problematic according to Melugin, to conjecture the setting(s) of the earlier events prior to the textually portrayed setting. To further this discussion, it may be a legitimate and helpful task to clarify the differentiation (if not redefinition) of these terms:

19. Note a similar remark by James Crenshaw, *Joel*, 28: "To some extent such endeavors to establish a historical context for a biblical book constitute exercises in futility. Much of the argument moves in the realm of probability, often resting on one hypothesis after another about the development of the language and religion of the Bible. I do not think we can accurately date most books in the canon, nor do I believe it possible to determine the exact history of any Hebrew word."

20. Roy F. Melugin, "Recent Form Criticism Revisited in an Age of Reader Response," in this book.

*Sitz im Leben, Sitz im Text, Sitz im Buch, Sitz im Literati (Literatur),* and *Sitz im Reder.*

Second, Ehud Ben Zvi's recent commentary on Micah has offered another groundbreaking understanding of the tasks of form criticism. In a nutshell one may reiterate Ben Zvi's argument in this way: if we start with the final written form of a text to study its structure and genre, why not for its setting as well? As the extant form of a text is what we have now, it would make sense to focus on the setting of the "primary readership . . . and the original communities of readers of the book."[21] This approach clearly benefits from paying close attention to the ingeniously interwoven phrases or sentences that function as "signposts" or "catchwords."[22] These "signposts" connect many pieces or subunits in such subtle and complicated ways that they make it difficult for us to identify any *originally* independent subunits.

We can find similar instances in the book of Joel. The call for the "ground" not to fear but to rejoice (2:21) nicely connects its text (2:21-27) to chap. 1, where 1:10 already informs that "the ground mourns" (cf. also 2:18). The mention of various kinds of locusts (2:25) likewise alludes to 1:4. Furthermore, YHWH's "great army" (2:25) refers to the northern army in 2:20 (cf. 2:1, 11), which thus tightly connects to the preceding unit in chap. 2. Similarly, the words "sons" and "daughters" in 2:28 coincide with the "sons of Zion" (2:23), thus tying the connection to the following unit. Finally, even the authorial pattern of listing more than one item recurs in various places — for example, "rain of righteousness," "autumn rain," "spring rain," and "former rain" in 2:23; "swarming locust," "hopper," "destroyer," and "cutter" in 2:25; "sons," "daughters," "old men," "young men," and "male and female slaves" in 3:1 (Eng. 2:28); "wonders," "blood," "fire," and "pillars of smoke" in 3:3 (Eng. 2:30) — as if the whole was written or finalized by one author/redactor.[23] Thus it becomes inevitable that we render the setting of its complete written form as one composition.

Third, nevertheless, form criticism may lose much of its inherent methodological significance if it only means "*final* form criticism." Literary critics

21. Ben Zvi, *Micah,* 6.

22. For the former see ibid.; for the latter, Hans W. Wolff, *Joel and Amos* (trans. W. Janzen, et al.; Hermeneia; Philadelphia: Fortress, 1977), 7-8; James D. Nogalski, "Intertextuality and the Twelve," in *Forming Prophetic Literature: Essays on Isaiah and the Twelve in Honor of John D. W. Watts* (ed. J. W. Watts and P. R. House; JSOTSup 235; Sheffield: Sheffield Academic Press, 1996), 112-16.

23. For a succinct review of scholarship on the unity of the book of Joel, mainly from Bernhard Duhm (two-part authorship) to Hans W. Wolff ("near-perfect" symmetry of the whole book), see Crenshaw, *Joel,* 29-34.

have already taught us that "a text has a life of its own." In other words, even as a text becomes finalized and read, it still is not static but becomes reinterpreted by (subjective) rereaders of various subsequent eras. From another angle, however, we need to note that "this text has a life (or stages of life) it depicts as well."[24] If a text portrays life forward as well as in the present, it also portrays it backward. Otherwise, that text loses its account of history, of the past. In order to give full account to its historicality, we must study the past, present, and future of the text — not one or two aspects only.

Here we need to differentiate the notions of historicity and historicality. Historicity implies the idea that a text has a real historical event, in the sense of a fact (e.g., the event relations between David and Ps 51 or Moses and Ps 90). Historicality denotes the idea that an event may not have occurred as the text depicts and yet the text invites or compels readers to associate it with the possible setting/context of the past (e.g., the setting relations between David and Ps 51 or Moses and Ps 90). The form-critical study of setting(s) of a text may not be oriented toward reconstructing or proving the historicity (or factuality) of the past events but rather be directed toward correlating or interpreting the historicality (or contextuality) of the possible past events — even in the notion of the written texts and not oral texts. In other words, the issue is not so much about restoring the accurate layers of the past stages. Rather, it should be about understanding how the text could have *functioned* against those possible stages of settings.

Why is this helpful or necessary? The biblical text has history in it in many cases. As long as form criticism identifies and (re)orients its root to historical-critical scholarship, it needs to wrestle with the historicality of the ancient sacred texts, no matter how ambiguous its face may appear to be.[25] Also, it is because other biblical disciplines, such as redaction criticism, canonical criticism, and reader-response criticism, have engendered and even reawakened the perception of the making — and interpreting — of texts not only as a product but also as a process. Redaction criticism has guided form-critical readers to pay attention to "the creative, authorial role of later redaction."[26] Applying both

24. See Knierim, "Criticism," 123: "It is the task of exegesis to interpret the Hebrew Bible as ancient literature, i.e., as written texts that came into existence in a distinct historical milieu and certainly do not exist without it."

25. For a recent theoretical reinvestigation of the (equally important) centrality of biblical historical criticism vis-à-vis literary criticism in the field of biblical studies, see F. W. Dobbs-Allsopp, "Rethinking Historical Criticism," *BibInt* 7 (1999): 235-71.

26. Marvin A. Sweeney, "Form Criticism," in *To Each Its Own Meaning: An Introduction to Biblical Criticisms and Their Application* (ed. S. L. McKenzie and S. R. Haynes; rev. ed.; Louisville: Westminster John Knox, 1999), 64.

synchronic and diachronic approaches, they intend not only to identify but also to follow through the layered strata of traditions and texts. Canonical criticism, in a brief definition, is a hermeneutical extension or adaptation of midrash. According to the hermeneutical triangle of the interpretive mode by James A. Sanders, sacred traditions have been transmitted into the subsequent context(s) that have shaped sacred texts vis-à-vis the various specific community's faith in God, by means of shifting, resignifying, or reconceptualizing those traditions for the new setting(s).[27] Reader-response criticism, in a similar line of thought (if not method), contributed to the matter of reconstructing possible settings of various audiences in the *Nachleben* (afterlife) of the text. The text thus can be read and reread by the varied subsequent generations of readers and rereaders, all associated with their own subjectivity.

Accordingly, we are not calling for "back to Gunkel" per se. Rather, the attention should be given both to the rereaders of the original composition and to the hearers of the texts of earlier redactional stages. The reason that we need not return to Gunkel's approach on setting is that we want to reconstruct the possible historical settings of the text as it is, rather than atomizing, taking bits and pieces apart.[28] For probability rather than certainty, we still have the invitation by the text (which often possesses the aspects of both history and story) to imagine or conjecture the various settings of the events, immediate audience, later tradents, final redactor, and beyond. One may do well considering only the setting of the final written form. However, to avoid the danger of anachronistic or one-dimensional reading of the setting, we ought not be forced to read all texts against only one setting.[29] On one extreme, giving up on the historicality of a text implies ahistoricism. On another extreme, at the same time, while admitting the sheer degree of hypothesis in any reconstruction of the past, our reconstruction of the setting of the final stage of a text may still be no more than mere conjecture.

What then would be a third possibility in the form-critical study of setting(s)? It is a plurality of settings. We may call it "stages of settings" (in a similar analogy with "strata" of the archeological stratigraphy) rather than a setting. These various stages should not be understood as a set of randomly speculated periods in the ancient history. Rather, they should be

27. James A. Sanders, *Canon and Community* (Philadelphia: Fortress, 1984), 77-78.

28. Knierim, "Criticism," 145: "The time is passing rapidly in which one could prematurely jump to conclusions about oral tradition before doing what must be done first: the form-critical assessment of the written text itself."

29. Crenshaw, *Joel*, 39: "I am fully aware of the difficulty involved in moving from a text to historical context, but I am not entirely skeptical about the possibility of imagining a reasonable setting for Joel."

understood as the minimal historical backgrounds against which a text may share both direct and indirect contact. Because the text does not offer the unequivocal *one* setting to us — in fact, the text often does not give us any setting at all (as in the case of the book of Joel), our task needs to be to find the best possible setting and then retrieve the other possible settings.[30] In analogy, both synchronic and diachronic approaches should be implemented for the study of settings.[31] We must start with the synchronic dimension. Yet instead of stopping at the synchronic reading of a setting, which too is a reconstruction of probability than factuality, we can move backward in the diachronic dimension.

Let us look at an example in Joel 2. Just like many psalms that do not offer superscriptions or historical narrative accounts, the book of Joel does not give clues for a historical setting. It is precisely for this reason that we need to pay attention to various stages of life pregnant in this text. It may be helpful to find various "signposts" not only of textual interconnection but also of historical clues to reconstruct various pertinent backgrounds of the making of that text. In this analysis I emphasize understanding the *function* of the possible settings rather than the *verification* (or facticity) of the settings.[32] Marvin A. Sweeney's commentary on Joel, for example, gives a fuller account of the various possible stages of life in the text.[33] The notions, such as accusation against the elders, priests, and ministers (1:2, 9, 13, 14), call to return/repent (2:12-13), promise of restoration (2:18, 25; 4:1 [Eng. 3:1]), passages that display intertextual adaptation of Obadiah (Joel 3–4 [Eng. 2:28–3:21]) and Amos (cf. Joel 4:16, 18 [Eng. 3:16, 18]), and the like, are some of the signifiers of possible settings. Even the mention of the

---

30. Thus Melugin points out the tangency of even reconstructing the particular setting of the readers rather than the authors: "But his [Ben Zvi's] emphasis on the polyvalence of the text and on the activity of rereading complicates the recovery of what these Persian-period readers actually did. The most Ben Zvi can do is to imagine the meanings they *might* have produced as they read and reread and came up with ever-different meanings as the various rereadings were undertaken" (Melugin, "Recent Form Criticism," 60).

31. See Knierim, "Criticism," 139, 145, 154.

32. Note a systematic definition of "function," and its distinction from other categories, by Knierim: "The same is true for 'function' (e.g. the way a genre, or a text-type or text operates in a communication event) and 'intention' or 'intentionality' (e.g. the goal a speaker or writer wants to achieve, or the goal a text achieves)" ("Reconsidered," 466).

33. Sweeney, *Twelve Prophets*, 1:149-50. Note also Sweeney, "The Place and Function of Joel in the Book of the Twelve," *SBLSP* (Atlanta: Scholars Press, 1999), 582: "Joel presents its scenario of threat and deliverance in anonymous terms; it therefore constitutes a basic pattern of threat and divine response to threat that can be read in relation to any particular historical situation in which the same patterns apply."

"Greeks" (4:6 [Eng. 3:6]) is an important clue to reconstruct the final stage of the setting.

First, with regard to a synchronic reading, most scholars date this text "between 500 and 350 B.C.E.,"[34] that is, the final stage of the written form in terms of the final redactor (stage 1). In light of this context, the book of Joel can be read as "a document of priestly ministry" with the function of a "learned prophecy" that "takes up the received eschatological message with a burning passion for knowledge, and with the help of sapiential training, and gives it new expression in intense expectation of Yahweh's future."[35] Second, reading diachronically, we can conjecturally reconstruct the settings of the postexilic community (stage 2). There is one unique feature in the book of Joel: the term "elders" (הזקנים) for the addressees. This term occurs rarely in other prophetic books.[36] It is for this reason that we may read this text against the setting of a postexilic community of hierocracy or theocracy. Third, as with many other prophetic books, this text too betrays the setting of exile, for example, the time of Jeremiah (stage 3). The call to repent (2:12-17) offers a tone of message that can be read against the context of the early exile, in addition to the late postexilic time. The text would then function as a call to repent against the impending doom.

Last but not least, we could read this text, and the whole book of Joel, in light of the time of the eighth-century prophets, such as Amos and Hosea (stage 4). The reason for this earlier, more fluid stage of setting may come from a different signifier, that is, in light of the structure of the entire twelve prophetic books. Most scholars agree that finding a chronological order in the formation of the Twelve Prophets is an incomplete, if not unconvincing, task.[37] Hence most find a thematic link to be the key principle of the present order.[38] Nevertheless, a case can be made that all factors (e.g., chronology, size,

---

34. Elizabeth Achtemeier, "The Book of Joel," in *NIB* 7:301. Wolff dates it to "the first half of the fourth century" (*Joel and Amos*, 12), and Crenshaw to "a late sixth- or fifth-century date" (*Joel*, 26).

35. Wolff, *Joel and Amos*, 11-12.

36. Whereas this term occurs as the addressee in Joel (1:2, 14; cf. 3:1 [Eng 2:28]), it occurs elsewhere only in Zech 8:4 in the rest of the Twelve Prophets.

37. Sweeney, "Sequence and Interpretation in the Book of the Twelve," in *Reading and Hearing the Book of the Twelve* (ed. J. D. Nogalski and M. A. Sweeney; SBLSymS 15; Atlanta: SBL, 2000), 55: "A chronological principle does not provide the full rationale for the sequence of the Twelve Prophets in either the LXX or the MT." Likewise, see Nogalski, "Joel as 'Literary Anchor' for the Book of the Twelve," in *Reading and Hearing*, ed. Nogalski and Sweeney, 91: "More must be said than that the Twelve progresses chronologically."

38. For a compelling reading of the extant orders of the Twelve Prophets in the MT and LXX, see Sweeney, *Twelve Prophets*, 1:xxvii-xxxv; idem, "Sequence," 49-64.

theme, genre) were instrumental in shaping the present structural sequences of the Twelve Prophets in the MT and LXX.[39] The majority of the Tanak is formed in a rough chronological order. The obvious exception would be the Writings, which start with the Psalms. Even within the Prophets, Deutero-Isaiah and Zephaniah are two of the many apparent problems for this approach. Still, the Tanak starts with the very beginning of everything and moves through a line of history, even within the groupings of books that follow other factors, such as the size (e.g., Isaiah, Jeremiah, Ezekiel) and genre (e.g., the Former Prophets).[40] In light of this possibility, Joel, which stands as the second book in the MT and the fourth book in the LXX, may have been considered — if not treated — as a prophet of an earlier time at a certain stage of text making. In this view we may read that the notions of "locust" (1:4), "nation" (1:6), and "the northern army" (2:20; cf. 2:2, 11, 25) could signify — at one stage of setting — the impending punishment on Israel and/or Judah.[41] The fact that in chap. 1 the addressees are the elders and all inhabitants "of the land" (1:2, 14), unlike Zion in chaps. 2–4, can help us see how the message of Joel could function as an oracle of warning for the similar settings of Hosea and Amos.

To sum up, what mutual methodological correlations can we find in the dialogues of these orientations? First, in all these methods, we find common denominators, that is, reading against a (historical) context — though it is not a common context. Inasmuch as a text is meant to be read by the subsequent generations, it is also meant to be read against each changing, different,

---

39. Even the correlation of the number "twelve" for the early tribes of Israel and the Minor Prophets does not seem to be a mere coincidence.

40. In the canonical order of the LXX, note how Hosea, Amos, and Micah are grouped together — the three largest volumes with the similar historical background. Haggai and Zechariah are grouped together in both the MT and LXX by the common theme and context (cf. Ezra 5:1; 6:14). Likewise, in the LXX, Jonah and Nahum are grouped together, obviously by the same issue concerning Nineveh vis-à-vis Israel. More roughly, the mention of Edom at the end of Joel (4:19 [Eng. 3:19]) may have been a factor to group it with Obadiah in the LXX. In view of these multiple factors, it is possible to argue that the grouping of the Twelve in the LXX seems more intentional or facilitated than that in the MT. Note Sweeney, "Place," 592: "Joel's place in the LXX sequence of the book of the Twelve provides for a far more logically consistent progression among the individual books."

41. Although Wolff interprets "locust" and "army" as natural catastrophe (1:4-20) and "eschatological army" (*Joel and Amos*, 13), if read against the earlier settings — or even considering that the Greeks were coming from the north — the army can contain a double entendre, including the meaning of the army in its literal sense. For an earlier dating, see Rex Mason, *Zephaniah, Habakkuk, Joel* (OTG; Sheffield: JSOT Press, 1994), 116: "Nothing demands a post-exilic date for 1.1–2.27." Cf. also "the valley of Jehoshaphat" in Joel 4:2, 12 (Eng. 3:2, 12) as a possible signifier of the 9th-century setting (Sweeney, "Sequence," 53).

and yet unique historical background. Second, in all of them we find an understanding of the biblical text as a constantly flowing stream of events, ideas, and peoples. The biblical text encompasses the past, present, and future. In a rough analogy, we may correlate redaction criticism to the past, canonical criticism to the contemporary (i.e., of a specifically designated set of settings or contexts), and reader-response criticism to the future. Third, consequently, in that constant flow, what becomes important would be to read a text against the established or identified setting. If we need to construe and interpret (i.e., retell) a text not only as a product but also as a process, in dialogue with the input of those criticisms, we as readers may have a cautious task (as well as freedom) to reread the text against various historically reconstructed or imagined texts, just as the ancient rereaders reread it in their own past, present, and future.

## Concept

Structure connects setting, genre, and concept. Yet it is concept that is more fundamental than the others. Concept even controls structure. Concept may not be the foundation of a building, nor is it the desks, chairs, or peoples inside that building. Rather, concept is like the blueprint of a building, without which nothing would stand in such a specific form. Structure is like Form as concept is like Idea in the philosophical understanding of Plato. In the analysis of a text, concept implies the subsurface level of a text. In the biblical texts, a text often contains concepts, not *the* concept. A text may easily engender not one but many ideas, implications, and even many sermon titles. Some of those divergent concepts are internally conflicting to one another. Inasmuch as other aspects of a form have been crucial in understanding the text, such as genre, structure, and setting, concept (which is usually discussed in the section of "intention" in the FOTL commentaries) deserves a more careful examination. To do so, we may need to dialogue with other criticisms, especially intertextuality. A model example of a study of conceptuality as well as textuality has been made by Rolf Knierim on Lev 1:1-9.[42] Similar studies need to be made on the larger units, such as Isaiah 40–55 or beyond.

Here we should note that unity or unified composition in a text or book does not necessarily mean that the author intended all elements, themes, or concepts to be coherent. Rather, often author/redactor somehow deliberately

---

42. Knierim, *Text and Concept in Leviticus 1:1-9: A Case in Exegetical Method* (FAT 2; Tübingen: Mohr, 1992).

left the tension of concepts together, making the whole ambiguous and multivalent. We may not know exactly why such is the case, except to ponder that in most cases, the biblical texts were not created by a single author out of a vacuum but rather compiled by the transmission of a long string of traditions, be they oral or written or a combination of both. Form criticism started from paying attention to these very processes, such as sagas, folktales, legends, and myths, through oral traditions. Perhaps many elements were so common to the immediate audience or readers that the author/redactor did not have to worry about juxtaposing coherently. Or perhaps the author/redactor had such piety that altering or subtracting some of the contents was less tolerable than adding on. Or perhaps the author/redactor was not concerned so much with making a book within the canon, but rather creating a collection of stories, histories, and oracles. Be that as it may, the biblical texts as we have now exhibit both coherent and, equally frequently, ambivalent concepts.

With regard to conceptual unity and diversity, at least two aspects need to be considered: internal and external — both in the mode of either tension or correlation. As for the internal aspects, for example, even in a concise book like Joel, we have the metaphors of creation restored (2:21-24) as well as creation reversed (3:3-5 [Eng. 2:30-32]). To press forward an argument, we have at least three distinct understandings of the coming restoration. In light of 2:21-27, the restoration of YHWH's people entails healing of the land and nature. In light of 3:1-5 (Eng 2:28-32), restoration encompasses an element of apocalyptic intervention, as if destruction would return, presumably on the cosmic scale. Then, in light of 4:1-8 (Eng. 3:1-8), restoration involves the divine lawsuit against the enemy nations, especially Tyre, Sidon, and the Philistines. On the one hand, these subunits signify divergent concepts, as if one offers a counterargument over another. At the least, they do not seem to correlate well. On the other hand, the extant form nicely connects these subunits together through the temporal phrases, such as "after this" (3:1) and "in those days" (4:1). Read together, each subunit can be delineated by the succeeding subunit. YHWH's way of "shalom" (2:25) will encompass the judgment on the nations (4:1-8 [Eng. 3:1-8]). The dreams and visions of all flesh (3:1-2) will include "the portents in the heavens and on the earth" (3:3-4). Even on the viewpoint of retrospect, just as the "elderly" who will dream dreams (3:1) makes a reversal of the condemnation against the "elders" (1:2, 14), so the "sons" and "daughters" who shall prophesy (3:1) depict a dramatic shift of the time when "boys" and "girls" were sold among the nations (4:3).

An example of the conceptual tension or correlation in terms of external aspect can show more congruence with intertextuality. Recent scholarship has contributed to the importance of reading a book within the place of the whole Twelve Prophets as a single entity. Read this way, a phrase, metaphor, or concept in a book can be read in connection with another. Thus, as Nogalski convincingly suggests, Joel can be read as a conceptual bridge between Hosea and Amos. Hosea's call for Israel's repentance is "dovetailed" with a call to repentance in Joel, and then Joel's oracle against the nations is concatenated with the oracle against the nations in Amos.[43] In this correlation we find conceptual similarities as well as differences.

Additionally, by the same token, Joel 4:9-19 (Eng. 3:9-19) shares the interconnection with Mic 4:1-5. The motif of Mt. Zion amid the mountains correlates Joel 4:16-18 (Eng. 3:16-18) with Mic 4:1-3. The notion that YHWH is to "sit to judge all the surrounding nations" (Joel 4:12 [Eng. 3:12]) echoes Mic 4:3 (cf. Ps 82). Even the motif that "everyone who *calls* on the name of YHWH shall be saved" in Joel 3:5 (Eng 2:32) is reiterated in the confession of the people who are said to "*walk* in the name of YHWH" in Mic 4:5. Most importantly, the concept of beating "plowshares into swords and pruning hooks into spears" (Joel 4:10 [Eng. 3:10]) recurs with its opposite concept in Mic 4:3-4. It is noteworthy that Joel immediately follows Micah in the LXX, whereas Micah comes three books after Joel in the MT. In either sequence, read synchronically, the concept of peace in Micah's vision is contrasted with the concept of war in Joel's vision. Reading diachronically, we can pose how one textual tradition was reconceptualized in another by the phraseological, metaphorical, and conceptual interconnections and shifts.[44]

In summary, just as a text may depict more than one inherent structure, genre, or setting, it also signifies many themes, metaphors, and concepts. Some of them are nicely correlated within a text. Others are in tension with one another not only within the text but also in connection with other texts. Moreover, a text contains many conceptual signals that point to many internal and external similarities and shifts in its intertextual connections with other books in the Hebrew Bible. Paying attention to these aspects can further enrich both synchronic and diachronic readings.

## Conclusion

Form criticism has made enormous contributions to biblical scholarship in the last century. Like the root of a tree, it has produced many branches of

43. Nogalski, "Joel as 'Literary Anchor,'" 91-109.
44. For a fuller discussion and interpretation of this relationship, see Sweeney, "Place," 589-95.

subdisciplines. As a parent, it has yielded many children. At the dawn of a new century, what should form criticism look like? In what areas shall it grow? In what other areas will it not succeed and thereby need to change or modify?

As for its changing face, it should continue to grow and extend in association with many other disciplines. Form criticism will remain one discipline; yet, externally, it will and should continue to share mutual interactions with other criticisms, such as redaction criticism, textual criticism, rhetorical criticism, canonical criticism, literary criticism, sociological criticism, archeology, intertextuality, comparative studies (both the ancient Near East and other ancient cultures), and reader-response criticism. The interaction should be mutual, the criticisms influencing, challenging, and correcting one another. At the same time, internally, within its own internal discipline, form criticism further needs to be sharpened by its subdisciplines. Admittedly, we do not wish to have compartments become more independent — as if we need to have more criticisms such as genre criticism, structure criticism, setting criticism, or concept criticism — when one of the remarkable features of the postmodern era is the very existence of multifaceted methods, theories, and perspectives. What must remain vital in this discipline is to weave those subdisciplines together rather than deconstruct completely.

What then would the changed face of form criticism look like? On the one hand, its face will probably be constantly changing. Postmodernism has contributed significantly to this aspect. Because of the unceasing rise of new ideas, different methods, and opposing perspectives, it would be most likely that form criticism's orientations and methods will not stay in one place. Like the ever-flowing stream, it has to and will become new, be outdated, and then revitalized, and so on. On the other hand, however, we may be able to get a glimpse of its shape every now and then, that is, amid the constant fluctuation of its shaping and reshaping. It is for this punctual stage that we may project a possible face. If we use an analogy, I wonder if its earliest stage may be depicted as a face drawn by Cézanne. It looked clear, clean, and quite simple. In the similar analogy, I wonder if the face of the upcoming era may resemble that of a face drawn by Picasso. It would look multifaceted, complex, and complicated, as it displays a face seen from many angles. The face is one, just as the text is one in its completed written form of a manuscript. Yet its drawing portrays many dimensions just as the biblical text often portrays multidimensional textuality and conceptuality.

In this shape of the face, we may no longer describe the components of form criticism as structure, setting, and concept. For that matter, genre should be considered likewise. Then we may have to call these components structures, genres, settings, and concepts, a multidimensional building for a multilayered text. Each task may require more scrutiny and imagination. Nevertheless, this cohesive approach may do better justice to the text that itself has grown out of a long stream of retelling, rewriting, and rereading.

PART II

# THE BIBLE AND
# ANCIENT NEAR EASTERN LITERATURE

# Inscriptional Evidence and the Question of Genre

## MARTIN RÖSEL

A short description of two phenomena shall serve as the background of the following considerations: the first observation is that especially in a German perspective one has to state an ongoing decline of the usage and importance of the form-critical method. This neglect can easily be seen when looking at the latest commentaries on the psalms by Frank-Lothar Hossfeld and Erich Zenger, especially when compared to the older one by Hans-Joachim Kraus or the commentaries of Erhard Gerstenberger in the FOTL series.[1] The same is true for attempts to understand the prophetic literature; it may suffice to refer to the latest book by Uwe Becker in comparison with the commentary by Marvin Sweeney.[2]

Several reasons have led to this development.[3] One important factor has been the work of Sigmund Mowinckel and his "cult-historical method," which led older scholarship to hold confidence in the possibility for a recon-

---

1. F.-L. Hossfeld and E. Zenger, *Die Psalmen I. Psalm 1–50* (NEB 29; Würzburg: Echter, 1993); F.-L. Hossfeld and E. Zenger, *Psalmen 51–100* (HTKAT; Freiburg: Herder, 2000); H.-J. Kraus, *Psalmen* (BKAT XV/1-2; 6th ed., Neukirchen-Vluyn: Neukirchener Verlag, 1989); ET: *Psalms* (trans. H. C. Oswald; 2 vols.; Minneapolis: Augsburg, 1988-89); E. Gerstenberger, *Psalms, Part 1; with an Introduction to Cultic Poetry* (FOTL 14; Grand Rapids: Eerdmans, 1988); idem, *Psalms, Part 2; Lamentations* (FOTL 15; Grand Rapids: Eerdmans, 2001).

2. U. Becker, *Jesaja — Von der Botschaft zum Buch* (FRLANT 178; Göttingen: Vandenhoeck & Ruprecht, 1997); M. A. Sweeney, *Isaiah 1–39; with an Introduction to Prophetic Literature* (FOTL 16; Grand Rapids: Eerdmans, 1996).

3. Cf. J. Barton, "Form Criticism. OT," *ABD* 2:838-41; M. Rösel, "Formen/Gattungen II. Altes Testament," *RGG*[4] 186-200.

---

I would like to dedicate this article to my *Doktorvater* and friend Klaus Koch on the occasion of his seventy-fifth birthday for having introduced me to the field of form criticism.

struction of a cultic *Sitz im Leben* of the texts (also for prophetic texts) that can no longer be justified. Another point was that scholars often undervalued the tension between the idealized forms they established (in the German sense of *Gattung*) and the individual texts.[4] We now have to accept a broader variety within the forms and a more complex history of the forms *(Gattungsgeschichte)*. The last reason to be named in this short (and necessarily rough) survey is the shift of interest in exegetical studies from preliterary, oral stages of the texts to their literary development.

Thus one may conclude that especially in German exegesis redaction-critical studies are predominant while the form-critical method has lost its former status. This leads to the consequence that the question for an actual *Sitz im Leben* of the texts has widely been abandoned; in the commentaries of Hossfeld and Zenger most of the psalms are understood as mere literary products without a significant relationship to cultic practices or the temple. The situation in American exegesis is somewhat different. The focus of interest has shifted to the finished form of the text, but the results are comparable: the method has lost its former status.

The second observation is that this neglect of the possibilities of the form-critical method can also be seen in research concerning the inscriptions or larger texts that have been found in recent years. These documents have caused much scholarly discussion because of their historical or religious implications. One may remember the inscription from Tel Dan and the discussions between "minimalists" and "maximalists" it has caused;[5] the problem of "YHWH and his Asherah" in the findings from Kuntillet Ajrud or Khirbet el-Qom;[6] and most recently the inscriptions from Ekron.[7] But these discussions

4. See, e.g., F. -L. Hossfeld, "Hymnus II. Altes Testament," *RGG*[4] 3:1975; and the criticism of the method in Hossfeld and Zenger, *Psalmen I,* 17-25. It should be noted that the important article by R. Knierim, "Old Testament Form Criticism Reconsidered," *Int* 27 (1973): 435-68, did not receive the attention it has deserved in German exegesis.

5. A translation of the text of the stele can be found in *COS* 2.39. The most convincing interpretation can be found in I. Kottsieper, "Die Inschrift vom Tell Dan und die politischen Beziehungen zwischen Aram-Damaskus und Israel in der 1. Hälfte des 1. Jahrtausends vor Christus," in *"Und Mose schrieb dieses Lied auf"* (Fest. O. Loretz; ed. M. Dietrich and I. Kottsieper; AOAT 250; Münster: Ugarit-Verlag, 1998), 475-500.

6. Cf. the most recent survey by R. K. Gnuse, "The Emergence of Monotheism in Ancient Israel: A Survey of Recent Scholarship," *Religion* 29 (1999): 315-36; or the important volume by W. Dietrich and M. A. Klopfenstein, eds., *Ein Gott allein? JHWH-Verehrung und biblischer Monotheismus im Kontext der israelitischen altorientalischen Religionsgeschichte* (OBO 139; Fribourg: Universitaires; Göttingen: Vandenhoeck & Ruprecht, 1994).

7. See V. Sasson, "The Inscription of Achish, Governor of Eqron, and Philistine Dialect, Cult and Culture," *UF* 29 (1997): 627-39; R. G. Lehmann, "Studien zur Formgeschichte

have focused primarily on the contents of the findings, very seldom on their genre.

In my view this is regrettable, because in these inscriptions one has access to genres in their primary usage, while in the Hebrew Bible we can find them inserted only in secondary contexts, which are therefore altered in different respects. Thus I try to demonstrate that working on these texts with the more traditional questions and methods of form criticism can give new insights — results that are also important for biblical exegesis. I pay special attention to texts in Hebrew or cognate languages from Israel or its closest neighbors, because parallels from Egyptian and Mesopotamian sources have already been examined by older form-critical research and are still the source of interest.[8]

## Formulations of Blessings

As a starting point I choose the formulations of blessings. Most of the texts are well known because of the lively discussion on the emergence of monotheism in Israel and the question whether the God of Israel had a *parhedra* in preexilic times.[9] Despite the ongoing discussion the focus of this contribution is only on the form-critical aspects of these texts. The inscriptions on the pithoi from Kuntillet Ajrud read as follows:[10]

---

der 'Eqron-Inschrift des 'kyš und den phönikischen Dedikationstexten aus Byblos," *UF* 31 (1999): 255-306.

8. For more recent studies, see W. Burkert and F. Stolz, eds., *Hymnen der Alten Welt im Kulturvergleich* (OBO 131; Fribourg: Universitaires; Göttingen: Vandenhoeck & Ruprecht, 1994); M. Emmendörffer, *Der ferne Gott: Eine Untersuchung der alttestamentlichen Volksklagelieder vor dem Hintergrund der mesopotamischen Literatur* (FAT 21; Tübingen: Mohr-Siebeck, 1998). Still valuable is W. Mayer, *Untersuchungen zur Formensprache der babylonischen "Gebetsbeschwörungen"* (Studia Pohl, Series Major 5; Rome: Biblical Institute Press, 1976).

9. The scholarly literature on these texts is immense. It may suffice to refer readers to O. Keel and C. Uehlinger, *Götter, Göttinen und Gottessymbole: Neue Erkenntnisse zur Religionsgeschichte Kanaans und Israels aufgrund bislang unerschlossener ikonographischer Quellen* (4th expanded ed.; Freiburg: Herder, 1998), 237-82, §§129-47.

10. The best edition of the texts is J. Renz and W. Röllig, *Handbuch der Althebräischen Epigraphik*, vols. I, II/1, III (Darmstadt: Wissenschaftliche Buchgesellschaft, 1995), hereafter abbreviated *HAE*. Cf. the translation of the texts in *COS* 2.

Pithos 1: (*HAE* I:61; cf. *COS* 2.47A)

1. אמר א[.. ה.[.. ה.[..]ך אמר ליהל[..] וליועשה ו.[..] ברכת אתכם
He has said [   ] speak to [   ] and to Yauʿāśā [   ] I bless you by

2. ליהוה שמרן ולעשרתה
YHWH of Samaria and by his Asherah

Pithos 2: (*HAE* I:62; cf. *COS* 2.47B)

1-3. אמריו אומר ל אדני ו השלם א[ת]
Amaryau: Speak to my lord: Are you in peace?

4-7. ברכתך לי הו[..] ו ולאשרתה יבורך וישמרך
I bless you by YHWH (of Teman?) and by his Asherah. May he
bless you and keep you

8-9. ויהי עם אד[ו]
and may he be with my Lord

One interesting fact is the grammatical distinction that is made in these formulas. Although the blessing that is spoken of a human being ("I bless you by
YHWH") is formulated as ברכתך ל in the AK/perfect conjugation, the hope
that the Lord is blessing a human ("He may bless you") is written in the PK/
imperfect.

Only seldom are the wall inscriptions of Kuntillet Ajrud referred to.
Here one can read at least one similar formula in inscription no. 3 (*HAE* I:59;
cf. *COS* 2.47D):

1. [..] ובזרח אל וימסן הרם [..]
[..] When God is rising, the mountains are melting [..]

2. [..] ברך בעל בים מלח[מה..]
[..] Blessed be Baʿal on the day of the war [..]

3. [..] לשם אל בים מלח[מה..]
[..] by the name of God on the day of the war [..]

These remains of a once longer text are a fragment of a hymnic song that can
be compared to descriptions of God's theophany. The verbs used (מסס ;זרח)
are attested in biblical texts, such as Deut 33:2; Mal 3:20 (Eng. 4:1); or Mic
1:4.[11] Again, the interest of this investigation is in the formulation of the
blessing only.

In this context, one should also mention the difficult inscription from
the grave in Khirbet el-Qom. Its text is very close to those on the pithoi in
Kuntillet Ajrud (*HAE* I:207-11; cf. *COS* 2.52):

11. Cf. the title in *COS* 2.47D, p. 173, "A Theophany of the Day of Battle."

1. אריהו העשר כתבה

Uriyahu the rich wrote it

2. ברך/ברכת אריהו ליהוה

blessed be/I bless[12] Uriyahu by YHWH

3. ומצריה לאשרתה הושע לה

For from his enemies he has saved him by his Asherah

4. לאניהו

by Oniyahu

One of the problems of this text is that it is very unusual for a grave inscription. Most of the other inscriptions from Khirbet el-Qom and from other graves follow the usual pattern "this grave belongs to X, son of Y." That is why Bill Dever has tried to reconstruct this type of inscription here too, but this theory has not been accepted.[13]

It has to be noted that there are no exact parallels to these formulations in the Hebrew Bible. Occasionally some formulas call a blessing upon YHWH himself, such as ברוך אדני/יהוה in doxologic formulas in Ps 68:20 (Eng. 19) (a praise spoken by the whole nation) or 72:18-19 (the conclusion of the second book of the Psalter).[14] One can also find the wishful expression "May N be blessed by/before YHWH" (ברוך ליהוה), for example, in Gen 14:19; Judg 17:2; feminine in Ruth 3:10.[15] All these biblical texts are formulated with the passive בָּרוּךְ,[16] which clearly distinguishes them from the inscriptional evidence (the wall inscription with the blessing of Baal is an exception). But they all share the strange use of the *lamed* in ליהוה,[17] which in the Hebrew Bible is never combined with a finite form of ברך.

12. Z. Zevit, "The Khirbet el-Qôm Inscription Mentioning a Goddess," *BASOR* 255 (1984): 44, reads ברכת instead of ברך. This would fit nicely with the other examples of the formula. Nevertheless, this reading is far from certain; cf. *HAE* I:205, 208; J. M. Hadley, "The Khirbet El-Qom Inscription," *VT* 37 (1987): 54.

13. W. D. Dever, "Iron Age Epigraphic Material from the Area of Khirbet el-Kôm," *HUCA* 40/41 (1969-70): 139-204. See the detailed discussion in *HAE* I:204-11; Hadley, "Khirbet el-Qom," 52ff.

14. See Gerstenberger, *Psalms, Part 1*, 18; C. W. Mitchell, *The Meaning of brk "to Bless" in the Old Testament* (SBLDS 95; Atlanta: Scholars Press, 1995), 152-53, 158-59.

15. Cf. also 1 Sam 15:13; 23:21 (pl.); 2 Sam 2:5; Ruth 2:20. See I. Lande, *Formelhafte Wendungen der Umgangssprache im Alten Testament* (Leiden: Brill, 1949), 9-11.

16. Mitchell, *Meaning*, 110-18, who came to the result that the *bārûk* formula should best be understood as an optative wish (pp. 111-12); see already GKC §116r.

17. For the use of the *lamed* in biblical texts, cf. the divergent positions of G. Wehmeier, *Der Segen im Alten Testament: Eine semasiologische Untersuchung der Wurzel brk* (diss.; Basel, 1970), 110; Mitchell, *Meaning*, 111-12. In my view it is obvious that the *lamed* should be seen as a *lamed auctoris* or *agentis*; see *IBHAS* §11.2.10g, p. 210.

Thus one should look for an even closer parallel. Because of the characteristic beginning of the texts on the pithoi, the openings or prescripts of Hebrew and Aramaic letters should be considered. As an example, the initial address and greeting of the letter on ostracon 16 from Arad reads (*HAE* I:379, 6th century):

1-3. אחך חנניהו שלח לשלם אלישב ולשלם ביתך ברכתך ליהוה ועת
Your brother Hananyahu sends greetings to Elyashib and your household. I bless you by YHWH. And now . . .[18]

The same blessing is found on Arad ostracon 21,[19] while the ostraca from Lachish have a different greeting, reading (ostraca 2, 3, 4, 5, 8, 9; see *HAE* I:411-30):

(Ostr. 1:1-3): ישמע יהוה את אדני שמעת שלם
may YHWH let my lord hear good news . . .[20]

Perhaps one can think of a territorial diversity in using those formulas, because all of the *bārak lᵉ*-formulas come from the south. It is noteworthy that the form ברכתך in these ostraca appears only in a finite verbal form, "I bless you," not as a passive as in the biblical formulas.

This special initial greeting of a letter is also attested in the Phoenician language in a sixth-century papyrus from Saqqara (*KAI* 50):

1+2. ברכתך לבועל צפן ולכל אל תחפנחס
I bless you by Baʿal Zaphon and all Gods of Tachpanchas[21]

In Aramaic the blessing can be found in several letters from the sixth and fifth centuries from Hermopolis (Hermopolis 1 + 2 + 3 + 4 + 6; Lindenberger, *Letters*, 26-32): ברכתכי לפתח, "I bless you by Ptah"; in letter 5 even in plural formulation: ברכנכן לפתח, "We bless you by Ptah." Another parallel can be found on an Edomite ostracon from Horvat Uza (late 7th century, Lindenberger, *Letters*, 118). It is also possible to reconstruct this blessing in a fifth-century letter

18. Translation from J. M. Lindenberger, *Ancient Aramaic and Hebrew Letters* (SBLWAW 4; Atlanta: Scholars Press, 1994), 110. Cf. pp. 6-7 on the form of the letters.

19. M. Weippert, "Zum Präskript der hebräischen Briefe von Arad," *VT* 25 (1975): 202-12, has seen this formula also in ostraca 1, 2, and 15.

20. Lindenberger, *Letters*, 110-15.

21. Ibid., 119-20.

from Elephantine (Lindenberger, *Letters*, 45: [ב]ברכתך ליהה ולחנן, "I bless you by YHH and Khnum (!)."

The evidence from these letters is unambiguous. One must therefore conclude that the blessings from Kuntillet Ajrud and Khirbet el-Qom are written in the form of the initial greeting formulas of letters.[22] In a form-critical perspective this leads to interesting results, because we can see a very important shift of the *Sitz im Leben* of such a formula from the personal, individual usage in a letter to a more public use in the Kuntillet Ajrud inscriptions and another shift to the use in a grave as in the Khirbet el-Qom material. Even if we do not know exactly why the formulas were written on the pithoi, we can assume a kind of dedicatory function in a semi-official or private stratum of the Israelite religion. The shift from the use of the formula in letters to the usage on pithoi and walls is understandable if we assume that *scribes*, but not other officials such as priests, were responsible for these dedications. This consideration gains support from the fact that on pithos 2 remnants of several alphabets, which obviously were practice or exercises of a scribe, can be seen (*HAE* I:63). But that does not mean that the texts as a whole were mere exercises without a deeper meaning.[23] Perhaps we even know the name of one of these scribes, Oniyahu, who obviously wrote the inscription of Khirbet el-Qom.

The formulations taken from the prescripts of the letters invoke the blessing of YHWH onto the mentioned individuals in Kuntillet Ajrud. One can not be sure whether they were taken from real letters that were sent to the south from Samaria or Teman (as Keel and Uehlinger have proposed),[24] but the possibility remains. It is noteworthy that in any instance the formulation of the blessing refers to the name of the deity as the true source who grants the blessing. Thus the effectiveness of the blessing does not depend on the one who utters or writes the blessing, but on the power of the deity. Therefore these formulations can be compared to those biblical texts in which people invoke God's blessing on other humans (e.g., Gen 27:27-29; 28:3; 48:15-16);[25] these texts did preserve the more private formulations attested by the inscriptions.

---

22. Admittedly, this observation is not entirely new; cf. *HAE* II/1:11-16, 24; J. Naveh, "Graffiti and Dedications," *BASOR* 235 (1979): 27-30.

23. In *HAE* I:62 (obviously following A. Lemaire, *Les écoles et la formation de la Bible dans l'ancien Israël* [OBO 39; Fribourg: Universitaires; Göttingen: Vandenhoeck & Ruprecht, 1981], 28) the content of the text on pithos 2 is given as *Schülerübung* (students' exercise), which is in my view not a sufficient description; cf. Keel and Uehlinger, *Götter*, 275.

24. *Götter*, 274n243.

25. According to Mitchell, *Meaning*, 79, these blessings should be named "declarative human blessings"; cf. pp. 79-131 for an exhaustive discussion of the problem and the scholarly debate.

Another problem is the function of the blessing in a grave. Here one should also consider the difficult inscriptions in the grave from Khirbet Beit Lei (Inscription B, *HAE* I:248; cf. *COS* 2.53), פקד יה אל חנן נקה יה יהוה, "Intervene, O compassionate God! Absolve, O YHWH!" and the well-known silver amulets from Ketef Hinnom (*HAE* I:447-56; *COS* 2.83). They obviously show the more official, priestly formulation of a blessing, but they share the wishful phrase יברכך וישמרך, "may he bless you and keep you," with the inscription on pithos 2 from Kuntillet Ajrud. The different texts supply evidence that already in preexilic times the power of God's blessing was not restricted to the lifetime of the faithful.[26]

One last fact is interesting to note with respect to biblical exegesis. The letters in the Hebrew Bible are never transmitted with an opening as we have seen it in Arad or Hermopolis,[27] with the possible exception of ועתה in 2 Kgs 5:6; 10:2. This can be seen as a hint that these texts were newly formulated or at least reworked when they were inserted into the current context.[28]

## Royal Inscriptions and Punic Votive Inscriptions

If it is probable that the inscriptions from Kuntillet Ajrud that we have examined were used as dedications or votive inscriptions, one should look for more texts with a comparable function. Two important inscriptions from a royal context should be mentioned. The first is the Aramaic prayer of King Zakkur from Hamat (*KAI* 202; *COS* 2.35, ca. 800 BCE).[29] In the text of the stele, the king reports the danger he experienced when ten kings were attack-

---

26. This is not the place to begin a discussion about the background of the idea of resurrection in the HB, but in my view there are more and more hints (including the above-mentioned texts) arguing against the widely held position that this concept is a very late development. It may suffice to refer interested readers to K. Spronk, *Beatic Afterlife in Ancient Israel and the Ancient Near East* (AOAT 219; Neukirchen-Vluyn: Neukirchener Verlag, 1986); or M. Albani, "Der Herr tötet und macht lebendig; er führt in die Unterwelt und wieder herauf. Zur Problematik der Auferstehungshoffnung im AT am Beispiel von 1 Sam 2,6," *Leqach* 1 (2001): 22-55.

27. Cf. 2 Sam 11:15; 1 Kgs 21:8-11; 2 Kgs 5:5-6; 10:1-7; etc. See Lindenberger, *Letters*, 6, for a helpful diagram of the form of the letters.

28. According to D. Pardee, "Letters (Hebrew)," *ABD* 4:285, "the brevity and sobriety [of the biblical letters] . . . bespeaks authenticity of form if not necessarily of content," but this is hardly convincing.

29. For a form-critical investigation of this text cf. H. J. Zobel, "Das Gebet um Abwendung der Not und seine Erhörung in den Klageliedern des Alten Testaments und in der Inschrift des Königs Zakir von Hamath," *VT* 21 (1971): 91-99.

ing his city. In this situation he raised his hands to Baal-Shamen, who then answered his complaint and told him that he would be saved. Thus this inscription shows the classical basic structure, complaint-petition-praise, like most of the individual biblical complaint psalms (cf. Ps 13),[30] including the acknowledgment of the divine response. Unfortunately the exact wording of the prayer is not handed down to us nor any accompanying rituals.

The same structure of praising God after the experience of salvation can be seen in the famous inscription of King Mesha from Moab (*KAI* 181; *COS* 2.23; ca. 835 BCE). The text belongs to the genre of building inscriptions; the king states that he has built this sanctuary because his god Chemosh saved him after his anger came against the land. Again, nothing is said about accompanying cultic practices, but perhaps 2 Kgs 3:27 has kept the information about the ritual the king celebrated when calling to his god — he offered his son. This brings us to the Phoenician religion.

A very interesting yet seldom studied source for dedications are the Punic votive inscriptions.[31] The motifs used in these inscriptions are stereotyped, the sequence is flexible. The texts belong to a special, heavily disputed kind of offering, the *mlk* offering.[32] Obviously these offerings have been celebrated in situations of trouble or affliction (see *COS* 1.198, 4-5, *nsb mlkt bmsrm*, "a stele of an offering in affliction"). Sometimes these offerings seem to accompany a ceremony of thanksgiving and blessing (*KAI* 98):

לאדן לבעל חמן [נצ]ב מלך בעל אזרם
אש נדר בעלשלך בן עזרבעל בן מתר כ שמא קל יברכא
To the lord, to Baʿal Hammon, a stele of an offering instead of an infant, which vowed BʿLSHLK, son of ʿZRBʿL, son of MTR, because he has heard (his) call, may he bless him.

Cf. also the vow in *KAI* 97:

אש נדר מגן בן אנתחן
(This is) what MGN, son of ʾNTHN, has vowed.

---

30. Cf. Gerstenberger, *Psalms, Part 1*, 11-16, for the genre; 83-86 for Ps 13.

31. For the following cf. H.-P. Müller, "Punische Weihinschriften und alttestamentliche Psalmen im religionsgeschichtlichen Zusammenhang," *Or* 67 (1998): 477-96.

32. H.-P. Müller. "Genesis 22 und das *mlk*-Opfer: Erinnerung an einen religionsgeschichtlichen Tatbestand," *BZ* 41 (1997): 237-46; Klaus Koch, "Molek astral," in *Mythos im Alten Testament und seiner Umwelt* (Fest. H.-P. Müller; BZAW 278; Berlin and New York: de Gruyter, 1999), 19-50.

Very close to biblical pleas like Ps 27:7 ("Hear, O Lord, my voice; have mercy and answer me"; cf. *KAI* 33.3; 77.3-4) are inscriptions that explicitly state, "for he has heard his voice" (*KAI* 103; cf. also 104, 105):

מלך אדם נדר אש נדר בעלפדא בן מגן שמא קלא ברכא

an offering of a man, a vow that vowed B'LPD', son of MGN,
(because) he has heard his call (and) blessed him.

The inscriptions often end with a blessing, a rare phenomenon that can be seen also in Ps 129:8. Again, these inscriptions can be compared to elements of biblical psalms, such as the songs of thanksgiving or the vows to praise God in the complaint psalms, which are often combined with the promise that an offering will be celebrated (Ps 27:6; 54:8-9 [Eng. 6-7]). The brevity of the inscriptions and the stereotyped formulations indicate that the texts stem from an originally oral use. Eventually they were written on the stelae. Perhaps, as H.-P. Müller has assumed, all these dedications and psalms were written after the one uttering the prayer had experienced God's intervention.[33] This would easily explain why the complaint is often followed by praise; it is a characteristic of the genre that refers back to an actual *Sitz im Leben,* a cultic ceremony of thanksgiving. This speaks against the widely held theory that the *Stimmungsumschwung* (transition or change of mood) in these psalms is a psychological development in the process of a prayer.[34]

The biblical psalms as we have them today show only traces of this development, and one cannot regain the once-felt confidence to reconstruct in detail the specific sociological contexts from which they came.[35] In any case, comparison with the evidence of the above-mentioned inscriptions makes clear that the original *Sitz im Leben* of these psalms cannot be described without the cultic or ritual background.

33. "Punische Weihinschriften," 487.

34. See most recently Hossfeld and Zenger, *Psalmen 51–100,* 92, on Ps 54:8-9 (Eng. 6-7); although an offering is clearly mentioned in v. 8, Hossfeld speaks only about the prayer and the question whether it was uttered in the temple. M. E. Tate, *Psalms 51–100* (WBC 20; Dallas: Word, 1990), 45, 48, realizes the importance of the thanksgiving ceremony and clearly distinguishes vv. 8-9 from the rest of the psalm.

35. Cf. also the reservations expressed by R. C. Van Leeuwen, pp. 72-73, 80-82 in this volume.

## Larger Compositions

In the last section of this essay I turn to larger textual units. One of the most important findings is the Balaam inscription from Tell Deir Alla, because here mention is made of a seer named Balaam ben Beor (*COS* 2.27). There can be no doubt that this inscription from the ninth or eighth century refers to the same Balaam as the biblical account in Numbers 22–24.[36] What interests us here is the form-critical assessment of the text. The first line, written in red, is the highlighted heading, reading, ספר בלעם בן בער, "This is the *sefer* of Balaam, son of Beor." Then follows an account about this visionary in the third-person singular (ll. 2-17), and after that a vision can be read. Because of the damage the inscription has suffered, one can only guess whether the text once ended with this visionary experience or whether it comes back to the narration.[37]

The genre of this text has to be seen in the context of prophetic stories.[38] More specifically it can be called a "prophetic apophthegma."[39] According to the definition by Rudolf Bultmann, this is a story that ascribes a specific saying to a concrete person. In the Hebrew Bible we have one example for this genre in Amos 7:10-17, a narration centered on the prophecy against the king of Israel and the question whether Amos is a prophet.[40] One can also think of the visionary account in Isaiah 6 pointing to v. 9, "Hear, but understand not; and see, but perceive not," or of Isaiah 7, pointing to v. 9, "If ye will not believe, surely ye shall not be established." Another late example may be seen in the book of Jonah with its single prophecy against Nineveh in 3:4.

Even more interesting is that the text was inscribed on a wall. Although the function of the room cannot be described with certainty, one should as-

---

36. See the most recent studies by M. Rösel, "Wie einer vom Propheten zum Verführer wird: Tradition und Rezeption der Bileamgestalt," *Bib* 80 (1999): 506-24; and B. A. Levine, *Numbers 21–36* (AB 4A; New York: Doubleday, 2000), 241-75.

37. See Levine, *Numbers 21–36*, 275, who states, "It is tempting to regard Combination II as a dramatic description of Balaam's own tragedy."

38. Cf. Sweeney, *Isaiah 1–39*, 20-22.

39. So M. Weippert, "Der "Bileam"-Text von *Tell Dēr ʿAllā* und das Alte Testament," in *Jahwe und die anderen Götter* (FAT 18; Tübingen: Mohr-Siebeck, 1997), 174.

40. As for Amos 7:10-17 see most recently J. Werlitz, "Amos und sein Biograph: Zur Entstehung und Intention der Prophetenerzählung Am 7,10-17," *BZ* 44 (2000): 233-51. Although he argues that the text is a late composition, serving as "redaktionelle Bucheinschreibung" (p. 250), he concludes that the statement in v. 14, "I am no prophet, nor a prophet's son; but I am a herdsman, and a dresser of sycamore trees," should be seen as an older tradition because of its poetic style and underivable diction. This fits perfectly the definition of an apophthegma.

sume that it was a meeting place of a group of prophets, $b^e n\hat{e}$ $n^e b\hat{i}\hat{i}m$, where the visions and deeds of that Balaam were remembered.[41] It should be noted that this relatively long text was written in comparatively early times. This could serve as an argument against the tendency to date similar biblical texts to very late times. Moreover, we have a hint to the *Sitz im Leben* of these texts. First, one can certainly assume that the wall inscription is a kind of secondary usage of the text, for it must have been composed on other material like papyrus that is now lost.[42] Second, that the writing appeared on a wall means that its content could be known by a lot of people, not only by scribes. Although it is true that illiteracy was normal at these times, one should assume that even illiterate persons would ask about this inscription and that the text had been commemorated by the $b^e n\hat{e}$ $n^e b\hat{i}\hat{i}m$. Thus the text and the visionary became well known, even in Israel, as Numbers 22–24 proves.

One more consideration can be added. When working with biblical texts we often assume a shorter or longer history of oral transmission prior to its literary recording. The inscriptional evidence confronts us with the phenomenon of wall inscriptions in more public rooms. We have seen the phenomenon in Kuntillet Ajrud, Deir Alla, and on the stelae of Zakkur and Mesha as well. One could also recall the Tell Dan stele (*COS* 2.29), the Ekron inscription (*COS* 2.42), or the inscription from the Ophel in Jerusalem.[43] This necessarily leads to the assumption that even a written text can have an ongoing oral tradition until it is newly written down. From a methodological standpoint, this assumption makes things more complicated but historically more adequate. A second problem is that we should also consider the possibility that texts we now have in the Bible were initially composed to serve as a kind of wall inscription. There are enough indications that those

41. So convincingly R. Wenning and E. Zenger, "Heiligtum ohne Stadt — Stadt ohne Heiligtum? Anmerkungen zum archäologischen Befund des *Tell Dēr ʿAllā*,*" ZAH* 4 (1991): 171-93, esp. 189-92. The problem is that there are no contemporary characteristics of sacral or cultic architecture and equipment; therefore they conclude that the building probably served as a meeting place for a group of prophets.

One should remember 2 Kgs 8:4, the retelling of the $g^e d\hat{o} l\bar{o}t$ that Elisha had done, or the important text Isa 8:16 concerning the sealing of the teaching among the disciples, which — interestingly enough — is embedded in a larger prophetic instruction (Sweeney, *Isaiah 1– 39,* 179).

42. M. Nissinen, "Spoken, Written, Quoted, and Invented: Orality and Writtenness in Ancient Near Eastern Prophecy," in *Writings and Speech in Israelite and Ancient Near Eastern Prophecy* (ed. E. Ben Zvi and M. H. Floyd; SBLSymS 10; Atlanta: SBL, 2000), 250.

43. M. Ben Dov, "A Fragmentary First Temple Period Hebrew Inscription from the Ophel," in *Ancient Jerusalem Revealed* (ed. H. Geva; Jerusalem: Israel Exploration Society, 1994), 73-75.

inscriptions were known to biblical authors; cf. the plaster inscription from Deut 27:2; Daniel 5; or Job 19:23-24, in which Job wishes that his words were recorded and graven with an iron pen and lead in the rock.[44] One can easily assume that prophetic texts such as a model of Amos 7:10-17 or his visions might once have been used in this or a similar way,[45] even after the confirmation of the prophecies following the events of 722 BCE.[46] One can also think of a *sēper milḥāmōt YHWH* (Num 21:14) or the *sēper hayyāšār* (Josh 10:13; 2 Sam 1:18). Another important candidate could be the dedication of the temple by Solomon in 1 Kgs 8:12-13, which according to the longer and probably more original LXX version is written in the "book of the song [corrected to *yāšār*]."[47] Likewise, the *sēper* of the kings of Israel and Judah (2 Chr 16:11) may have originated in wall inscriptions in the palace in Jerusalem.[48] Obviously there was a pattern for those texts,[49] and since monumental inscriptions like these are well known from Israel's neighbors, it is hard to tell whether they would have been influential in Judah or Israel.[50] As a support for these considerations it should be noted that according to a recent study by Siegfried Kreuzer, even the structure of the story of King David can be explained in the light of West Semitic royal inscriptions.[51] Margaret S.

44. Cf. also 1 Sam 15:12, in which Saul set up a monument for himself (לוֹ מַצִּיב וְהִנֵּה יָד), or 2 Sam 8:13, in which David won a name (שֵׁם דָּוִד וַיַּעַשׂ). Even the Siloam Tunnel Inscription can be mentioned here; see *COS* 2.28.

45. One should remember the לוּחַ from Isa 30:8; Jer 17:1; Hab 2:2. See also the הַזֶּה סֵפֶר in Jer 25:13 and Isa 8:16 (see above n. 41).

46. Admittedly, this is speculation only. But seen before the background of the evidence collected by Nissinen, "Spoken," 250-51, 270, this assumption is probable. The divine messages would be archived and later interpreted and applied. This does not necessarily mean that the text of those inscriptions was identical with the biblical texts as we have them today; the scribal activity surely went on in the process of tradition and reception. The question to what extent one has to assume later expansions remains disputed.

47. 1 Kgs 8:12-13, בְּעַרְפֶל לִשְׁכֹּן אָמַר יְהוָה שְׁלֹמֹה אָמַר אָז: מָכוֹן לָךְ זְבֻל בַּיִת בָּנִתִי בָּנֹה: עוֹלָמִים לְשִׁבְתְּךָ; LXX + οὐκ ἰδοὺ αὔτη γέγραπται ἐν βιβλίῳ τῆς ᾠδῆς [הַשִּׁיר > הַיָּשָׁר?]. Cf. already M. Noth, *Könige (1,1–16)* (2d ed.; BKAT IX; Neukirchen-Vluyn: Neukirchener Verlag, 1983), 172-73.

48. Cf. N. Na'aman, "Royal Inscriptions and the Histories of Joash and Ahaz, Kings of Judah," *VT* 48 (1998): 333-49.

49. A. S. Kapelrud, "Two Great Rulers and Their Temple Buildings," in *Text and Theology* (Fest. M. Sæbø; ed. A. Tångberg; Oslo: Verbum, 1994), 135-42.

50. See the important article by S. B. Parker, "Did the Authors of the Books of Kings Make Use of Royal Inscriptions?" *VT* 50 (2000): 357-78, who collects the evidence but comes to a negative conclusion. In his view the authors of Kings did not use royal epigraphic monuments (p. 375), although he accepts the possibility that an Israelite king list was used.

51. S. Kreuzer, "'. . . und der Herr half David in allem, was er unternahm.' Die

Odell has attempted to explain the book of Ezekiel with Assyrian building inscriptions.[52]

Only short mention can be made of Papyrus Amherst 63, which only of late has come to the attention of scholars. This is a considerably long papyrus from the fourth century written in the Aramaic language with Demotic script.[53] It should interest the scholarly community because in col. 12 one can find a clear parallel to Psalm 20, and in col. 13 to Psalm 75. Moreover, in my view, col. 8:7 mentions YHWH and Asherah as a divine couple, but whether the papyrus reads YHW is heavily disputed.[54]

In its latter parts it gives proof for a consideration that was more or less speculative until now, that is, that a monumental inscription has made its way to a completely different literary composition. Here a story about the fight between Assurbanipal and his brother Shamash-shum-Ukin (652-648 BCE) is recorded that has previously been known from monumental reliefs and inscriptions in Nineveh.[55] Moreover, this interesting papyrus shows the arrangement of individual songs (laments and hymns as well) in a larger collection that can be compared to the early stages of the formation of the Psalter, such as the songs of Asaph or Korah. But since research has just begun, nothing more can be said at this time.[56]

The results of this brief investigation can easily be summarized. It is evident that the use of form-critical questions and methods can give new insights into the inscriptional material and the biblical texts as well. It could be demonstrated that the inscriptions allow us to draw some careful conclusions

---

Davidgeschichte in ihrem inneren Zusammenhang und im Licht der westsemitischen Königsinschriften," in *Verbindungslinien* (Fest. W. H. Schmidt; ed. A. Graupner, H. Delkurt, and A. B. Ernst; Neukirchen-Vluyn: Neukirchener Verlag, 2000), 187-205.

52. Pages 162-76 in this volume.

53. The translation in *COS* 1.99 is, according to the translator R. C. Steiner, "an interim progress report" (p. 310). The text is extremely difficult.

54. As an introduction to the problems of this papyrus and the history of research, see M. Rösel, "Israels Psalmen in Ägypten? Papyrus Amherst 63 und die Psalmen XX und LXXV," *VT* 50 (2000): 81-99. Here arguments can be found that the reading/translation "YHW/YH" is the most probable.

55. See S. M. Streck, *Assurbanipal und die letzten assyrischen Könige bis zum Untergang Niniveh's*, part 1, *Einleitung*; part 2, *Texte* (Leipzig: Hinrichs'sche Buchhandlung, 1916), 260-74, 288-300; R. C. Steiner and C. F. Nims, "Ashurbanipal and Shamash-Shum-Ukin: A Tale of Two Brothers from the Aramaic Text in Demotic Script," *RB* 92 (1985): 60-81, pls. I-IV.

56. To get an impression of the problems, one could consult I. Kottsieper, "Anmerkungen zu Pap. Amherst 63, I: 12,11-19 — Eine aramäische Version von Psalm 20," *ZAW* 100 (1988): 217-44; idem, "Teil II-V," *UF* 29 (1997): 385-434.

about the *Sitz im Leben* and the use of related biblical texts. Although it is true that reconstructing the actual sociological context of the texts is hardly ever possible, we have access to a more original use of comparable texts. Thus we are able to reconstruct the development from those older, extrabiblically attested texts to the form of the texts as they now appear in the Bible. This can prevent exegetes from regarding the biblical texts too easily as mere literary constructions without a meaningful relation to a historical reality. Thus the inscriptional evidence brings us back to one of the most important insights of the form-critical method, that the texts cannot be separated from the social life of the community from which they come.

# Fear Not: A Study on an
# Ancient Near Eastern Phrase

## MARTTI NISSINEN

## A Brief History of Research

The identification of fixed formulaic expressions and the search for their sociocultural origin, or *Sitz im Leben,* is characteristic of traditional form criticism. In the study of the "basic forms of prophetic literature," fixed formulas have been taken as structural elements, the origin of which is not necessarily prophetic but can be traced back to nonprophetic contexts. The prime example of such a formula is "Thus says the Lord" *(kōh 'āmar YHWH),* the so-called *Botenformel.* In the biblical prophetic literature, this formula typically introduces divine speech, but its original context has been found in a profane communication situation, the transmission of a message from one person to another by an intermediary who forwards the message to the addressee, introducing it with the words "Thus says N." This form-critical observation was of permanent value for the study of prophecy, since it sustained the understanding of the role of the prophet as an intermediary and prophecy as communication.[1]

A more complicated case is presented by another well-known formula, "fear not" (*'al-tîrā',* etc.). In the Hebrew Bible this phrase is often, though by no means exclusively, used in prophetic contexts, with a notable concentration in Second Isaiah.[2] Hugo Gressmann, a leading figure of the early days of

---

1. See Ludwig Köhler, *Deuterojesaja stilkritisch untersucht* (BZAW 37; Giessen: Töpelmann, 1923), 102-5; Claus Westermann, *Grundformen prophetischer Rede* (Munich: Kaiser, 1960), 70-82; ET: *Basic Forms of Prophetic Speech* (trans. Hugh Clayton White; repr. Louisville: Westminster/John Knox, 1991), 98-128.

2. Isa 40:9; 41:10, 13, 14; 43:1, 5; 44:2; 51:7; 54:4; cf. Isa 7:4; 8:12; 10:24; 35:4; 37:6; Jer 1:8; 10:5; 30:10; 42:11; 46:27, 28; Ezek 2:6; 3:9; Joel 2:21, 22; Zeph 3:16; Hag 2:5; Zech 8:13, 15; Dan 10:12, 19.

form criticism, identified it as an element of revelatory oracular speech (*Offenbarungsrede*) common to ancient Near Eastern sources. In his literary analysis of Second Isaiah, published in 1914, he quoted several examples of oracles, known today as Assyrian prophecies,[3] to show the stereotyped character and the cheering and comforting function of the respective Akkadian phrase *lā tapallaḫ*, as well as its proximity to the divine self-identification "I am . . . DN."[4] All this Gressmann saw was fully compatible with Second Isaiah, who, according to him, used the formula under "Babylonian" influence.[5]

Gressmann's idea of the Mesopotamian background of the "fear not" formula was soon refuted by Ludwig Köhler, who also related it with theophany but derived it from the numinous experience of the presence of the divine rather than from oracular practices.[6] Köhler's contribution met with little approval,[7] whereas the theory of Joachim Begrich, published fifteen years later in 1934, became all the more influential.[8] Begrich traced the Deutero-Isaianic "fear not" oracles back to a cultic context similar to that of the individual lament psalms *(Klagelieder des Einzelnen)*. He rested his argument on the observations of Hermann Gunkel,[9] according to whom the sudden change of mood from lament to consolation and encouragement, typical

3. Simo Parpola, *Assyrian Prophecies* (SAA 9; Helsinki: Helsinki Univ. Press, 1997).

4. Hugo Gressmann, "Die literarische Analyse Deuterojesajas," *ZAW* 34 (1914): 254-97, esp. 287-90. The texts quoted are SAA 9 1.1; 1.4; 1.8.

5. "Die Abhängigkeit des im Exil lebenden Deuterojesaja von babylonischen Vorbildern wird damit zur Gewissheit erhoben; denn wie will man dies in der israelitischen Literatur der Propheten bis dahin unerhörte Nebeneinander der Formeln 'Ich bin Jahwe' und 'Fürchte dich nicht' und ihre Verknüpfung mit dem Hymnenstil der ersten Person einleuchtender erklären als durch den Einfluss der babylonischen Orakelliteratur, in der gerade diese drei Erscheinungen von jeher zu beobachten sind?" (Gressmann, "Die literarische Analyse Deuterojesajas," 290).

6. Ludwig Köhler, "Die Offenbarungsformel 'Fürchte dich nicht' im Alten Testament," *SThZ* 36 (1919): 33-39.

7. Cf., however, Wilhelm Pesch, "Zur Formgeschichte und Exegese von Lk 12,32," *Bib* 41 (1960): 25-40, esp. 26-31; *HAL* 413.

8. Joachim Begrich, "Das priesterliche Heilsorakel," *ZAW* 52 (1934): 81-92; repr. in *Gesammelte Studien zum Alten Testament* (ed. Walther Zimmerli; TB 21; Munich: Kaiser, 1964), 217-31.

9. Hermann Gunkel, *Einleitung in die Psalmen: Die Gattungen der religiösen Lyrik Israels* (completed by Joachim Begrich; Göttingen: Vandenhoeck & Ruprecht, 1985⁴), 246-47. Begrich does not mention F. Küchler, who made the same argument on similar grounds already in 1918 (Friedrich Küchler, "Das priesterliche Orakel in Israel und Juda," in *Abhandlungen zur semitischen Religionsgeschichte und Sprachwissenschaft: Wolf Wilhelm Grafen von Baudissin zum 26. September 1917 überreicht von Freunden und Schülern* [ed. Wilhelm Frankenberg and Friedrich Küchler; BZAW 33; Giessen: Töpelmann, 1918], 285-301).

of these psalms, corresponds to the prayer of the individual and the subsequent divine answer spoken by the priest (cf. also Lam 3:57). Begrich considered this "priestly oracle of salvation" *(priesterliches Heilsorakel)* an established pattern, familiar to and consciously taken over by Second Isaiah, who adapted the prayers of the individual to his own purposes, addressing his people as a collective in singular form.

Begrich's theory of the priestly oracle was ingenious enough to become the most quoted explanation of the phrase "fear not" and the salvation oracles of Second Isaiah in decades to come, as demonstrated, for example, by studies devoted to the concept of the fear of God in the Hebrew Bible.[10] It did not remain unchallenged, though. More detailed form-critical investigations, performed by Walther Zimmerli, Claus Westermann, and others, substantially refined the analysis of the structural elements of the salvation oracle, whereby Begrich's idea of the priestly oracle was modified and enriched with new viewpoints and alternative patterns of the oracle of salvation.[11] Westermann, for example, did not question the priestly oracle as such, but he found it insufficient to explain the proclamation of Second Isaiah. He made a distinction between the oracle of salvation *(Heilszusage)* derived from cultic practices of priests, and the proclamation of salvation *(Heilsankündigung)*, which he considered a purely prophetic function. The "fear not" oracles and their extrabiblical parallels he placed in the first category.[12]

---

10. S. Plath, *Furcht Gottes: Der Begriff* jr' *im Alten Testament* (AzTh 2/2; Stuttgart: Calwer, 1963), 119; Joachim Becker, *Gottesfurcht im Alten Testament* (AnBib 25; Rome: Pontifical Biblical Institute Press, 1965), 52-53; L. Derousseaux, *La crainte de Dieu dans l'Ancien Testament: Royauté, Alliance, Sagesse dans les royaumes d'Israël et Juda. Recherches d'exégèse et d'histoire sur la racine yârê* (LD 63; Paris: Cerf, 1970), 97.

11. Walther Zimmerli, "Ich bin Jahwe," in *Geschichte und Altes Testament* (FS Albrecht Alt; BHT 16; Tübingen: Mohr, 1953), 179-209, esp. 193-203; repr. in idem, *Gottes Offenbarung: Gesammelte Aufsätze* (TB 19; Munich: Kaiser, 1963), 11-40, esp. 24-34; Claus Westermann, "Das Heilswort bei Deuterojesaja," *EvT* 24 (1964): 355-73 (summarized in idem, *Forschung am Alten Testament* [TB 24; Munich: Kaiser, 1964], 117-24); cf. *Prophetische Heilsworte im Alten Testament* (FRLANT 145; Göttingen: Vandenhoeck & Ruprecht, 1987), 33-53; ET: *Prophetic Oracles of Salvation in the Old Testament* (trans. Keith Crim; Louisville: Westminster/John Knox, 1991), 39-66; Hans-Eberhard von Waldow, "Anlass und Hintergrund der Verkündigung des Deuterojesaja" (diss.; Univ. of Bonn, 1953); Henning Graf Reventlow, *Liturgie und prophetisches Ich bei Jeremia* (Gütersloh: Gütersloher Verlagshaus, 1963); Anton Schoors, *I Am God Your Saviour: A Form-Critical Study of the Main Genres in Is. xl–lv* (VTSup 24; Leiden: Brill, 1973); Roy F. Melugin, *The Formation of Isaiah 40–55* (BZAW 141; Berlin and New York: de Gruyter, 1976); Jean Marcel Vincent, *Studien zur literarischen Eigenart und zur geistigen Heimat von Jesaja, Kapitel 40–55* (BBET 5; Frankfurt am Main: Lang, 1977).

12. Westermann, "Das Heilswort bei Deuterojesaja," passim; cf. ibid., *Prophetische Heilsworte*, 35-36 (= *Prophetic Oracles*, 39-40).

Some scholars called into question Begrich's theory as a whole, for example, Edgar W. Conrad, who found the "priestly oracle of salvation" — both the *Gattung* and the *Sitz im Leben* — to be ill founded altogether and traced the "fear not" oracles of Second Isaiah back to two different genres, the war oracle and the patriarchal oracle.[13] In spite of the criticism, the priestly oracle held out quite well among other explanations of the "fear not" formula, as can be seen from relevant articles in theological dictionaries.[14]

The popularity of Begrich's theory is striking, considering that he himself wisely admitted that his evidence was indirect, presenting his theory modestly as a working hypothesis.[15] The hypothesis was well spoken and comprehensible enough to catch on with subsequent studies, but was it really comprehensive enough to make out a certain case for the priestly oracle, and did it even attempt an exhaustive explanation of the origin of the phrase "fear not"? The following points call for attention: (1) There is no single occurrence of the phrase in the individual lament psalms.[16] If the use of the salvation oracle in Second Isaiah is tied to these psalms,[17] the origin of "fear not" must be sought elsewhere. (2) Begrich's intention was primarily to demonstrate the existence of the priestly oracle, not the origin of the phrase "fear not." Apparently for this reason he confined himself to Second Isaiah, making no argument of the use of the phrase in other contexts. (3) The designation of the oracle as "priestly" rests solely on the implied assumption that it was spoken by

13. Edgar W. Conrad, "Second Isaiah and the Priestly Oracle of Salvation," *ZAW* 93 (1981): 234-46; idem, "The 'Fear Not' Oracles in Second Isaiah," *VT* 34 (1984): 129-52. For earlier criticism see, e.g., Rudolf Kilian, "Ps 22 und das priesterliche Heilsorakel," *BZ* 12 (1968): 172-85; Rosario Pius Merendino, "Literarkritisches, Gattungskritisches und Exegetisches zu Jes 41,8-16," *Bib* 53 (1972): 1-42.

14. H.-P. Stähli, "ירא *jr'* fürchten," *THAT* 1:765-78, esp. 772-73; Günther Wanke, "φοβέω κτλ. B. φόβος und φοβέομαι im Alten Testament," *ThWNT* 9 (1973): 194-201, esp. 199; ET: *TDNT* 9:197-205, esp. 203; H. F. Fuhs, "ירא *jārē'*," *ThWAT* 3:869-93, esp. 884-85; ET: *TDOT* 6:290-315, esp. 305-6; cf. also Werner Grimm and Kurt Dittert, *Deuterojesaja: Deutung — Wirkung — Gegenwart* (Calwer Bibelkommentare; Stuttgart: Calwer, 1990), 457-60.

15. "Da ein Beweis nach Lage der Dinge hier nur indirekt geführt werden kann, muss das Ergebnis, das sich dem Verfasser herausgestellt hat, hier notwendig kurz vorgenommen werden, freilich nur im Sinne einer Arbeitshypothese, die dem Leser das Ziel unserer Ausführungen deutlich machen soll und deren Recht allein von der Schlüssigkeit und Überzeugungskraft der Beweisführung abhängt" (Begrich, "Das priesterliche Heilsorakel," 81).

16. The only occurrence in the Psalter, Ps 49:17, hardly bears any relevance to the matter in hand: "Do not envy *('al tîrā')* a man who becomes rich."

17. "Dass Deuterojesaja gerade auf diese Gattung zukam, hat seinen entscheidenden Grund darin, dass er selbst aufs tiefste in seiner Frömmigkeit und in seinem Denken mit der Psalmenfrömmigkeit verbunden ist" (Begrich, "Das priesterliche Heilsorakel," 92).

a priest after the prayer of the individual. Here the argument is indirect indeed, since the relevant psalms — or Lam 3:57, or any other text where the phrase occurs — make no mention of any kind of a priest, whatever is concretely meant by this word. (4) The extrabiblical sources are completely ignored by Begrich, who refers to Gressmann's article only once to reproach him for the failure of identifying the alleged priestly context of Second Isaiah's use of the phrase.[18] Consequently, he fails to recognize the relevance of prophecy in defining the origins of the salvation oracle in Second Isaiah.

By the time Begrich wrote his article, the Assyrian oracles quoted by Gressmann had virtually fallen into oblivion. One can only speculate whether these texts would have been taken more intensively into consideration had they been called prophecies instead of "oracles." In subsequent treatments they were quoted time and again for the sake of comparison, even by the critics of the priestly oracle theory, but this was done in discussion with Begrich and his followers, and the texts were not acknowledged as prophecies.[19] This is true even in the case of Philip B. Harner, whose contribution was important in rehabilitating Gressmann's argument of the oracular pattern common to the Mesopotamian texts and Second Isaiah, in expanding it with new relevant material, and in pointing out the royal focus of the Assyrian oracles, but who overlooked the prophetic nature of the extrabiblical evidence, taking it as an external confirmation of Begrich's theory.[20]

The first form-critical analysis that took full advantage of the extrabiblical material, including the Assyrian prophecies, was the dissertation of Meindert Dijkstra (1980), whereas the first comprehensive study of the Assyrian prophecies was published by Manfred Weippert in 1981.[21] Both Dijkstra and Weippert found the Assyrian prophecies most relevant parallels to the salvation oracles of Second Isaiah, but Weippert labeled these texts as "royal

---

18. "H. Gressmann hat (. . .) zwar die Formel richtig als zur Offenbarungsrede gehörig erkannt, jedoch den grösseren Zusammenhang nicht gesehen, aus dem sie Deuterojesaja entnommen hat" (Begrich, "Das priesterliche Heilsorakel," 83n1).

19. E.g., Zimmerli, "Ich bin Jahwe," 194-95; Plath, *Furcht Gottes*, 121; Westermann, "Das Heilswort," 360-62; Merendino, "Literarkritisches," 29-31; Schoors, *I Am God*, 39-45.

20. Philip B. Harner, "The Salvation Oracle in Second Isaiah," *JBL* 88 (1969): 418-34.

21. Meindert Dijkstra, *Gods voorstelling: Predikatieve expressie van zelfopenbaring in Oudoosterse teksten en Deutero-Jesaja* (Dissertationes Neerlandicae, Series Theologica 2; Kampen: Kok, 1980), esp. 136-70; Manfred Weippert, "Assyrische Prophetien der Zeit Asarhaddons und Assurbanipals," in *Assyrian Royal Inscriptions: New Horizons in Literary, Ideological, and Historical Analysis* (ed. F. M. Fales; Orientis Antiqui Collectio 17; Rome: Istituto per l'Oriente, 1981), 71-115; cf. idem, "De herkomst van het heilsorakel voor Israël bij Deutero-Jesaja," *NedTT* 36 (1982): 1-11.

oracles" *(Königsorakel)* rather than priestly oracles, since they were addressed to the king and spoken by prophets rather than priests. Weippert questioned explicitly the viability of Begrich's theory of the priestly oracle as a mere commonplace in the traditio-historical analysis of Second Isaiah,[22] doubtless presenting the most forcefully argued alternative to it, especially from the point of view of prophecy in the ancient Near East. Recently, in a thorough comparison of the Neo-Assyrian prophecies and Second Isaiah, Weippert has reaffirmed that in Second Isaiah the prophetic royal oracle is employed, independently from the Neo-Assyrian prophecies but clinging to a common ancient Near Eastern tradition.[23]

The form-critical study of the phrase "fear not" has been strongly connected with the study of Second Isaiah. However, there are plenty of biblical occurrences of "fear not" in other contexts, such as the patriarchal narratives (Gen 15:1; 21:17; 26:24; 46:3) and the Deuteronom(ist)ic literature (Deut 1:21; 7:18; Josh 8:1; 10:8; 11:6; etc.). Otto Kaiser, for instance, combined the salvation oracle with a fearsome theophany experience, not forgetting the Assyrian parallels.[24] Gerhard von Rad, in his classic study on the holy war in ancient Israel, listed "fear not" among the typical phraseology of holy war language, and several scholars after him accepted its belonging to this alleged institution.[25] Cognate expressions were found in a military context even in extrabiblical sources, such as the Mari letters and the Aramaic Zakkur inscription.[26] This not only suggested that the holy war ideology was not re-

---

22. Weippert, "Assyrische Prophetien," 91-92, 108-11; cf. idem, "De herkomst," 5.

23. Manfred Weippert, "'Ich bin Jahwe' — 'Ich bin Ištar von Arbela.' Deuterojesaja im Lichte der neuassyrischen Prophetie," in *Prophetie und Psalmen: Festschrift für Klaus Seybold zum 65. Geburtstag* (ed. Beat Huwyler, Hans-Peter Mathys, and Beat Weber; AOAT 280; Münster: Ugarit-Verlag, 2001), 31-59.

24. Otto Kaiser, "Traditionsgeschichtliche Untersuchung von Genesis 15," *ZAW* 70 (1958): 107-26, esp. 111-13.

25. Gerhard von Rad, *Der Heilige Krieg im alten Israel* (Zurich: Zwingli, 1951), 7-8; ET: *Holy War in Ancient Israel* (trans. Marva J. Dawn; Grand Rapids: Eerdmans, 1991), 45, lists the following occurrences: Exod 14:13-14; Deut 20:3; Josh 8:1; 10:8, 25; 11:6; Judg 7:3; 1 Sam 23:16-17; 30:6; 2 Sam 10:12. Becker, *Gottesfurcht*, 52, takes the war oracles as a secondary application of the priestly oracle of salvation, whereas Derousseaux, *La crainte de Dieu*, 97, on the other hand, sees the war oracle as the primary context of the formula; similarly Merendino, "Literarkritisches."

26. On Mari see Jean-Georges Heintz, "Oracles prophétiques et 'guerre sainte' selon les archives royales de Mari et l'Ancien Testament," in *Congress Volume: Rome 1968* (VTSup 17; Leiden: Brill, 1969), 112-28, esp. 121-25. The texts quoted by Heintz are ARM 13 114 (= ARM 26 210): 11-14: *Dagan išpuranni šupur ana bēlīk[a l]ā Iḫâš u mā[tum]ma [lā] Iḫâš,* "Dagan has sent me. Write to your lord that he should not be anxious, and [neither] should the la[nd] be

stricted to ancient Israel[27] but also that the alleged priestly oracle was not the only *Sitz im Leben* of the formulaic use of the expression "fear not."

More recently, Karel van der Toorn has demonstrated the prophetic contribution to the ancient Near Eastern ideology of war with ample evidence of what he called the "oracle of victory," including the Assyrian "fear not" oracles.[28] The contribution of van der Toorn, like that of Weippert, is significant in illuminating the issue from both the ancient Near Eastern and the Hebrew prophetic point of view.

In today's discourse the currency given to traditional form-critical issues is substantially decreased, and the quest for a single, definable *Sitz im Leben* of fixed formulas seems to be obsolescent. In the case of "fear not," little has happened during the past two decades. In spite of the criticism, Begrich's theory is still quoted often, and little attention is paid to his complete ignoring of the extrabiblical sources and his failure to recognize the prophetic

anxious"; and ARM 10 80 (= ARM 26 197): 26-27: *ana ramānīšu ištanarrar ana ramānīka la taštanarra[r]*. The translation of the last text is uncertain. According to the suggestion of Durand, the verb *šarārum* means here "to shine brilliantly" (Jean-Marie Durand, *Archives épistolaires de Mari I/1* [ARM 26/1; Paris: Éditions Recherche sur les Civilisations, 1988], 424); hence the translation, "I have heard people saying: 'He is always distinguishing himself.' Do not try to distinguish yourself!" The alleged stereotyped character of the "fear not" formula in Mari letters was immediately refuted by P.-E. Dion, who found the evidence too narrow to sustain Heintz's argument (Paul-Eugène Dion, "The 'Fear Not' Formula and Holy War," *CBQ* 32 [1970]: 565-70), whereas Heintz's examples of the so-called Übergabeformel "I [the god] deliver the enemies into your [the king's] hand" (Heintz, "Oracles prophétiques," 125-29), were found to rest on more solid ground (Dion, "Fear Not," 569-70). Cf. below, n. 93. On Zakkur see James F. Ross, "Prophecy in Hamath, Israel, and Mari," *HTR* 63 (1970): 1-28, esp. 8-9; cf. Hans-Jürgen Zobel, "Das Gebet um Abwendung der Not und seine Erhörung in den Klageliedern des Alten Testaments und in der Inschrift des Königs Zakir von Hamath," *VT* 21 (1971): 91-99, who found here another representative of Begrich's priestly oracle.

27. This was argued especially by Manfred Weippert, who used ample evidence from Assyria to demonstrate the broader context of the idea of divinely promoted warfare; see "'Heiliger Krieg' in Israel und Assyrien: Kritische Anmerkungen zu Gerhard von Rads Konzept des 'Heiligen Krieges im alten Israel,'" *ZAW* 84 (1972): 460-93. Cf. also Moshe Weinfeld, "Divine Intervention in War in Ancient Israel and in the Ancient Near East," in *History, Historiography and Interpretation: Studies in Biblical and Cuneiform Literatures* (ed. Moshe Weinfeld and Hayim Tadmor; Jerusalem: Magnes, 1983), 121-47; R. J. van der Spek, "Assyriology and History: A Comparative Study of War and Empire in Assyria, Athens, and Rome," in *The Tablet and the Scroll: Near Eastern Studies in Honor of William W. Hallo* (ed. Mark E. Cohen, Daniel C. Snell, and David B. Weisberg; Bethesda, Md.: CDL Press, 1993), 262-70; Lori L. Rowlett, *Joshua and the Rhetoric of Violence: A New Historicist Analysis* (JSOTSup 226; Sheffield: Sheffield Academic Press, 1996).

28. Karel van der Toorn, "L'Oracle de victoire comme expression prophétique au Proche-Orient ancien," *RB* 94 (1987): 63-97.

component of the "priestly" oracle. If the Assyrian oracles are referred to as parallels at all,[29] this is done as a matter of routine, usually even without recognizing them as prophecies. With regard to our increased knowledge of ancient Near Eastern sources and the state of publication improved by the new edition of the Assyrian prophecies by Simo Parpola (SAA 9) as well as other sources from the Assyrian archives, the fundamental observations made already by Gressmann and improved by, for example, Weippert and van der Toorn deserve renewed attention and confirmation.

On the other hand, the distribution of "fear not" in the ancient Near Eastern sources is wide and has hitherto not been fully investigated. There are numerous attestations of "fear not" in Akkadian *(lā tapallaḥ)*, many of which have remained unexplored so far, and at least one in Old Aramaic *('l tzḥl)*.[30] Therefore, to find new facets to an old problem and to broaden the scope of the discussion, a study dedicated to the occurrences of this expression in ancient Near Eastern (mainly Mesopotamian) documents suggests itself.

## Fear Not, but Fear: Semantic Viewpoints

The semantic field of verbs for fear, like Hebrew *yr'* or Akkadian *palāḥu*, is twofold, covering both "fear" in the sense of fright, horror, or anxiety, and "respect," denoting reverence, respectful behavior, obedience, or, especially in theological contexts, veneration.[31] Correspondingly, the object of fear is either any kind of threat or menace to the subject's safety, or an authority, human or divine. In the latter case, the fear is usually motivated by the superior position and the powers vested in the authority in question, as in the case of

---

29. They are completely ignored by Klaus Baltzer, who in his new voluminous commentary on Second Isaiah (*Deutero-Jesaja* [KAT 10/2; Gütersloh: Gütersloher Verlagshaus, 1999]; ET *Deutero-Isaiah: A Commentary* [Hermeneia; Minneapolis: Fortress, 2001]) neither discusses the Assyrian prophecies nor pays any special attention to the "fear not" formula.

30. See, e.g., Old Assyrian: *TCL* 19 47:10; Old Babylonian: *TCL* 1 23:15; 18 80:18; *PBS* 7 17:21; Middle Babylonian: *KBo* 1 13 r. 5; *BWL* 50:35; *PRU* 4 35:5; 36:32; Standard Babylonian: *Cuthaean Legend* 157; Neo-Assyrian/Babylonian: *Poem of Erra* iv 27; Ashurbanipal Prism B v 46; *ABL* 523:16; 541 r. 9; 944 r. 3; 1022:12; 1186:8; *OIP* 114 98:20; SAA 3 13:24; SAA 9 1 i 5, 24, 30; ii 16, 33; iii 30; v 21; 2 i 13, 15; iii 17, 19, 29; iv 28, 30; 4:5; 7:2, r. 6, 11; SAA 10 171:14; 278 r. 7; 320:11; SAA 15 104 r. 17; 306:5; Late Babylonian: RAcc 144: 434. This list is based on the preliminary draft of the forthcoming *CAD* P (sub *palāḥu*) and the files of the Neo-Assyrian Text Corpus Project in Helsinki. I am indebted to Dr. Raija Mattila and Prof. Simo Parpola for making these resources accessible to me. For Old Aramaic see *KAI* 202 A 13.

31. For Hebrew consult the dictionaries and cf. Becker, *Gottesfurcht*; Stähli, *THAT* 1; Fuhs, *ThWAT* 3; for Aramaic cf. Dan 6:27, etc.; for Akkadian, see *AHw* 2:812-13.

an obstinate governor: *ipallaḥ issu pān šarri išamme*, "He will become afraid of the king and obey."[32] In theological contexts "fear" is virtually synonymous to devotion and worship, or even to a proper way of life: *[p]alāḥ ilāni damāqu ullad [p]alāḥ Anunnakī balāṭu uttar*, "Fear of the gods creates kindness, fear of the Anunnaki returns life."[33] On the other hand, fear can be misplaced if it is motivated by improper authorities, as in Isa 57:11 (NEB):

> Whom do you fear so much *(dā'agtā wattîrě'î)*, that you should be false,
> that you never remembered me or gave me a thought?
> Did I not hold my peace and seem not to see,
> while you showed no fear of me *(wě'ôtî lō' tîrā'î)?*[34]

Due to the semantic variability, expressions for fear, or lack thereof, denote different attitudes. For this reason not every prohibitive construction involving a verb for "fear" can be taken as a specimen of a fixed formula. In private discourse, such expressions may occur in contexts where a person is forbidden to obey inappropriate authorities, or to show loyalty to wrong directions, as in a Neo-Babylonian letter from Nippur:

> *[a]na muḥḥi mīni nasīk Ubūlu umma šum ili šu[l]ā Bāniya ul tapallaḥ*

> [O]n wh[at] account is the sheikh of the Ubulu tribe saying: "Sw[ea]r an oath by god to me that you will not fear Baniya"?[35]

A similar expression may be used when reproaching a person with disrespectful behavior or negligence, as in the Old Babylonian letter of King Ammiditana to a Sippar merchant:

> *ana mīnim šipāt enzim nēmettaka ana Bābili lā tušābilam/ana epēšim annîm kî lā taplaḥ/kīma ṭuppi annia[m] tammar[u] šipāt enzim nēmettaka ana Bābili šūbilam*

---

32. SAA 10 285 r. 3-4; see Simo Parpola, *Letters from Assyrian and Babylonian Scholars* (SAA 10; Helsinki: Helsinki Univ. Press, 1993), 221.

33. SAA 10 188 r. 9-10; see Parpola, *Letters from Assyrian and Babylonian Scholars*, 155; and cf. Prov 1:7: *yir'at YHWH rē'šît da'at*, "Fear of the Lord is the beginning of knowledge; 9:10: *těhillat ḥokmâ yir'at YHWH*, "Fear of the Lord is the beginning of wisdom"; 14:27: *yir'at YHWH měqôr ḥayyîm*, "Fear of the Lord is the source of life"; etc.

34. For a prohibition against fearing, i.e., venerating, other gods, see also Judg 6:10; 2 Kgs 17:34-39; Jer 10:5.

35. OIP 114 98:16-20; see Steven W. Cole, *Nippur IV: The Early Neo-Babylonian Governor's Archive from Nippur* (OIP 114; Chicago: Oriental Institute, 1996), 205.

Why have you not sent the goat's wool, your duty, to Babylon?/How could you not be afraid to act like that?/As soon as you see this tablet, send goat's wool, your duty, to me to Babylon![36]

In this case *lā taplaḫ* is used as a fixed phrase,[37] not as a prohibitive, however, but corresponding to the phrase "how dare you!" A similar shade of meaning is expressed as a prohibition in the passage of the *Poem of Erra*, where the governor of Babylon becomes enraged and incites the leader of the army to outrageous crimes:

*ana āli šâšu ša ašapparūka atta amēlu*
*ila lā tapallaḫ lā taddar amē[la]*
*ṣeḫra u rabâ ištēniš šumitma*
*eniq šīzib šerra lā tezziba ayyamma*
*nakma būšē Bābili tašallal atta*

You are the man whom I shall send to that city!
You shall respect neither god nor man.
Put young and old alike to death.
You shall not leave any child, even if he still sucks milk.
You shall pillage the accumulated wealth of Babylon.[38]

The lack of fear implies here extreme arrogance, impiety, and moral corruption, which sets this and similar[39] occurrences of the phrase "fear not" apart from its use in expressions of encouragement and comfort, which are the main context of the use of this phrase and the principal source material of this essay. Nevertheless, the semantic ambiguity of the concept of fear is not without implications for understanding the phrase "fear not."

Mayer I. Gruber has pointed out the difference between justified "fear" and unjustified "anxiety."[40] While the individual, for the sake of her or his

36. Arthur Ungnad, *Babylonische Briefe aus der Zeit der Hammurapi-Dynastie* (VAB 6; Leipzig: Hinrichs, 1914), no. 82:14-22 (p. 74).

37. Cf. the same phrase in ibid., no. 71 (p. 64): *ana mīnim adi inanna puḫādī nēmettaka ana ekallim lā ublam/ana epēšim annîm kî lā tapla[ḫ]*, "Why have you not sent the lambs to the palace up to now?/How could you not be afrai[d] to act like that?"

38. *Erra* iv 26-30; see Luigi Cagni, *L'Epopea di Erra* (Studi Semitici 3; Rome: Istituto di Studi del Vicino Oriente, 1969), 136-37. Translation from Stephanie Dalley, *Myths from Mesopotamia: Creation, The Flood, Gilgamesh and Others* (Oxford: Oxford Univ. Press, 1989), 303-4 (= COS 1.412).

39. Cf. Luke 18:2: "There was once a judge who did not fear God and did not care about people *(ton theon mē phoboumenos kai anthrōpon mē entrepomenos)*."

40. Mayer I. Gruber, "Fear, Anxiety and Reverence in Akkadian, Biblical Hebrew and Other North-West Semitic Languages," *VT* 40 (1990): 411-22.

own safety, should have fear in front of a legitimate authority, royal or divine, he or she should not be anxious when confronting anything that should not be feared. This becomes crystal clear in texts to be quoted below, in which the one to be feared — the god(dess) or the king — tells the one(s) addressed not to be anxious about people or things that must not be feared. Hence "fear not" is never a demand not to revere the speaker but an exhortation to show fearlessness before illegitimate powers and to give up unjustified anxiety, which causes a state of paralysis and inability to act.[41] As such, it can appropriately be called an "encouraging formula" *(Ermutigungsformel)*.[42]

However, "fear not" refers not only to earthly powers. The close proximity of the formula to the divine self-identification "I am Ištar of Arbela" (etc.) alone suggests that it is by the same token intended as a "soothing formula" *(Beschwichtigungsformel)*, easing the frightening experience of the revelation of the divine.[43] In the Hebrew Bible, this is conclusive from Exod 20:18-21 (NEB):

> When all the people saw how it thundered and the lightning flashed, when they heard the trumpet sound and saw the mountain smoking, they trembled *(wayyarʾ hāʿām wayyānūʿû)* and stood at a distance. "Speak to us yourself," they said to Moses, "and we will listen; but if God speaks to us, we shall die." Moses answered, "Do not be afraid *(ʾal-tîrāʾû)*. God has come only to test you, so that the fear of him *(yirʾātô)* may remain with you and keep you from sin." So the people stood at a distance, while Moses approached the dark cloud where God was.

Thus God should be feared, but the divine presence should not cause anxiety. In theophany the distance between God and humans, characterized as "fear," becomes apparent and must be reduced for the moment when God speaks to humans.

---

41. Cf. SAA 9 1.1 i 25: "Fear not! You are paralyzed, but I, in the midst of wailing, will get up and sit down." See also Gruber, "Fear," 416-17, who points out the parallelism between Akk. *palāḫu*, "to fear," and *nīd aḫi*, "throwing down of the arm" (Rykle Borger, *Die Inschriften Asarhaddons, Königs von Assyrien* [AfO Beiheft 9; Graz: Selbstverlag], §2 iii 44, p. 3), and the corresponding Heb. *yrʾ* and *rph ydym* (Zeph 3:16).

42. See Weippert, "Ich bin Jahwe," 37.

43. Thus Weippert, "Assyrische Prophetien," 78-79. Cf. already Köhler, "Offenbarungsformel"; and Kaiser, "Traditionsgeschichtliche Untersuchung," 111-13.

## Private Discourse

In private correspondence "fear not" points to different kinds of fearlessness, depending on the object or the reason of fear. At its mildest, it is said or written by one person to another without any specific threat in mind and regardless of these persons' positions in relation to each other. In these cases "fear not" equals "don't worry" and may be taken as belonging to colloquial communication between humans, as it appears in two Old Babylonian letters:

[k]īma Nūr-Ilabrat u Gemūtum tušakkali anāku īde/mimma lā tapallaḥi/ a[n]āku šalmāku u awīlum šalim/u šunātūa [m]ādiš [d]amqā

I know how you support Nur-Ilabrat and Gemutum./Fear [fem.] nothing!/ I am well, the gentleman[44] is well,/and my dreams are very good.[45]

u mimma lā tapallaḥā/šulumkunu šuprānimma libbī linūḥ

Fear [pl.] nothing!/Your well-being convinces me that I can be with a peaceful mind.[46]

In both cases these wishes follow the subject matter of the letter as a kind of a personal appendix, independent of the actual message. Without naming any specific cause of anxiety, the writers simply want to assure that all is well with them, and express their conviction, based on dreams or personal knowledge, that the same holds true for the addressee.

A similarly phrased word of encouragement is uttered by another Old Babylonian writer who urges the addressee to go before his gods without fear:

ana maḥar Zababa u Ištār alāka mimma lā tapallaḥ

Do not be at all afraid to enter before Zababa and Ištar![47]

---

44. In spite of the singular forms, two persons appear as the senders of the letter (l. 3; both names are broken). The "gentleman" may refer to the other writer, or, if the actual writer is a woman, to her husband.

45. *PBS* 7 17: 21-25; see M. Stol, *Letters from Collections in Philadelphia, Chicago and Berkeley* (AbB 11; Leiden: Brill, 1986), 10-11.

46. Lit. "Your well-being [or: your greeting] announces to me that my heart should calm down," *TCL* 1 23:14-18; see Ungnad, *Babylonische Briefe*, no. 129, pp. 106-9.

47. *TCL* 18 80:15-18; see the copy in G. Dossin, *Lettres de la première dynastie babylonienne II* (TCL 18; Paris: Geuthner, 1934), pl. 47. I owe the reading of the first divine name as Zababa to Walter Sommerfeld, *Der Aufstieg Marduks: Die Stellung Marduks in der babylonischen Religion des zweiten Jahrtausends v. Chr.* (AOAT 213; Kevelaer: Butzon & Bercker; Neukirchen-Vluyn: Neukirchener Verlag, 1982), 119n2.

It is not clear whether the encounter with the deities is enough to frighten the addressee or whether the writer has something more specific in mind. The letter ends here, and if the writer hints at any particular need of the addressee to go to Zababa and Ištar,[48] for example, to consult them through a diviner in a personal distress, this is hidden between the lines.

An Old Assyrian letter from Anatolia is a little more explicit, since the verb *palāḥu* clearly implies the addressee's concern for the logistics of an important message:

*mimma lā tapallaḥ miššum têrtaka ana Burušḥattim mātima lā illikam*

Do not be at all afraid that your message would not reach Burušhattum![49]

In the above examples, the potential sources of anxiety, whether or not specified, belong to the sphere of private life, and *mimma lā tapallaḥ* (etc.) is used in discourse between humans, in which the social standing of the persons involved plays no role. These texts also provide the oldest attestations of the phrase that I know and speak for a primary use of "fear not" in colloquial speech concerning everyday cares. A similar use of analogous expressions is well known, not only from the Hebrew Bible (e.g., *'al-tîrĕ'î* in Gen 35:17; Ruth 3:11; *'al-tîrā'û* in Gen 43:23), but probably from countless languages and literatures independent of one another. This context is too broad to be defined as *Sitz im Leben,* since the use of "fear not" cannot be shown to be restricted to any specific situations or forms of speech or literature.

## Royal Discourse

### Letters to the King

When used in communication between humans in Neo-Assyrian and Neo-Babylonian sources, the phrase "fear not" occurs in royal correspondence, where the anxieties of the private life and the fear of the royal authority overlap. An unknown officer of Sargon II reports to the king what he has said to another, likewise unknown person:

48. These particular deities are probably chosen as gods of the city of Kiš, where the addressee is supposed to live; thus Sommerfeld, *Der Aufstieg Marduks,* 119.

49. *TCL* 19 47:10-15; see the copy in J. Lewy, *Tablettes cappadociennes, troisième série, première partie* (TCL 19; Paris: Geuthner, 1935), pl. 44. For Burušhattum (Hitt. Purushattum), see Sanna Aro, "Tabal: Zur Geschichte und materiellen Kultur des zentralanatolischen Hochplateaus von 1200 bis 600 v. Chr." (Ph.D. diss., Univ. of Helsinki, 1998), 53.

*ittalka iqtibīya m[ā . . .]/dibbi ṭābū issīy[a idubbub mā] atâ Nāṣib-ilu kî an[nie . . ./libbu] assakanšu nūk lā ta[pallaḫ . . .] ekalli lallik*

He came and said to me: "[. . . . . .]."/[He spoke] kindly with m[e but said]: "Why [does] Naṣib-ilu [. . .] in this ma[nner]?"/I encouraged him, saying: "F[ear] not! I will go to the palace [and . . .]"[50]

The writer is obviously in the position to say a good word for his friend in front of the king. When he claims to have told his friend not to fear, he is anticipating a similar word from the mouth of the king, accompanied by actions that should remove all concern about what the certain Naṣib-ilu had done to the writer's comrade.

If "fear not" is said to the king himself, it is phrased differently: instead of *lā tapallaḫ*, the writers use the more courteous form *šarru (lū) lā ipallaḫ*, "the king should not be afraid," which reflects the unequal status of the correspondents. In both of the cases at hand, the cause of worry is mentioned explicitly. The chief exorcist Nabû-nadin-šumi allays the king's fears caused by an untoward portent:

*u ina muḫḫi itti annīti šarru bēlī [issi lib]bīšu lū [l]ā idabbub/Bēl u Nabû ammar ittu šētuqi maṣû ana šarri bēlīya ušettuqū/šarru bēlī lū lā ipallaḫ*

The king, my lord, should not be worried about this portent./Bel and Nabû can make a portent pass by, and they will make it bypass the king, my lord./ The king, my lord, should not be afraid.[51]

Similarly, Urad-Nanaya, the physician, soothes the feelings of the father of a sick child:

*šulmu adanniš ana Aššūr-mukīn-palūʾa/ḫuntu anniu ša šanīšu šalšīšu [i]ṣbatušūni šarru lā ipallaḫ/sa[kik]kûšu šulmu tariṣ/šulmu šū*

Aššur-mukin-pale'a is doing very well./The king should not be afraid of this fever which has two or three times seized him;/his pulse is normal and sound;/he is well.[52]

50. SAA 15 104 r. 14-18; see Andreas Fuchs and Simo Parpola, *The Correspondence of Sargon II, Part III: Letters from Babylonia and Eastern Provinces* (SAA 15; Helsinki: Helsinki Univ. Press, 2001), 71.

51. SAA 10 278:12-r. 7; see Parpola, *Letters from Assyrian and Babylonian Scholars*, 217.

52. SAA 10 320:7-12; see Parpola, *Letters from Assyrian and Babylonian Scholars*, 258. Aššur-mukin-pale'a was the son of King Esarhaddon, probably born shortly after his enthronement, who seems to have been in poor health as a child; see Karen Radner, Aššur-

Functionally, the use of "fear not" in these letters is similar to the previously mentioned occurrences in Old Babylonian correspondence. The cause of anxiety has to do with the king's personal safety or private life, and the writers base their assurances on their own conviction and expertise.

### The Royal Word

The exhortation not to fear becomes a significantly different tone when it is spoken by the king himself. In such cases the use of the phrase is inseparable from the position of the king as the supreme authority. In the Hebrew Bible a royal word of this kind is spoken, for example, by David to Mephibosheth (Meribaal) in 2 Sam 9:7 (NEB):

> David said: "Do not be afraid *('al tîrā');* I mean to show you kindness for your father Jonathan's sake, and I will give you back the whole estate of your grandfather Saul; you shall have a place for yourself at my table."[53]

According to the story, Mephibosheth could count on this royal promise, which for him meant a permanent change in his social status.

An opposite experience can be found in the letter of an unknown astrologer who is worried about his employment in the service of the king of Assyria:

> *mīnū ḫiṭṭūa šarru itti ummānīšu rēšā ul išši/šarru iqtabi umma lā tapallaḫ umma rēška anašši/u la libbi kî ēlû adi muḫḫi enna šarru rēšā ul išši*

> What is my fault that the king has not summoned me with his scholars?/ The king said: Have no fear, I will summon you./But when I departed from there, up to now the king has not summoned me.[54]

---

mukīn-palē'a, in Karen Radner and Heather D. Baker, eds., *The Prosopography of the Neo-Assyrian Empire* (Helsinki: Neo-Assyrian Text Corpus Project, 1998-2000), 1/I:197-98 (hereafter *PNA*).

53. For 2 Sam 9 see Timo Veijola, "David und Meribaal," in *David: Gesammelte Studien zu den Davidüberlieferungen des Alten Testaments* (Publications of the Finnish Exegetical Society 52; Helsinki: Finnish Exegetical Society; Göttingen: Vandenhoeck & Ruprecht, 1990), 58-83 (= *RB* 85 [1978]: 338-61), according to whom this speech of David is the turning point of the story (pp. 70-71). Cf. also Joseph's words to his brothers in Gen 50:21: "Do not be afraid *('al-tîrā'û).* I will provide for you and your dependents."

54. For SAA 10 171:11-17 see Parpola, *Letters from Assyrian and Babylonian Scholars*, 131. The name of the writer of the letter is broken away. The same concern is expressed by the as-

The writer expresses openly the concern for his future, totally dependent on the king's favor. He also makes clear that, in spite of the king's assurances, he still has every reason to fear, because his life is in the hands of the king who has failed to keep his promise. The words *lā tapallaḫ* mean here more than neighborly consolation or encouragement; they are royal words coming from the one who himself is to be feared and whose "fear not" should inspire one with particular confidence in powers vested in him. In other words, the people have only the king to fear; otherwise they have nothing to fear. This is what the king himself affirms to his subjects, for instance, in *ABL* 541:

> [. . . . . . *taš]puranni mā šēpēka niṣbat/mā palḫāni issu pān šagalûti ša māt Aššūr/issu pān turrūte ša kutalli ana Elamti/ūmâ kî ša taqbianni ina pān Bēl-iqīša alkāni/kaqquru bēt tara"imāni lušaṣbitkunu/ina libbi šîbâ urdānīya attunu bīrtu ša* LÚ.*r[u] issi Bēl-iqīša uṣrā/ina libbi ilānīja attama šumma anāku ušaggalukkanūni šumma ana kutalli usaḫḫarukkanūni ana Elamti/assaprakkunu lā tapallaḫā* [. . . . . .]

> [. . . . . . *Concerning what* you w]rote: "We wish to grasp your feet, we are afraid of getting deported by Assyria and of being exposed to Elam"— now, in accordance with what you said, come before Bel-iqiša and let him settle you in a territory that you like./Stay there as my servants and guard the fortress of . . . with Bel-iqiša!/I swear by my gods that I shall not deport you and not expose you to Elam./I am writing to you: have no fear! [. . . . . .][55]

Assuming that Bel-iqiša is identical to the leader of the Gambulu tribe inhabiting the area between Babylonia and Elam, this letter reflects the politically delicate status of the Gambuleans between Elam and Assyria/Babylonia.[56] Bel-iqiša had submitted to Esarhaddon, who treated him favorably and who, having concluded a treaty with Urtaku, king of Elam, in the year 674, was on good terms also with Elam.[57] The letter may be read as the answer of the new

trologer Bel-ušezib in SAA 10 109; see Martti Nissinen, *References to Prophecy in Neo-Assyrian Sources* (SAAS 7; Helsinki: Neo-Assyrian Text Corpus Project, 1998), 89-95.

55. *ABL* 541:2-r. 9. The transcription and translation are based on the draft of the forthcoming Correspondence of Assurbanipal volume of the SAA series. I am grateful to Prof. Simo Parpola for the opportunity of using this material.

56. See Heather D. Baker, "Bēl-iqīša," *PNA* 1/II:315-16; Grant Frame, *Babylonia 689-627 B.C.: A Political History* (Uitgaven van het Nederlands Historisch-Archaeologisch Instituut te Istanbul 69; Istanbul: Nederlands Historisch-Archaeologisch Instituut, 1992), 81, 111, 118-20.

57. Cf. Borger, *Inschriften Asarhaddons*, §27 iii 71-83 (pp. 52-53); §27 v 26-33 (pp. 58-59); cf. Matthew W. Waters, *A Survey of Neo-Elamite History* (SAAS 12; Helsinki: Neo-Assyrian Text Corpus Project, 2000), 42-45.

king Ashurbanipal to some Gambuleans who were concerned about their status after the transfer of power, which always meant a redistribution of royal favors. In this context "fear not" is a royal promise of loyalty toward people whose submission has been accepted. The letter was certainly written before Urtaku and his allies, Bel-iqiša among them, probably in the year 664, unexpectedly invaded Babylonia, thus breaking up their loyalty to Assyria with fatal consequences.[58]

In the correspondence of Ashurbanipal, the phrase "fear not" occurs repeatedly, always in letters written by the king to his subjects or vassals. With the probable exception of *ABL* 541 quoted above, their dates are close to the time of the revolt of his brother Šamaš-šumu-ukin, the subordinate ruler of Babylonia, with whom he was at war from 652 to 648. Not surprisingly, the king's exhortation not to fear calls for perseverance and loyalty in the ever changing conjunctures of war. In a letter dated to the 5th of Tishri (VII), 652 and concerning men of two Babylonian cities, Cutha and Surmarrati, Ashurbanipal says to Zakir and Kabtiya[59] that they should not be afraid (*ABL* 944). The letter is too badly broken to yield a solid interpretation, but it is imaginable that the addressees of the letter held a responsible, probably military position in or near Cutha, a strategically important city, which fell into the hands of Šamaš-šumu-ukin less than a year later.[60]

A better-preserved message from the king is presented by *ABL* 523:

> *ana Sîn-tabni-uṣur/ina muḫḫi Sîn-šarra-uṣur ša ta[qbûni] mā annūri nik[lu] inakkil/samku ina mu[ḫḫ]īja ikarrar/lā t[apallaḫ]/mīnu ḫappu anniu ina muḫḫīka iqabbi/anāku lā uddâ ša [. . .] u taddanūni x [x maṣṣartī] taṣṣurūni [. . .] u tasmûni mī[nu ḫīṭu]/u tablaṭanni ina muḫḫi bēt bēl[ēka]/šû mīnu iqabbi ina muḫḫīka u ina libbimma anāku atâ ašamme/lā tapallaḫ tuāršu/napšatka ibašši ina pānīya/u ina muḫḫi alākīka ša taqbûni mā rabūti iktallūni/šalaš šanāti tattitiz maṣṣartu tattaṣar zikirka ina pānīya tuddammiq/ūmâ simān taqāni ša māti/maṣṣartaka tuk[tīn] tettiqa tallaka/ūlâ itiz maṣṣartaka uṣur adi mātu ta[tqanūni]/u ina ūmēšu tallaka pānīya ḫaddute tammar [. . .] u tasaḫḫur ina šal[imte] tallak*

---

58. For the unsuccessful invasion of Urtaku, supported by Bel-iqiša, Nabû-šumu-ereš, the governor of Nippur, and Marduk-šumu-ibni, a Babylonian general of Urtaku, see Rykle Borger, *Beiträge zum Inschriftenwerk Assurbanipals: Die Prismenklassen A, B, C = K, D, E, F, G, H, J und T sowie andere Inschriften* (Wiesbaden: Harrassowitz, 1996), 94-96 (Prism B iv 18-53// C v 24-61); and cf. Frame, *Babylonia*, 118-21; Waters, *Survey*, 45-47.

59. For this person, see Heather D. Baker, "Kabtîa," *PNA* 2/I:594. Probably the same person writes in another letter (*ABL* 202) about Babylonians taking a loyalty oath.

60. See Frame, *Babylonia*, 144, 146.

To Sîn-tabni-uṣur:/Concerning Sîn-šarra-uṣur about whom you s[aid]: Now then, he is devising a scheme/and *spreading rumors*[61] against me/have no f[ear]!/What can this *fool*[62] say against you?/Don't I know what you [*do*] and deliver, *h[ow] you have kept* [my watch . . . ]ed, . . . ed *without bl[ame]*,/ and lived for the house of [your] lord[s]?/What could he say against you? And in the middle of it, why should I listen to it?/Do not fear his return!/ Your life is with me!/As to your coming about which you said: "The magnates have held me back,"/it is the third year now that you have stood by and kept my watch, making yourself a good name in my presence./Now, at the moment that the country is getting safe, you could move on to come, having estab[lished] your guard./Alternatively, stay there and keep [your] wat[ch] until the country has been put up in order;/then you can come, see [my] beaming [face], and return in safe[ty].[63]

Both Sîn-tabni-uṣur and Sîn-šarra-uṣur were sons of Nikkal-iddina, governor of the city of Ur, which most of the time was "a bastion of pro-Assyrian sentiment in southern Babylonia, an area whose tribal groups frequently provided support for rebel movements."[64] Sîn-šarra-uṣur followed his brother Sîn-balassu-iqbi as the governor of Ur, probably just before Šamaš-šumu-ukin rose up in arms and with his consent, whereas Ashurbanipal would have supported Sîn-tabni-uṣur.[65] The letter quoted here is not the only one to give the impression that Sîn-tabni-uṣur was given preference over Sîn-šarra-uṣur by Ashurbanipal, who, after having consulted diviners, replaced Sîn-šarra-uṣur by his brother at some turn during the war — in 650 at the latest but probably earlier.[66] Since the king gives Sîn-tabni-uṣur the credit for keeping guard of the city for three years without release and now gives him permission to leave the city, the letter is certainly written after Ur was relieved by Ashurbanipal in 650, but not necessarily before the war was over. As in *ABL* 290, the king en-

---

61. The word *samku* is probably derived from *samāku*, "to cover up," and may here refer to secrets or malicious gossips.

62. Lit. perhaps: "stinker."

63. For transcription and translation, see n. 56.

64. Frame, *Babylonia*, 101.

65. See Jean-Marie Durand, "Note à propos de la date d'*ABL* 290," *RA* 75 (1981): 181-85; cf. Frame, *Babylonia*, 126.

66. In addition to *ABL* 523, cf. *ABL* 290, 947, and 1002. On consulting diviners see SAA 4 300-301 (Ivan Starr, *Queries to Sungod: Divination and Politics in Sargonid Assyria* [SAA 4; Helsinki: Helsinki Univ. Press, 1990], 282-84). Ashurbanipal also asked whether Sîn-šarra-uṣur should be appointed over the Babylonian Sealand (SAA 4 302), but there is no evidence that he actually did so. On the date see J. A. Brinkman, "Ur: 721-605 B.C.," *Or* 34 (1965): 241-58, esp. 253-55.

courages the governor, giving his word that he will not believe the bad rumors circulated by Sîn-šarra-uṣur. Having once been pardoned by the king in spite of having submitted to the enemy during a famine in the city,[67] Sîn-tabni-uṣur would have had every reason to trust in this royal word.

Due to the damaged state of the tablet, the historical background of *ABL* 1186 is not explicit in the extant wording of the letter. To all appearances, it is written to the inhabitants of a city, threatened by the forces of someone who is himself shut up in another city and surrounded by the army of the author of the letter. This leaves little doubt that the person in question is Šamaš-šumu-ukin and that Ashurbanipal has authored the letter during the siege of Babylon in the years 650-648:

> [. . . . . .] *u attunu atâ kî anniu tāmurāni ša duāki lā tadūkā ša ṣabāte lā taṣbatā/ša illikūninni šunû ina muḫḫīkunu maʾdū/ūmâ lā tapallaḫā/maṣṣartu ša bēt ilānīya uṣrā/šû gabbīšuma ina libbi āli esir u emūqīya labiūšu/ūmâ bēt mār šiprīšu tammarāni/ša duāki tadūkā ša ṣabāte ṣabtā [. . . . . .]*

> [. . . . . .] But you [pl.], when you saw this, why did you not kill those who were to be killed and seize those who were to be seized?/Certainly (the troops) who came were not more numerous than you!/Now fear not, but guard my temples!/He is shut up in the city with all his forces, and my army is surrounding him./Now wherever you see a messenger of his, kill those who are to be killed and seize those who are to be seized! [. . . . . .][68]

Again, the king pronounces his *lā tapallaḫā* to people whom he knows or believes to be in an emergency, demanding loyalty. It seems that the addressees have lent an ear to messages from the adversary and not offered enough resistance, but the king is willing to forgive this, if they remain loyal to him even under the threat of an aggressor. The king himself seems not to be operating near the city in question, so he cannot promise any military backup but only assure that the enemy will soon be slain. In this context fearlessness requires faith without seeing (cf. Isa 7:4, 9), supposing the people's confidence in the king's sovereignty, which is ultimately of divine origin; hence the king's "fear

---

67. In the letter *ABL* 1274, the citizens of Ur assure the loyalty of their governor in spite of the fact that he had no other option than to surrender because of starvation; cf. Frame, *Babylonia*, 166.

68. *ABL* 1186: 3′-14′ (for transcription and translation, see n. 55 above). A fragment of a royal order with similar content has been preserved in SAA 15 306: 2-6 (Fuchs and Parpola, *Correspondence of Sargon II, Part III*, 192): [. . .] "the fort sho[uld be . . . . . .] it [should] be watched over; and [. . . . . .] fetc[h] for your watch [. . . . . . F]ear [not], be con[fident! . . .] Gua[rd] this [fo]rt!"

not" can be trusted as if it were a divine word. In Ashurbanipal's letters, this phrase always has political overtones: it reminds the addressees of their position and connotes a demand for fidelity to the king.

## King to King

The turbulences of the Šamaš-šumu-ukin revolt affected not only Babylonia but also Elam, whose rulers changed at a brisk pace, and so did their loyalties to Assyria.[69] A prime example is provided by Tammaritu II, who ruled 651-649 after having killed his predecessor and uncle Humban-nikaš II, a puppet of Assyria who before his short rule had been granted asylum by Ashurbanipal, but who went over to Šamaš-šumu-ukin when the revolt began. Tammaritu remained on Šamaš-šumu-ukin's side, but when he, in turn, was toppled by Indabibi, he survived by fleeing to Assyria.[70] Ashurbanipal protected Tammaritu who even dwelt in his palace.[71] There are discordant records concerning Ashurbanipal's relation to Indabibi,[72] who ruled only until the next year (648). He was killed by the Elamites who put Humban-haltaš III on the throne. By this time Babylon fell and the war was over, but Ashurbanipal soon attacked Elam, forcing Humban-haltaš to flee, and giving Tammaritu a second chance.[73] The long letter from Ashurbanipal to Tammaritu, *ABL* 1022, probably dates from this period of time, since it mentions the names Humban-haltaš (Ass. Ummanaldasi, l. r. 5) and Nabû-bel-šumati (l. 15), the right hand of Šamaš-šumu-ukin who was protected by Humban-haltaš after the fall of Babylon. The context of the phrase "fear not" (*lā tapallaḫ*, l. 12) is broken, but the remaining text suggests an account concerning the threat constituted by people from Raši, the area between Elam and northern Babylonia, and the coming of Ashurbanipal's troops to assistance:

69. For an overview of the complicated circumstances in Elam during the years 652-645, see Waters, *Survey*, 62-80.

70. Borger, *Beiträge zum Inschriftenwerk Assurbanipals*, 110-12 (Prism B vii 43-76).

71. Ibid., 110-11 (Prism B vii 58-63).

72. Prism B 77-92, completed by the time Indabibi gained power, tells about his assurances of goodwill and peace (Borger, *Beiträge zum Inschriftenwerk Assurbanipals*, 112-13), and in the letter *ABL* 1151, Ashurbanipal calls Indabibi his "brother." However, Prism C ix 58-86, compiled two or three years later, gives a less harmonious impression of the Assyrian-Elamite relations at that time (Borger, *Beiträge zum Inschriftenwerk Assurbanipals*, 153-55). See Waters, *Survey*, 66.

73. Borger, *Beiträge zum Inschriftenwerk Assurbanipals*, 45-48 (Prism A iv 110–v 35). Waters, *Survey*, 69-70, dates the campaign either to 648 or 657; the month of Sivan (III) is given in the inscription.

*[ṭuppi Aššūr-bāni-apli] šar [māt Aššūr] a[na Tamma]rītu šar Elamti šulmu
ana yāši lū šulmu a[na kāša]/ina muḫḫi emūqī annūti ša [. . .] lā immagāni
[. . .]/ina muḫḫi Rāšāja [. . .] ša ina kutallīkunu [. . .] ina muḫḫi kabbusi ša
māti/šū [. . .] ūmâ issi māt Aššūr urru adi [. . .] ittalkū u ammaka [. . .]
ušamḫirūni/ulâ [. . . i]zzazū lā tapallaḫ [. . . . . .]*

[A tablet of Ashurbanipal], king [of Assyria], t[o Tamma]ritu, king of
Elam: I am well, may [you, too], be well./Concerning these troops that
[*were . . .*] *they were* not [. . .] in vain!/As to the Rašeans, [. . .] who [. . .] in
your back [. . .] to subjugate the country:/they have now . . . from Assyria
and gone as far as [. . .] and [. . .] there. [The . . . who] have done correspondingly,/or [. . . are s]taying [. . .]./Fear not! [. . . . . .][74]

A better-preserved part from the conclusion of the letter probably refers to a
treaty between Ashurbanipal and Tammaritu:

*ša abu ana mar'i lā eppašūni anāku [ētapaš] attannakka/atta [. . .] ḫussa
ṭābāte annā[te . . .] epuš dilip šallimanni/u [adê] ša ina pān ilāni ša šamê u
kaq[qiri . . .] utammûkāni [. . .]*

What even a father has not done for a son, I have [done] and given to you!/
As for you, remember [this], unremittingly strive to return to me these
[*many*] favors,/and [*keep*] the [treaty] that I have made you swear before
[*all*] the gods of heaven and earth![75]

Both the encouraging "fear not" and the reference to a treaty suggest that
Ashurbanipal was quite serious about Tammaritu's renewed rulership. Whatever his political plans were, they did not work out, though. Tammaritu's second tenure in Elam lasted only a few months, after which he was captured
and brought back to Assyria; he is mentioned later among other captured
vassals who were forced to pull Ashurbanipal's carriage.[76] Presumably, he
failed to return to the great king his favors, hence the divine-royal "fear not"
was no longer in force.

Ashurbanipal's correspondence with his vassal has an earlier counter-
part in the letter of the Hittite king Šuppiluliuma to Niqmadu II, king of
Ugarit, dating to the first half of the fourteenth century.[77] At that time,

74. *ABL* 1022: 1-12 (for transcription and translation, see n. 55 above).

75. *ABL* 1022 r. 19-24.

76. Borger, *Beiträge zum Inschriftenwerk Assurbanipals,* 70-71 (Prism A x 6-30); cf. Waters, *Survey,* 72.

77. RS 17.132; see Jean Nougayrol, *PRU IV: Textes accadiens des archives sud* (Mission de
Ras Shamra 9; Paris: Imprimerie nationale and Librairie C. Klincksieck, 1956), 35-37.

Šuppiluliuma was confronted by a coalition of Syrian kings supported by Mitanni. King Niqmadu of Ugarit, rather than joining this anti-Hittite league, chose to conclude a treaty with Šuppiluliuma, which in concrete terms meant vassalage under the Hittite king.[78] The letter begins with the following words:

*umma Šamši šarri rabî ana Niqmanda qibima/enūma Nuḫaš u Mugi[š] ittīya nakrūma/u atta Niqmandu lā tapallaḫšunu itti ramānīka lū putqu-dāta/kî ša ultu maḫirî abbūka itti Ḫatti šalmū u lā nakrū/anumma atta Niqmandu lū akannama/itti nakrīya lū nakrāta itti šalāmīya lū šalmāta/u šumma atta Niqmandu amāte annâti ša šarri rabî bēlīka tašamme u tanaṣ-ṣaršina/u šarrumma tammar dumqa ša šarru rabû bēlka udammiqakku*

Thus the Sun, the great king; speak to Niqmadu: Nuhašše and Muki[š] are now at war with me./You, Niqmadu: Do not be afraid of them, trust in yourself!/As your fathers before were my allies and not enemies,/let it now be the same way with you, Niqmadu:/may you be the enemy of my enemies and the ally of my allies!/And if you, Niqmadu, listen to these words of the great king, your lord, take heed of them,/you, king, will see the good deeds that the great king, your lord, will do to you.[79]

After having urged Niqmadu to remain faithful and to trust in his word,[80] Šuppiluliuma writes:

*u šumma šarrānu gabbūšunu ṣābī mimma ana ḫabāti ša mātīka umaššarū/u atta Niqmandu lā tapallaḫšunu/ḫamutta mār šiprāka ana muḫḫīya šupram-ma lillikka*

And if all those kings send any troops to plunder your country,/you, Niqmadu, be not afraid of them,/but send immediately a messenger of yours to me![81]

No reader will miss the paternalistic tone of this letter, very similar to the language Ashurbanipal or any Assyrian king would use when writing to their vassals. While animating Niqmadu to self-reliance, he makes clear that he himself is the one who is to be feared, not the kings involved in anti-Hittite

78. For the treaty, see ibid., 37-48; cf. Manfried Dietrich and Oswald Loretz, "Der Vertrag zwischen Šuppiluliuma und Niqmadu," *WO* 3 (1966): 206-45.

79. Nougayrol, *PRU* IV:35-36, ll. 1-18.

80. Ibid., 36, ll. 28-29: *Niqmandu ina arki ūmi amāte ša šarri rabî bēlīka taqâp*, "Niqmadu, from day to day trust in the word of the great king, your lord!"

81. Ibid., 36, ll. 30-34.

undertakings. Again, one is reminded of the biblical exhortations not to be afraid of the enemy, spoken by God (Num 21:34; Deut 3:2) or by Moses or Joshua (Exod 14:13; Num 14:9; Deut 1:29; 3:22; Josh 10:25). It has been noted that Šuppiluliuma speaks in his letter like a god.[82] Indeed, the great king seems to relate to his vassal as gods do to him, just as, for example, Ashurbanipal relates to Gyges, king of Lydia, who allegedly sent his messenger (mār šipri) to tell him about a dream of his concerning his obeisance to Ashurbanipal's sovereignty.[83]

A certain kind of king-to-king communication is represented also by the "Cuthaean Legend of Naram-Sin," a tale preserved in several manuscripts of the Old Babylonian and Standard Babylonian (Neo-Assyrian) recensions.[84] In this fictional autobiography, Naram-Sin, the legendary king of Akkad, narrates in first person about his battle against hordes of heavenly creatures that entirely devastate his forces. According to the Standard Babylonian recension, Naram-Sin finally gains a victory, but is not allowed to annihilate the enemy. The recension concludes with an admonition to a future ruler, the message of which is that he should live in peace, taking good care of everyday pursuits and not engage in violent enterprises:

> atta mannu lū iššakku u rubû lū mimma šanāma
> ša ilānu inambûšu šarrūta ippuš . . .
> narâ annâ amurma ša pī narê annâ šimēma
> lā tessiḫḫu lā tenniššu
> lā tapallaḫ lā tatarrur
> išdāka lū kīna

> You, whoever you are, be it governor or prince or anyone else,
> Whom the gods will call to perform kingship. . . .
> Read this stele! Hearken unto the words of this stele!
> Be not bewildered! Be not confused!
> Be not afraid! Do not tremble!
> Let your foundations be firm![85]

---

82. Hans Wildberger, "'Glauben' im Alten Testament," *ZTK* 65 (1968): 129-59, esp. 136; cf. Dion, "Fear Not," 566.

83. Borger, *Beiträge zum Inschriftenwerk Assurbanipals*, 30-31 (Prism A ii 95-110), 181-83 (E prisms); cf. Mordechai Cogan and Hayim Tadmor, "Gyges and Assurbanipal: A Study in Literary Transmission," *Or* 46 (1977): 65-85; Nissinen, *References to Prophecy*, 57-58.

84. See Joan Goodnick Westenholz, *Legends of the Kings of Akkad: The Texts* (Winona Lake, Ind.: Eisenbrauns, 1997), 263-331.

85. Lines 149-50, 154-58; see Westenholz, *Legends*, 326-27.

One cannot help comparing *lā tapallaḥ lā tatarrur* with the structurally similar Deuteronomistic phrase, "Do not be afraid, do not be discouraged" *('al/lō' tîrâ wĕ'al/lō' tēḥāt)*, especially when said by Moses to his follower Joshua (Deut 31:8), or to the Israelites (Deut 1:21; cf. God to Joshua, Josh 8:1; Joshua to the people, Josh 10:25). The setting is different in that Joshua and the Israelites are called up to fight, whereas the follower of Naram-Sin is urged not to engage in war.[86] Fearlessness appears in the Cuthaean Legend among qualities of a peaceful leadership, which gives "fear not" a tone rather different from its use in military contexts. There is no fundamental ideological clash, however, since the very message of the Cuthaean Legend is essentially convergent with the general idea of divine warfare, advocated by the Deuteronomists as well, in which the role of the humans is auxiliary at best. This ideology becomes a pronounced form when "fear not" is used in divine discourse.

### Divine Discourse

#### Ludlul bēl nēmeqi

The oldest attestation of *lā tapallaḥ* in divine discourse is probably to be found in *Ludlul bēl nēmeqi,* or The Poem of the Righteous Sufferer.[87] This literary work is conventionally dated to the Kassite period (i.e., 15th-12th centuries), although the extant manuscripts are all Neo-Assyrian/Babylonian.[88] The implied author, having described his miseries (illness, loss of his formerly esteemed position and futile endeavors to find relief), tells in the third tablet of the poem about a series of dreams that finally promised well. In the first dream, "a remarkable young man of extraordinary physique" appears, but the text is too fragmentary to reveal what he says to the sufferer. In the second dream, he becomes cleansed by another remarkable young man, whereas in the third dream a female being speaks to him:

---

86. Cf. Rowlett, *Joshua*, 100.

87. W. G. Lambert, *Babylonian Wisdom Literature* (Oxford: Oxford Univ. Press, 1960; repr. Winona Lake, Ind.: Eisenbrauns, 1996), 21-62; cf. the translation of Benjamin R. Foster, "The Poem of the Righteous Sufferer," *COS* 1:486-92 (no. 1.153). Note also *KBo* 1 13, a somewhat later Middle Babylonian text from Anatolia, in which *lā tapallaḥ* occurs in a broken context. The text is too badly broken to be interpreted; cf. the transliteration and translation of Sommerfeld, *Der Aufstieg Marduks*, 198-99. According to him, the text may be part of an otherwise unknown mythological narrative or a historical-literary poem (p. 197).

88. See Lambert, *Babylonian Wisdom Literature,* 29.

*ašlušma šuttu anaṭ[ṭal] ina šutti aṭṭulu mūšīt[īya]*
*ištē[t] batūltu banû zī[mūšu]/nišiš x x x iliš ma[šlat]*
*šarrat nišī [. . . . . .]/īrubamma itta[šba . . . . . .]*
*qibâ aḫulapī [. . . . . .]/lā tapallaḫ iqbâ*
*mimmu šutta īṭul [. . . . . .]*
*iqbima aḫulapī magal šum[ruṣma]*
*ayyumma ša ina šāt mūši ibnû bī[ra]*

A third time I sa[w] a dream, in [my] nightly dream I saw
A certain young woman of shining coun[tenance],/ . . . like a human be-
ing, eq[ual] to a god,
A queen of the peoples [. . . . . .]./She entered and [sat down], [. . . . . .]
"Speak my deliverance [. . . . . .]!"/"Fear not," she said, [. . . . . .]
Whatever of a dream one has seen [. . . . . .]
She spoke my deliverance: "Most wre[tched] is he,
Whoever he is, the one who saw the nightly vision."[89]

The speech of the female dream goddess, best described as an oracle of salvation,[90] anticipates the fourth and final dream, in which a diviner speaks an
oracle of Marduk, the supreme god, who then releases the sufferer from his
distress; the diviner *(mašmaššu)* assumes a remarkably prophetic role, holding a tablet in his hands and saying: "Marduk has sent me" (*Mardukma
išpuranni;* iii 41-42). The climax of the story, the turn for the better, is marked
with oracular experiences, in which the exhortation "fear not" is embedded in
a divinatory context.

### Ištar to Ashurbanipal

In Ashurbanipal's letters "fear not" is reminiscent of words of Moses, who encourages the people not to be afraid in face of the enemy because the divine
force behind them is greater (e.g., Exod 14:13; Deut 1:29; 3:22; 20:1; 31:6; cf. also
Neh 4:8 [Eng. 4:14]). But they also remind one of divine words, which according to Ashurbanipal's own account were spoken to him by Ištar in a critical
situation. Since several manuscripts of *Ludlul bēl nēmeqi* belonged to
Ashurbanipal's library, it is not far-fetched to assume that the above quoted
section has influenced the following passage, which even repeats the word order *lā tapallaḫ iqbâ:*

89. Tablet iii, ll. 29-38; see Lambert, *Babylonian Wisdom Literature,* 48-51 (cf. the correction on p. 345); Foster, "Poem," 490.
90. Cf. Harner, "Salvation Oracle," 422.

*inḫēya šunūḫūti Ištār išmēma lā tapallaḫ iqbâ/ušarḫiṣanni libbu/ana nīš qātēka ša taššâ ēnāka imlâ dimtu artaši rēmu*

Ištar heard my desperate sighs and said to me: "Have no fear!"/She made my heart confident (saying):/"Because of the hand-lifting prayer you said, your eyes being filled with tears, I have mercy upon you."[91]

Ashurbanipal's tears were caused by the surprise attack of Teumman, king of Elam, in 653, after which he claims to have uttered a long prayer with the above quoted divine reaction. The answer of the goddess implies an essentially similar role division as in Ashurbanipal's letters, only the king now assumes the role of the distressed whereas the goddess plays the part of the sovereign. Like the Gambuleans in *ABL* 541, Ashurbanipal begs his superior for help, and the goddess utters the queenly "fear not" to her "son" who has shown his fidelity to her, just as he himself pacifies his faithful servant Sîn-tabni-uṣur in *ABL* 523.

In a dream expanding this answer, Ištar promises to take care of the warfare, telling the king to relax.[92] Without directly corresponding to the message of Ashurbanipal in *ABL* 1186, the dream renders a similar idea: the people should not be frightened, but trust in the one who alone should be feared. But the dream, being a divine message, says more: whereas Ashurbanipal tells the people to "kill the one to be killed and seize the one to be seized," Ištar urges the king to make merry and leave all fighting to her. This statement represents hyperbolically the idea that reserves all warfare to divine intervention. The "quietist" aspect of the ideology of divine warfare can be found already in Mari prophecies, but it is also observable in the Cuthaean legend, in the Hebrew Bible, and, as we shall see, in Neo-Assyrian prophecies.[93]

---

91. Borger, *Beiträge zum Inschriftenwerk Assurbanipals,* 100 (Prism B v 46-49).

92. Ibid., 100-101 (Prism B v 49-76).

93. On Mari see, e.g., ARM 26 237:22-26: *muḫḫūtum ina bīt Annunītim [i]tbêma/ ummāmi Zimri-Lim ana gerrim lā tallak/ina Māri šibma u anākūma ātanappal,* "A *muḫḫūtum* arose in the temple of Annunitum and spoke:/'Zimri-Lim, do not go on campaign!/Stay in Mari, and I shall continue to answer.'" The word "quietism" is used by William L. Moran with regard to this text in "New Evidence from Mari on the History of Prophecy," *Bib* 50 (1969): 15-56, esp. 40. At Mari there are no attestations of *lā tapallaḫ,* but the idea of fearlessness in a threatening situation is certainly there; of the two texts brought into discussion by Heintz, "Oracles prophétiques," 121-25, ARM 26 210 is still conclusive in spite of Dion's criticism (cf. above, n. 26); here I concur with Rowlett, *Joshua,* 98. For the OT see esp. Exod 14:13-14 (NEB): "'Have no fear *('al tîrā'û),'* Moses answered, 'stand firm and see the deliverance that the Lord will bring you this day. . . . The Lord will fight for you so hold your peace.'"

The inscription of Ashurbanipal is noteworthy in two further respects. First, "fear not" is presented in a formulaic manner. In the clause *lā tapallah iqbâ*, the word order makes the words *lā tapallah* the object of the verb *qabû* rather than a direct speech, which indicates a formulaic use of words perceived as a fixed compound. Second, "fear not" is part of a divine speech, an oracle of salvation presumably transmitted by a prophet.[94] This brings us to the use of the phrase in the Neo-Assyrian prophetic oracles.

## *"Fear not" in Prophecy*

More than in any other extant source, *lā tapallah* is used in Neo-Assyrian prophecies (SAA 9), where it has nineteen occurrences in twelve different oracles; this makes up approximately half of the attestations of the phrase that I am aware of. Hence it is not by chance that these texts, if any, are mentioned as parallels of biblical "fear not" oracles. Furthermore, even the assumption of a fixed formula with a definable *Sitz im Leben* may be appropriate with regard to these oracles. The density of the phrase allows manifold observations of the place and function of *lā tapallah* in divine discourse.

1. Any reader of the Assyrian prophecies will notice at first glance that "fear not" often assumes a structural function as the opening or closing formula, just as it does in Second Isaiah.[95] Quoting this phrase is one of the most frequent ways to begin an oracle. In these cases it is always combined with the name of the addressee, for example: *Aššur-ahu-iddina lā tapallah*, "Esarhaddon, fear not!"[96] and once preceded by the name of the prophet and the speaking deity: *Mullissu-kabtat raggintu/[m]ā abat šarrati Mullissu ši/mā lā tapallah Aššur-bāni-apli*, "Thus the prophetess Mullissu-kabtat:/This is the word of Queen Mullissu:/Fear not, Ashurbanipal!"[97] In a few cases "fear not"

94. See Weippert, "Assyrische Prophetien," 97-98; Parpola, *Assyrian Prophecies*, xlvi-xlvii; Nissinen, *References to Prophecy*, 53-54.

95. See Parpola, *Assyrian Prophecies*, lxvi; Weippert, "Ich bin Jahwe," 37-41. For the OT see Isa 41:14; 43:1; 44:2 (opening formula); 41:13 (closing formula).

96. SAA 9 2.5 iii 19; cf. SAA 9 1.1 i 4-5 *[Aššur-ahu-]iddina šar mātāti [lā t]apallah*, "[Esarh]addon, king of the lands, [f]ear [not]!"; SAA 9 1.2 i 30: *šar māt Aššur lā tapallah*, "King of Assyria, fear not!"; SAA 9 1.4 ii 16: *lā tapallah Aššur-ahu-iddina*, "Fear not, Esarhaddon!"; SAA 9 2.2 i 15: *[lā tapa]llah Aššur-ahu-iddina*, "[Fe]ar [not], Esarhaddon." Moreover, in SAA 9 1.8 v 21 the actual oracle to Esarhaddon begins with *šarru lā tapallah*, "O King, fear not!"

97. SAA 9 7:1-2.

is placed at the end of the oracle as a closing formula, for example, in the same oracle as above: *atta lā tapallaḥ mūrī ša anāku urabbûni*, "Fear not, you, my calf whom I rear."[98]

Another typical and formulaic feature in several Assyrian prophecies is the divine self-identification *anāku Issār ša Arbail*, "I am Ištar of Arbela" (etc.), again corresponding to *'ănî YHWH*, "I am Yahweh" (etc.), in Second Isaiah.[99] It is used independently of "fear not," but in the oracles of the collection SAA 9 1, both formulas tend to appear close to each other.[100] Even in the other tablets of the corpus, where the formulaic self-identification of this type is not attested,[101] the divine *anāku* always accompanies the exhortation "fear not,"[102] marking the divine discourse and leaving the addressee with no uncertainty about who the speaker is.

As a structural element framing the oracles, "fear not" is used in a genuinely formulaic way. Besides the semantic content of the phrase as such and its immediate surroundings, it connotes more: it functions as a signifier of a prophecy, encapsulating the whole substance of the following or preceding oracle. In fact, when used together with the divine self-predication and the name of the addressee (cf. above, SAA 9 7:1-2), "fear not" alone is enough to constitute a prophecy. Nevertheless, it always has a context from which it becomes a specific tone: encouragement before the enemy, promises for future support, or the special relationship of the king to the goddess.

2. The Neo-Assyrian prophecies have sometimes been classified as "war oracles" because of the frequent divine encouragements concerning the king's

---

98. SAA 9 7 r. 11; cf. SAA 9 2.1 i 13: *[lā tapa]lliḥi ummi šarri*, "[Fe]ar [not], mother of the king!"; SAA 9 2.4 iii 17: *lā tapallaḥ ina ṣilli Aššūr-aḥu-iddina šar māt Aššūr*, "Fear not! Esarhaddon is in my protection."

99. See Parpola, *Assyrian Prophecies*, lxv; Weippert, "Ich bin Jahwe," 42-49. For the OT see Isa 41:13; 43:3 (close to *'al tîrā'*); cf. 42:6, 8; 43:11, 15; 44:24; 45:3, 5, 7, 18, 21; 48:17; 49:23, 26; cf. *'ānōkî 'ēl*, "I am God," Isa 43:12; 45:3; 46:9.

100. SAA 9 1.1 i 18, 20-21; 1.4 ii 30; 1.6 iii 7: *anāku Issār ša Arbail*, "I am Ištar of Arbela"; cf. SAA 9 1.1 i 11-12; 1.2 i 36 (?): *Bēlet rabītu anāku anāku Issār ša Arbail*, "I am the great Lady, I am Ištar of Arbela"; 1.8 v 12: *anāku Bēlet Arbail*, "I am the Lady of Arbela." Only in SAA 9 1.4 does the self-identification involve other divine names: *anāku Bēl*, "I am Bel" (ii 17); *anāku Nabû*, "I am Nabû" (ii 38).

101. Save SAA 9 3.3 ii 24-25: *lēmurū lūna"idūni akī Aššūr bēl ilāni anākūni*, "Let them see it and praise me, for I am Aššur, lord of the gods!" and, provided that the restoration is correct, SAA 9 2.3 i 36-38: *[anāku B]ēlet Arbail [Aššūr-aḥu-iddina šar] māt Aššūr [lā tapallaḥ]*, "[I am the L]ady of Arbela! [Esarhaddon, king] of Assyria, [fear not!]."

102. Cf. the oracles SAA 9 2.1; 2.2; 2.4; 2.5; SAA 9 4; SAA 9 7.

encounter with his enemies.[103] Inadequate though it is to maintain that Assyrian prophecy in its entirety would fall under this kind of a *Gattung* (not every Assyrian prophecy has to do with war), enemies are a recurring theme in the oracles, some of which are actually spoken in critical situations. This is especially true for the collection SAA 9 1, the oracles of which derive from the time when Esarhaddon was expatriated and at war against his brothers before his victory and enthronement.[104] The first — and most frequently quoted — prophecy of this collection serves as a prime example of "fear not" proclaimed in the midst of a battle:

> *[Aššūr-ahu-]iddina šar mātāti [lā t]apallaḥ/[a]yyu šāru ša idibakkāni aqappušu lā aksupūni/nakarūtēka kî šahšūri ša Simāni ina pān šēpēka ittangararrū/*
> *Bēlet rabītu anāku anāku Issār ša Arbail ša nakarūtēka ina pān šēpēka akkarrūni/ayyūte dibbīja ša aqqabakanni ina muḥḥi lā tazzizūni/*
> *anāku Issār ša Arbail nakarūtēka ukāṣa addanakka/anāku Issār ša Arbail ina pānātūka ina kutallīka allāka/*
> *lā tapallaḥ atta ina libbi muggi anāku ina libbi ūʾa atabbi uššab*

> [Esarh]addon, king of the lands, fear [not]!/What is the wind that has attacked you, whose wings I have not broken?/Like ripe apples your enemies will roll before your feet./
> I am the great Lady, I am Ištar of Arbela who will throw your enemies before your feet./Have I spoken to you any words that you could not rely upon?/
> I am Ištar of Arbela, I will flay your enemies and deliver them up to you./I am Ištar of Arbela, I go before you and behind you./
> Fear not! You are paralyzed, but I, in the midst of wailing, will get up and sit down.[105]

The well-structured and highly stylistic interplay of "fear not" and the divine self-identification has a single focus: the divine intervention at the critical moment when Esarhaddon is "paralyzed," that is, unable to act (and not yet even a king!).[106] This makes the oracle, as well as other "fear not" oracles in SAA 9 1,[107] a full-fledged representative of the ideology of divine warfare: the

---

103. Cf. Stähli, *THAT* 1:773; Rowlett, *Joshua*, 116-19.

104. For the historical background, see Nissinen, *References to Prophecy*, 14-34.

105. SAA 9 1.1 i 4-27.

106. Parpola, *Assyrian Prophecies*, 5, comments: "The king is here pictured as a baby crying violently (to the point of paralysis) in its distress, the goddess as mother rushing to help it."

107. Cf. SAA 9 1.2 i 30-32: *šar māt Aššūr lā tapallaḥ/nakru ša šar māt Aššūr ana ṭabaḫḫi*

"getting up" and "sitting down" seem to express the whole action of the goddess, who rises to the king's rescue, fights for him, and finally returns to her place. Even Naqia, Esarhaddon's mother, who did her best for her son (and against his brothers) during the war,[108] received a prophetic assurance that the Lady of warfare and battle will have the last word:

*anāku Bēlet Arbail/ana ummi šarri kî taḫḫurīninni mā/ša imitti ša šumēli ina sūnīki tassakni/mā īyû ṣīt libbīja ṣēru tussarpidi/ ūmâ šarru lā tapallaḫ/šarrūtu ikkû danānu ikkûma*

I am the Lady of Arbela!/To the king's mother, since you implored me, saying:/"The one on the right and the other on the left you have placed in your lap./My own offspring you expelled to roam the steppe!"/ Now, king, fear not!/Yours is the kingdom, yours is the power![109]

The use of "fear not" in this prophecy deserves attention not only as a response to a prayer, for which see below, but also as the beginning of the actual oracle, which is addressed directly to Esarhaddon, though physically delivered to his mother, who received prophecies on behalf of her son during his absence (cf. SAA 9 1.7; SAA 9 5). Later on, when Esarhaddon was ruling in Nineveh, she herself, in turn, was encouraged by the same words in prophecies addressed to her son; this indicates the importance of her political role as well as her close relationship to the prophets:

*Aššūr-aḫu-iddina šar māt Aššūr/[nakarūtēka] usappak [ina šēpēya] ukabbas/[lā tapa]lliḫi ummi šarri*

Esarhaddon, king of Assyria!/I will catch [your enemies] and trample them [under my foot]./[Fe]ar not, mother of the king![110]

---

*addana,* "King of Assyria, fear not! The enemy of the king of Assyria I will lead to the slaughter"; SAA 9 1.6 iii 30–iv 4: *lā tapallaḫ šarru/aqṭibak lā aslīk[a]/utakki[lka] lā ubâš[ka]/nāru ina tuqunni ušēbar[ka],* "Fear not, king! I have spoken to you, I have not let yo[u] down!/I have inspi[red you] with confidence, I have not caused [you] to come to shame!/I will lead [you] safely across the River."

108. For her see Nissinen, *References to Prophecy,* 22-24; Sarah C. Melville, *The Role of Naqia/Zakutu in Sargonid Politics* (SAAS 9; Helsinki: Neo-Assyrian Text Corpus Project, 1999).

109. SAA 9 1.8 v 12-23.

110. SAA 9 2.1 i 10-13; cf. SAA 2.6 iv 28, where the preserved *[l]ā tapalliḫi* is probably addressed to Naqia.

3. The previous prophecy begins the collection SAA 9 2, which is composed of oracles from the beginning of Esarhaddon's rule. In this collection, too, "fear not" is repeated frequently, however, in an atmosphere different from the momentous tone of the SAA 9 1 prophecies. These oracles are not true "war oracles," since the war is over, and the oracles orient toward the future, assuring the divine support and protection:

> *[lā tapal]lah̬ Aššūr-ah̬u-iddina/[akī m]allāh̬i damqi ina kāri ṭābi [eleppu uk]alla/akī ša pānīti [lū ina u]rkīti/ina batbattīka [asah̬h̬u]r maṣṣartaka anaṣṣar*

> [Fe]ar not, Esarhaddon!/[Like] a skilled [p]ilot [I will s]teer [the ship] for a good harbor./[Let the f]uture be like the past!/[I will circl]e around you, I will stand guard for you.[111]

The enemies are now looked upon from the perspective of the safety of the king and his prosperous future, guaranteed by reconciliation of heaven and earth (SAA 9 2.3 ii 1-5, etc.). Because of the shift of perspective into the future, even the neighboring states are envisioned as potential adversaries rather than an actual menace:

> *atta lū qālāka Aššūr-ah̬u-iddina/ṣīrāni Elamāya Mannāya abīar/Urarṭāya šiṭrīšu abarrim/igib ša Mugalli ubattaq/mannu ēdu mannu h̬ablu/lā tapallah̬ ina ṣilli Aššūr-ahu-iddina šar māt Aššūr*

> You, Esarhaddon, keep silent!/I will select the emissaries of the Elamite king and the Mannean king,/I will seal the messages of the Urartean king,/I will cut off the heel[112] of Mugallu.[113]/Who is now lonely, who is now wronged?/ Fear not! Esarhaddon is in my protection.[114]

The "quietist" idea of the divine warfare thus is in force even when there is no actual military situation, and the change of perspective does not alter the fundamental ideology behind the "fear not" exhortation.

4. One of the central aspects of Begrich's theory of the priestly oracle was that the salvation oracle is spoken in response to the prayer of a person in distress.[115] Two such cases have indeed been discussed in this article. Both the

---

111. SAA 9 2.2 i 15-19.
112. I interpret the word in the same meaning as *eqbu*, "heel."
113. Mugallu was the king of Melid in Anatolia.
114. SAA 9 2.4 iii 12-17.
115. Begrich, "Das priesterliche Heilsorakel," 82-85.

inscription of Ashurbanipal reporting his request for help in a military situation and the subsequent answer of Ištar, and the prophecy in response to the plea of Naqia, the queen mother,[116] not only explicitly mention that the prayers have been uttered but even quote their words.

Another well-known example is the Aramaic inscription of Zakkur, king of Hamath, who reports to have received a response from his patron deity Ba'alšamayim through prophetic intermediaries. After describing how he was besieged in the city of Hazrak by seventeen kings, he says:

*w'š' ydy 'l b'lš[my]m wy'nny b'lšmy[n/w ymll] b'lšmym 'ly [b]yd ḥzyn wbyd 'ddn [wy'mr 'ly] b'lšmym/'l tzḥl ky 'nh hml[ktk w'nh 'q]m 'mk/w'nh 'ḥṣlk mn kl [mlky' 'l zy] mḥ'w 'lyk mṣr*

I lifted my hands to Ba'alša[mayi]m, and Ba'alšamayim anwered me./ Ba'alšamayim [spoke] to me [thr]ough seers and messengers[117] [and] Ba'alšamayim [said]:/"Fear not! I have made [you] king [and I will st]and by [you]./I will rescue you from all [these kings who] have laid a siege against you!"[118]

This reminds one not only of the previously quoted inscription of Ashurbanipal, but also of Esarhaddon's report on his rise to power, where he, having heard about his rebelling brothers' evil deeds, claims to have prayed with raised hands to the great gods with the following response: *alik lā kalâta idāka nittallakma ninâra gārêka*, "Go ahead, do not hold back! We go by your side, we annihilate your enemies."[119] This oracle of encouragement *(šīr takilti)* is probably the result of extispicy, and hence no prophecy, but the report echoes the prophecy SAA 9 3.3;[120] neither source employs the phrase "fear not," but the setting is essentially the same as in inscriptions of Zakkur

116. See, respectively, Borger, *Beiträge zum Inschriftenwerk Assurbanipals*, 99-100 (Prism B v 15-49); SAA 9 1.8.

117. For the interpretation of the word *'ddn*, see Ross, "Prophecy," 4-8.

118. *KAI* 202 A 11-15. For this text see also Ross, "Prophecy"; Zobel, "Das Gebet"; Simon B. Parker, *Studies in Scripture and Inscriptions: Comparative Studies on Narratives in Northwest Semitic Inscriptions and the Hebrew Bible* (New York and Oxford: Oxford Univ. Press, 1997), 106-12; André Lemaire, "Oracles, politique et littérature dans les royaumes araméens et transjordaniens (IX^e-VIII^e s. av. n.è.)," in *Oracles et prophéties dans l'antiquité. Actes du Colloque de Strasbourg 15-17 Juin 1995* (ed. Jean-Georges Heintz; Université des sciences humaines de Strasbourg, Travaux du Centre de recherche sur le Proche-Orient et la Grèce antiques 15; Paris: De Boccard, 1997), 171-93, esp. 172-75.

119. Borger, *Die Inschriften Asarhaddons*, § 27 i 53-62 (p. 43).

120. See Nissinen, *References to Prophecy*, 24-28.

and Ashurbanipal. Furthermore, a comparable situation — Ashurbanipal's war against Šamaš-šumu-ukin — is to be found behind the Dialogue of Ashurbanipal and Nabû,[121] in which the king's prayers alternate with divine responses. Even *lā tapallaḥ* appears once, in the answer of Nabû mediated by a ghost or a dream god *(zaqīqu)*:[122] *lā tapallaḥ Aššūr-bāni-apli . . . pīya ammiu ša ṭābu iktanarrabka ina puḫur ilāni rabûti*, "Fear not, Ashurbanipal! . . . My pleasant mouth shall ever bless you in the assembly of the great gods."

These documents can be quoted in support of one essential aspect in Begrich's theory of the priestly oracle; as a matter of fact, they express the divine response to the prayer much more explicitly than the biblical lamentation psalms do.[123] However, the priestly component of the salvation oracle remains no less vague than in Begrich's argumentation. In Esarhaddon's inscription, the *šīr takilti* probably comes from a diviner; whether the *bārû* should be called "priest" is a matter of definition. In the Zakkur inscription, as well as in SAA 9 1.8, the oracle is clearly prophetic. Who, then, is imagined to mediate the divine responses in the Dialogue of Ashurbanipal and Nabû? First, one should remember that the text is a poetic construction and need not to be understood as an exact report of any actual "dialogue between the king and the god." However, it is probable that Ashurbanipal, in his distress during the Šamaš-šumu-ukin war, prayed to the goddess in her temple more than once, and was certainly also provided with divine words in response. The dialogue SAA 3 13 may constitute a poetic compilation reflecting such situations, and it is evident that the language used by the scribe is essentially the same that the same scribe used for prophetic words in SAA 9 9.[124]

5. In several cases the exhortation not to fear is accompanied with the reconciliation of Assyria and its king with gods — an idea unseparable from the special relationship of the king with Ištar/Mullissu. In the case of SAA 9 2.5, the reconciliation of the exiled gods of Babylon, much propagated by the prophets,[125] is presented as an analogy to, if not the prerequisite of, the stabilization of Assyria and Esarhaddon's rule:

121. See Parpola, *Assyrian Prophecies*, lxxi.

122. SAA 3 13:24, 26; cf. the appearance of the dream goddess in *Ludlul bēl nēmeqi*.

123. Cf. Westermann, "Das Heilswort bei Deuterojesaja," 360-61, with a reference to SAA 3 13; and Zobel, "Das Gebet," 98, with regard to the Zakkur inscription.

124. See Beate Pongratz-Leisten, *Herrschaftswissen in Mesopotamien: Formen der Kommunikation zwischen Gott und König im 2. und 1. Jahrtausend v. Chr.* (SAAS 10; Helsinki: Neo-Assyrian Text Corpus Project, 1999), 75.

125. See Martti Nissinen, "City as Lofty as Heaven: Arbela and Other Cities in Neo-Assyrian Prophecy," in *"Every City Shall Be Forsaken": Urbanism and Prophecy in Ancient Is-*

*Aššūr-aḫu-iddina lā tapallaḫ/māt Aššūr utaqqan/ilāni zenûti [is]si māt Aššūr ušal[l]am*

Esarhaddon, fear not!/I will put Assyria in order,/I will reconcile the angry gods [wi]th Assyria.[126]

The divine speaker, even though not indicated, is doubtless Ištar, who enacts the reconciliation also in SAA 9 1.4, where the prophet(ess?) Bayâ acts as the mouthpiece of three different deities. In this oracle, which proclaims the legitimacy of the kingship of Esarhaddon from his very birth, Ištar assumes the role of the mediator between the king and the gods, all incorporated in Aššur.[127] By the same token, she assures Esarhaddon that she took him in her custody already when he was a child:

*anāku Issār ša Arbail Aššūr issīka ussallim/ṣeḫerāka attaṣakka/lā tapallaḫ na"idanni*

I am Ištar of Arbela. I have reconciled Aššur with you./I already carried you when you were a baby./Fear not, praise me![128]

Both aspects, the stabilization of the country and the reconciliation with gods, are combined in the letter of Aššur-hamatu'a, priest of the temple of Ištar in Arbela, to Ashurbanipal:

*[anāku] Bēl ētarba issi Mu[ll]issu assilim/Aššūr-bāni-apli šar māt Aššūr ša turabbīni [l]ā tapallaḫ/[anā]ku Bēl artēanki/Aššūr-bāni-apli ina māti ša kēnu/kēni šû adi mātīšu artēanki*

[I] am Bel, I have entered and reconciled with Mullissu./Ashurbanipal, king of Assyria, whom she raised: Fear not!/I am Bel, I have had mercy on you [fem.]./Ashurbanipal is in a country that remains loyal. I have had mercy on you, together with his country.[129]

---

*rael and the Near East* (ed. Lester L. Grabbe and Robert D. Haak; JSOTSup 330; Sheffield: Sheffield Academic Press, 2001), 170-207, esp. 193-200.

126. SAA 9 2.5 iii 19-20.

127. For Aššur as the totality of gods, see Simo Parpola, "Monotheism in Ancient Assyria," in *One God or Many? Concepts of Divinity in the Ancient World* (ed. Barbara Nevling Porter; Transactions of the Casco Bay Assyriological Institute 1; Casco Bay, Maine: Casco Bay Assyriological Institute, 2000), 165-209, esp. 168-73.

128. SAA 9 1.4 ii 30-33.

129. SAA 13 139:1-9.

The letter rather atypically begins with an oracle, this time presented as the word of Bel, or Marduk, the supreme god of Babylonia who in this letter seems to take the position Aššur has in the previously quoted oracle; this may indicate that the country that "remains loyal" to Ashurbanipal is Babylonia. The role division between Bel, Mullissu, and Ashurbanipal calls for attention. The triangle Bel-Mullissu-Ashurbanipal fully corresponds here to Aššur-Ištar-Esarhaddon in SAA 9 1.4. Bel, presumably presented as the head of the divine council, is speaking to the king and to the goddess simultaneously. "Fear not" is addressed to the king; however, Bel reconciles with the goddess and has mercy on her, who stands there on behalf of the king and country. Hence the words *lā tapallaḥ* come to the king through the mediation of the goddess who "raised" him. The same idea can be found in the prophecy SAA 9 9 (where *lā tapallaḥ* is not attested), as well as in the Dialogue of Ashurbanipal and Nabû (SAA 3 13), in which the phrase "fear not" is used in the context of Ashurbanipal's struggle before the divine council, and followed by the idea of him as the child of Mullissu (queen of Nineveh).[130]

The special relationship of the king with the goddess finds multiple expressions in prophecies, and even the phrase "fear not" is repeatedly embedded in this context, as the following two examples demonstrate:

> *ša Mullissu ummašūni lā tapallaḥ*
> *ša Bēlet Arbail tārīssūni lā tapallaḥ . . .*
> *atta lā tapallaḥ mūrī ša anāku urabbûni*

> You whose mother is Mullissu, fear not!
> You whose nurse is the Lady of Arbela, fear not! . . .
> Fear not, you, my calf whom I rear.[131]

> *anāku abūka ummaka/birti agappīya urtabbīka nēmalka ammar/lā tapallaḥ*
> *Aššūr-aḫu-iddina/birti iziriya ammāteya ašakkanka/ina libbi ū'a nakarūti ša*
> *šarrīya aka[šša]d/māt Aššūr utaqqan šarr[ūtu ša] šamê utaqqa[n . . .]*

> I am your father and mother./I brought you up between my wings, I will see how you prosper./Fear not, Esarhaddon!/I will place you between my arm and forearm./In the midst of distress, I will va[nqu]ish the enemies of my

---

130. See, respectively, SAA 3 13:24-26 (see the quotation above); SAA 3 13 r. 6-7: *ṣeḥru atta Aššūr-bāni-apli ša umašširūka ina muḫḫi šarrat Nīnua/lakû atta ša ašbāka ina burki šarrat Nīnua*, "You were a child, Ashurbanipal, when I left you with the queen of Nineveh,/you were a baby, Ashurbanipal, when you sat in the lap of the queen of Nineveh."

131. SAA 7 r. 6, 11 and SAA 9 2.5 iii 29-34.

king./I will put Assyria in order, I will put the king[dom of] heaven in orde[r . . .]

The position of Ištar/Mullissu as the one who puts both Assyria and the kingdom of heaven in order conflates with her role as the mother of the king and intercessor before the divine council. Moreover, the role of Mullissu as the spouse of Ashur makes her the principal intercessor on behalf of the king and humankind.[132] Her "fear not" to the king is based on the conviction that the divine council will decide in his favor. On the other hand, the position of the king as the child of the goddess makes him a partly divine figure, through whom the people participate in divine favors.[133] Hence, when the king himself says "fear not" to his subjects or vassals, as Ashurbanipal does in the above-discussed letters, he does so with divine authority, passing down the very word spoken to himself by the gods.

6. The last example of the use of "fear not" as an element of prophetic language is the Late Babylonian ritual text from Hellenistic Uruk.[134] The text is a compilation of hymns, prayers, and ritual acts to be performed before Bel (Marduk) by *šešgallu*, the high priest of Uruk, on the occasion of the New Year Festival from the 2d through the 5th of the month of Nisan (I). At a certain point of the ritual, the king enters the presence of Bel and, stripped of his royal insignia by the high priest, affirms his faithfulness in performing his duties.[135] The divine response follows after a lacuna of a few lines:

> *lā tapallaḫ [. . .] ša Bēl iqtabi [. . .] Bēl ikribka [ilteme . . .] ušarbi bēlūtka [. . .] ušaqqa šarrūtka [. . .]/ina ūm eššēši epu[š . . .] ina pīt bābi ubbib qāt[ka . . .] urri u mūši lū [. . .]/ša Bābili ālšu [. . .] ša Esaggil bīss[u . . .] ša mārē Bābili ṣāb kidin[nīšu . . .]/Bēl ikarrabku [. . . an]a dāri[š] uḫallaq nakarku ušamqat zāmānku/enūma iqbû šarru kabāt appi ginûšu i[ppuš]/ḫaṭṭa kippata miṭṭa agâ ušeṣṣima ana šarri [inamdin]/lēt šarri imaḫḫaṣ*

---

132. This was a central idea in rituals of divine love, in this case in the love ritual (*quršu*) of Mullissu; see Martti Nissinen, "Akkadian Rituals and Poetry of Divine Love," in *Mythology and Mythologies* (ed. R. M. Whiting; Melammu Symposia 2; Helsinki: Neo-Assyrian Text Corpus Project, 2001), 93-136, esp. 95-97.

133. See Parpola, *Assyrian Prophecies*, xxxvi-xlvi; idem, "Monotheism," 192-95.

134. F. Thureau-Dangin, *Rituels accadiens* (Paris: Ernest Leroux, 1921), 129-46; cf. Harner, "Salvation Oracle," 421; van der Toorn, "L'Oracle," 93; idem, "Mesopotamian Prophecy Between Immanence and Transcendence: A Comparison of Old Babylonian and Neo-Assyrian Prophecy," in *Prophecy in Its Ancient Near Eastern Context: Mesopotamian, Biblical, and Arabian Perspectives* (ed. Martti Nissinen; SBLSymS 13; Atlanta: SBL, 2000), 71-87, esp. 77.

135. Thureau-Dangin, *Rituels accadiens*, 144, ll. 415-27.

*enūma lēssu [imḫaṣ]/šumma dimātūšu illik Bēl sal[im]/šumma dimātūšu lā
illakā Bēl ezzi[z] nakru itebbamma išakkan miqissu*

"Fear not! [. . .] of Bel has said [. . .] Bel [has heard] your prayer [. . .] He
has enlarged your rule [. . .] He will exalt your kingship [. . .]!/On the day of
the *eššēšu* festival, do [. . .]! Upon the opening of the gate, purify [your]
hands [. . .]! May [. . .] day and night! [You], whose city Babylon is, [. . .],
whose temple Esaggil is, [. . .], whose [. . .] the people of Babylon, the privi-
leged citizens are: Bel will bless you [. . . fo]r eve[r]! He will destroy your
enemy, he will annihilate your adversary!"/When he [the high priest] has
spoken this, the king p[erforms] his regular offering in a dignified manner./
He (the high priest) takes the scepter, the ring, the divine weapon, and the
crown and [gives] them to the king./He slaps the face of the king./If, when
he [slaps] his face, his (the king's) tears flow, Bel is favor[able]; if his tears
do not flow, Bel is angr[y], and an enemy will rise and cause his downfall.[136]

Although the oracle resembles the extant prophetic oracles known to us, it is
not spoken by a prophet but by the high priest, the central figure of the ritual
who here assumes a divinatory role. The oracle is not an independent, much
less a spontaneous uttering, but an integral part of liturgy, which goes on with
offerings of the king, to whom his royal insignia are returned, and with an act
of divination, which is a kind of final test of Bel's acceptance of his rule. The
oracle provides itself as an example of a reuse of prophecy[137] in a liturgy, in
which the ideological heritage of Mesopotamian kingship is carried on under
the rule of Seleucid kings.[138] The function of "fear not" remains unaltered: it
begins an oracle of salvation, compressing its contents in a nutshell. In this
case the oracle is indeed spoken by a priest, but clearly designed after a prophetic model.

### "Fear Not" in the Hebrew Bible: Reinterpretation of the Royal Ideology

In Assyrian prophecy, as we have seen, "fear not" is more than an encouraging
or soothing formula; it is a signifier of the position of the king as the point of

---

136. Ibid., 144-45, ll. 434-52.

137. It is called "frozen" prophecy by van der Toorn, "Mesopotamian Prophecy," 77.

138. One is tempted to ask whether the Seleucid kings actually attended the New Year
rituals at Uruk at all, and if not, who represented them.

convergence between heaven and earth. As such, this formula belongs firmly to the language of the Assyrian royal ideology as a sign of the divine acceptance of the king's rule. The inventory of the phrase "fear not" shows that, whenever part of the divine discourse, it is seldom uttered to anyone else than to kings and other royal figures in Mesopotamia. This holds good even for the few non-Mesopotamian documents, the letter of Šuppiluliuma and the inscription of Zakkur.

In Second Isaiah Israel or Jacob typically appears as the addressee of prophecies very similar to those spoken to kings of Assyria, which, as demonstrated by Weippert, present a reinterpretation of the traditional ancient Near Eastern royal oracle.[139] This makes it worthwhile to ask whether the royal focus of the ancient Near Eastern use of the phrase "fear not" could be compared to the state of affairs elsewhere in the Hebrew Bible. The private discourse notwithstanding, the phrase occurs either (1) in direct divine speech, (2) in divine words transmitted by an intermediary, or (3) in the mouth of an authority who speaks to the people as a collective.

1. When God says "fear not" directly to a person, the addressee is sometimes a prophet like Jeremiah (Jer 1:8), Ezekiel (Ezek 2:6, 3:9), or Daniel (Dan 10:12, 19), who is encouraged not to be anxious before the opponents of the divine word he is commissioned to speak.[140] Otherwise this happens either to patriarchal figures in the narratives of Genesis (Abraham: Gen 15:1; Hagar: 21:17; Isaac: 26:24; Jacob: 46:3), or to Moses (Num 21:34; Deut 3:2) and Joshua (Josh 8:1; 10:8; 11:6) in Deuteronomistic texts. In both cases, as Edgar W. Conrad has shown, the divine words bear close resemblance with regard to both form and content to the "fear not" oracles in Second Isaiah.[141] However, Second Isaiah hardly combines two existing genres employing the "fear not" formula as Conrad argues; it is more likely that both the patriarchal oracles and the war oracles, like Second Isaiah, owe their use to the ancient Near Eastern royal pattern, here applied to patriarchs as corporate personalities or to divinely authorized leaders like Moses and Joshua.

2. In several cases "fear not" is part of a divine word transmitted by an intermediary, sometimes an angel but mostly a prophet; this is in line with

---

139. Weippert, "Assyrische Prophetien," 108-11; idem, "De herkomst," passim; idem, "Ich bin Jahwe," 49-51. See Isa 41:10, 13, 14; 43:1, 5; 44:2; cf. Jer 30:10; 46:27-28, the close affiliation to Second Isaiah of which has been noticed (see William McKane, *A Critical and Exegetical Commentary on Jeremiah*, vol. 2 [ICC; Edinburgh: T&T Clark, 1996], 762, 1137). In Isa 54:4 the addressee is Jerusalem; cf. Zeph 3:16.

140. This applies even to Elijah, to whom the divine word is spoken by an angel in 2 Kgs 1:15.

141. Conrad, "Fear Not," passim.

the assumption that the phrase is part and parcel of prophetic, rather than priestly, discourse. It is addressed either to the people (Isa 8:12; 10:24; Jer 42:11; Zech 8:13, 15; 2 Chr 20:15, 17)[142] or to its leaders (angel to Gideon: Judg 6:23; Isaiah to Ahaz: Isa 7:4; Isaiah to Hezekiah: 2 Kgs 19:6//Isa 37:6; Haggai to Zerubbabel: Hag 2:5). The only "ordinary" people to receive the divine "fear not" are the widow of Zarephath (1 Kgs 17:13) and the disciple of Elisha (2 Kgs 6:16); in both cases the word is spoken by prophetic figures, Elijah and Elisha, respectively.

3. In some cases leaders of people like Samuel (1 Sam 12:20), David (2 Sam 9:7; 1 Chr 22:13; 28:20), or Nehemiah (4:8 [Eng. 4:14]) say "fear not" to the people without explicitly presenting it as a divine word. Especially in the cases of Moses (Exod 14:13; 20:20; Deut 1:21, 29; 3:22; 7:18; 20:1; 31:6, 8) and Joshua (Num 14:9; Josh 10:25) it is evident, however, that they do it under divine authority, and the words they speak essentially correspond to oracles spoken directly by God or through intermediaries.[143] In the case of Moses, this is compatible with his role as a prophet and intermediator between God and the people.[144]

The short survey of the occurrences of "fear not" in the Hebrew Bible pays no attention to the relative chronology and the ideological affiliation of the texts, and hence is too brief to explain exhaustively the various aspects of this phrase in biblical environments. I hope, however, to have provided some support for the argument that 'al-tîrā' and lā tapallaḥ are historically, ideologically, and institutionally related, and the formulaic use of the phrase is essentially rooted in the institutions of kingship and prophecy.

## Conclusion

On the basis of the above analysis, I contend that "fear not" is a standard expression in the ancient Near East, with a clear emphasis on the Neo-Assyrian period and in an oracular, especially prophetic, context.

Like the prophetic Botenformel, "Thus says the Lord," which can be

---

142. Here the Levite Jahaziel assumes the role of a prophet.

143. In Deut 20:3 the delivering of the "fear not" oracle is interestingly delegated to a priest; the oracle itself, however, is a full-fledged representative of the "war oracle" to be found in the mouth of God or Moses elsewhere in Deuteronomy.

144. See Lothar Perlitt, "Mose als Prophet," EvT 31 (1971): 588-608 (repr. in idem, Deuteronomium-Studien [FAT 8; Tübingen: Mohr Siebeck, 1994], 1-19); Timo Veijola, Moses Erben: Studien zum Dekalog, zum Deuteronomismus und zum Schriftgelehrtentum (BWANT 149; Stuttgart: Kohlhammer, 2000), 216-18.

traced to a profane communication situation, the phrase "fear not" can be found in human and in divine speech alike in the ancient Near Eastern sources. In private discourse, which probably constitutes the primary context of its use, it cannot be called a formula with a clearly definable *Sitz im Leben*.

The institutionalized, formulaic use of "fear not" as an encouraging and soothing formula is clearly connected with divine speech, usually transmitted by prophets, predominantly to royal figures or leaders of the people. In Assyrian prophecy the formula signifies the position of the king between heaven and earth: even in the mouth of the king, "fear not" is uttered by the supreme authority whose word is regarded equal to the divine word from the point of view of the addressee. In the Hebrew Bible, too, the use of "fear not" has a clear emphasis on the leaders of the people (patriarchs, Moses, Joshua, kings, etc.), or on the people as a collective, which is typical to the reinterpretation of the royal ideology in Second Isaiah. Both ancient Near Eastern and biblical sources hence point to the origin of the "fear not" formula in the institutions of kingship and prophecy.

The phrase "fear not" can be spoken in response to a prayer, but there are only a few ambiguous signs of priestly use of the phrase; hence Begrich's theory of the priestly oracle finds little support in the ancient Near Eastern sources, and also the allegedly indigenous origin of the biblical "fear not" oracles becomes improbable. On the other hand, and in support of the previous work of Gressmann and his followers, the ancient Near Eastern, especially prophetic, background of "fear not" is amply demonstrated.

# Ezekiel Saw What He Said He Saw:
# Genres, Forms, and the Vision of Ezekiel 1

## MARGARET S. ODELL

Elsewhere I have argued that the book of Ezekiel achieved its coherence as the result of a sophisticated appropriation of the three-part Assyrian building inscription genre. That argument rested on the following observations: (1) Compelling explanations for the coherence of Ezekiel are lacking in the biblical tradition; (2) Ezekiel's familiarity with the conventions of Neo-Assyrian statecraft, iconography, and literary traditions makes it plausible to suggest that he was also acquainted with the building inscription genre; and (3) not only does the book of Ezekiel roughly resemble the genre in its general outline, in a number of details it also resembles one particular set of exemplars, Esarhaddon's inscriptions on the rebuilding of Babylon.[1]

One problem for my thesis is that the stylistic features of Ezekiel 1 do not conform to the generic features of the royal self-introduction of building inscriptions. The building inscription genre involves a first-person recounting of epithets by which the king extols his power and majesty. By contrast, Ezekiel 1 is Ezekiel's account of what *he* sees, not God's own narrative self-disclosure. This fundamental difference would therefore seem to invalidate my argument.

The difficulty can be resolved by redefining the nature of genre so that it allows for a greater range of comparisons between the Assyrian inscriptional context and the book of Ezekiel. I will, accordingly, follow the lead of several literary critics who have proposed a definition of genre that depends on the identification of "family resemblances," or a clustering of traits between and

---

1. Margaret S. Odell, "Genre and Persona in Ezekiel 24:15-24," in *The Book of Ezekiel: Theological and Anthropological Perspectives* (ed. Margaret S. Odell and John T. Strong; SBLSymS 9; Atlanta: SBL, 2000), 195-219.

among different literary texts. The elucidation of the genre of Ezekiel 1 according to these traits depends on a close reading of the entire unit, as opposed to the detection of an underlying structure, or form, that is typical of form criticism. When all of the elements of Ezekiel 1 are so examined, it becomes possible to read Ezekiel 1 in light of the architectural context of the Assyrian royal inscriptions. Against the usual form-critical assumption that Ezekiel 1 authorizes Ezekiel's call, I argue that Ezekiel 1 is more properly understood as the initial programmatic statement of the book's theme of Yahweh's campaign to bring the rebellious house of Israel once again under his rule.

## Form Criticism and Ezekiel 1

One of the difficulties in appropriating form criticism in the analysis of Ezekiel is that the method is primarily concerned with identifying oral forms that serve a particular function in living sociopolitical situations. The method privileges pattern over detail and consequently devotes little attention to a text's unique features. In addition, because the method assumes that such forms have been generated by a societal setting, literary texts can be forced into hypothetical contexts that may or may not have been part of the text's prehistory or, for that matter, necessary or relevant for its interpretation in its current literary context.

The effect of this method is evident in the form-critical treatment of Ezekiel's vision in chap. 1. Thanks to Walther Zimmerli's study of call narratives in his commentary on Ezekiel 1–3, this chapter is by common consensus regarded as an integral element of Ezekiel's call.[2] According to Zimmerli's reconstruction, the pattern of this type of call combines a throne vision and a

---

2. Walther Zimmerli, *Ezekiel 1: A Commentary on the Book of the Prophet Ezekiel, Chapters 1–24* (trans. Ronald E. Clements; Hermeneia; Philadelphia: Fortress, 1979), 95-100. See also, e.g., Leslie Allen, *Ezekiel 1–19* (WBC 28; Dallas: Word, 1994), 14; Daniel I. Block, *The Book of Ezekiel, Chapters 1–24* (NICOT; Grand Rapids: Eerdmans, 1997), 78-79, 111; Joseph Blenkinsopp, *Ezekiel* (IBC; Louisville: John Knox, 1990), 23; Ronald E. Clements, *Ezekiel* (Westminster Bible Companion; Louisville: Westminster John Knox, 1996), 8-10; Keith Carley, *The Book of the Prophet Ezekiel* (CBC; Cambridge: Cambridge Univ. Press, 1974), 9; H. F. Fuhs, *Ezechiel 1–24* (NEchtB; Würzburg: Echter, 1986), 19; Moshe Greenberg, *Ezekiel 1–20* (AB 22; Garden City, N.Y.: Doubleday, 1983), 80; Ronald Hals, *Ezekiel* (FOTL 19; Grand Rapids: Eerdmans, 1989), 15; Bruce Vawter and Leslie J. Hoppe, *A New Heart: A Commentary on the Book of Ezekiel* (ITC; Grand Rapids: Eerdmans, 1991), 23-24; John W. Wevers, *Ezekiel* (NCB; repr. Grand Rapids: Eerdmans, 1982), 12-13, esp. 40.

commissioning ceremony. As evidence for this pattern, Zimmerli cited 1 Kgs 22:19-23, Micaiah's account of Yahweh's deliberations with the host of heaven to bring about the death of Ahab, and Isa 6:1-13, Isaiah's temple vision in the year that King Uzziah died. Detecting this pattern also in Ezek 1:4–3:15, Zimmerli believed that he had established an inherent connection between the vision in Ezekiel 1 and the subsequent call material.

One notes, however, that only the last three verses of Ezekiel 1, the climactic description of the "appearance of the likeness of the glory of God," are essential to this structure. Other key features of the vision — its unique language, its extensive description of the living beings, wheels, and so on — fall outside Zimmerli's discussion of form. They do not fall outside his interpretation; but rather than treating them as elements of the genre, Zimmerli regarded these specific features as evidence of the uniqueness of Ezekiel's visionary experience.

Despite this apparent inattention to the literary features of the text, at least in the identification of genre, a literary question had prompted Zimmerli's analysis. In the first half of the twentieth century, critical studies of the book had employed literary criticism in order to retrieve the genuine prophetic words of the prophet Ezekiel from his book. Ezekiel 1 had not fared well; Volkmar Herntrich had excised the vision as nonprophetic; and even those who claimed that the vision was authentic to Ezekiel thought it came from a period later in his ministry.[3]

Responding to this state of affairs, Zimmerli asked whether it was possible to show that the vision of 1:1-28 was integrally connected to the succeeding call material of 2:1–3:15. Although he acknowledged that the vision differed significantly from the call material, he sought to demonstrate that 1:1–3:15 was a coherent call account. He employed form criticism to do that: "Is such a connection between the account of the commissioning of a prophet in the strict sense and an elaborate vision of God to be found elsewhere? Can we in general discover anything about *customs of style* and *given traditions* in the presentation of the prophetic experiences of being commissioned?" (emphasis added).[4] Identifying the structure as a "type of commissioning narrative,"[5] Zimmerli was then able to posit that the coherence of 1:1–3:15 was due to the skeletal framework provided by this narrative type.

Zimmerli had used form criticism not only to solve a literary problem

3. Volkmar Herntrich, *Ezechielprobleme* (BZAW 61; Giessen: Töpelmann, 1933), 75-79; Zimmerli, *Ezekiel 1*, 95-97.

4. Zimmerli, *Ezekiel 1*, 97.

5. Ibid., 99.

but also to claim yet more of the book as a record of authentic prophetic experience. It is worth noting that his interpretation was motivated primarily by a desire to rehabilitate both the prophet and his book. In order to do that, he assumed that he needed to demonstrate that Ezekiel 1 was rooted in prophetic traditions.[6]

## Oral Form or Literary Genre?

Even though Zimmerli employed form criticism to solve a problem in the written form of Ezekiel 1–3, it has for a long time been recognized that there are methodological problems in the application of form criticism to written materials.[7] Especially in the case of Ezekiel, which is increasingly being treated as a written text as opposed to a repository of originally oral materials,[8] the usefulness of identifying an earlier oral form behind the written text seems open to question.

As Zimmerli practiced it, form criticism does not adequately identify literary genres. Stan Rummel has criticized the method for its tendency to reduce text to an "ideal type." By "imposing patterns through partial association,"[9] he noted, form critics ran the risk of misinterpreting texts. With respect to Zimmerli's identification of an underlying pattern in Isaiah 6, 1 Kgs 22:19-23, and Ezek 1:1–3:15, one notes several difficulties. First, neither Isaiah 6 nor 1 Kgs 22:19-23 is necessarily or only to be regarded as a call.[10] Zimmerli had acknowledged that fact in the case of 1 Kings 22; and his identification of the genre avoided the designation of call. But there are other difficulties. All

6. It is worth noting that Zimmerli's analysis has its own historical context: he was employing what was then the reigning method to address a problem that had been created by a mode of criticism that had by then become passé. This has not been acknowledged in subsequent citations of his study of the call narrative; as a consequence scholars tend to treat Zimmerli's findings positivistically as assured facts. See Burke O. Long, "Prophetic Call Traditions and Reports of Visions," *ZAW* 84 (1972): 494-500; idem, "Reports of Visions Among the Prophets," *JBL* 95 (1976): 353-65; Marvin A. Sweeney, *Isaiah 1–39; with an Introduction to Prophetic Literature* (FOTL 16; Grand Rapids: Eerdmans, 1996), 19-20.

7. See esp. Rolf Knierim, "Old Testament Form Criticism Reconsidered," *Int* 27 (1973): 435-68.

8. Ellen F. Davis, *Swallowing the Scroll: Textuality and the Dynamics of Discourse in Ezekiel's Prophecy* (BLS 21; JSOTSup 78; Sheffield: Almond Press, 1989); Thomas Renz, *The Rhetorical Function of the Book of Ezekiel* (VTSup 76; Leiden: Brill, 1999).

9. Stan Rummel, "Narrative Structures in Ugaritic Texts," *RSP* 3:226.

10. For 1 Kgs 22:19-23 see Zimmerli's qualifications, *Ezekiel 1*, 98. For the problems in designating Isa 6 as a call narrative, see Sweeney, *Isaiah 1–39*, 135-36.

three texts differ significantly from one another and, moreover, serve entirely different functions within their respective literary contexts. For example, both Isaiah 6 and 1 Kgs 22:19-23 revolve around the disclosure of a divine secret, both involving the mysterious ways that prophecy accomplishes divine ends. Even though Zimmerli discusses the presence of the motif in these accounts, he does not factor it in to his identification of the genre. One suspects that doing so would have diminished the points of comparison that he sought to establish with Ezekiel 1.

By the same token, one can ask whether Zimmerli's "type of commissioning account" adequately explains the features of Ezekiel 1. The phrase מַרְאוֹת אֱלֹהִים (NRSV "visions of God") is itself an unusual term as an introduction to a prophetic vision, for which nouns derived from the verb root חזה are more typical.[11] Even Ezekiel uses חָזוֹן when he speaks of prophetic revelations;[12] and with one exception, which will be discussed below, he uses מַרְאוֹת/מַרְאֶה only in the visions of chaps. 1, 8–11, and 40–43. The terminology alone suggests that Ezekiel 1 is something other than a prophetic vision.

More importantly, the details of the theophany in Ezekiel 1 are unlike anything found in prophetic literature. Isaiah sees Yahweh Sabaoth in the temple, but Ezekiel sees into the opened heavens.[13] Isaiah sees seraphim surrounding the Holy One, but Ezekiel sees living beings *below* the firmament; their closest parallels are found in contemporaneous Mesopotamian iconography.[14] Although these features may be crucial to understanding the genres of the respective texts, form criticism as it has traditionally been employed treats them as irrelevant. Whether the vision is called a חָזוֹן or a מַרְאֶה, or whether it incorporates details from Assyrian iconography or not, appears to be beside the point. What matters to form critics is the pattern. Since, in prophetic literature, theophanies introduce either call narratives (as in the case of

11. In prophetic superscriptions, see Isa 1:1; Obad 1; Nah 1:1; cf. an analogous use of the verb חזה in superscriptions in Amos 1:1; Mic 1:1; Hab 1:1. Elsewhere in the prophetic literature see Mic 3:6-7; Jer 14:14; 23:16; Hos 12:11. For a discussion of this term, see A. Jepsen, "חָזָה, *chāzāh*," *TDOT* 4:280-90. See also Long, "Prophetic Call Traditions," whose list of terminology for prophetic visions does not include מַרְאֶה.

12. Ezekiel 12 provides evidence for Ezekiel's use of the noun חָזוֹן to refer to prophetic visions (12:22, 23, 24, 27; cf. 7:26). In addition, 7:13 self-referentially speaks of the oracle of chap. 7 as חָזוֹן, while the references in chap. 13 refer to false visions (13:6, 7, 8, 9, 16, 23; cf. 21:34 [Eng. 29]; 22:28).

13. The commentators have noted this unique occurrence in Ezekiel; see Zimmerli, *Ezekiel 1*, 116-17; Block, *Ezekiel 1–24*, 85; Greenberg, *Ezekiel*, 41; Allen, *Ezekiel 1–19*, 22.

14. O. Keel, *Jahwe-Visionen und Siegelkunst: Eine neue Deutung der Majestätsschilderungen in Jes 6, Ez 1 und 10 und Sach 4* (SBS 84/85; Stuttgart: Katholisches Bibelwerk, 1977), 125-273.

Isa 6) or proclamations of judgment,[15] that must be what Ezekiel's theophany is doing in chap. 1.

Taking up Rummel's critique, I propose that we base our identification of the genre of Ezekiel 1 on all of its literary features, and not just on those elements that it shares with other call narratives. My suggestion differs from James Muilenburg's proposal to use rhetorical criticism as a complement to form criticism. Inherent in his proposal was the idea that the rhetorical features represented an aesthetic development of a form or genre that could still be identified through the use of form criticism.[16] Instead, I propose that the distinctive literary features in Ezekiel 1 *are* generic, and that their identification as such is crucial to understanding the purpose of the chapter.

My proposal takes its cue from Alastair Fowler's discussion of the nature of genres.[17] He challenges the notion that genres represent fixed classes of literature and proposes instead that they be thought of as types evidencing a clustering of traits. He invokes Wittgenstein's notion of family resemblances[18] to describe the manner in which such traits reveal a text's genre: "Representations of a genre may then be regarded as making up a family whose septs and individual members are related in various ways, without necessarily having any single feature shared in common by all."[19] According to this theory of

15. For the former see Zimmerli, *Ezekiel 1,* 95-11; Greenberg, *Ezekiel,* 80-81; for the latter, Allen, *Ezekiel 1–19,* 41.

16. James Muilenburg, "Form Criticism and Beyond," *JBL* 88 (1969): 1-18.

17. Alastair Fowler, *Kinds of Literature: An Introduction to the Theory of Genres and Modes* (Cambridge: Harvard Univ. Press, 1982), 37-53.

18. "We see a complicated network of similarities overlapping and criss-crossing: sometimes overall similarities, sometimes similarities of detail" (Ludwig Wittgenstein, *Philosophical Investigations* [trans. G. E. M. Anscombe; Oxford: Blackwell, 1953], 1:66-67).

19. Fowler, *Kinds of Literature,* 41. To illustrate how the identification of a genre by way of a clustering of traits might work, let me use an example from my family. My middle brother, with his bald blondness, blue eyes, large nose, and tall ranginess, looks nothing like the rest of us brown-haired, hazel-eyed, nasally compact, and short-statured Odells. With apologies to my mother and Bayville Farms, he could claim paternity from the milkman. But when my brother attends an Odell funeral, the clustering of resemblances among cousins and uncles definitively establishes the genetic source of my brother's nose; and when we are among four generations of my maternal grandmother's family, he fits right in among the lanky great-uncles and second cousins — in fact, he looks more like them than we do. As a description of family resemblances, my example underscores not only the flexibility of this conception of genre, but also the relationship of a text's particularity to its generic context. Of course, the Odells have no doubt that my brother is a member of the family; but if there were any question, it is the entire clustering of his physical traits, not any single one, that reveals his genetic identity. Furthermore, it is when these traits are set against an *extended* familial context that the resemblances become identifiable. So also in a literary text: not only

genre, a single text may have some but not all of the identifying traits; and in a collection of texts associated with a particular genre, there may be overlapping traits but also some significantly distinct elements. Situating a text within a particular genre requires the identification of traits that bring it into association with these other texts. Fowler lists such elements as scale (e.g., a sonnet cannot be the length of the *Oxford English Dictionary*), subject, values, mood, occasion, attitude, mise en scène, character, style, and task.[20]

In "Old Testament Form Criticism Reconsidered," Rolf Knierim anticipated Fowler in two key areas. Proposing that form criticism keep its categories of genre and setting as heuristic models, Knierim suggested that the question of genre should involve the analysis of a range of typicalities in the text, as well as the determination of which typicalities govern a text.[21] If these questions were asked of Ezekiel 1, the resemblance between Ezekiel's vision and Isaiah 6 and 1 Kgs 22:19-23 may remain relevant but would be considered only one of a number of significant typicalities and possibly not the governing one. Other features of the text, such as its unique terminology, may be more important.

Second, Knierim proposed replacing the conception of "setting" with "matrix." The latter term allowed for a more flexible and, in his view, more accurate way of defining a text's relation to its historical context: "If . . . setting means basically the matrix which produces the structural models, we can ask whether this matrix could not be something other than a setting in the traditional form-critical . . . sense."[22] Under the influence of structuralism, Knierim went on to propose that such matrices may be understood as the "basic structure of an existential human situation" — that is, processes that are primarily located in the human mind, as opposed to social institutions. One infers from his discussion that the spiritual, intellectual, and political influences of the age can be regarded as the manifestations of those processes.

## The Generic Elements of Ezekiel 1

In light of the above discussion, the first step toward the identification of the genre of Ezekiel 1 is a close reading of its particular features in order to estab-

---

do all of the traits of a text contribute to its genre, one must also often seek resemblances beyond the text's nuclear family, so to speak, and pay attention to the entire network of clustering traits and contexts.

20. Ibid., 61.

21. Knierim, "Reconsidered," 451-56, esp. 456.

22. Ibid., 446.

lish its typicalities. For Ezekiel 1, the most prominent recurring feature is the use of two words, מראה, "appearance," and דמות, "likeness."[23] Ezekiel introduces the vision as מראות אלהים and then methodically proceeds to describe what he saw. A storm theophany opens to reveal forms (דמות) that have certain appearances (מראה). These terms yield two important insights into Ezekiel's account of his vision.

First, Ezekiel has a decided preference for the masculine term מַרְאֶה, "appearance," as opposed to the feminine term מַרְאָה, "vision." This has not always been taken into account, perhaps because of the form-critical interest in classifying Ezekiel 1 as a vision. It is worth noting, however, that even though the plural מראות in 1:1 suggests that Ezekiel is using the feminine term, intratextual references back to 1:1 always use the masculine singular term, מַרְאֶה (8:4; 43:3). It is possible, then, that מראות is the plural of the masculine מַרְאֶה.

The difference between the masculine and feminine terms is illustrated by their juxtaposition in Num 12:6-8:

> If any one among you is a prophet,
>> I make myself known to him in a vision (מַרְאָה)
>> by means of dreams I speak to him.
> Not so with my servant Moses . . .
>> face to face I speak with him,
>>> in plain sight (מַרְאֶה) and not in riddles. (Num 12:6-8)

The feminine מַרְאָה is associated with prophets and dream revelations; this is consistent with its admittedly rare usage elsewhere (Gen 46:2; 1 Sam 3:15; Dan 10:7-8, 16).[24] By contrast, the masculine מַרְאֶה is associated with face-to-face encounters that do not have the dreamlike ambiguity of prophetic revelation. John Kutsko has argued that the term is often used in the description of "quite concrete objects."[25] The difference between the two terms is crucial. While the feminine term is associated with prophetic revelations and dreams, the masculine מַרְאֶה signifies something else entirely. It is not that the one is invalid and the other true; rather, what is at stake is the directness of the en-

---

23. מַרְאֶה: Ezek 1:5, 13 (twice), 14, 16 (twice), 26 (twice) 27 (twice), 28 (three times); דמות: 1:5 (twice); 10, 13, 16, 22, 26 (three times), 28.

24. The only other biblical occurrence of מַרְאָה, in Exod 38:8, has the connotation "mirror" (cf. 1QM 5:5).

25. John F. Kutsko, *Between Heaven and Earth: Divine Presence and Absence in the Book of Ezekiel* (Biblical and Judaic Studies from Univ. of California, San Diego, 7; Winona Lake, Ind.: Eisenbrauns, 2000), 67.

counter. The preference for the term מַרְאֶה throughout Ezekiel 1 suggests that the account describes a direct encounter that differs distinctly from a prophetic visionary experience.

Even though these terms are a recurring feature of Ezekiel's vision, they have not been treated as a "typicality," that is, as a clue to habits of speech or thought that may be fruitfully explored within a particular setting or matrix. The terms have instead been treated as evidence of Ezekiel's mental state. As such, they indicate Ezekiel's restraint in introducing analogies to describe the indescribable.[26] Greenberg's comment is typical: "The use of $k^emar'e$ (and of $k^e$'en and $d^emut$ also) signifies an unwillingness to commit oneself to the substantial identity of the seen with the compared. It looked like torches, sapphire, and a human being, but that is not to say that torches, sapphire, and a human being were actually there."[27] In Greenberg's view, then, these terms function analogously, with little difference in meaning.

But the words מַרְאֶה and דמות are complementary terms, not synonyms. The latter term denotes an object's form or representation (see 2 Kgs 16:10),[28] while the former signifies what that form looked like. As Ezekiel describes each successive part of his vision, this distinction between form and appearance is sustained (see also 8:2-3). The one exception may be Ezekiel's description of the wheelwork, which Ezekiel introduces without reference to its form. The term דמות does eventually appear in his description of the wheelwork in v. 16, where it denotes a pattern to which all the wheels conform. But even this latter usage reflects a concrete meaning, since a pattern would be a drawing or representation of an object (see 2 Kgs 16:10). In any case it is important to note that each דמות, or likeness, has a מַרְאֶה, or appearance.

Ezekiel maintains this distinction between form and appearance elsewhere, in his description of Oholibah's lust for the Babylonians (23:14b-16). In that account the term דמות refers to a concrete depiction of the Chaldeans, which NRSV translates as a "picture." Since the term דמות is parallel with צלם, image, it signifies a sculptural representation; and Ezek 23:14b implies that the pictures were wall reliefs. The *appearance* of these images is further defined by the details of flowing turbans, brilliant colors, waist sashes, and the like: "she saw male figures carved on the wall; images of the Chaldeans (צלמי כשדיים) portrayed in vermilion, with belts around their waists, with

26. Allen, *Ezekiel 1–19*, 26.

27. Greenberg, *Ezekiel*, 53. Blenkinsopp calls it the "language of indirection and approximation" (*Ezekiel*, 21); Carley exquisitely describes the language as the evocation of the "eerie half-knowledge of a dream" (*Ezekiel*, 19). See also H. D. Preus, "דָּמָה *dāmāh*; דְמוּת *d^emûth*," *TDOT* 3:257-60.

28. Kutsko, *Between Heaven and Earth*, 66.

flowing turbans on their heads, all of them looking like officers (שָׁלִשִׁים כֻּלָּם
מַרְאֵה) — a picture (דְּמוּת) of Babylonians whose native land was Chaldea"
(23:14b-16). Ezekiel's use of these terms in this context suggests that the distinction between form and appearance was at home in discourse about representational art. Far from indicating restraint, the terms דְּמוּת and מַרְאֵה are
readily identifiable as discourse about concrete, aesthetic representations.

The literary context of 23:15-16 also sheds light on the larger cultural
and political context of such descriptions of visual art. The description of
these pictures of the Babylonians appears in an allegory of the infidelity of
the sisters Oholah and Oholibah. Although Oholah belongs to Yahweh, she
lusts after the Assyrians (23:5); accordingly, Yahweh resolves to give her over
to her lovers. Oholibah's behavior is even worse: Not only does she lust after
the Assyrians, she adulterates this adultery by falling in love with the
Chaldeans, about whom she learns by seeing these pictures on the walls. Once
these pictures trigger her lust, she defies her Assyrian lord and initiates her se-
duction of Babylon.

One wishes that the allegory contained a few more details: Where does
Oholibah see these representations? What is their intended function? Given
the allegory's focus on Oholibah's dangerous liaison with the Assyrians, one
may suggest that Oholibah has seen these representations while in the company of her lovers the Assyrians. The architectural context of such representations is the Assyrian royal palace, which combines royal inscriptions extolling
the pious valor of the king and sculptural reliefs depicting his mighty deeds in
behalf of the god Ashur.

In the palace inscriptions, a king introduces himself using a series of epithets that emphasize his royal characteristics. The inscriptions then recount
his rise to power and the execution of his responsibilities, particularly
through his military campaigns, and finally conclude with an account of the
building of his palace.[29] The inscriptions saturated the palace and communicated the royal ideology not just to those who could read Akkadian but to any
and all who entered the royal precincts.[30]

Sculptural reliefs on the palace walls also conveyed the royal ideology by
depicting episodes from the inscriptions.[31] If the writing was inaccessible to

29. Edward L. Greenstein, "Autobiographies in Ancient Western Asia," *CANE* 4:2421-32.

30. John Malcolm Russell, *The Writing on the Wall: Studies in the Architectural Context
of Late Assyrian Palace Inscriptions* (Mesopotamian Civilizations 9; Winona Lake, Ind.:
Eisenbrauns, 1999), 230.

31. For the connection between text and image, see Irene Winter, "Royal Rhetoric and
the Development of Historical Narrative in Neo-Assyrian Reliefs," *Studies in Visual Communication 7* (1981): 34n18.

diplomatic visitors and subject peoples, the reliefs were not. In fact, as Assyria extended the reach of its empire, the quantity of text to sculptural representation was reduced. By the time of Sennacherib, little more than captions were inscribed on the reliefs.[32]

The wall reliefs conveyed to vassals their place in the Assyrian cosmic and political order.[33] They could submit willingly and bring tribute, or they could rebel and face certain destruction, as the numerous battle scenes made clear. Ezek 23:14b-16 suggests that Ezekiel understood the rhetorical and ideological function of these pictures. Although the Assyrians had depicted the Chaldeans so as to magnify their own power as rulers over these magnificent peoples, Oholibah has flagrantly misread the writing on the wall, as it were, and sought to replace her lovers the Assyrians with these new objects of her desire.

One further element of palace decoration that contributes to the generic matrix of Ezekiel's vision is the ritualized portrait of the king. Two identical, highly stylized and symmetrical portraits were placed in two key focal points in the throne room, opposite the entrance and above the throne.[34] In the earlier throne rooms of Ashurnasirpal and Sargon, the portraits appear in orthostats positioned in these two focal areas. Although these areas are left blank in the palaces built after Sargon, Julian Reade suggests that for all the Neo-Assyrian palaces, "It is hard to avoid the suspicion that all . . . had similar ritual scenes: some carved in stone, others shaped or woven in some magnificent material supported on the main slabs behind."[35] In any case these two areas supplied the dominant portraits of the king. By depicting the king worshiping his god and surrounded by protective deities, the portraits become the lenses through which the narrative reliefs are to be viewed. It is through his piety and because of Ashur's support that the king is victorious over his enemies.[36]

Many of the unusual features of Ezekiel 1 suggest that Ezekiel is patterning his vision after this portrait of the Assyrian king. The aesthetic and sociopolitical contexts of מַרְאָה and דמות have already been discussed. Other features, which appear only in Ezekiel, seem to reflect the conventions of this

---

32. Russell, *Writing on the Wall,* 244-45.

33. Winter, "Royal Rhetoric," 3; Mario Liverani, "The Deeds of Ancient Mesopotamian Kings," *CANE* 4:2355.

34. Winter, "Royal Rhetoric," 10.

35. Julian Reade, "The Architectural Context of Assyrian Sculpture," *Baghdader Mitteilungen* 11 (1979): 81.

36. Winter, "Royal Rhetoric," 10-11. For a schematic drawing of throne room decoration, see pp. 4-5. See also Reade, "Architectural Context," 81.

broader ancient Near Eastern context. First, Ezekiel introduces his vision with a statement unique to prophetic literature: "the heavens were opened (פתח, niphal), and I saw divine sights."[37] The use of פתח (niphal) in this context may have been motivated by the idea of entrances into royal and divine residences (פֶּתַח). Zimmerli and Block have noted this peculiarity and have suggested that the vision affords the prophet a glimpse into the heavenly throne room.[38]

Second, the use of the term חשמל (NRSV "amber"), which occurs only in 1:4 and 27, indicates that Ezekiel's vision would remind readers of a particular type of sculptural representation, a divine image. As he describes the storm cloud that comes out of the north, Ezekiel employs several elements that are known from the biblical theophanic tradition. But he augments this traditional language with the use of this Akkadian loanword. The word appears again in Ezekiel's description of the appearance of the form that sits on the throne. Daniel Bodi has suggested that the term is equivalent to the Akkadian *elm šu*, which appears in some texts as a quasi-mythical stone and in others as material used to refurbish divine statues.[39] Along with typical terminology for representations (דמות), Ezekiel has here employed a term that would have been readily familiar to his readers as the material that would be used in the construction of a divine image. Taken together, this evidence suggests that Ezekiel is describing a heavenly representation of God.

In Ezekiel's tour of the temple in chap. 8, several intriguing correspondences to chap. 1 support the suggestion that Ezekiel is describing a representation of the divine glory, and not the glory itself. As in chap. 1, Ezekiel stands at an opening and looks north (8:5). From that vantage point, he sees yet another representation of a divine being, this time the Image of Jealousy. While it is not possible within the confines of this essay to explore the significance of this image, it is worth noting that Ezekiel's use of the rare term סמל, "image," is the only time that Ezekiel calls an idol what it is, a representation or a likeness of a divine being.[40] The visions of chaps. 1 and 8 are thus counterparts: the one presents a heavenly and therefore accurate representation of the glory of God, while the other presents a limited, hence perverted, representation that becomes the source of all the other abominations in the temple.

37. Zimmerli, *Ezekiel 1*, 116; Block, *Ezekiel 1–24*, 184n35; Allen, *Ezekiel 1–19*, 22; Greenberg, *Ezekiel*, 41.

38. Zimmerli, *Ezekiel 1*, 116; Block, *Ezekiel 1–24*, 184.

39. Daniel Bodi, *The Book of Ezekiel and the Poem of Erra* (OBO 104; Göttingen: Vandenhoeck & Ruprecht, 1991), 82-94.

40. Christoph Dohmen, "Heisst סמל 'Bild, Statue'?" *ZAW* 96 (1984): 263-66.

To summarize: In chap. 1 Ezekiel sees what he says he sees, a *depiction* of the glory of God.[41] To be sure, the representation has come to life: it is full of vitality and energy; and flames of fire flash between and among the living beings. Even so, Ezekiel does not see the glory of God directly. His use of the terms מַרְאָה and דְמוּת are not equivocations, an unwillingness to pin himself down, but a forthright attempt to describe this heavenly representation. That these terms do not indicate Ezekiel's restraint is corroborated by their absence in his other references to the glory of God. At these other points, Ezekiel speaks quite directly about his encounters with the divine glory (3:23; 8:2, 4; 9:3; 10:4, 18, 19; 11:22, 23; 43:2, 4, 5). What distinguishes Ezekiel 1 from these references is that Ezekiel is describing a representation of the divine glory, and not the glory itself.

As a representation, the vision incorporates several aesthetic features comparable to those in the ritualized portrait of the Assyrian king in the Assyrian throne room. First, Ezekiel's vision preserves a sense of separateness. Irene Winter points out that the emblematic depiction of the king is visually and spatially separated from the historical reliefs by being set about one-third above the lower register. Similarly, in Ezekiel's vision, the enthroned glory appears above and apart from the earth. The vision also evokes the symmetricality of the royal portrait, with its careful and indeed torturous description of the four living beings, their four faces, and their wheels. Finally, the sense that what Ezekiel sees is a representation of God, and not God himself, is suggested by the placement of sounds and voices within the vision. When Ezekiel falls on his face in 1:28, he hears "someone speaking" (מדבר). Now, while the account had earlier described a "voice" or, better, "sound" (קול) coming from above the firmament, the account does not identify the "one speaking" with either the sound or the vision. Given the unusual concentration of prepositions and directional phrases in chap. 1, this ambiguity is significant. The disembodied voice can be explained in terms of the layout of the throne room. When Ezekiel stands at its threshold, he sees a likeness of the glory of God in front of him; but the voice comes from another direction that is inaccessible to his sight.[42]

Finally, as in the Assyrian throne room, this representation is not simply a portrait of the king, but a portrait of the king in relation to the world. The

---

41. Walther Eichrodt has anticipated this interpretation, seeing the vision as a "mere copy or reproduction of the glory of his power" (*Ezekiel: A Commentary* [trans. Cosslett Quin; OTL; Philadelphia: Westminster, 1970], 59).

42. John Strong has noted a similar phenomenon in Ezek 43:5-6; see "God's *Kābôd*: The Presence of Yahweh in the Book of Ezekiel," in *Book of Ezekiel*, ed. Odell and Strong, 83.

tableau in Ezekiel brings the heavenly and earthly worlds together in its portrayal of a bilevel universe in which the firmament (רָקִיעַ, 1:22, 25, 26) separates the enthroned glory from the living beings, who are clearly subordinate to God. Unlike the heavenly spirits of other biblical throne visions, these attendants are creatures, living beings, and their placement below the firmament signifies their subordination to the divine will. Ezekiel may have been acquainted with Mesopotamian myths about rebels whom the gods had subdued and then put into service to do battle against the remaining elements of chaos in the cosmos.[43] If these myths lie behind Ezekiel's description of the four living creatures, then the vision anticipates the end of Israel's rebellion. Yahweh will be king, and this cosmic tableau is proof of that final victory.

## Conclusion

The Assyrian royal inscriptions and their architectural context, the palace and its throne room, establish a matrix in which to interpret the vision of Ezekiel 1. That matrix highlights the significance of the terms דמות and מַרְאֶה as a type of discourse about representational art and raises the possibility that Ezekiel 1 is a schematic tableau of divine rule.

Even without a knowledge of the ancient Near Eastern parallels, some critics have arrived at similar conclusions. When Herntrich had dismissed Ezekiel 1 as nonprophetic, he had labeled it as a type of display.[44] Similarly, when Long rejected the interpretation of call narratives as texts of legitimization, he had observed that the vision was "a kind of visionary tableau."[45]

What the ancient Near Eastern parallels do provide, however, is the context for understanding how such a visionary tableau could have been construed as a schematic and organizing representation of Ezekiel's book. What is important is not that the vision is now accurately classified and pigeonholed, but that its literary and cultural contexts have been enlarged so as to evoke the political, cultural, and aesthetic range of associations that would have made it intelligible to Ezekiel's readers.

The vision remains squarely within the Israelite theophanic tradition; nevertheless, Ezekiel's familiarity with Assyrian royal ideology and iconogra-

43. F. A. M. Wiggerman, *Mesopotamian Protective Spirits: The Ritual Texts* (Cuneiform Monographs 1; Groningen: Styx, 1992), 143-88, esp. 148-49, 179-82, 174-79.

44. Herntrich, *Ezechielprobleme*, 79.

45. Long, "Prophetic Authority as Social Reality," in *Canon and Authority: Essays in Old Testament Religion and Theology* (ed. Burke O. Long and George W. Coats; Philadelphia: Fortress, 1977), 12.

phy allows him to enlarge upon the Israelite theophanic tradition in several respects. When Ezekiel sees directly into the divine throne room, he does not see God directly. Where the older theophanic visions of Micaiah ben Imlah and Isaiah depict Yahweh seated on his throne and the prophet ushered directly into the presence of God, Ezekiel tells us that what he sees are appearances and representations. This expansion allows the vision into the throne room to become significantly more than an episodic moment in a prophet's career. Certainly, the book links Ezekiel's call with the vision, and it is clear that Ezekiel receives his commission within the context of this initial vision of the throne room. But the vision also prepares for the rest of the book, in much the same way that the royal portrait organizes the many discrete scenes of battle and conquest that are portrayed on the walls of the Assyrian throne room. If Ezekiel's inaugural vision does not bring the prophet face-to-face with God, it does bring the prophet into the realm of God's rule. In Yahweh's heavenly throne room, the story of Yahweh's victories is complete. Ezekiel's task is to carry that message out of the throne room and back into the world that Yahweh intends to rule.

Finally, this interpretation of Ezekiel 1 explains why the great visions of chaps. 1, 8–11, and 40–48 lend coherence to the book. All three visions are concerned with the proper representation of Yahweh's rule. In chap. 1 Ezekiel sees a throne room properly adorned with the "appearance of the likeness of the glory of God." In his vision of Yahweh's earthly home in chap. 8, however, he sees the "anti-likeness," the Image of Jealousy, which is the root of the alienation between God and the house of Israel. Finally, the vision of chaps. 40–48 reveals a world so conformed to Yahweh's rule that there is no longer any need for representation, as the divine glory itself comes to dwell in the temple. By interpreting Ezekiel 1 as the prophet's vision of the proper representation of the divine glory, we are able to see that the goal of the book of Ezekiel is to get earthly life to imitate a cosmic art.

# Israelite Genres in Their
# Ancient Near Eastern Context

## TREMPER LONGMAN III

Much debate surrounds the genesis of the Bible, both how and when its component parts were brought into existence. Regardless of the answer to these difficult and enigmatic questions, we know that it did not drop out of heaven in a form totally unique to Israel. The Bible does not transcend culture but appears in the context of an ancient Near Eastern world. In other words, the Bible does not appear in a cultural vacuum, and this principle applies to its literary genres. Generic conventions cross cultural boundaries in antiquity as well as today, and we do well to study the Bible's genres in the light of their ancient Near Eastern counterparts. Nonetheless, readers, particularly scholars, need to do so consciously and mindful that there may be differences between two cultures' use of the same generic tradition even in the midst of similarity. These similarities and differences inform and deepen our reading of biblical texts.

Analogies may be drawn with our study of the Hebrew language. Hebrew was not a language created for the production of the Bible. It served everyday use. It is also a language related to other languages in its cultural environment. We may debate the nature of the exact relationship between Hebrew and Ugaritic, Akkadian, and Arabic, but we cannot debate that they are all members of the same linguistic family tree. Similarly, no one doubts that our discovery of, say, Ugaritic has enriched our knowledge of Biblical Hebrew. This in spite of the fact that there were certain excesses of comparison that did not attend to differences between the languages.[1]

Reading and writing take place in the context of literary conventions

---

1. The most notable instance is, of course, M. J. Dahood, as may be seen in such works as his three-volume Psalms commentary (AB 16-17A; Garden City, N.Y.: Doubleday, 1965-70).

exploited by both authors and readers. Genre is such a convention. Writers may not always be conscious of the generic tradition that is driving their writing. For instance, a contemporary mystery writer may not be able to articulate well a definition of his or her genre, but previous reading has provided the background needed in order to write something that readers will recognize as a member of that genre.

Indeed, readers would be lost if an author utilized a writing vehicle that was totally unique with no literary connections with what preceded it. It is hard to imagine what such a writing would look like. Authors thus naturally write within a generic tradition to give the reader some guidance as to "how to take" the writing on the page. In a sentence, genre triggers reading strategy. Genre signals are embedded in the text to evoke in the reader the proper response.

One commonly cited example drawn from the modern reading experience is the opening line "Once upon a time." These words trigger an expectation of a fairy tale in the reader that then guides one's interpretation of the following lines.

Heather Dubrow offered a powerful example of how this works. She cites the first paragraph of a literary piece that she entitled "Murder at Marplethorpe": "The clock on the mantelpiece said ten thirty, but someone had suggested recently that the clock was wrong. As the figure of the dead woman lay on the bed in the front room, a no less silent figure glided rapidly from the house. The only sounds to be heard were the ticking of that clock and the loud wailing of an infant."[2] After reading this text, we would likely identify the woman as the murder victim and suspect that the silent figure was the murderer. We would also recognize the infant's wailing to be the result of the disturbance created by the crime. We would make these interpretive moves because of our genre identification based on the title.

Dubrow then invites the reader to reread the paragraph, but this time as the opening of a book entitled "The Biography of David Marplethorpe." Most readers would then assume that the wailing infant was Marplethorpe and the dead woman was his mother who passed away while giving birth. The silent figure would likely be the doctor or the midwife.

The point of the preceding is that the more we learn about the genre of a biblical text, the better our reading will be. It is the contention of this essay that as we see biblical genres in their broader ancient Near Eastern context, we will better understand the biblical genre.

Finally, by way of introduction, the reader should note that the ap-

2. See H. Dubrow, *Genre* (Critical Idiom; New York: Methuen, 1982), 1-3.

proach to genre assumed here is synchronic rather than diachronic. We are also dealing with whole texts and not their parts. The first point should not be taken as a rejection of the idea of the development of the text or the possibility that form criticism may throw light on that subject. In regard to the second point, many of the points discussed below will apply to forms that are used to create whole texts. The ideas that follow relate equally well to the identification of Nah 3:1-3 as a woe oracle and of the whole book as a war oracle against a foreign nation.[3]

## Ancient Genres and Modern Terminology

To my knowledge, the first theoretical discussion of the concept of literary genre took place among the ancient Greeks, specifically in the writings of Plato and Aristotle.[4] We have nothing equivalent from the Old Testament period either in Hebrew literature or the literature of the ancient Near East. Indeed, some scholars have suggested that Israelite and other Near Eastern scribes were not concerned with a precise and self-conscious generic classification of their literature.[5]

From the description of the idea of genre above, we note that it is not necessary for writers or speakers to be self-conscious about the type of written or oral utterance that they bring into existence. They may be unaware of the category of writing/speech that their writing falls into and totally unable to articulate on a theoretical level that their writing is, say, a love poem or a biography, for it to be received as such. In short, it is not at all necessary to show that the writers and readers of ancient Israel understood the concept of genre for it to be at play and, therefore, significant for interpretation.

As it is, however, the scribes of Mesopotamia, Egypt, and Israel left traces of their awareness of genre, particularly in the labels that they applied to the written compositions that are left to us. As we survey this evidence, however, we will see that the ancient generic labels, if that is what they are, do not always conform to our expectations. In other words, the labels are attached to compositions that strike us as decidedly different. This may be seen

---

3. As I argued in "Nahum," in *The Minor Prophets*, vol. 2 (ed. T. E. McComiskey; Grand Rapids: Baker, 1993), 765-829.

4. Plato in his *Republic* and Aristotle in his *Poetics;* cf. G. N. G. Orsini, "Genres," *Princeton Encyclopedia of Poetry and Poetics* (ed. A. Preminger; Princeton: Princeton Univ. Press, 1965), 307-9.

5. A. K. Grayson, *Babylonian Historical-Literary Texts* (Toronto: Univ. of Toronto Press, 1975), 5.

in the widespread use of *za-mi,* "praise," in Sumerian literature. This phrase occurs in texts of various genres (hymns, myths, epics, *Lehrgedicht*).[6] Other names assigned to individual texts by the native scribes (*tigi,* etc.) principally concern musical accompaniment, not generic relationships. Still other native labels reflect the method of recitation *(sir-gid-da).*

A second locus of native literary classification occurs in the literary catalogues.[7] Yet here too the classificatory principle is not systematically generic. While texts of the same genre are occasionally listed together in a catalogue,[8] usually they are not. In a catalogue from Ur published by S. N. Kramer,[9] for example, many different genres are represented — hymns, epics, myths, laments, and so on.

In biblical literature the frame narrator of Ecclesiastes comments that Qohelet was as conscious of how he wrote things as he was of what he said: "Qohelet sought to find words of delight and to write honestly words of truth" (12:10). Furthermore, Qohelet is complimented for his ability to investigate and put in good order many "proverbs," a broad generic category in the Bible.[10] Moreover, to note an awareness of different types of psalms, one need look only at the titles of the psalms, admittedly late additions, where we find words of debated reference like *miktām, maśkîl,* and so forth.

I conclude, therefore, that, though we have no theoretical reflections on genre from the ancient Near East, there was clearly a knowledge of the concept and its practice, even though the generic labels of antiquity are not always applied in a way that conforms to our expectations.

While the Israelite and other Near Eastern peoples were not concerned as far as we know with genres on a theoretical level, their writings are conducive to a generic approach, perhaps even more than modern literature. The latter frequently prides itself in being innovative and iconoclastic, but ancient Near Eastern literature was much less so.[11] Thus generic similarities do exist in ancient texts.

Here the distinction between emic and etic approaches to language and

---

6. See, respectively, Hymn to Enlil, the All-Beneficent, *ANET* 573-76 (l. 170); Enki and Ninhursag, *ANET* 37ff. (l. 279); Gilgamesh and Agga, *ANET* 44ff. (l. 115); J. Cooper, *The Return of Ninurta to Nippur* (AnOr 52; Rome: Biblical Institute Press, 1978), 5.

7. J. Krecher, "Literarische Kataloge," *RLA* 5 (1976-80): 478-85.

8. W. W. Hallo, "On the Antiquity of Sumerian Literature," *JAOS* 83 (1963): 168-69; idem, "Another Sumerian Literary Catalogue?" *StudOr* 46 (1977): 77-80.

9. S. N. Kramer, "The Oldest Literary Catalogue," *BASOR* 88 (1942): 10-19.

10. See G. Wilson, "*mšl,*" *NIDOTTE* 2:1134-35, which indicates that the word is associated with literature that we would classify as proverb, parable, fable, allegory.

11. R. Knierim, "Old Testament Form Criticism Reconsidered," *Int* 27 (1973): 435-36.

literature may prove helpful.[12] The emic describes native designations and classification of literature. This approach has the advantage of giving the researcher insight into the native consciousness of a particular text and also the relationship between that text and others bearing the same designation. The etic view of literature imposes a nonnative grid or classification scheme not necessarily defined in their language. The focus of this essay is on the utility of an etic approach to genres that may or may not coincide with the emic.

## A Communicative-Semiotic Approach to Genre

Although revolutionary in biblical studies, H. Gunkel introduced what was already by his time an obsolete model of genre into the discussion in biblical studies. His influence came from folklorists like P. Wendland, E. Norden, and most famously, the brothers Grimm, all representing a neoclassical model of genre current in the nineteenth century.[13] This affected his method in at least four areas.

First, Gunkel believed that genres are pure, that they are separate categories of literature. This doctrine of the purity of genres, well known from his negative evaluation of mixed genres in the Psalms,[14] was not current in his own day, but rather was the predominant opinion of neoclassical literary scholars of the nineteenth century who were repeating an Aristotelian view of genre.[15]

Second, Gunkel set up certain criteria for the identification of the genre of texts. He examined three factors in order to generically classify a text: (a) the mood and thought(s) of the text, (b) the linguistic forms (grammar and vocabulary), and (c) the social setting *(Sitz im Leben).*[16]

Third, form criticism as developed by Gunkel and others was primarily

12. K. Pike, *Language in Relation to a Unified Theory of Human Behavior* (The Hague: Mouton, 1967), chap. 2; and V. S. Poythress, "Analysing a Biblical Text: Some Important Linguistic Distinctions," *SJT* 32 (1979): 113-37. The emic/etic distinction was first proposed in linguistics, where it was used to distinguish native understanding of language from the analysis of a language by linguists or other outsiders. Pike was the first to generalize the distinction into a principle that could be used in the study of any aspect of culture. Poythress further refined the concept. For the tendency of taking linguistic categories and applying them to other disciplines, see J. Culler, *The Pursuit of Signs* (Ithaca: Cornell Univ. Press, 1981), 27-29.

13. As noted by G. Tucker, *Form Criticism of the Old Testament* (GBS; Philadelphia: Fortress, 1971), 4-5; and M. J. Buss, "The Study of Forms," in *Old Testament Form Criticism* (ed. J. H. Hayes; TUMSR 2; San Antonio: Trinity Univ. Press, 1974), 50.

14. H. Gunkel, *The Psalms* (trans. T. M. Horner; Philadelphia: Fortress, 1967), 36-9.

15. Orsini, "Genres," 307-9.

16. Gunkel, *Psalms,* 10.

applied to literature that was believed to be oral in origin. Indeed, Gunkel considered the writing down of an oral composition to result in the degeneration of the text.

Fourth, Gunkel's approach to genre has diachronic interests rather than synchronic. That is, he used his analysis of *Gattung* as part of a program to recover the original shape of a text.

In a word, Gunkel's approach to genre was rather rigid and diachronic in its concerns. His approach still claims many advocates and practitioners today. On the other hand, more recent articulations of form-critical method have renewed dialogue with literary theory and adopt a more fluid and synchronic analysis of genre.[17]

Influenced by these studies, I here employ a communicative-semiotic approach to genre.[18] In the act of reading, a transaction takes place between the author and the reader, a transaction that is a form of communication. To communicate effectively, the author must use forms that are understandable to the reader and direct the reader "how to take" what is written.[19] Forms are recognized by the reader on the basis of earlier reading experience, and authors write in certain literary traditions, though they may stretch and expand the boundaries of previous works. Genre theorists employ various analogies for their understanding of genre: institution,[20] contract,[21] game,[22] code, deep structure, and patterns of expression.

In summary, I underline three points concerning genre: (1) genre explains the possibility of communication in a literary transaction; (2) genre rests on expectations that arise in readers when they confront a text; (3) authors can be coerced in composition to conform to genre expectations.

---

17. Representative articles include W. G. Doty, "The Concept of Genre in Literary Analysis," *SBLSP* (2 vols.; 1972), 2:413-48; idem, "Fundamental Questions about Literary Critical Methodology: A Review Article," *JAAR* 40 (1972): 521-27; P. D. Hanson, "A Response to J. J. Collins' Methodological Issues in the Study of I Enoch," *SBLSP* (1978); Knierim, "Reconsidered," 435-68; F. Letzen-Deis, "Methodologische Überlegungen zur Bestimmung 'literarischer Gattungen' im Neuen Testament," *Bib* 62 (1981): 1-20.

18. See K. Hempfer, *Gattungstheorie* (Munich: W. Funk, 1973).

19. "The individual is ineffable"; see Buss, "Study of Forms," 32; and R. Pascal, *Delight and Truth in Autobiography* (Cambridge: Harvard Univ. Press, 1960), 2.

20. R. Wellek and A. Warren, *Theory of Literature* (3d ed.; New York: Harcourt Brace Jovanovich, 1977), 226.

21. T. Todorov, *The Fantastic: A Structural Approach to a Literary Genre* (Ithaca: Cornell Univ. Press, 1981), 11-12, 37.

22. E. D. Hirsch Jr., *Validity in Interpretation* (New Haven: Yale Univ. Press, 1987), 68-71.

## The Fluidity of Genres

Traditional form criticism as given impetus by Gunkel treated genres as forms that were discrete entities. His neoclassical approach gave the impression that genres were pure and fixed, also that they existed at only one level of abstraction.

Genres are abstractions from particular texts. Similarities are highlighted as literary texts are placed into groups. Genres are not categories that are fixed in nature, but rather are based on the observation of textual similarities of a number of different types. The fluidity of genres derives from the fact that a researcher/reader can attend to a small number of similarities, thus producing a large category, or a large number of similarities, which will result in a small category of texts. Thus with T. Todorov it is possible to speak of genres on a scale that ranges from one text ("jedes Werk stellt eine eigene 'Gattung' dar") to the maximum ("alle Texte gehoren zu einer 'Gattung'").[23]

## Comparative Method

In this essay I argue that the study of biblical genres is enriched by comparison to their cognates in the broader ancient Near East.[24] This statement raises all manner of methodological issues that I cannot fully address here, but I will at least draw out the main lines of the discussion and give some justification for the approach that I advocate.

First, it raises the question of the relationship between the literatures of related cultures. A wide exposure to ancient as well as modern society reveals surface similarities. Reading the Egyptian instruction genre *(sby3t)* with a knowledge of Proverbs provides a good example. One cannot help but notice the similar dynamic of a father instructing a son as well as the occasional bit of identical advice.

Such similarities have led many scholars and others less qualified to overemphasize the similarities between the Bible and the literature of the an-

---

23. Cited by Hempfer, *Gattungstheorie*, 137.

24. For helpful studies on a comparative approach to genre, see F. W. Dobbs-Allsopp, *Weep, O Daughter of Zion: A Study of the City Lament in the Hebrew Bible* (BibOr 44; Rome: Pontifical Biblical Institute Press, 1993); W. W. Hallo, "Individual Prayer in Sumerian: The Continuity of a Tradition," *JAOS* 88 (1968): 71-89; H. L. J. Vanstiphout, "Some Thoughts on Genre in Mesopotamian Literature," in *Keilschriftliche Literaturen. Ausgewählte Vorträge der XXXII. Rencontre Assyriologique Internationale* (ed. K. Hecker and W. Sommerfeld; Berlin: D. Reimer, 1986), 1-11.

cient Near East.[25] The superficiality of the comparisons resulted in other scholars reacting against the comparative method, S. Sandmel labeling the earlier interpretive strategy as parallelomania and B. Landsberger suggesting that each culture and its literature are independent of others.[26] This was clearly an overreaction, but the viewpoint served a useful function in getting the field to question the previous tendency to emphasize similarities.

The next move might well be anticipated. If surface similarities were to be avoided and radical contrast ruled out as unreasonable, then the best solution would be in the middle. W. W. Hallo has championed a version of the comparative method that he calls the contextual approach, which studies similarities in the context of differences.[27] This idea is simple in conception if not always easy to carry out, and it has produced fruitful and interesting results. The reception of Hallo's ideas has been more favorable among biblical scholars than among his fellow Assyriologists, who may fear their field becoming a subsidiary of biblical studies.[28]

Hallo's approach, of course, is relevant not only for genre studies, but for comparison of many other aspects of biblical and ancient Near Eastern culture and literature. However, I understand it more like a principle that guides the interpreter than anything else. That principle is to observe similarities as well as differences and be aware that even the similarities may have different functions or purposes in a different cultural tradition.

---

25. The classic study is F. Delitzsch, *Babel und Bibel* (Leipzig: Hinrichs, 1903). P. Jensen, *Das Gilgamesch-Epos in der Weltliteratur* (Strassburg: Trubner, 1906), is an early example of viewing the Gilgamesh Epic as the precursor to much biblical literature.

26. S. Sandmel, "Parallelomania," *JBL* 81 (1962): 1-13; B. Landsberger, "The Conceptual Autonomy of the Babylonian World," *MANE* 1/4 (Malibu: Undena, 1976).

27. Hallo's method and influence may be seen in part in the series of four volumes that carry the subtitle *Scripture in Context* and represent the collected papers of four years of teaching an NEH summer course primarily for professors of Hebrew Bible. His work as editor (along with Lawson Younger) of the three-volume *Context of Scripture* (Leiden: Brill, 1997-2002) also indicates his interest in the comparative method. For a single article that explains and applies his comparative/contextual approach, see his "Biblical History in Its Near Eastern Setting: The Contextual Approach," in *Scripture in Context: Essays on the Comparative Method* (ed. C. D. Evans, W. W. Hallo, and J. B. White; PTMS 34; Pittsburgh: Pickwick, 1980), 1-26.

28. Unfortunately, in the United States the greater danger is that the field of ancient Near Eastern studies, particularly Assyriology, will die out due to the neglect of even well-funded major research universities.

## Previous Studies of the Biblical Genres
## in the Light of the Ancient Near East

Studying the genres of the Bible in the light of their ancient Near Eastern analogues is not new. Indeed, some of the most important advances in understanding texts has come as a result of an association that has been made through comparative studies. The list is long, but the following are a selection of the most interesting.

1. Reports of covenant making that bear at least a vague structural relationship to treaty texts from Hatti and Assyria.[29]
2. Lamentations in the light of the city laments of Sumer (i.e., the Lamentation over the Destruction of Ur).[30]
3. The Song of Songs in connection with Egyptian and Mesopotamian love poetry.[31]

To illustrate my particular approach to the subject, I have chosen to study the book of Ecclesiastes, and in particular, Qohelet's speech in the light of the genre of Akkadian autobiography.

## Qohelet's Speech (Eccl 1:12–12:7) as Fictional Autobiography

During my graduate program at Yale University, W. W. Hallo, my advisor, encouraged me to study a group of texts that he suspected fell into a single genre

29. Most notably G. E. Mendenhall, *Law and Covenant in Israel and the Ancient Near East* (Pittsburgh: Presbyterian Board of Colportage of Western Pennsylvania, 1955); D. J. McCarthy, *Treaty and Covenant* (AnBib 21; Rome: Pontifical Biblical Institute Press, 1963); D. R. Hillers, *Covenant: The History of a Biblical Idea* (Baltimore: Johns Hopkins Univ. Press, 1969). See also M. G. Kline, *Treaty of the Great King* (Grand Rapids: Eerdmans, 1963); idem, *By Oath Consigned: A Reinterpretation of the Covenant Signs of Circumcision and Baptism* (Grand Rapids: Eerdmans, 1968); idem, *The Structure of Biblical Authority* (Grand Rapids: Eerdmans, 1972).

30. Dobbs-Allsopp, *Weep*; P. W. Ferris, *The Genre of the Communal Lament in the Bible and the Ancient Near East* (SBLDS 127; Atlanta: Scholars Press, 1992); T. F. McDaniel, "The Alleged Sumerian Influence upon Lamentations," *VT* 18 (1968): 198-209, as well as all recent commentaries on Lamentations. For a complete survey of the ancient Mesopotamian evidence see W. W. Hallo, "Lamentations and Prayers in Sumer and Akkad," *CANE* 3:1871-81.

31. See the discussion in T. Longman III, *Song of Songs* (NICOT; Grand Rapids: Eerdmans, 2001). Indeed, the discovery of an ancient Near Eastern love poetry tradition helped turn the tide against an allegorical reading of the biblical text.

category. I prepared translations of these texts and discussed their literary interrelationships. As I reflected on the latter, I came to realize that, though they
were all autobiographical texts, there were differences among them that allowed me to divide them into four subgenres.[32]

All fifteen texts that I studied began with what A. Poebel had identified
as a self-introduction.[33] It was usually short and simple, as in the case of the
Autobiography of Idrimi: "I am Idrimi, the son of Ilimilimma, the servant of
Adad, Hebat, and Istar, the lady of Alalah, my ladies." This brief introduction
was followed by a lengthier first-person narration that told a story about the
life of the speaker. In the case of Idrimi, it recounts how the royal family of
which he is a member must flee his hometown of Aleppo for some unspecified reason and then how they take up residence at Emar. Later he decides to
reassert his rights in Aleppo but sojourns for a period among the *ḫabiru* or
social outcasts. Idrimi eventually returns and becomes a successful ruler.

All fifteen texts have a third part, but here is where the similarity ends.
There are four different possible endings. Idrimi is a text that is most like a
typical royal inscription and ends with blessings and curses (see also the
Sargon Birth Legend). A second group made up of the Cruciform Monument
of Manishtusu, the Agum-kakrime Inscription, and the Kurigalzu Inscription
conclude with fraudulent donations to the cult. This subgenre is similar to a
more recent and well-known text, namely the Donation of Constantine.
Third, we have texts that end with some sort of look into the future (Text A,
Marduk Prophecy, Shulgi Prophecy, Uruk Prophecy, Dynastic Prophecy).
Whether these texts are to be considered prophecies or apocalypses is still debated but unimportant for our present purposes. Most significant for a study
of Ecclesiastes, there are three autobiographical texts that conclude with advice. This advice flows from the first-person experiences narrated in the first
two sections of the text. The three compositions are the Cuthaean Legend of
Naram-Sin, the Sin of Sargon text, and the Adad-guppi Inscription.

The Cuthaean Legend is purportedly about Naram-Sin of Akkad (ca.
late 23d–early 22d century BCE), but is very clearly written at a later time. This
text is relatively well preserved, and thus we can provide a good summary of
its contents.[34] We can make sense of the opening, but it is the most difficult

---

32. My dissertation was finished in 1982 and published as *Fictional Akkadian Autobiography* (Winona Lake, Ind.: Eisenbrauns, 1991).

33. A. Poebel, *Das appositionell bestimmte Pronomen der 1. Pers. Sing. In den
westsemitische Inschriften und im Alten Testament* (AS 3; Chicago: Oriental Institute, 1931).

34. There are four different sources of the Cuthaean Legend; the best known is from
the Neo-Assyrian period. In addition, we have an Old Babylonian copy, two prisms written in
Akkadian from Boghazköy, and a Hittite version. See J. J. Finkelstein, "The So-called 'Old

part of the text. He speaks of a distant predecessor, Enmerkar, and seems upset that he did not leave advice to kings who followed him.

The issue confronting Naram-Sin was a ferocious people described in dramatic fashion as: "Troops with the body of cave-birds, men with raven-faces, the great gods created them in a land whose city the gods created. Tiamat nursed them; Belit-ili, their mother, treated them well. In the midst of the mountains they grew up, became adults and acquired good looks" (ll. 31-37). These wild troops were conquering great swathes of territory, and Naram-Sin wondered whether he should resist them. As a good king, he consulted the liver omens to determine the will of the gods, but when the response was negative, he presumptuously proclaimed: "What lion practiced divination? What wolf questioned a dream-interpretress? Let me go like a robber wherever I desire and let me seize the *luddu* of Ninurta" (ll. 80-84).

Thus Naram-Sin engaged them in combat and was roundly defeated losing great numbers of troops. He persisted until he realized that his efforts were of no avail and that the gods were against him. After all, he disobeyed the first principle of holy war, which was to follow the guidance of the gods.[35]

The next section is broken, but from the fact that the text mentions both further divine inquiry as well as Naram-Sin's overcoming of troops, the best interpretation is that, after some time, the divine will changed and encouraged Naram-Sin to go to battle. Thus he won, though further inquiry indicated that he should not extend his victory to the point that the enemy was completely exterminated. Defeat was turned into victory as Naram-Sin became attentive to the divine oracles.

At this point, the focus of the text shifts again, this time from narration to admonition. Naram-Sin will not follow the pattern of Enmerkar and leave his successors without some guidance. He leaves a stele that will impart wisdom to those after him.

As mentioned, it is this third section that distinguishes this subgenre from the others. In the case of the Cuthaean Legend, the advice takes the form of an encouragement to promote home interests and to restrain from foreign adventurism. In good wisdom fashion (Prov 1:8; 3:1-2; 4:1; and throughout

Babylonian Kutha Legend,'" *JCS* 11 (1957): 83-88; and O. R. Gurney, "The Sultantepe Tablets IV: The Cuthaean Legend of Naram-Sin," *AnSt* 5 (1955): 93-113 (cf. *AnSt* 6 [1956]: 163-64); and C. B. F. Walker, "The Second Tablet of *tupsenna pitema*: An Old Babylonian Naram-Sin Legend?" *JCS* 33 (1981): 191-95.

35. See T. Longman III and D. G. Reid, *God Is a Warrior* (Grand Rapids: Zondervan, 1995); and S.-M. Kang, *Divine War in the Old Testament and in the Ancient Near East* (Berlin and New York: de Gruyter, 1989).

chaps. 1–9) the admonition section instructs its readers to pay attention to what follows:

> Read this stele!
> Heed the wording of this stele! (152-53)

Illustrative of the wisdom that promotes domestic policy and discourages foreign wars is the following advice:

> Let him neglect (your) herds, do not check on it! (165)

> Be meek, be humble. Answer them, "Yes, my lord." To their wickedness, repay kindness. To (their) kindness (repay with) gifts and the realization of (their) wishes. (168-71)

The one admonition that appears to be out of context in this last section actually confirms the view that the advice as a whole amounts to political isolationism:

> Do your task in your wife's embrace. (157)

But, for our purposes, the specific content of the third section is not as important as its function as advice that derives from the autobiographical narrative presented earlier in the text.

The same threefold structure may be observed in the so-called Inscription of Adad-guppi.[36] Adad-guppi, as presented in her autobiography, is a fascinating figure. She was the mother of the last Babylonian king, Nabonidus. She died during his reign at the age of 104. Her long life meant that she lived during the beginning of what we today call the Neo-Babylonian period (beginning in 626 BCE). After her autobiographical introduction, she tells the story of her life on the background of the reigns of Nabopolassar, Nebuchadnezzar, Awel-Marduk, Neriglissar, and her son Nabonidus.[37]

The focus of her life story is on her devotion to the cult of the moon god Sin and his cult site at Harran (the Ehulhul). As is well known, Nabonidus, her son, promoted the cult of Sin over that of Marduk, leading to great tension during his reign. This text, clearly written after Adad-guppi's death

---

36. The text has been transliterated and translated by C. J. Gadd ("The Harran Inscription of Nabonidus," *AnSt* 8 [1958]: 35-92), but no copy has yet been made. The two texts are known as Nab. H 1, A and Nab H 2, A. See also the Latin translation by E. Vogt, "Nabonidi novae inscriptiones," *Bib* 40 (1959): 88-102.

37. The text does not mention the short-lived Labashi-Marduk, the son of Neriglissar.

(since it mentions it and her funeral), was probably part of Nabonidus's pro-Sin propaganda. The advice that flows from Adad-guppi's life story has to do with the maintenance of the Sin cult:

> [Whoever] you are — whether king, prince [ ] in the land. [Continually stand watch] for Sin, the king [of the gods], the lord of the gods of heaven and earth, his great divinity, and reverence [the divinities of heaven and] earth who [ ] dwell in Esagil and Ehulhul and pray (to the divinities) in heaven and earth and [ ] the command of Sin and Ishtar who saves [ ] keep your see safe and forever and ever. (ll. 44ff.)

The third text that represents the subgenre of fictional Akkadian autobiography with a didactic ending is the Sin of Sargon text, which I prefer to call a Sennacherib autobiography.[38] This text is not as fully restored as the others, so I will not describe it as extensively. In this composition Sennacherib, speaking in the first person, expresses his concern that he will meet the same fate as his father, Sargon. Sargon died and was not buried in his tomb. Sennacherib makes oracular inquiry as to why his father came to this untoward end, so he might avoid the same fate. Again, the text is broken and difficult at times to follow. What emerges at the end, however, are a series of admonitions that apparently flow from this experience.

In conclusion, these three Akkadian texts reveal a three-part structure: (1) an autobiographical introduction leads to (2) a lengthy personal narration recounting some significant episodes from the speaker's life; and (3) from these experiences the autobiographical speaker imparts advice to the readers.

As I worked on these texts I almost immediately noted a similarity with the book of Ecclesiastes. To be more exact, I observed that Qohelet's speech in Ecclesiastes had the three components of the Akkadian texts with which I was working. Further research encouraged me that the connection was a valid one and that the comparison illuminated my understanding of the biblical text. In the dissertation, I suggested a connection, but it was not appropriate to develop it.[39]

---

38. H. Winckler, *Sammlung von Keilschrifttexten* (Leipzig: Pfeiffer, 1894), 2:52-53; H. Tadmor, "The Sin of Sargon," *ErIsr* 5 (1958): 150-62 (Hebrew).

39. See further T. Longman III, *Ecclesiastes* (NICOT; Grand Rapids: Eerdmans, 1998). C. L. Seow independently pursued a similar connection with Near Eastern autobiography with an emphasis on Northwest Semitic inscriptions. See his "Qohelet's Autobiography," in *Fortunate the Eyes That See* (Fest. D. N. Freedman; ed. A. Beck, et al.; Grand Rapids: Eerdmans, 1995), 275-87, as well as his *Ecclesiastes* (AB 18C; Garden City, N.Y.: Doubleday, 1997).

When Qohelet speaks for the first time in the book, he introduces himself in a way that is clearly recognizable as the start of an autobiography:

I, Qohelet, was[40] king over Israel in Jerusalem. (1:12)

This introduction is followed by a lengthy self-reflection on Qohelet's search for meaning.[41] While the emphasis is on his intellectual quest, at points his comments sound similar to a royal inscription, particularly as he recounts his great achievements and fabulous wealth:

Still guided by wisdom I mentally explored by cheering myself with wine and embracing folly until I could see what was good for people to do under heaven during the few days of their life.

I did great works. I built for myself houses and planted for myself vineyards. I made for myself gardens and parks. I planted every kind of fruit tree in them. I made for myself pools to water the flourishing forest of trees. I acquired male and female servants, and I had more house-born servants as well. I also acquired herds and flocks. I had more than anyone before me in Jerusalem.

I also amassed for myself silver and gold, the treasure of kings and provinces. I gathered for myself male and female singers and many concubines — the pleasure of humankind.

I surpassed all who lived before me in Jerusalem, and all the while, my wisdom stayed with me. (2:1-9)

After recounting all his accomplishments and acquisitions, he concludes that they are "all meaningless and like trying to catch the wind. There was no profit under the sun" (2:11). The search does not end here, but continues to explore other areas including wisdom (2:12-17), work (2:18-23; 4:2-6), political power (4:13-16), wealth (5:9–6:9). Each time he concludes that life lacks meaning and then resignedly encourages his hearers to grab whatever form of enjoyment that is possible in their lives (2:24-26 and elsewhere throughout the book).

Indeed, it is with these last passages, the so-called *carpe diem* passages, that we note the third aspect of the subgenre that we have observed in the Akkadian texts, the didactic element. In other words, Qohelet imparts advice to his readers based on his experience of searching for meaning.

The Akkadian genre might lead us to expect that the didactic element in

---

40. Or perhaps "have been." See B. Isaksson, *Studies in the Language of Qoheleth* (Studia Semitica Uppsaliensia 10; Uppsala: Uppsala Univ. Press, 1987), 50-51.

41. See O. Loretz, "Zur Darbietungsform der 'Ich-Erzählung' im Buche Qohelet," *CBQ* 25 (1963): 46-59.

the text might be in a third and separate part, and it is interesting to note that the preponderance of advice and wise observations occur in the third section of the book (the latter of which are often cast in proverbial form [see 7:1-14]). However, there is also advice in the second part, as well as autobiographical narration all the way to the end of Qohelet's speech.

In fact, Qohelet's first-person speech ends in 12:1-7 with an anticipation of death, a likely place to conclude a meditation on the meaning of life. Indeed, it is death that has pervaded the earlier part of the book as the factor that renders every life status and accomplishment as meaningless (see 2:12-17; 3:16-22). Even in the final description of death, however, we find instruction ("Remember your creator in the days of your youth," 12:1).

## Implications for Reading Ecclesiastes

It is interesting enough simply to recognize the ancient Near Eastern generic connections of a biblical book like Ecclesiastes. The large central portion of the book, Qohelet's speech, bears resemblance to a genre of literature, didactic fictional autobiography, in Mesopotamia that has three known members, coming from the Old Babylonian, Neo-Assyrian, and Neo-Babylonian periods. Besides being interesting, however, the connection helps us read the book correctly.

First, it supports M. Fox's suggestion that the book has two voices.[42] In one sense we might say that this point is obvious enough. After all, it is the most natural reading of a text where the same person speaks in the first person and is spoken about (1:2; 7:27; 12:8-14). However, the ancient Near Eastern background permits the reader to see the two voices clearly and thereby to determine a macrostructure for the book.

This is true particularly for the prologue. Most scholars fail to treat 1:2-11 as a unit and attribute it to the second unnamed wisdom teacher. In the light of the structure of Mesopotamian autobiographies, however, I prefer to take 1:12 as the beginning of Qohelet's speech, while 1:2-11 anticipates his reflections. Since these verses anticipate Qohelet's conclusions as well as reflect his somber mood, they have been confused with Qohelet's section. But the change from third-person address to first-person does not take place until 1:12, and this should be respected in one's analysis. Thus we end up with the following structure to the book:

42. For the first time in his "Frame-Narrative and Composition in the Book of Qohelet," *HUCA* 48 (1968): 83-106.

| 1:1 | Superscription |
| 1:2-11 | Frame narrator introducing and anticipating Qohelet |
| 1:12–12:7 | Qohelet's autobiographical reflections |
| 12:8-14 | Frame narrator's summary and evaluation of Qohelet's viewpoint |

Thus, in terms of the final form of the text at least, the authorial voice is that of the unnamed wisdom teacher who is instructing his son using Qohelet's words as a foil. Elsewhere, I argue that the frame narrator both affirms and critiques Qohelet's words, finally leading the son (and thus the reader) to consider what is truly important in life: "The end of the matter. All has been heard. Fear God and keep his commandments, for this is the whole duty of humanity. For God will bring every deed into judgment, including every hidden thing, whether good or evil" (12:13-14).

Furthermore, the connection with fictional Akkadian autobiographies helps us understand the ancient context of the Solomon fiction perhaps more clearly. Most scholars do not even discuss the traditional viewpoint that identifies Qohelet and Solomon, even though a number of highly competent conservative scholars continue to hold that position.[43] In my opinion the text itself makes clear that the association is not one of identity and the book is not a testimony of a late-life return of that king to Yahwism. Rather, Qohelet is a wise man who exploits an association with Solomon in the first part of his book in order to explore different avenues of meaning in life, including pleasure, work, wisdom, wealth, and women. After all, Solomon was the one who had these things in abundance and ended up dying an apostate. If Solomon could not find it, then who could? After all, "what can anyone who comes after the king do but that which has already been done?" (2:12).

Just using the name Qohelet signals the reader of this fictional exploiting of Solomon's life. If it was Solomon, why not simply use that name? But the name associates the character with Solomon, since the root *qhl* ("to assemble") is a *Leitwort* in an important story in the Solomon narrative (1 Kgs 8:1, 2, 14, 22, 55). The use of the nickname and the fact that later passages in the book distance Qohelet and the kingship (Eccl 4:1-3; 5:7-8 [Eng. 8-9]; 10:20) are clear indicators that Qohelet and Solomon are not to be identified. The genre indicates that the composer utilized a well-known genre to communicate this fiction. Whether Qohelet was an actual wise man known to the

---

43. W. C. Kaiser, *Ecclesiastes: Total Life* (Chicago: Moody Press, 1979); D. A. Garrett, *Proverbs, Ecclesiastes, Song of Songs* (Nashville: Broadman, 1993).

frame narrator or whether he himself was a fictional creation to represent a particular viewpoint he wanted to critique is impossible to decide.[44]

The ancient Near Eastern genre category in which I have placed Qohelet's speech has, in my opinion, helped us understand how the book would have been read in antiquity. However, the comparison takes us only so far. For instance, it tells us nothing about date. For one thing, it is not at all clear that this form was borrowed or learned from the Babylonians and Assyrians at all. But even granted that the influence came from that direction, the genre in its three attestations comes from the Old Babylonian to the Neo-Babylonian period, and who is to say whether there are unknown examples even beyond that time period? Indeed, there are other fictional Akkadian autobiographies from as late as the Seleucid period (the Dynastic Prophecy for one). Indeed, I believe that comparative studies have been wrongly used to try to establish a date for a biblical text.[45] Literary genres tended to be conservative.[46]

## Limits and Controls

The Hebrew Bible is not isolated from its broader environment. Similarities in language, custom, institutions, metaphors, and, as we have observed in this essay, genre are obvious between Israel and the cultures of Mesopotamia, Egypt, Hatti, Ugarit, and so on. However, there are also differences. Indeed, some of the similarities may be superficial, with the result that unfortunate comparison can be made to the detriment of our understanding of the literature. As noted earlier, most scholars today would judge the work of M. Dahood as overzealous in the area of comparative philology.[47] However, most of his critics did not reject the method of comparative philology as a result, but rather worked toward establishing methodological controls.[48] The

44. See Fox, "Frame-Narrative," 94-96, who suggests an analogy with Uncle Remus in the Brer Rabbit story cycle.

45. For instance, the old debates over whether the covenant/treaty forms in the Bible were more like the Hittite examples from the mid-3d millennium or the Neo-Assyrian texts from the 7th century BCE, particularly as applied to the book of Deuteronomy.

46. Language and the mood expressed in the book lead me to lean toward a late date for the book.

47. J. Barr, *Comparative Philology and the Text of the Old Testament* (Oxford: Clarendon, 1968); J. C. de Moor and P. van de Lugt, "The Spectre of Pan-Ugaritism," *BiOr* 31 (1974): 3-26.

48. P. C. Craigie, "The Poetry of Ugarit and Israel," *TynBul* 22 (1971): 3-31.

following principles have an eye toward comparative genre study, but are in many ways extensions of P. Craigie's basic ideas.[49]

1. Along the lines discussed above, contrasts as well as similarities must be taken into account when comparing cultures.
2. The genres being compared must be understood as thoroughly as possible in their original cultural context before being compared. Sandmel's strictures against "parallelomania" are directed against superficial, noncontextual comparative work and should be heeded.
3. The closer the two genres are to one another temporally, the more likely the comparison is valid.
4. The closer the two cultures that produced the texts are geographically, the more likely it is that they influenced one another.
5. If the two generic traditions are written in closely related languages, then it is more likely that the literatures interacted with one another.

Some scholars may note an omission from the above list. They may well expect some comment on positing a mechanism for literary borrowing. That is, a time and a place where the Israelites may have been influenced by another culture. In one sense, the five points above are indirect ways of positing such a mechanism or gauging the likelihood that there was a mechanism. However, our knowledge of the history of literature of these ancient Near Eastern cultures is sketchy at best (how many other examples of fictional autobiographies from other time periods were there that are now lost to us?). Thus, if similarities between texts are strong and unique, then we should not hesitate to suggest, with humility to be sure, that there is a generic relationship.[50]

In any case, these guidelines do not bring scientific precision to the endeavors of comparative research, but adherence to them increases the probability of a valid comparison. The words of A. Etzioni and F. L. Dubow should be borne in mind: "As in most areas of science, the student approaching this field with a romantic notion of finding great precision, high objectivity, and

49. See my *Fictional Akkadian Autobiography*, 30-31, for my first attempt at suggesting methodological guidelines. I have also recently benefited from a lecture given by Lawson Younger, "The 'Contextual Method': Some West Semitic Reflections," delivered at a conference entitled "The Future of Biblical Archaeology: Reassessing Methodologies and Assumptions," held on August 12-14, 2001, at Trinity International University.

50. One might suggest the example of the Sumerian lamentations at the turn of the 2d millennium BCE that are clearly related generically to the biblical book of Lamentations (6th century BCE).

the accumulation of verified truth will find these attributes to some extent, but will also find an exciting struggle to gain a foot-hold on slippery slopes, a considerable measure of conflict and even intellectual turmoil, and, occasionally, a genuine insight."[51]

51. A. Etzioni and F. L. Dubow, "Introduction," in *Comparative Perspectives: Theories and Methods* (ed. Etzioni and Dubow; Boston: Little, Brown, 1970), 15.

# PART III

# NARRATIVE LITERATURE

# Kaleidoscopic Patterns
# and the Shaping of Experience

SUE BOORER

Can form criticism, with its roots in a romantic view of history and its functioning within a historical-critical framework throughout the twentieth century, still play a role in the current climate where ahistorical approaches to interpretation are exerting their influence? Is it possible for form criticism to make a constructive contribution in relation to newer literary approaches in which historical background and reconstruction (however defined) are not important? If so, what shape might form criticism take when divorced from its traditional association with historical-critical interests where texts are interpreted in relation to their supposed original contexts?

It is my purpose here to examine form criticism in relation to one specific newer literary approach, namely a reader-response approach. Within reader-response criticism I take the particular stance that the meaning of the text emerges from the interaction or dialogue between both the reader *and* the text.[1] I will argue that form criticism in its essentials as having to do with the

---

1. Among a range of philosophies, the particular philosophy of reader-response criticism that provides the context within which form criticism and the shape that it would take are explored here is specifically that outlined by W. Iser in "The Reading Process: A Phenomenological Approach," in *Reader-Response Criticism: From Formalism to Post-Structuralism* (ed. J. Tompkins; Baltimore: Johns Hopkins Univ. Press, 1980), 50-69. For Iser the meaning is cocreated by the literary text and the reader, or the literary work is actualized through the convergence of text and reader. In this process the reader will experience the text like a mirror reflecting back to himself his own presuppositions and dispositions and also leave behind his preconceptions to experience a reality different from his own, the unfamiliar world of the literary text. Thus Iser (56-57) states, "The manner in which the reader experiences the text will reflect his own disposition, and in this respect the literary text acts as a kind of mirror; but at the same time the reality which this process helps to create is one that

form of expression (comprised of the interplay of structure and content) as inseparably linked with life setting or experience ("life situation")[2] has a role within this type of reader-response interpretation: that it can function within it, albeit in a different manifestation from its praxis within a historical-critical framework. I hope to show that, in the shift from historical criticism to a reader-response interpretation, while the form-critical analysis of the text in terms of structure or pattern remains consistent, the locus of the connection to life, the "life situation," and the corresponding function are transformed. Within this transformation, however, form criticism remains true to itself. This is possible because of the philosophy at the heart of form criticism where

---

will be different from his own. . . . Thus we have the apparently paradoxical situation in which the reader is forced to reveal aspects of himself in order to experience a reality which is different from his own. The impact this reality makes on him will depend largely on the extent to which he himself actively provides the unwritten part of the text, and yet in supplying all the missing links he must think in terms of experiences different from his own; indeed it is only by leaving behind the familiar world of his own experience that the reader can truly participate in the adventure that the literary text offers him."

This has some affinities with the hermeneutical process described by P. Ricoeur (*Interpretation Theory: Discourse and the Surplus of Meaning* [Fort Worth: Texas Christian Univ. Press, 1976]), and indeed I will later use Ricoeur's terminology of the "world of the text." In Ricoeur's framework, however, the reader or interpreter reaches full understanding by an appropriation of the "world of the text" (arrived at by moving through the "sense" of the text) that involves dispossessing the self and allowing the "secondary intentionality" or "world of the text" to inform self-understanding. The way in which I use the "world of the text" and the dynamics of interpretation that I will use here are similar, but whereas for Ricoeur the "world of the text" seems to be more "objective," inhering in the text, the "world of the text" as unfolded here is that which is *perceived* by the reader through moving through the perceived literal sense such that the "world" that emerges is the result of the interaction between text and reader, one that is cocreated through the convergence of text and reader in line with Iser. Thus I shall refer to the *perceived* "world of the text." In addition, then, the appropriation of this perceived "world of the text" also may involve more the interaction of the self with the perceived world of the text, rather than the dispossession of the self.

Finally it should be noted that Iser's philosophy of reader-response criticism that forms the basis of this paper is to be differentiated sharply from the later stance of S. Fish, as outlined for example in "Interpreting the Variorum," in *Reader-Response Criticism,* ed. Tompkins, 164-84; idem, *Is There a Text in This Class?* (Cambridge: Harvard Univ. Press, 1980), which maintains that the reader, or more precisely the interpretive strategies of the interpretive communities, constitutes (or makes, or gives shape to) text.

2. I will use the terminology "life situation" to describe that aspect of form criticism that connects texts to life in its social and psychological dimensions, whether in the form of sociological setting or more general life experience, including the inner life of the individual, both of which were the focus of Gunkel's concern. See M. Buss, *Biblical Form Criticism in Its Context* (JSOTSup 274; Sheffield: Sheffield Academic Press, 1999), 214, 238.

the life situation as inseparably linked to the form of expression reflects the commonality of human experience across culture and time.

## I

Within the praxis of form criticism in a historical-critical framework in the twentieth century, a double focus on the general and the particular can be seen. These two aspects, which are not always integrated, are evident especially in relation to the life situation.[3] For example, the flood story has been analyzed form critically by C. Westermann in general terms as a story with a common pattern occurring across cultures — namely, announcement of the flood with the commission to construct the means of salvation, the coming of the flood and its effect, the preservation of one, the end of the flood, and the preservation of humanity[4] — that reflects the common human experience or life situation of "the threat to human existence and at the same time . . . its permanence."[5] It has also been seen in its particular manifestation in J as part of the recurring pattern of crime and punishment of the "primeval history" as it functions within J as a whole within preexilic monarchic Israel.[6] Or

3. This goes back to the roots of form criticism, as evidenced in the work of H. Gunkel himself. For Gunkel forms, reflected primarily in the structure but as this interplays with linguistic expressions and content, arose out of and functioned within typical human experiences or settings. Gunkel engaged in a search for the original pure forms behind the concrete examples of patterns found in the text, and the associated typical settings of these pure forms. Indeed, in line with a romantic view of history, Gunkel's primary interest was in the earliest oral (and for him more pure) forms behind the written text and their sociological settings. Alongside this there was in Gunkel's work also a quest for the inner life of the individual as discerned through the particular form of the text he or she articulated or composed. Although Gunkel engaged in the reconstruction of particular sociopolitical situations within the life of Israel as reflected in the texts and their forms (such as cultic occasions peculiar to the state of Israel), his focus tended to be on the commonality of the life situations behind the text, whether on a sociological or individual level. Indeed, his belief in the commonality of human experience across time and culture, on both an individual and a collective level, was central to, and the basis of, how he conceived of the task of interpretation. Gunkel saw the task of the interpreter as getting back into the experience that gave rise to the text, through its form and by an aesthetic relationship with it, reliving that experience or life situation in him- or herself and thus interpreting it in the present, a task that is possible only if human experience is seen as universal in a transcultural and transchronic sense. See Buss, *Biblical Form Criticism*, 209-62.

4. C. Westermann, *Genesis 1–11* (Minneapolis: Augsburg; London: SPCK, 1984), 405.

5. Ibid., 395.

6. C. Westermann, *The Promises to the Fathers: Studies in the Patriarchal Narratives* (Philadelphia: Fortress, 1980), 44-55.

again, form criticism has encompassed in its method the setting of the various types of psalms within specific reconstructed cultic festivals in monarchical Israel,[7] and Westermann's analysis of the psalms of praise and lament as prayer reflecting and arising out of the existential and general life situation of the related polarities of joy and sorrow.[8]

The dimension of general or common life experience has been somewhat overshadowed by an emphasis on the particular, or the specific cultural and political situation or Israelite cultic festival within which texts originally functioned, in the twentieth-century practice of form criticism in a historical-critical framework. But it is precisely this general dimension, intrinsic to the philosophy of form criticism, that has the potential to allow form criticism to survive and function within ahistorical newer literary approaches. For the common life situation, as reflected in the structure of the text as it interplays with the content, is transcultural and transchronic. As such it allows form criticism to transcend the historical-critical framework and operate within such approaches as reader-response criticism that has no interest in reconstructing the original situation within which the text functioned.

Within the particular type of reader response we will explore here, however, form criticism assumes a different shape from its guise within a historical-critical framework. It still involves the essentials of analysis, or perception, of form (as interplay between structure and content) and the inextricable connection of this to life situation. But the locus and role of the life situation are changed and correspondingly so is the function that emerges in relation to this.

The life situation becomes no longer the original life setting or experience out of which the form arose and in which it originally functioned, but the *perceived* "world of the text."[9] Picking up on Ricoeur's terminology and hermeneutics, but placing it in a deliberately reader-response framework (along the line of the phenomenologist W. Iser[10]), the dynamic of interpreta-

---

7. See, e.g., S. Mowinckel, *The Psalms in Israel's Worship* (trans. D. R. Ap-Thomas; 2 vols.; Nashville: Abingdon; Blackwell: Oxford, 1962).

8. C. Westermann, *Praise and Lament in the Psalms* (trans. K. Crim and R. Soulen; Atlanta: John Knox; Edinburgh: T&T Clark, 1981), esp. p. 267.

9. This is P. Ricoeur's terminology; see P. Ricoeur, *The Symbolism of Evil* (Boston: Beacon, 1967); idem, *Interpretation Theory;* and n. 1 above. See also J. Roffey, "Beyond Reality: Poetic Discourse and Psalm 107," in *A Biblical Itinerary: In Search of Method, Form and Content* (ed. E. Carpenter; JSOTSup 240; Sheffield: JSOT Press, 1997), 60-76, esp. 62-66.

10. W. Iser, "The Reading Process: A Phenomenological Approach," in *Reader-Response Criticism*, ed. Tompkins, 50-69; and see n. 1 above.

tion, still true to form criticism, looks something like this. The reader's perception of the form of the text results from the perceived interplay of structure and content emergent from the interaction of the text itself with the reader and her life situation. The reader then moves through this perceived form (akin to Ricoeur's "literal sense") into the world of the text as she perceives it. This perceived world of the text is the life situation of the text. This then interacts with the life situation of the reader. It is in this interaction that the text and its perceived world, or life situation, function. It does this by mirroring back and/or transforming the life situation of the reader.

As with Gunkel, the interpreter in this type of reader-response framework relates to the text (aesthetically), moving through its form to the life situation.[11] For both, interpretation can occur only because of the commonality or universality of human experience, of life situation. But within the historical-critical framework the form is inherent to the text. For this reader-reponse framework it emerges in the interaction of the text and the perception of the reader. For Gunkel the interpreter was to relive *the* original past-life experience that gave rise to the form and within which it functioned. But the reader-response interpreter interacts with the life situation of the text as the world of the text perceived out of her own life situation, and in this the function emerges in the present. Because the life situation of the reader may change from moment to moment and with different readers, the possibilities with regard to the text's perceived life situation and its function are multiple.


## II


As a concrete example of the nature of form criticism, and how it might operate, within this reader-response framework, I will use the story of the failure of the Mosaic generation to enter the promised land right at the point of standing on its edge and surveying it as found in the pentateuchal text in Numbers 13–14; 32:7-15; Deut 1:22–2:1. For this reader, experienced in diachronic analysis of these texts, the multiple versions of this story comprise: the non-P (or J) text of Numbers 13–14;[12] the P text of Numbers 13–

---

11. See n. 3 above.

12. Designated from now on as Num 13–14* (non-P), and comprising (following M. Noth) 13:17b-20, 22-24, 27-28, 30-31; 14:1aβb, 4, 11a(11b-23a)23b-24, 25b, 39-45. See S. Boorer, *The Promise of the Land as Oath: A Key to the Formation of the Pentateuch* (BZAW 205; Berlin and New York: de Gruyter, 1992), 332-55; and, for the text, A. F. Campbell and M. O'Brien, *The Sources of the Pentateuch* (Minneapolis: Fortress, 1993), 153-55.

14;[13] the final form of Numbers 13–14; Num 32:7-15; and Deut 1:22–2:1.[14]

In the perception of this reader, these accounts have a common structure or pattern:

> the exploration of the land;
> what the surveyors said or did to the people;
> the negative reaction by the people;[15]
> Yahweh's response to the people, comprising the judgment that this people will not go into the land — the promise of the land will not be fulfilled for that generation in general,[16] but only in the future.

The life situation, or world of the text, that this reader perceives through this common structure is: the experience of never having quite arrived; of perhaps glimpsing something of what the future goal might be, but the full reality ever remaining only a future hope; of always being existentially between promise and fulfilment, the now but not yet; and the guilt and/or blame associated with this failure to arrive.

Different nuances of this general pattern can be seen in the interplay of

---

13. Designated from now on as Num 13–14* (P), and comprising (following M. Noth) 13:1-3a(3b-17a)17b, 21, 25-26, 32-33; 14:1aa, 2-3, 5-10, 26-29(30-34)35-38. See Campbell and O'Brien, *Sources*, 80-82.

14. Designated from now on as Deut 1*. One might expect that in a reader-response framework these texts, in particular Num 13–14, would be interpreted here in their final form only, i.e., synchronically. However, it seems to me to be valid to offer here an analysis in reader-response terms of three levels of Num 13–14, i.e., non-P, P, and final form, even though these have been identified by diachronic analysis. This is because the perception of the reader is, of course, vital in the interpretation of texts in a reader-response framework, and this particular reader, because of having analyzed these texts, and in particular Num 13–14 diachronically in some depth previously (see Boorer, *Promise*), perceives and reads Num 13–14, almost automatically, at three different levels. Their relative chronological order, which probably looks something like the following —

|  | Num 13–14* (non-P) |  |
|---|---|---|
| Deut 1* | Num 13–14* (P) |  |
|  | Num 13–14 (final form) |  |
| Num 32:7-15 |  |  |

(see Boorer, *Promise*, for arguments regarding the relative order of Num 13–14* [non-P]; Deut 1*; Num 32:7-15)

— is not, however, relevant here within a reader-response framework, as will become clear in the ensuing discussion.

15. Implicit only in Num 32:9b.

16. The exception is limited to the individual, e.g., Caleb, or Caleb and Joshua.

the particular structures and content of the specific accounts. Through each of these is opened up a uniquely nuanced life situation as perceived by the reader.

There are many specific differences between these accounts: for example, with regard to who initiates the exploration of the land (Moses,[17] or Yahweh whom Moses obeys,[18] or the people with whom Moses complies[19]); what it is about the land that the surveyors are to explore (the nature of the land, inhabitants and cities,[20] simply the land in general,[21] or the route and cities[22]); the area explored (a local area in the south,[23] or the whole land[24]); Yahweh's initial reaction to the people (anger,[25] or complaint[26]); the particular expression of Yahweh's judgment (not seeing the land and going back into the wilderness,[27] death in the wilderness,[28] or both[29]); those for whom the land promise will be fulfilled in the future (Caleb and his descendants only,[30] or the whole of the next generation and Joshua as well as Caleb[31]).

In this reader's perception, however, at the present time the main difference between these accounts lies in their particular portrayals of who is primarily responsible for the failure of that generation to enter the promised land and how. The varying nuances with regard to this are reflected in differences both in the structures between these accounts and in the details in content. These differences occur specifically in the subsections of the accounts regarding the responses, by the people and/or surveyors on an individual level or as a whole group, to the content of the report or action of the surveyors: that is, in the subsections I.C and II of the structures of Numbers 13–14 (non-P); Numbers 13–14 (P); Numbers 13–14 (final form); Deuteronomy 1*; and subsection II of the structure of Num 32:8-13, as outlined in the appendix. The differences in the order, as well as the content, of the responses of the

17. Num 13–14* (non-P); Num 32:7-15.
18. Num 13–14* (P) and Numbers 13–14 (final form).
19. Deut 1*.
20. Num 13–14* (non-P).
21. Num 13–14* (P); Num 32:7-15.
22. Deut 1*.
23. Num 13–14* (non-P); Deut 1*; Num 32:7-15.
24. Num 13–14* (P).
25. Deut 1*; Num 32:7-15.
26. Num 13–14* (non-P); Num 13–14* (P).
27. Num 13–14* (non-P), in line with their wish to go back to Egypt; and Deut 1*.
28. Num 13–14* (P), in line with their wish to have died in the wilderness.
29. Num 32:7-15.
30. Num 13–14* (non-P).
31. Num 13–14* (P); Num 13–14 (final form); Deut 1*, where Caleb's descendants inherit a small area of the whole land that the next generation of the nation will possess.

people and/or surveyors as this interplays with the specific content of the surveyors' report (or action) after exploring the land reflect the different portrayals, in this reader's perception, of where responsibility for failure lies and why. This issue and the subsections of the text relating only to this will form the center of our focus.

## Numbers 13–14* (non-P)

In the narrative of Numbers 13–14* (non-P),[32] the surveyors' report (13:27-28) speaks of the fertility of the land but also of the strength of the people and the cities. In response, first Caleb and then the other surveyors speak, followed by the response of the people. Caleb exhorts the people to go up and occupy the land confident they are able to overcome it (13:30); but the rest of the spies react in opposition to this, stating that they cannot go up, for the people of the land are stronger (13:31). In response to these two different perspectives the people choose to believe the negative one with the majority of spies, over against Caleb's positive position: they weep and want to go back to Egypt (14:1b, 4), and consequently Yahweh sends them back into the wilderness away from the land.

The responsibility for the failure of that generation to enter the land in this account lies with both the majority of spies and the whole people. The spies fail in lacking confidence to enter the land in the face of the strong inhabitants. The people fail by being swayed by the majority and with them taking a defeatist view.

The life situation suggested to this reader moving through the interplay of structure and content of the text as she perceives it is of choosing a pessimistic outlook on life that gravitates toward the negative perspective or option — whether through a lack of confidence that there can be a positive outcome, or lack of courage to try to bring it about, or simply because of being swayed by the majority negative opinion around — thus leading in a self-fulfilling way to failure.

## Numbers 13–14* (P)

In the narrative of Numbers 13–14* (P)[33] the surveyors' report (13:32-33) does not speak of the fertility of the land: on the contrary, the report slanders the

32. For the structure, see Appendix, p. 214.
33. For the structure, see Appendix, pp. 214-15.

promised land itself (13:32a), describing it as a killer, "a land that eats up its inhabitants" (13:32bα). What is more, these inhabitants are giants (13:32bβ-33). In response to this totally negative report of the land, first the people react, then Joshua and Caleb, and then the people once more. The people believe entirely the surveyors' negative report of the land, and believing they will be killed in the land, raise a loud cry of complaint against Moses and Aaron, and Yahweh for his action in the exodus, expressing their wish to have died in Egypt or the wilderness (14:1a, 2-3). In response, Joshua and Caleb offer a positive perspective and reassurance to the people. They contradict the surveyors' negative report of the land by describing it as very good; and they counter the people's fear of being killed in the land with the reassurance that Yahweh is with them and therefore there is nothing to worry about in relation to the people of the land (14:6-9). The people, however, violently reject this positive perspective and reassurance, responding to Joshua and Caleb by threatening to stone them (14:10).

In this P account, the responsibility for the failure of that generation to enter the land again rests on both the surveyors and the people, but more blame is placed here on the majority of surveyors, who are primarily responsible. It is totally understandable for the people initially to react negatively to the promised land after hearing an entirely negative picture of it by the surveyors who slander it. Indeed, at the end of this account the surveyors who slander the land are described as *making* the congregation complain, hence the immediate death of these surveyors (14:36-37). The people, however, also play an important part in the failure, for they rigidly hang on to their first negative reaction, refusing to change their minds when given a positive perspective. Indeed, far from being open to the reassurance given by Joshua and Caleb, they seek to annihilate them and their positive point of view.

The text's life situation seen by this reader through its perceived structure, with its double negative reaction of the people to a totally negative report that slanders the land and then a positive report that values it, is as follows. Failure to move into a positive future can be due to a failure to perceive the value of the promised gift, and hence the people reject the goal, a situation that may come about through colluding with those who denigrate the divine gift and rejecting those who value it and believe it can be embraced even in the face of empirically difficult odds.

## Numbers 13–14 (final form)

In the narrative of the final form of Numbers 13–14,[34] the initial mixed report of a fertile land but strong people and cities (13:26-29) is followed by a brief but positive speech by Caleb, exhorting the people to go into the land (13:30), and then a lengthy speech by the other spies in the negative. They maintain it is not possible to go into the land, now not only because of the stronger inhabitants, but indeed because the land itself is a killer, devouring even its giant inhabitants (13:31-33). The extended negative opinion and report of these surveyors leads to the negative response of the people who cry and complain against Moses, Aaron, and Yahweh. They not only want to go back to Egypt but, believing they will be slaughtered in this killer land, wish they had already died in Egypt or the wilderness (14:1-4). Even though Joshua and Caleb now try to persuade them otherwise, offering a contrary and hopeful countermessage by describing the land as very good and reassuring them in the face of their fear of death in the land that Yahweh is present with them (14:6-9), the people reject this positive perspective, threatening to annihilate its bearers (14:10).

Again, responsibility for failure lies with both the majority of the surveyors and the people, but primarily with the surveyors. The people fail in initially disregarding the positive aspects presented to them of fertile land and possibility of entry, preferring to believe the contradictory and more heavily weighted negative view of the land and impossibility of entry; they also fail in continuing to embrace this view and its attendant fear by blotting out any further attempts to present the positive and faithful perspective.

The life situation suggested to this reader moving through the interplay of structure and content of the text as she perceives it is that of living as if there is no hope, and therefore failing to move into and embrace the positive promised future. This paralysis might be due to multiple factors: a pessimistic attitude that gravitates toward the negative option, maybe through lack of confidence that there could be a positive outcome; or a rigidly stubborn adherence to this defeatist outlook that allows no other more positive perspective, or hope, to be heard or believed in, because of an underlying fear; or a failure to perceive the value of the promised future, rejecting the goal itself, perhaps through colluding with the majority with their cynical and derogatory opinions, or even perpetuating them.

34. For the structure, see Appendix, p. 215.

## Numbers 32:7-15

The reported speech of Moses to the Reubenites and Gadites in Num 32:7-15 aligns the next generation of these tribes with the spies of the previous generation who are used as a precedent to warn them not to behave in the same way and reap the same disastrous consequences for their whole generation.[35] In this rather summary account of the action of the spies in the past and its consequences (32:8-13), the content of the report and the reactions to it are not given explicitly. To say that the "fathers" (i.e., the spies) saw the land (32:9a) is sufficient here, for the accent falls on what the spies did in relation to the people as a consequence of this. This is summarized in the statement, "they discouraged the hearts of the people from going into the land that the Lord had given them" (32:9b). It is this that led to the failure of that whole generation to see the land.

In the account of the spying out of the land here, as held up as a precedent to instruct the next generation, the responsibility for the failure of the whole generation to enter the promised land rests squarely on a subgroup of that generation, the spies: it is their leadership that drags their whole generation down. The spies are *actively* responsible in discouraging the people from wanting to go into the land and for their not going in; the people are only *passively* responsible in letting themselves be discouraged in relation to embracing Yahweh's gift.

The life situation opened up here in the perception of this reader and possible in any generation has to do with the experience of how poor or corrupt leadership can lead to the demise of the whole group.

## Deuteronomy 1*

Finally, the first-person speech of Moses in Deuteronomy 1* addresses the next generation as "you" and therefore as if they *are* the generation of people associated with the surveying of the land.[36] The account of the failure of that generation to enter the land is thus presented as a warning to the present generation that the same can happen to them if they repeat what the preceding generation did. In this account, in stark contrast to Numbers 13–14* (P), the content of the surveyors' report is purely positive, evaluating the promised land as Yahweh's gift as good (1:25). This is followed by a response of the peo-

---

35. For the structure, see Appendix, pp 215-16.
36. For the structure, see Appendix, p. 216.

ple only with no mention of any reaction by individual surveyors. The people's response is totally negative, an irrational and unfounded response to the entirely positive report of the surveyors (1:26-28): they are unwilling to go up into the land, and this is interpreted as rebellion against the command of the Lord their God (1:26). The people's response is based on their perception of Yahweh as hating them so that he brought them to this land to kill them (a reversal of holy war imagery). They have formed this belief not on the basis of the reality of the report of the good land, but on seemingly unfounded hearsay and rumor regarding the strength of the people and cities in the land (1:27-28). Though Moses reassures the people that they need not fear the people of the land, since, in true holy war imagery, Yahweh will fight for them (rather than killing them!) and guide them as they have seen him doing in Egypt and in the wilderness, they do not trust in Yahweh. Again this lack of trust in Yahweh is irrational and unfounded, since they know empirically from past experience that Yahweh can be trusted to guide and protect them. So they miss out on Yahweh's gift of the promised land; it will be fulfilled only for a future generation.

In contrast to Num 32:7-15, where Moses claims that the spies are responsible for the failure because they led the people astray, in Deuteronomy 1* it is the people themselves alone who are responsible. Here only the people blame the spies for discouraging them, by way of rumor, and since the people are portrayed entirely negatively in this account, this lacks credibility. The way in which this whole generation fails is in preferring to believe negative hearsay rather than believing the reality of the good report and most importantly trusting in Yahweh, whose protection and guidance they have experienced in the past.

The life situation of this text perceived by this reader through the perceived interplay of structure and content has to do with the experience of blindness to positive reality in the face of negative hearsay, and an irrational tendency to believe the worst even though the empirical evidence points overwhelmingly to the contrary. Lurking at the heart of this unfounded rejection of the future gift and hope is an irrational lack of trust in the good experiences of the past and their Giver.

What then might be the effect on the reader — this reader at various times or other readers — of the life situations of the worlds of these texts perceived through the perceived interplay of structure and content? Or, in other words, how might these texts *function* in the present?

This depends on how these perceived life situations, already influenced by the life situation of the reader, interact with the reader's life situation. The reader's life situation does not remain static and, of course, will differ with different readers. Thus the way in which these texts function in the present will vary with different readers and with the same reader over time.[37] What, then, might some of the possibilities be?

The reader, with a general existential angst of not having arrived at a promised or hoped-for future in his or her particular life situation at the present time, in line with the perceived life situation of the common structure underlying these texts, may selectively gravitate toward one of the particular accounts of this general scenario.

This might be because its life situation or "world" as she perceives it co-heres with her present life situation or way-of-being-in-the-world. This inter-action, then, may function to articulate and clarify her life situation by mir-roring it back to her.

For example, a reader whose general existential angst of never having arrived takes the form of a lack of hope that her vocational goals will ever be fulfilled might gravitate toward Num 32:7-15. There she might see mirrored in its perceived life situation of the downfall of the whole group because of the actions of a few of its leaders her own situation of being undermined in the working environment by a few managers at the top who discourage her goals.

Or perhaps a reader might gravitate toward a particular text because of its perceived potential to open up a fresh perspective, or this at least may be the effect of the interaction of the reader with this text. It may be that the per-ceived life situation of the text interacts with the reader's present life situation in such a way as to open up another alternative and thus transform it. For ex-ample, a reader, prone to blame others, or those in power, for the failure of her goals may have her horizons broadened by the perceived life situation of Numbers 13–14 (whether the non-P text, the P text, or the final form) where the leaders *and* the people are to blame. In perceiving that the people collude with the pessimism of the leaders and refuse to hear the positive, the reader might then take more responsibility for failure and defeatism in her own life situation. She might even look for a positive side and begin to grasp it instead of pushing it away.

Yet again, after reading Deuteronomy 1* a reader who can imagine only a bleak future may see herself mirrored in the irrationally fearful and negative people. But then, taking seriously this perceived world of Deuteronomy 1* as a warning, she may shift toward perceiving the positive experiences of the past and present, previously ignored, as a basis for future hope.

Furthermore, since there are multiple accounts of this scenario, the reader, with a general sense of having failed to arrive, might gravitate toward a

---

37. As might the perception of the life situation of the text.

combination of these texts. The life situations perceived from moving through a complex text made up of a combination of these differently nuanced and structured accounts will depend on what particular complex pattern is perceived — the specific combination selected, and perception of the complex pattern, and the life situation perceived from it. This will be influenced by the life-situation lens of the reader in the present time. Like the turning of a kaleidoscope a reader may see one complex pattern comprising a particular combination of varying accounts at one time and at another time something different; and a different reader may pick up the kaleidoscope at the same turn or at a different turn. The life situation perceived for each complex patterning of texts may vary with the perception of different readers or the same reader over time. Again, the life situation, or perceived world, of this complex text may mesh with or mirror the reader's experience or life situation and/or provide a dynamic alternative that may shift or transform the reader's present life situation. Let us explore some of the possibilities that this reader perceives by way of illustration.

For example, one reader may read Numbers 13–14 (final form); Num 32:7-15; and Deuteronomy 1* in the sequence of the literary text and, in moving through the nuanced patterns as she sees them, interact with the dynamic of guilt and blame of their perceived worlds as follows. Initially identifying with the shared blame of leaders and people in Numbers 13–14, she may be relieved to move to a more radical blame of others, a small group with power, as in Num 32:7-15. But in the end she may come to realize that the buck really stops with the whole people as in Deuteronomy 1* because of an overriding pessimism symbolized in the spies of Numbers 13–14 and 32 but integral to the whole, that expects the worst and ignores the positive through a lack of trust in the promised divine future. This may enlighten the reader to her desire to shift responsibility, and finally she will acknowledge that it is her own underlying lack of trust that leads to failure.

Yet another reader, or the same reader at a different time, may read Deuteronomy 1* in combination with Num 32:7-15 and perceive a complex kaleidoscopic pattern where the latter corrects the former and whose perceived world involves the shifting of blame entirely from the people in general to a small subgroup of leaders. If this reader is feeling particularly guilt prone but with little power or authority in her present life situation, this perception may free her from self-blame to a different (and perhaps more helpful?) place of feeling caught up in a situation outside herself, about which she can do little.

Or yet another reader, or the same reader at a different time, might perceive a complex pattern in which Numbers 13–14* (non-P) and Numbers 13–

14* (P) are read sequentially rather than in the final form and conclude that the experience of failure to move into a positive future at present is not entirely due to a lack of courage or defeatist attitude as initially believed, but a lack of desire for, or rejection of, this hoped-for future, either because of an initial taste of it or because of believing the denigration of it by the dominant voice that is around. This perception of the life situation of this complex text may simply function to help mirror and articulate the life situation of the reader at more depth or perhaps have a transformative effect, since the real reason behind the reader's present situation is now clear to her.

The permutations and combinations, the perceived kaleidoscopic patterns and their perceived life situations, could be multiplied. The ways in which these perceived patterns, whether of individual texts or a complex combination of texts, and their perceived life situations might function in the varying life situations of the readers, by mirroring or transforming, are legion. Enough has been said, however, to illustrate the way in which form criticism may operate within this framework of reader-response interpretation by present and future generations of readers.

## III

In conclusion, form criticism as practiced within this reader-response framework is identifiable as such since, as with its praxis within a historical-critical framework, it is true to its essential nature of relating form of expression to its connection with life (or life situation). Its praxis in both frameworks involves a focus on structure, both common and particular, as it interplays with content. At its heart the life situation is common or general in its dimensions, being both transcultural and transchronic. Indeed it is this commonality of the life situation in the philosophy of form criticism that allows it to operate in a historical-critical framework *and* in a reader-response interpretive framework.

In its guise within the particular reader-response framework chosen here, where meaning is seen to emerge through the interaction of both text and reader, the life situation becomes the perceived world of the text, rather than, as in a historical-critical framework, the original life setting or experience, however typical. Correspondingly, the hermeneutical move becomes not, as with Gunkel, for the interpreter to get back into the original life situation of the text, reexperience it, and then interpret it in the present, but for the present life situation of the interpreter to interact in the present, from moment to moment, with the life situation of the text as she perceives it. It is, then, in this interaction that the text and its perceived life situation function, to mirror and/or transform the life situation of the reader in whatever way that may emerge.

In this new guise within this reader-response framework, then, form criticism can thrive and play a constructive role where the interpretive task is inextricably related to life experience in the present and into the future.

## Appendix: Structure of the Stories

### Numbers 13–14* (non-P)

| | | |
|---|---|---|
| I. | Survey of the land | 13:17b-20, 22-24, 27-28 |
| | A. Command to make survey | 13:17b-20 |
| | B. Survey | 13:22-24 |
| | C. Report by all the surveyors: | 13:27-28 |
| |    1. Positive (land fertile) | 13:27 |
| |    2. Negative (people and cities strong) | 13:28 |
| II. | Response to the survey | 13:30-31; 14:1b, 4 |
| | A. By surveyors | 13:30-31 |
| |    1. Caleb: positive (let us go up, we are able) | 13:30 |
| |    2. Others: negative (we are not able because people are stronger) | 13:31 |
| | B. By people: negative (weep and want new leader to take them back to Egypt) | 14:1b, 4 |
| III. | Yahweh's response to the people: judgment (this people will not see the land, except Caleb) | 14:11-25 |
| IV. | Unfolding of Yahweh's judgment | 14:39-45 |

### Numbers 13–14* (P)

| | | |
|---|---|---|
| I. | Survey of the land | 13:1-21, 25-26, 32-33 |
| | A. Command to make survey | 13:1-20 |
| | B. Survey | 13:21, 25 |
| | C. Report by surveyors in general: | 13:26, 32-33 |
| |    1. Concerning the land as devouring killer | 13:32a |
| |    2. Concerning its inhabitants as giants | 13:32b-33 |
| II. | Response to the survey | 14:1a, 2-3, 5-10a |
| | A. By people: negative (complaint against Moses, Aaron, and Yahweh; wished they had died in Egypt or wilderness; and desire to go back to Egypt) | 14:1a, 2-3 |
| | B. By Moses and Aaron: prostrate | 14:5 |

    C. By Joshua and Caleb: positive counterreport
       (the land is very good and Yahweh will give it;
       exhortation not to fear the people of the land
       because Yahweh is with Israel in cultic warfare)       14:6-9
    D. By congregation: negative (want to stone Joshua
       and Caleb)       14:10a
  III. Yahweh's response to the people: judgment (this people
      will die in the wilderness as they wished except Caleb
      and Joshua — next generation will know land)     14:10b, 26-35
  IV. Unfolding of Yahweh's judgment       14:36-38

## Numbers 13–14 (final form)

    I. Survey of the land       13:1-33
    A. Command to make survey       13:1-20
    B. Survey       13:21-25
    C. Report       13:26-33
      1. By all the surveyors: positive (land fertile)
        and negative (strong inhabitants)       13:26-29
      2. Caleb's advice: positive (we are able)       13:30
      3. Other surveyors: negative (we are not able,
        the land is a killer, and the inhabitants are large)     13:32-33
   II. Response to the survey       14:1-10a
    A. By the people: negative (rejection of Yahweh
       and the land)       14:1-4
    B. By Moses and Aaron: prostrate       14:5
    C. By Joshua and Caleb: positive perspective,
       and exhortation and reassurance (good land
       and Yahweh is with us in cultic warfare)       14:6-9
    D. By the people: negative (want to kill Joshua
       and Caleb)       14:10a
  III. Yahweh's response to the people: judgment
      (this generation will not see the land but will die
      in the wilderness, except Joshua and Caleb —
      next generation will see the land)       14:10b-35
  IV. Unfolding of Yahweh's judgment       14:36-45

## Numbers 32:8-13

    I. Survey of the land       32:8-9a
    A. Sending of the "fathers" to see land       32:8
    B. Survey       32:9a

II. What the "fathers" (surveyors) did: discouraged
the hearts of the people from going into the land
Yahweh had given them     32:9b

III. Yahweh's response to the people: judgment
(this generation will not see the land except
Caleb and Joshua)     32:10-12

IV. Unfolding of Yahweh's judgment     32:13

**Deuteronomy 1:22–2:1**

I. Survey of the land     1:22-25
  A. Request to survey the land     1:22-23
  B. Survey     1:24-25a
  C. Report by all the surveyors: positive (good land)     1:25b

II. Response to the survey     1:26-33
  A. By the people: negative     1:26-28
    1. General statement: unwilling to go up/rebellion
      against Yahweh's command     1:26
    2. Reported speech of people:     1:27-28
      a. Yahweh hates us to bring us here to be killed     1:27
      b. What spies were rumored to have said to make
        them fear — strong inhabitants     1:28
  B. By Moses     1:29-33
    1. Reassurance: Yahweh fights for them as he
      has before     1:29-31
    2. Accusation: People still not trusting Yahweh
      as protector and guide     1:32-33

III. Yahweh's response to the people: judgment (this
generation will not see the land except Caleb and
Joshua — next generation will enter land)     1:34-40

IV. Unfolding of Yahweh's judgment     1:41–2:1

# The Exclusion of Moses from the Promised Land: A Conceptual Approach

## WON LEE

As the title indicates, this exegetical paper has a twofold focus. First, it introduces a particular direction taken in the recent development of form criticism, namely conceptual analysis. Conceptual analysis is not so much a new and separate approach; it is rather in alliance with or an extension of traditional historical criticisms, since all these methods deal with matters that are textual as well as infratextual. In particular, it is rooted in traditional form criticism; yet it moves beyond Gunkel's classic definition by focusing on conceptual aspects of texts. The task of conceptual analysis is to reconstruct the generative concept underneath the text that is operative in the text, that is the structure of the text. Second, this paper illustrates how conceptual analysis works in an actual exegesis. In so doing, the paper intends to show how exegesis of a text and conceptualization as a method complement and even enhance each other. The chosen topic is the exclusion of Moses from the promised land. Num 20:1-13, representing the priestly traditions (Num 20:24; 27:12-14; Deut 32:48-52), reports that Moses and Aaron were punished with death outside the promised land because of their transgression at the waters of Meribah. What does the text say about the exact nature of their sin? How can it be understood in comparison to the seemingly conflicting explanation in Deuteronomy? There Moses was excluded because of the sin of the people (Deut 1:37; 3:23-29; 4:21-22). How do the exegetes interpret the juxtaposition of these two different explanations, if they consciously begin with the extant text so that the text's own voice can be heard? The application of conceptual analysis on the topic reveals that the generative concept of these traditions is the role of responsible leadership of Moses (and Aaron). Yet both traditions stand side by side, each reflecting one of two aspects of the leadership: Moses' (and Aaron's) role in representing God to the people in the case of the priestly traditions, and Moses' role in lead-

217

ing the people for accomplishment of God's plan in the case of the Deuteronomic traditions. Hence one should neither choose one tradition at the ex-
pense of the other, nor harmonize or collapse the two into one.

## Conceptual Analysis

Form criticism has played an instrumental role in the interpretation of biblical
texts since its inception by H. Gunkel. His interests in identifying and classifying the smallest units of biblical texts and in reconstructing the societal setting
out of which these units came launched a new direction in historical criticism.[1] Until the mid-twentieth century his formulation remained normative
for providing the framework of subsequent discussion on form-critical research, though many modified it with different emphases. Some preferred to
focus on larger textual units than Gunkel's small and self-contained ones,
while others expanded the definition and function of setting, and paid special
attention to the role of genre in the formation of texts.[2] However, the contemporary practices of form criticism indicate such a significant departure from
its traditional position that one wonders whether Gunkel's form criticism is
still viable today. These practices are part of a larger paradigm shift in biblical
studies from the diachronic approaches to the synchronic approaches. Particularly, form-critical research, interacting with literary analysis and structural linguistic analysis, has begun to focus on the structure of the text, the role
of language in the formation and identification of genres, and multiple set-

1. For a historical overview of the traditional historical methods, see H.-J. Kraus,
*Geschichte der historisch-kritischen Erforschung des Alten Testaments* (Neukirchen-Vluyn:
Neukirchener Verlag, 1956), esp. 309-34 for his treatment on Gunkel.

2. J. Barton expresses succinctly Gunkel's definition of form criticism: "In the OT,
form criticism is a method of study that identifies and classifies the smaller compositional
units of biblical texts, and seeks to discover the social settings within which units of these
types or literary genres were originally used" ("Form Criticism," *ABD* 2:838). For examples of
diverse modifications, see G. von Rad, *The Problem of the Hexateuch and Other Essays* (trans.
E. W. Trueman Dicken; New York: McGraw-Hill, 1966); S. Mowinckel, *The Psalms in Israel's
Worship* (trans. D. R. Ap-Thomas; 2 vols.; Nashville: Abingdon, 1962); A. Alt, "The Origins of
Israelite Law," in *Essays on Old Testament History and Religion* (trans. R. A. Wilson; Garden
City, N.Y.: Doubleday, 1967), 101-71; C. Westermann, *Basic Forms of Prophetic Speech* (trans.
H. C. White; Philadelphia: Westminster, 1967); M. Noth, *A History of Pentateuchal Traditions*
(trans. B. W. Anderson; repr. Atlanta: Scholars Press, 1981). One of the latest concise summa-
ries of the history of form criticism can be found in M. Sweeney, "Form Criticism," in *To
Each Its Own Meaning: An Introduction to Biblical Criticisms and Their Application* (ed. S. L.
McKenzie and S. R. Haynes; Louisville: Westminster John Knox, 1999), 58-89.

tings.[3] For example, M. Sweeney redefines form criticism as "a method of linguistic textual analysis . . . [which] focuses especially on the patterns of language that appear within the overall linguistic configuration or form of a text and the role that these patterns play in giving shape and expression to the text."[4] This definition is heavily influenced by text-linguistic structuralism and literary-synchronic analysis of biblical texts. After reviewing the history of development of form criticism from Gunkel to Knierim, Sweeney argues for the analysis of forms, genres, settings, and intentions of literature based on the present biblical text first, rather than within the source documents; he considers the extant text as constitutive for the determination of the possibility of earlier forms; and he warns form critics of the multiplicity of these aspects in its literary history. For him, this refinement of form criticism is not only a viable mode of biblical interpretation, but an indispensable one that will continue to serve as "a fundamental method" to address "both synchronic and diachronic issues in the interpretation of the biblical text."[5]

Sweeney's claim can be justified by recent developments in R. Knierim's exegetical program. Knierim has broadened the ways to identify and classify genres, so that the typicality of certain forms may arise from "underlying matrices which the human mind generates" other than specific sociolinguistic settings; he argues for the structure analysis of the individual texts as a means for identifying their genre; consequently he opens a door for diverse types of genres and settings as well.[6] Knierim further stresses the importance of structure analysis, arguing that it is an integral part of the form-critical method and should be treated as an initial step of its process. Hence a form criticism that incorporates such structure analysis into its methodology provides the basis for a unified exegetical system that conceptualizes the correlation of various methodological steps.[7] He has not yet articulated, however, how to

---

3. For the recent forms of form-critical works, see the twelve volumes in the FOTL series edited by R. P. Knierim, G. M. Tucker, and M. Sweeney. D. Petersen reviews seven volumes of this series published up until his article, "Hebrew Bible Form Criticism," *RelSRev* 18 (1992): 29-33. He argues that the decisive departure from the traditional definition of form criticism was fueled by two articles, J. Muilenburg, "Form Criticism and Beyond," *JBL* 88 (1969): 1-18; and R. P. Knierim, "Old Testament Form Criticism Reconsidered," *Int* 27 (1973): 435-68. He concludes that these works show movement not only "in diverse directions" but also "beyond the classic Gunkelian approach."

4. Sweeney, "Form Criticism," 58.

5. Ibid., 68-69.

6. Knierim, "Reconsidered."

7. R. P. Knierim, "Criticism of Literary Features, Form, Tradition, and Redaction," in *The Hebrew Bible and Its Modern Interpreters* (ed. D. Knight and G. Tucker; Chico, Calif.: Scholars Press, 1985), 123-65.

adjudicate the hierarchical relationships among different structuring features in a text. For this question his recent works pave the way by focusing on infratextual conceptual aspects of a text.[8] Among various structuring elements, Knierim contends that concepts of a text, which are operative in that text, are more fundamental than the generically typical; thus they govern the analysis of the structure of the text.

This recent development of Knierim's program presupposes the nature of texts as conceptualized linguistic-semantic entities. It means that texts are comprised of words, sentences, groups of sentences, and larger blocks of material knit together in an identifiable layout. These features are explicit textual information that appear on the surface of a text, and they demand an analysis of the text's grammar, syntax, stylistic and rhetorical features, genre elements, and themes. More than recognizing the linguistic nature of texts, this view of texts as conceptual entities also sees them as comprised of assumptions, presuppositions, or concepts that are directly and indirectly operative in their thought system. The presuppositions or concepts are inexplicit textual information located foundationally underneath the surface expression of a text. They are infratextual and stand at the subsurface level of a text. They are furthermore not general, indicating the text's view of reality; instead they are specific to an individual text in its individuality. This means that Knierim's program, conceptual analysis, deals with the infratextual concepts that are specific to a particular text and not abstractions from that text.[9]

Putting both explicit statements and implicit presuppositions of a text through a rigorous analysis, however, is not the end but the beginning of con-

---

8. R. P. Knierim, *Text and Concept in Leviticus 1:1-9: A Case in Exegetical Method* (FAT 2; Tübingen: Mohr [Siebeck], 1992); idem, "Interpretation of the Old Testament," in *The Task of Old Testament Theology: Substance, Method, and Cases* (Grand Rapids: Eerdmans, 1995), 57-138, esp. 58-71; idem, "Conceptual Aspects in Exodus 25:1-9," in *Task*, 389-99.

9. Knierim's observation on the dual aspects of a text is not particularly new, since most exegetes perceive that a certain system of assumptions lies beneath what the text says and contributes to what the text intends to say. In the process of interpreting a text, however, most exegetes tend to utilize this information in part intentionally and in part accidentally or unintentionally. Their practice of implicitly or even unconsciously reconstructing the infraconceptual framework results in a methodologically uncontrolled interpretation. This interpretation is potentially controlled by their own presuppositions of what the text ought to say. On the other hand, Knierim's observation is a launching pad for an advanced methodological discussion. He argues for the necessity of conscious use of the statements expressed at the surface of a text and presuppositions standing at the subsurface of a text. For Knierim, using this information is necessary, and should be given highest priority in order to grasp the meaning of the text. This knowledge must be methodologized, so that exegetes "do more than paraphrase what a text says" (Knierim, *Text*, 2).

ceptual analysis. Its next step is to investigate the relationship between the two. At issue is their "mutual convertibility" in a text. To investigate the interactions resulting from their influence, Knierim asks how the presuppositions are "implicitly operative" in the text and "generate and control its form and content." Thus, for him, the presuppositions of the text are more important than its statements. In other words, the linguistic and literary features of a text are in service to the composition and the structure of the text. This fact by no means undermines the significance of these explicit textual features in their own right, but it implies that their significance ultimately depends on how and on what basis they are related to the presuppositions of the text. The system of the conceptual presuppositions that lie underneath a text is responsible for all specific aspects of content and respective linguistic-semantic phenomena. This system is what Knierim calls the "structure" of the text.[10] Then,

---

10. Knierim's conceptual approach shares the similar methodological goal of structuralism, going below the surface of the text to a deep structural level (see D. Patte, "Structural Criticism," in *To Each Its Own Meaning*, ed. McKenzie and Haynes, 183-200; idem, *What Is Structural Exegesis?* [GBS; Philadelphia: Fortress, 1976]). With its understanding of the text as discourse, produced in a language, structuralism distinguishes linguistic signs that appear at a narrative level from the signifieds at the discursive level. The goal of structural exegesis is, then, to bring to light the interrelationship of values signified by signs. In focusing on a system, structuralism places its stress primarily on the mutual relations among components of the whole, paying little attention to the content of the individual components. Moreover, for structuralism, these mutual relations are governed by certain laws and rules, which determine the interaction among the individual elements. These laws and rules are located in the deep structure and are part of the semantic universe that determines all human communications. Structure analysis in a conceptual approach, on the other hand, deals with the implicit concepts that are specifically operative in a particular text, not the deep values that are abstracted from the surface of a text. Though structuralism talks about the semantic universe beneath the text, this universe is not necessarily specific to that text.

In addition, the conceptual approach focuses not only on the mutual relationships of the components of a text within the boundary that it permits, but also on the individual elements and the whole as well. Whereas in structuralism each component of the whole does not independently exist outside the system, and its relationship is understood only in terms of its function within the system of the whole, the conceptual approach starts with the uniqueness of the individual elements of the whole. For example, R. Jacobson understands the relationship of *parole*, the individual forms of expression on the surface of a text, and *langue*, the semantic rules, analogous to a chess game ("The Structuralists and the Bible," *Int* 28 [1974]: 147). For him, *langue* would represent the set of rules for chess that every player should know and is expected to follow, while *parole* would indicate individual moves or sets of moves that one makes. Conceptual analysis, however, acknowledges that there is more involved in a chess game than these two elements. It presupposes strategies (or concepts) that are specific to and responsible for the moves of a particular game. These strategies are con-

through a conscious reconstruction of the mutually convertible system of the text and of its assumptions, Knierim's program interprets a text in its own right and on its own terms.

Since Knierim's program, conceptual analysis, focuses on the structure of a text, it can be applied to virtually any written document, whether the document is perceived to be composed of various combinations of sources, or compiled of multiple layers, or a complete, self-contained unit. His choice of the extant text as the beginning of the investigation is an operational decision that the extant text is the realistic basis for a controlled investigation. A conceptual analysis must be done not only of the final form of the text but also of any stage of the text in its literary growth. Without a clear understanding of the text at any stage, not only the change of meaning of the text throughout its growth but also the meaning of its final form could be rendered confusing and ambiguous.

## An Illustration of Conceptual Analysis at Work

### Moses' and Aaron's Exclusion Because of Their Sin

J. Milgrom classifies numerous interpretations of the sin of Moses and Aaron (in Num 20:1-13) into three categories:

1. Moses' action in striking the rock: (a) that he struck it instead of speaking; (b) that he chose it although the people wanted another rock; (c) that he struck it twice instead of once.
2. His character, shown by (a) his blazing temper; (b) his cowardice (in fleeing to the sanctuary); (c) his callousness (in mourning for Miriam while his people died of thirst).
3. His words, (a) which in the form of a question were misconstrued as doubting God; (b) actually doubting God; (c) calling Israel "rebels"; (d) *nôṣî'*, "shall we draw forth. . . ?"[11]

---

sidered as parts of a game plan (conceptual system) that is not only necessary but also should be coherent in order to carry out a meaningful or successful game. Ultimately, each move on the board is generated according to this plan and reflects, however fragmentarily, the coherence of the plan without which it is meaningless.

11. J. Milgrom, *Numbers* (JPS Torah Commentary; Philadelphia: Jewish Publication Society, 1990), 448-56. For the latest work on this topic, see J. L. T. Kok, *The Sin of Moses and the Staff of God: A Narrative Approach* (Assen: Van Gorcum, 1997); idem, "Whose Staff Is It Anyway? Moses and Aaron," *BN* 85 (1996): 17-21.

Interpretations rarely posit a one-dimensional identification of Moses' and Aaron's sin. Most commentators have combined two or more of the explanations to justify God's judgment against Moses and Aaron. At first such an "all of the above" approach suggests that "none of the above" is entirely correct. Thus some resort to radical textual emendations and rearrangement to produce other explanations.[12] Others assume that the sin of Moses and Aaron has been lost in the tradition or deliberately obscured by the redactors so "as not to detract from the glory of Israel's founder."[13] However, Num 20:1-13 as a whole indicates that Moses and Aaron failed in their prophetic leadership and that God sentenced them accordingly, that is, removing them as leaders of the assembly rather than denying them the personal privilege to enter the promised land. As the representatives of God to the people, they misrepresented God's intent to provide the needed water to the people; this tended to mislead God's people about God's self-imposed promise to bring them into the promised land.

*Structure of Numbers 20:1-13*

**Report about Yahweh's denial of Moses' and Aaron's prophetic leadership**                                                  20:1-13

    I.  Setting: itinerary                                                                      20:1a

   II.  Two events                                                                             20:1b-13

       A.  First event: Miriam's death and burial                                     20:1b

       B.  Second event: Israel's quarrel against Moses and Aaron       20:2-13

           1.  Event proper                                                        20:2-12

              a.  Problem: people's complaint                               20:2-5

                  (1)  General statement                                  20:2

                  (2)  Specific content                                   20:3-5

              b.  Solution                                                        20:6-12

---

12. For harsh criticism on this approach, see E. Arden, "How Moses Failed God," *JBL* 76 (1957): 50-51; K. D. Sakenfeld, "Theological and Redactional Problems in Numbers 20:2-13," in *Understanding the Word* (Fest. B. W. Anderson; ed. J. T. Butler, E. W. Conrad, and B. C. Ollenburger; JSOTSup 37; Sheffield: JSOT Press, 1985), 136-37.

13. For example, G. B. Gray states in his commentary: "The truth is, the story is mutilated; and as any attempt to reconstruct it must be tentative, the exact nature of the sin of the leaders must remain doubtful" (*A Critical and Exegetical Commentary on Numbers* [ICC: Edinburgh: T&T Clark, 1903], 262). See the judicious comments of Milgrom, *Numbers*, 448; and of M. Margaliot, "The Transgression of Moses and Aaron — Num 20:1-13," *JQR* 74 (1983): 199.

On the surface level, this text has at least three distinctive elements. Verse 1 reports two things: Israel's travel itinerary and the event which happened at Kadesh (the death and burial of Miriam). Verses 2-12 shift the topic from v. 1 to Israel's quarrel with Moses and Aaron because of the lack of water, and these leaders' responses to Israel that bring about Yahweh's punishment for Moses and Aaron: they will not bring Israel into the promised land. Verse 13 ends the event with an extended etiological statement concerning the place-name, Meribah.

Is there structural integrity among these three elements, so that this text can be considered a complete unit? First, it is conceivable that 20:1 is the conclusion of 19:1-22 since the motif of death is present in both. Yet the death motif is also present and implied in the following units (vv. 3-4, 18-20, 22-29). At the same time, it is not entirely clear whether 20:1 is an organic part of what follows. If 20:1 is not a literary unit by itself,[14] however, then it is more closely related to 20:2-12 than to 19:1-22. This verse is generically more similar to 20:2-12, a story concerning the leadership of Moses and Aaron, than to 19:1-22, Yahweh's instruction for the water of purification. Second, 20:13 does not portray the entirely pure form of an etiology. It does not have typical patterns, such as ויקרא and כי clauses. It also adds another phrase, "by which he showed his holiness" (v. 13b), that is not directly connected with the name Meribah. Additionally, this verse provides the key to link v. 1 with vv. 2-12. It is the concept of holiness expressed in קדש. This term is the linguistic basis for Kadesh, where Israel stayed and where Miriam died and was buried (v. 1), and for Yahweh's reason for punishing Moses and Aaron (v. 12). As a whole, 20:1-13 reports that Moses and Aaron failed in their prophetic leadership by not showing the holiness of Yahweh to the people, and that Yahweh sentenced them accordingly, denying their future leadership of the assembly in the

---

14. T. B. Dozeman differentiates 20:1 from 20:2-13 and considers it as one of seven units in chaps. 20–21. However, he fails to provide the rationale for treating 20:1 as such ("The Book of Numbers," *NIB* 2:159).

promised land rather than simply denying them the privilege of entering the promised land.

The structure of 20:1-13 has two parts: the setting of the time and topographical locale (v. 1a) and the reports of the two events that occurred (vv. 1b-13). Verse 1a connects the following two events to the larger literary context of Moses' story (Exodus through Deuteronomy). In doing so, the text as a whole raises another question that can be answered in that larger context.[15] The first event is narrated very briefly (v. 1b), whereas the second is elaborated upon greatly so that it becomes the main event of the unit. These two are related to each other in that the characters of the event, that is, Miriam in the first and Moses and Aaron in the second, are the leaders of Israel and representatives of Yahweh for Israel's migration in the wilderness. Yet these two events differ in their operative concepts. The first event is interested in reporting a personal tragedy, the death of Miriam, but the second one points to the prophetic leadership of Moses and Aaron, although their deaths are implied as a consequence.

The second event contains two parts: the event proper (vv. 2-12) and a summary of the event (v. 13). These parts reveal three concepts that can be integrated into the dominant concept, the representativeness of Moses and Aaron, which is responsible for the structure of 20:1-13 in its entirety.

### Three Concepts in Numbers 20:1-13

**The Justifiable Complaint of the People**   The murmuring episodes can be divided into two different patterns of story line.[16] On the one hand, some

---

15. The question is whether God punishes Moses and Aaron justly. In light of Moses' status and dedication for constituting the Israelites as God's covenantal community and leading them into the promised land, could he be pardoned for the one mistake at the waters of Meribah? After all, has God not declared that Moses is the only one that God spoke to "face-to-face" (Num 12:8), and are there not more serious offenses among God's chosen leaders (and yet forgiven) in comparison to Moses? Since we know that God determines to call Moses as God's chief representative for the Israelites despite Moses' hesitations (Exod 3:1–4:17) and that God wants to make of Moses "a nation greater and mightier" than Israel (Exod 32:9-10; Num 14:12), was the sentence of God a condign punishment for Moses? This question should be discussed in light of the concepts that are operative beyond Num 20:1b-13 and in the entire Moses story.

16. These episodes are: the Red Sea (Exod 14:10-31), the waters of Marah (15:22-26), manna (Exod 16), waters from the rock (17:1-7), burning at Taberah (Num 11:1-3), quails (11:4-34), Miriam's and Aaron's jealousy (Num 12), incident with the spies (Num 13–14), Korah story (Num 16–17), bronze serpent (21:4-9). See B. Childs's division of two distinct patterns, *The Book of Exodus* (OTL; Philadelphia: Westminster, 1974), 254-64.

narratives tell a story of the people's need during the journey in the desert, and God's fulfilling of the need through Moses' mediation. On the other hand, other passages tell of unwarranted complaint on the part of the people and God's gracious provision (though the complaint was invalid), sometimes followed by a terrible punishment. The question is: in which category does Num 20:1-13 belong? The text clearly shows that the people quarreled with Moses (עִם־מֹשֶׁה, v. 3a) or with the Lord (אֶת־יְהוָה, v. 13aβ) because of the lack of needed water. The people's complaint and the divine instruction to Moses demonstrate that, in this instance, the people's murmuring was entirely justifiable.

First, the severity of the lack of water constitutes the main subject of the people's complaint. The statement that "there was no water" envelops their quarrel (vv. 2-5); the narrator states the absence of the water in v. 2 and the people restate it in v. 5. They expect to die, they even wish that they had died. The effect of their complaint is intensified by two questions, each clause longer than the preceding one and joined by conjunctions. No intervening narration separates the interrogation, which runs from v. 3b to the end of v. 5. The artistry of this intensifying effect is further heightened by the string of nouns joined by conjunctions. There was no water for people, none for cattle, none even for vegetation. Wouldn't such a quarrel be expected in a situation where people, having been wandering through a desert, are threatened with death by dehydration? G. Coats agrees on this line of inquiry by stressing the infertility of the land as a "much more prominent role" than the exodus theme in v. 5a.[17] The people not only perceived their station as "evil place" but also defined its character in terms of total infertility. The fact that אַיִן in the last statement of their complaint (v. 5bβ) stands after a noun in the absolute state indicates an emphasis of the thing denied, which is מַיִם.[18] This literary construction enhances the severity of the lack of water, as Coats claims: "the note about the lack of water in v. 5bβ still stands virtually as an anticlimax to the emphasis given by the list of plants."[19]

---

17. G. W. Coats, *Rebellion in the Wilderness: The Murmuring Motif in the Wilderness Traditions of the Old Testament* (Nashville: Abingdon, 1968), 76.

18. A. B. Davidson, *Hebrew Syntax* (3d ed.; repr. Edinburgh: T&T Clark, 1985), 172. Cf. Gen 2:5; 2 Kgs 19:3. The normal position of the particle אַיִן is before the word (noun or pronoun) that it negates in the construct state (thus it is usually אֵין).

19. Coats, *Rebellion*, 76. Moreover, comparing the nature of the complaint with that of Exod 17:1b-3 shows the same result. The narrator of the Exodus account introduces the problem of thirst in narrative form (v. 1bβ) with a natural place of the negating particle, and in imperative form for demanding of Moses to provide water so that the people may drink (v. 2aβ). The first words spoken by the Lord to Moses are also imperative instructions with

The characterization of the people's complaint as justifiable can be objected to by arguing the usage of רִיב. Coats concludes that the expression,

the result that the people may drink (vv. 5-6). This sequence seems to indicate that the focus of the quarrel would be on Moses' failure to provide needed water. But Moses' condemnation (v. 2) and the people's response (v. 3) raise an alternative for the central intention for the people's quarrel, namely the purpose of the exodus itself. Moses understood that their complaint in testing the Lord was whether the Lord was present in their midst (v. 7bβ). The presence of water indicates the presence of the Lord. This characterization of Moses is confirmed by the unusual placement of the people's concluding remark in v. 7bβ; "Is the Lord among us or not?" At first this question seems out of place. Logically it belongs before Moses' accusation (v. 2b). By the end of v. 7 the Lord has already affirmed his presence and provision. Why, then, does the question come at the end? The solution lies in the repetition of the אַיִן). While this key word introduces the physical problem in v. 1bβ, it punctuates the religious problem in v. 7bβ. This appears to be a deliberate stylistic device to accentuate the problem of "absence" at two levels. The first level is that the absence of water seems to be the way that the Lord again tests the people. The second is that the people test God by asserting God's absence in the light of this crisis. The first absence is part of narration, part of the givenness of the human situation. The second is the echo of a faithless assertion. Thus the repetition of אַיִן as the final word of the unit and the last spoken by the people artistically reveals the focal point of the narrative, the people's rebellious faithlessness toward God. The test of the presence of God is a question of the purpose of the exodus, as in the former stories.

Furthermore, the people's accusation in Exod 17:3b: "why did you bring us up out of Egypt to kill us and our children and our cattle with thirst?" indicates that the outcry of thirst is the result of Moses' bringing them out of Egypt. The main verb speech in v. 3b refers to the exodus (הֶעֱלִיתָנוּ). It is followed by an infinitive construct (לְהָמִית) whose purpose in this case is referring to the threat of dying from thirst. By stressing the syntactical position of לְהָמִית as a dependent infinitive construct clause, Coats argues that "the problem of thirst plays at best a minor role" (Coats, *Rebellion*, 60). Contrary to לְהָמִית in Exodus, לָמוּת in Numbers suggests the outcry of the people's given situation rather than their angry rebellion for Moses' past behavior, i.e., bringing them out of Egypt. Coats's argument, however, seems to ignore the emphatic position of וַיִּצְמָא at the beginning of v. 3, and the earlier demand of v. 2, which is based solely on the lack of water. But this ignorance cannot overrule Coats's strong argument, which is reinforced by the fact that לוּן with עַל in Exod 17:3a is more than simply "complain" but means "rebel against." Therefore, in Exod 17:3 Coats subordinates the threat of dying of thirst to the event of the exodus as the focal point of the complaint (*Rebellion*, 31-32). In addition, the Lord's response (vv. 5-6a) is rooted in the language of the exodus event. Note the facts that Moses is told (עבר; cf. Exod 12:12, 23); the elders of Israel are called as in Exod 3:16 and 4:29; the rod that struck the Nile making it undrinkable is to strike the rock (Exod 7:14ff.); the ḥōrēb of the burning bush and where Moses received his commission is again the scene of God's revelation. God's response serves mainly to reaffirm his deliverance of his people out of Egypt. Therefore, the crucial issue is that of the exodus, while the threatening situation of dying of thirst is an obvious part of the complaint. In the Numbers account the point is exactly opposite in that while the exodus is mentioned in v. 5aβ, the focal point of the complaint is the issue of lack of water. This distinction is persistent in the description of Moses' initial reaction and divine instruction, which I analyze later.

"תנסון את־יהוה" in Num 20:13aβ, "just as אשר־רבו בני־ישראל את־יהוה
מה in Exod 17:2b, must be taken in a negative light."[20] His main evidence for
this claim is that it is the only occurrence in which the Lord is the object of
this verb. But he misses the total picture of the nature of the people's quarrel.
The meaning of a single occurrence is always ambiguous. It may be interpreted in opposite ways according to an interpreter's purpose. The more obvious mistake of Coats is that he overlooks the crucial exegetical point that
ריב in the Numbers account does not conjoin with נסה as in the Exodus account. The legal concept associated with ריב is well established.[21] But in the
Numbers narrative, it is in a more general sense such as quarrel, dispute, or
conflict.[22] Quarreling with someone does not necessarily imply an unjust attitude on the part of the initiator. The issue is whether the content of the
quarrel is justified. Whereas the Exodus account (17:2, 7) combines ריב with
נסה "in order to indicate that the contention was not only unjustified but was
almost in the nature of a rebellion,"[23] the Numbers account employs only
ריב. Moreover, in the Numbers narrative there is no single occurrence for the
verbs that connote "unjustified complaints or wrong behavior in the judgment of the narrator."[24] With this solid evidence, the conclusion can be
reached that the people's complaint is justifiable in the face of their dying of
dehydration.

Second, the Lord's reaction to the people's complaint also indicates that
the nature of their complaint is justifiable. Verses 6-8 show Moses' and
Aaron's initial reaction followed by the Lord's instruction to Moses as his response to the people's complaint. If the people's quarrel is perceived as unjustifiable or rebellious, one might expect, as in the Exodus account, that Moses
and Aaron would respond critically (17:2) or cry out to God for help in the
face of death threats (17:4). In Numbers, however, they silently went from the
presence of the assembly and fell on their faces before the tent of meeting
(20:6a-bα). In response, the glory of the Lord appeared to Moses and Aaron,

20. Coats, *Rebellion,* 75. See the curse for those who strive with (ריב את) the Lord in
Isa 45:9. Note that unlike the people quarreling with Moses in v. 3a, and with Moses and
Aaron in vv. 4-5, they quarrel with the Lord in v. 13. With this, Margaliot ("Transgression,"
202-4) insists that the subject of הבאתם in v. 4 and העליתנו in v. 5 is Moses and Yahweh, not
Moses and Aaron. But it is not convincing in the whole context that equates the leadership of
Moses with the leadership of God. To rebel against Moses is to rebel against God. The two are
not the same, but the act is the same.

21. Coats, *Rebellion,* 32-37.

22. *HAL* 4:1141-44.

23. Margaliot, "Transgression," 217n66.

24. Ibid., 216n65.

and the Lord instructed Moses what to do (20:6bβ-8). This sequence shows that the divine appearance and instruction occur only to Moses (and Aaron), excluding the assembly. Moreover, this divine intervention is unique for murmuring situations and is characterized as positive.[25] Contrary to Num 14:11-12; 16:21; and 17:11 (Eng. 16:46), where divine punishment against the complainers is recorded, Exod 16:10-12 shows (as Num 20:7-8 intends) God's straightforward and gracious provision for the people's need. The crucial difference between Exod 16:10-12 and Num 20:7-8 lies in the grouping and arrangement of murmuring episodes on the basis of Sinai.[26] After Sinai, where the Israelites became the covenantal community equipped with clear divine instructions for the social and cultic life, only Num 20:1-13, among murmuring narratives, has punishment not for the complainers but instead for the leaders, Moses and Aaron. That the children of Israel quarreled with the Lord (20:13aβ) may encourage the readers to expect God's furious anger and deadly punishment, but no evidence of God's displeasure is reported. This uniqueness reinforces the characterization of the people's complaint as justifiable, and may direct the text's intention to highlight the justifiable divine punishment to Moses and Aaron for their misrepresenting the divine command.

The divine instruction itself exhibits God's desire to produce water for the people and their cattle. The last part (v. 8aβ-b) has four (out of six) verbs that are directly related to water: והשקית, והוצאת, ונתן, ודברתם. The imperative והקהל (v. 8a) is indirectly used to indicate who are to be involved in producing the water. This focus on the water becomes apparent in the three phrases that follow: that the rock will give its water, Moses will make water come out of the rock, and Moses will give water to the congregation and their cattle. It is surprisingly clear in comparison with the divine instruction in

25. In Exod 16:10-12 the glory of the Lord appears to "the whole congregation of the people of Israel," followed by a positive response to their murmuring. In some narratives, although the glory of the Lord appears to all people (Num 14:10b; 16:19), the consequence of this appearance is fatal punishment (14:11-12; 16:21). In an opposite way, when the consequence of the appearance of the glory is implied disaster (Num 17:11 [Eng. 16:46]), its appearance is only to Moses and Aaron (Num 17:7 [Eng. 16:42]).

26. Before Sinai, no serious punishments result when the people rebel against Moses (and Aaron). The Israelites are sharply reprimanded by Moses (and Aaron) or the Lord, but no one dies. After Sinai, on the other hand, each rebellion against Moses (and Aaron) results in a heavy punishment, usually death. Even in the case of the golden calf (Exod 32:1-35), it was Moses who could not control his anger and ordered the Levites to kill the people (32:25-28). In contrast, Yahweh was persuaded by Moses' intercession (32:14), and Yahweh further provided guidance and delayed the punishment (32:34). Although the text states that Yahweh sent a plague on the people, it mentions no report of any casualties related to that plague (32:35).

Exod 17:5-6b, which details the preparatory actions more than the production of water. Unlike the Exodus account, the consistent mention of cattle in Num 20:4 and 8 may indicate the text's care not to deviate from the focus on water.

The function for the first phrase, "take the rod," is at best ambiguous, however, because there is no further instruction for the rod. Whether the rod is supposed to be used for producing the water or for some other purpose is not clear in the divine instruction alone. But the context of the whole narrative grants sufficient clues to solve this question. First, the rod that the Lord commanded Moses to take is Aaron's rod, not Moses' own. The divine command states simply "the rod" (המטה) in v. 8a without specifying ownership. Whether the Lord intended this rod as Moses' or Aaron's or neither but simply a certain rod the text does not say. Without hesitation, however, Moses understood this rod as one belonging to Aaron, his brother.[27] The phrase מלפני יהוה in v. 9a is in all probability a direct reference to the record that narrates this rod had been placed לפני יהוה in Num 17:22 (Eng. 7) and had been taken מלפני יהוה in 17:24 (Eng. 9) and replaced לפני העדות in 17:25 (Eng. 10). Taking Aaron's budding rod is not Moses' voluntary act but following the Lord's command (20:9b). On the contrary, there is no reference anywhere to Moses' rod having been laid "before the Lord," though its use has been reported in connection with the plagues and the exodus, especially in Exod 17:1-7. In addition, this identification fits very well with the rest of the pericope, which recalls the Korah rebellion and its aftermath. The people's outcry in Num 20:3b, "would that we had died when our kindred died before the Lord!" is a reference to the disastrous result of Korah's rebellion (16:32-33; 17:14 [Eng. 16:49]). The verb גוענו (to expire, perish, die) recalls use of the same verb in 17:27 (Eng. 12). The optative particle ולו in 20:3b not only expresses "an unrealized wish" but also introduces "that which flows from what has gone before."[28] The specific case of "what has gone before" is the Korah incident, because the Korah rebellion and its aftermath are the preceding stories in the priestly source. Even reference to קהל יהוה in v. 4a recalls 16:3, further linking the quarrel of 20:1-3 to the context of chaps. 16–17. This linkage with the Korah incident makes it possible to understand the absence of further instruction for the rod and Moses' identifying the referred rod as Aaron's. Num 17:25 (Eng. 10) states: "And the Lord said to Moses, 'Put back the rod of Aaron before the testimony, to be kept as a sign for the rebels, that you may make an end of their murmurings against me, lest they die.'" Then

27. For the divided opinions among interpreters, see Kok, *Sin of Moses*, 156-66; idem, "Whose Staff," 17-21.

28. T. R. Ashley, *The Book of Numbers* (NICOT; Grand Rapids: Eerdmans, 1993), 376n2.

the Lord commanded Moses to take Aaron's rod in order to cease the people's complaint. The purpose is not to produce water by striking the rock with it. In this light, Moses' taking his own rod is itself considered part of his disobedience to God's instruction.[29]

Moreover, if the rendering of וְדִבַּרְתֶּם אֶל־הַסֶּלַע as "speak to the rock" is correct, what shall Moses and Aaron speak to the rock?[30] Speaking to a rock, at first glance, seems to be a strange thing to ask of someone. Since the text does not say anything, some speculation may be possible that "the rock" is understood in a metaphorical way for the Lord. The verb דבר occurs in the narrative only when the Lord speaks to Moses (v. 7) and Moses is commanded to speak to the rock (v. 8). Moses and Aaron are asked to speak to the rock "before their eyes" (לעיניהם). In v. 12 the Lord defines their failure in this way: they did not trust in the Lord to sanctify him "in the eyes of (לעיני) the children of Israel." The failure to speak to the rock and striking the rock instead are failures through unbelief to sanctify the Lord. Furthermore, the repetition of פנים is obvious in this text: the people wish they had died before (לפני) the Lord (v. 3bβ); Moses and Aaron go from (מפני) the assembly and fall on their faces (פניהם) at the door of the tent (v. 6); the rod is taken from before (מלפני) the Lord (v. 9a); the people are gathered before (אל־פני) the rock (v. 10a). All this exegetical information seems to point to "the rock" as standing for the Lord.[31] The divine statement: "Behold, I will stand before you there on the rock at Horeb" (Exod 17:6a) may support the metaphorical usage for the rock in Numbers. But one must concede that this theory is speculative, considering the lack of any direct textual evidence in Num 20:1-13.

In sum, the Lord's intention, reflected in his instruction, is clear. God sees his people's quarrel in the context of the threat of death by dehydration. In response to this justifiable complaint, God, without being angry or rebuking, appears only to his leaders; he instructs Moses step by step: first, to calm the complaint by showing Aaron's rod; second, to gather, along with Aaron,

---

29. Moses struck the rock "with his rod" (במטהו, v. 11a). It is clear that Moses is the antecedent for the 3d masculine singular suffix.

30. Margaliot prefers to translate this phrase as "speak about the rock" ("Transgression," 205-6n28). While Milgrom translates it as "by the rock" in "Magic, Monotheism, and the Sin of Moses," in *The Quest for the Kingdom of God: Studies in Honor of George E. Mendenhall* (ed. H. B. Huffmon, F. A. Spina, and A. R. W. Green; Winona Lake, Ind.: Eisenbrauns, 1983), 255-56, he translates as "order the rock" in his commentary (*Numbers,* 165). But rendering אֶל as if it were עַל is not necessary in consideration of the vast majority of cases, in which וְדִבַּרְתֶּם אֶל means "speak to."

31. Cf. J. de Vaulx, *Les Nombres* (SB; Paris: Gabalda, 1972), 223; G. J. Wenham, *Numbers: An Introduction and Commentary* (TOTC; Downers Grove, Ill.: InterVarsity Press, 1981), 151.

the congregation, and to speak to the rock before their eyes; and third, to bring forth water, and give drink to them and their cattle. The clear intention is that God wants to provide for the people's physical needs (the needed water in this case), as he has done before.

**The Unjustifiable Responses of Moses and Aaron**    Verses 9-10a portray the first two actions of Moses and Aaron that correspond exactly to the first two items in the divine instructions. Moses takes (v. 9 = singular verb in v. 8aα1) Aaron's rod, and Moses and Aaron assemble (v. 10a = singular verb in v. 8aα2, but it must be plural in sense because of the specification of subject: "you and Aaron your brother") the congregation. Next, in contrast, vv. 10b-11a report actions that neither correspond to nor have been specified by the divine instructions. The unspecified subject, in all probability Moses or Aaron, speaks to the people. Although the singular subject in v. 10b does not agree with the plural of v. 8aβ, it is understandable as one speaking for both indicated by "we" in the content of the speech. The clear nonconformance is that the leader speaks to the people, not to the rock. In addition, Moses' raising his hand and striking the rock twice with his own rod (v. 11a) are actions entirely of his own invention. Inexact obedience on the part of leaders is the same as disobedience: a part of the sins of Moses and Aaron. This is also hinted at by the awkward position of "as he [the Lord] had commanded him [Moses]" in v. 9b. Contrary to Exod 17:6b, "Moses did so, . . ." which indicates Moses' completing God's command, here this clause is inserted in the middle of Moses' and Aaron's actions, which suggests lack of precise obedience. It is another literary device to show the disobedience of the leaders at the outset.

The essential element behind these sins of the leaders goes beyond this imprecision. The words spoken by the leaders presuppose that they have mischaracterized the people's justifiable complaint; beyond that, they show that they mistrust God's fidelity to his own promise and plan for the people. Although God has been furious and punished the people for their constant murmuring, even after Sinai, the present text faults only the leaders for their anger and outburst. It is they who react negatively to both the people and God, who simply instructs them to quench the people's thirst. By calling the people "rebels," the leaders misjudged them. The people quarreled but had not rebelled. מרה is used mainly to describe negative reactions against the Lord.[32] While this word is used by one of the leaders to denounce the people,

---

32. Only two texts (Deut 21:18, 20) use it to deal with the rebellious son but not to deal with reaction against God. Cf. T. W. Mann, "Theological Reflections on the Denial of Moses," *JBL* 98 (1979): 484.

it is the Lord who uses this word to denote Moses' and Aaron's transgression in Num 20:24 and 27:14. Thus it is possible that using this word on the lips of one of the leaders here foreshadows the text's own intention for describing the leaders' sin in subsequent passages.

Milgrom claims that the act of speaking itself during the performance of a miracle is the nature of the transgression of Moses, because it does not distinguish Moses from any other magician who is simply doing a magic trick.[33] But he does not provide any explanation for the fact that speaking to the rock is God's own command. Milgrom also highlights the "we" of נוציא (v. 10b) as the essence of the sins of the leaders: from this prefix he infers that they are "setting themselves up in His place, arrogating to themselves the divine power to draw forth the water miraculously from the rock."[34] His argument, however, cannot be sustained in the light of God's own command. God says to Moses, "you shall bring forth (והוצאת) water for them from the rock." If the text wants to make clear that Moses replaces God by sinfully claiming the miraculous power, it ought to have God say "I shall bring (והוצאתי)," and have Moses proclaim that he will produce water, rather than ask an ambiguous question. The "we" in v. 10b is not emphatic and thus will not bear the weight of Milgrom's position.

Instead of picking one particular word spoken by one of the leaders, the whole rhetorical question should focus on the refusal by the leaders to provide water for the people by addressing the rock. The alliterative use of ה highlights the sarcastic and contemptuous tone of the refusal: המן־הסלע הזה המרים (v. 10b). That this rhetorical question is followed immediately by "Hear now, you rebels," suggests also the leaders' intention not to produce water.[35] Along with their misjudgment of the people's complaint as unjustifiable, the leaders perceive the people as unworthy to receive water.

The leaders' refusal has a deeper meaning. The words of Moses and Aaron would be understood by the people to mean that God was refusing to help them; after all, they know nothing about God's instructions to their leaders. By the speech they made, the leaders actually misrepresent God's inten-

---

33. Milgrom, *Numbers,* 453-56.

34. Ibid., 451-52. He actually does not interpret the text's own reason, namely, they did not trust to sanctify the Lord in the eyes of the people of Israel. Too much concentration on only one point leads him to leave everything else untouched, but only to serve to support his own opinion.

35. For many conceivable translations and implications for this rhetorical question, such as "Can we . . . ?" "Shall we . . . ?" "Must we . . . ?" or "Are we . . . ?" see Margaliot, "Transgression," 212-15; Sakenfeld, "Theological and Redactional Problems," 148-49. I prefer to translate as "Why should we . . . ?"

tions, and further mischaracterize God as being fed up with the people's constant quarrel, just as Moses and Aaron were fed up. Not knowing God's instructions to the leaders, the people are confused once again by Moses' actions, raising his hand and striking the rock twice with his rod. With the verb רום the raised hand is a symbol of power;[36] but it is also a symbol of defiance. In 15:30 anyone who does anything ביד־רמה is blaspheming the Lord and is to be cut off. Moses' presumptive use of power, striking the rock twice, solidifies the people's impression that it is the Lord's intention not to produce water for them. The speech to the people had indicated no water would be produced; now Moses' striking of the rock may suggest that even striking the rock would not bring forth water. It is not the striking itself, but striking twice that misleads the people, because they may expect Moses to strike only once, as in their previous experience (Exod 17:6). By striking the rock twice, Moses wants to prove that water would not come out of the rock. If this rendering is correct, how can the miracle of the water be explained? If the text wished to demonstrate the cost of sin by making a public example of leaders, then why did the text show the gushing forth of much water?

The water came not as a result of Moses' insolent action, but in spite of it. The conjunction in v. 11b may have an adversative force translated as "but": "And Moses raised his hand and he struck the rock with his rod twice, *but* much water gushed out." In spite of the words spoken by one of the leaders and actions done by Moses, God brings forth much water, showing his benevolent provision for the sake of the people. By paralleling "twice" and "much" the text wants to confirm that God does not abandon his promise to help his people on the one hand, and that the leaders misrepresented this intention of God for the people on the other. The people would have had no other way to understand the leaders' behavior except as God's own refusal to produce water.

**The Justifiable Punishment of the Lord**    Verse 12 specifically defines the sin of Moses and Aaron as their lack of trust in the Lord, which led them to fail to sanctify the Lord in the eyes of the people. The difficulties involved in interpreting the text's own characterization are constituted by the meaning of לא־האמנתם בי and להקדישני in this context. Concerning the phrase בי האמנתם, M. Margaliot presents some insightful information.[37] For him, the hiphil of the niphal נאמן must be translated as "to trust My faithfulness to you as my messenger to the people." By relating this word to the concept of

---

36. Deut 32:40; Isa 26:11; Ps 89:26 (Eng. 25), etc. See BDB 926.
37. Margaliot, "Transgression," 222-23.

covenant, he expands the idea that the leaders are supposed to impress on the people God's faithfulness to them as the God of their covenant. Locating בֿ נאמן in covenantal relationship, however, is not convincing due to lack of sufficient references. On the other hand, in the spy incident (Num 14:11), the Lord complains that the people "have not trusted in me" (לֹא־יַאֲמִינוּ בִי). This reference can be understood as God's anger against the people for their not trusting God's own plan, that is, to bring them into the promised land, and that they could rely on God to fulfill this plan.[38] Thus Num 20:12 reports that Moses and Aaron, like the Israelites on other occasions, failed to trust God's faithfulness to his own promise to bring the people into the promised land. This rendering is consistent in the usage of "sanctify" in God's understanding of the leaders' behavior.

Within the verses that concern Moses' and Aaron's sin by the water of Meribah the verb קדשׁ appears once in the niphal (Num 20:13), once in the piel (Deut 32:51), and twice in the hiphil (Num 20:12; 27:14). The piel is used only one other time to refer to sanctifying God. In Ezek 36:23 God will sanctify his name by restoring Israel from the nations. In the midst of helplessness and deep despair about God's dealings (i.e., the exilic situation) such a restoration must stem from God's fidelity to his own intrinsic nature. This is precisely what is ultimately meant by the sanctifying of his name.[39] Of the eleven occurrences of the verb קדשׁ in the niphal, ten refer specifically to God sanctifying himself.[40] Ezek 28:25 identifies God's sanctifying himself in the sight of the nations as the final fulfillment of his promise of the land to the ancestors, the proof of God's imperishable faithfulness. Five occurrences have a negative dimension. God sanctifies himself by harshly judging Sidon (Ezek 28:22), by sending Israel into exile (Isa 5:16), and by sending Gog against Israel (Ezek 38:16); in Lev 10:1-7 God sanctifies himself (v. 3) by devouring Nadab and Abihu with fire after they have offered unholy fire before God. This last usage, along with נאמן בֿ, indicates that the essence of the sin of the leaders is their misrepresentation to the people of God's fidelity to his promise to help his people. Moreover, this usage provides an adequate background for the under-

38. Even Deuteronomy characterizes the spy incident with the same word: "you did not trust in the Lord your God" (אֵינְכֶם מַאֲמִינִם בַּיהוה, 1:32).

39. The hiphil occurs in two other instances referring to people sanctifying God (Isa 8:13; 29:23). The context in Isa 8:13 suggests that the prophet calls on the people to make God the most significant fact of their existence, demonstrating by their attitudes and behavior that God is indeed holy.

40. Four times God shows himself holy by restoring the fortunes of Israel after the exile (Ezek 20:41; 28:25; 36:23; 39:27). Once God warns Israel not to profane his name because he will be sanctified (Lev 22:32).

standing of the final word of v. 13, בם. By whom or by what does the Lord assert/affirm his sanctity?[41] Some scholars answer "the children of Israel" due to its grammatical advantage, while others prefer "the waters of Meribah" due to its contextual meaning. But in consideration of the text's persistent use of literary devices, the plural suffix may suggest more than these obvious references, namely producing water and punishing the leaders. God affirms his sanctity in the eyes of the people by his demonstration of the power to produce much water and by his punishment of Moses and Aaron.[42]

As a result of this careful reading of Num 20:1-13 as it stands, the text's intention has been clearly stated. By the leaders' speaking as they did to the people, Moses and Aaron disobey God's command. The content of the speech suggests that the leaders misjudged the people's complaint as rebellious, while God found it justifiable. The most serious offense is that they mischaracterize God's nature as being irritated all the time without a proper cause, and thus they obscure God's gracious intention to help his people in time of need. This mispresentation is clearly shown to the people in Moses' presumptive use of power, and in his striking the rock twice with his own rod. In spite of this sin, God affirms his sanctity by producing much water for the people and their cattle, and by justifiably punishing Moses and Aaron by removing from them their anticipated role in leading the people into the promised land.

### Moses' Exclusion on Account of the People

Contrary to Num 20:1-13, the Deuteronomic traditions (Deut 1:37; 3:23-29; 4:15-24) narrate that Moses' exclusion from the promised land is on account of the people's unfaithfulness and rebellion. In the renarration of the spy incident (1:19-46), the text shows that God was angry with Moses because of the people (בגללכם, v. 37).[43] Generally the plural suffix of בגללכם is designated as referring to the rebellious people; thus on the people's account Moses was denied personal entrance to the promised land. However, the immediate context of v. 37, that is, 1:34-40, implies that the plural form of "on your account" refers to the spies who have been chosen from each tribe and returned with a

---

41. Where the Lord is the subject as here, ויקדש should be translated as reflexive rather than passive. Cf. Ashley, *Numbers*, 386.

42. For a detailed analysis concerning the sin of Aaron, see Sakenfeld, "Theological and Redactional Problems," 140-47; Margaliot, "Transgression," 209.

43. Only Deuteronomistic writers used the hithpael of אנף, and in every instance God is the subject and his anger is ready to erupt with awful consequences (Deut 1:37; 4:21; 9:8; 1 Kgs 11:9; 2 Kgs 17:18). Aaron is not found in the Deuteronomic narrative at all.

negative report about the land. Although the narrative begins and ends with the plural "you," indicating the people as a whole, vv. 35-38 focus particularly on leaders. That it is only Caleb who received a reward (v. 36) suggests "these men," to whom God's initial verdict is pronounced, can be exclusively the spies. It is followed by God's announcement of Joshua as the one who shall lead Israel to inherit the promised land (v. 38). In this context vv. 37-38 are not a case of personal tragedy for Moses, but instead his leadership cannot be completed as a result of God's anger with the chosen spies. Moreover, this understanding conjoins with Moses' poor judgment as a leader of the people in the beginning of the spy mission. Verse 23 reports that Moses not only agrees to the people's proposal to send spies but also takes initiative to select them. Rather than trusting the Lord, Moses misuses his leadership in compromising his integrity as God's chosen leader by approving the plan and appointing the twelve men. If this rendering is correct, God's denial of Moses is punishment for Moses' misusing responsibility for the Israelites.

Although the focus of Moses' exclusion is on his leadership, its cause is more the fault of the people than that of Moses himself. The Deuteronomic texts depict the people questioning God's ability to fulfill his promise (cf. Num 14:1-38), so that the entire people (כלכם, Deut 1:22), in contrast to the Numbers account (13:2, 17), initiated the request to Moses to send spies beforehand, even though they had just heard Moses' encouragement about God's presence (1:21). The people's request sets the fire of full-grown rebellion described with the word מרה: "you rebelled against the command of Yahweh" (1:26, 43). Their behavior was characterized as lack of trust in Yahweh (1:32). Then this larger context suggests that Moses as the leader of the people must accept their failure and even participate in their guilt. The sin of the people was so great that it engulfed even Moses and pulled him down with them.

### Harmonization in Psalm 106:32-33

The unavoidable question is, How are these conflicting traditions to be understood? If the Pentateuch is considered as one complete work, then neither the approach of choosing one while ignoring the other, nor the approach leaving the two traditions as unreconcilable, is appropriate. Ps 106:32-33 records some key elements of the two traditions, that is, anger on the people's account, and the speaking of rash words. Most interpreters assume that the psalmist attempts to harmonize the two: that the people's anger at Moses caused him to speak rash words to the people. It is possible, however, that the psalmist, despite knowing both traditions, inclines to the Deuteronomic tradition by attributing the severe punishment of Moses to the people's sin. First, there is no mention of Aaron. Second, the unidentified third-person masculine singular suffix and subject in vv. 32-33 can refer to God (conventionally it has been Moses): "They [the people] angered God at the waters of Meribah, and it went ill with Moses on their account; for they made God's spirit bitter and God spoke words that were rash." Third, the immediate context focuses on the people's continual sin. If this is the case, the psalmist utilizes the setting of the Numbers account to shift its concept completely: the people's quarrel was not justifiable but rebellious, and Moses was punished because of their sin.

But this rendering is reading too much into the text. Identifying the third masculine singular in this section as God creates an awkward relation between v. 32a and v. 32b and leaves an ambiguity as to whom God's rash word was spoken. The third masculine singular suffix of v. 32a is best identified as God; otherwise, it could be taken to refer to Phinehas, who is the subject of vv. 30-31. Then the third masculine singular in v. 33 should be Moses, following the clear mentioning of him in v. 32b. This clarification suggests that the psalmist presents a harmonized interpretation of the conflicting traditions, even utilizing the people's anger and Moses' emotional outburst in Exod 17:1-7.

## Concluding Remarks

Conceptual analysis of the priestly and the Deuteronomic traditions is a matter of Moses' position as leader *for the people* or his position as *representative of God* to the people. Moses as the representative of God to the people had the task of presenting the true intention of God, even if he perceived unworthiness on the part of the people. In times of despair and difficulty, whether its causes are a lack of water or a situation of exile, a representative of God must be able to lead God's people in trusting God's providence and wonder-working power. Even the seemingly impossible, for waters to gush out of a rock, or the Israelites' returning to their land, can be made possible. The role of a representative of God demands interpreting the present difficult situation as God's workplace to equip his own people for the future. Since the priestly traditions employ the trust motif that has been designated for the behavior of the people (Num 14:11; cf. Deut 1:32) and use the root מרה, which refers to the entire wilderness period (Deut 9:7, 24) and is related to the spy incident (Deut 9:23), on the lips of one of the leaders, it is possible that they knew this characterization of the people and transferred the same negativity to Moses and Aaron. When a representative of God fails in trusting and proclaiming the wonder-working power of God, he or she is no more or less than one individual who is punished for his or her own failure. On the other hand, Moses as the leader of the people is clearly shown in the Deuteronomic tradition. Moses suffers the same punishment that has been placed on the people throughout the forty-year wandering period. By locating Moses' punishment within the spy narrative, the Deuteronomic traditions succeed in their contention that Moses was certainly included in God's verdict.

Conceptual analysis is an exegetical approach to explain the text on its own terms and in its own right. The priestly traditions stress the leaders' representing God's intention to the people, whereas the Deuteronomic accounts focus on their guiding role for the people as they faced the corporate doom against which even Moses was helpless. The analysis allows interpreters to see the two traditions standing side by side while each is making its own theological claim. We should neither accept the two as unreconcilable nor collapse the two into one by scarifying the individuality. At best we can learn from the psalmist to integrate the two intertextually in a powerful hermeneutical statement that God has mercy on all sinful people.

# The Form-Critical Problem of the So-Called Deuteronomistic History

### THOMAS RÖMER

## Introduction

I still remember when I started my studies in Hebrew Bible and when I heard for the first time the magical words *Sitz im Leben*. At the time, it was presented as the very clue for understanding the OT: once you knew the form or the genre of a text, you would know the social and historical context in which it was produced. But if one dared to take a closer look, the so-called *Sitz im Leben* was often reduced to some obscure storytellers sitting around a campfire with memories like an elephant, which enabled them to recite oral traditions carefully preserved for hundreds of years. This encounter with form criticism was the source of my first real frustration in the realm of OT scholarship.

A second frustration was to appear much later. It still persists and is related to the so-called Deuteronomistic History, which I believed to be one of the most reliable constructs in OT research but which is now more and more disputed. Somehow, these two frustrations are related, inasmuch as the growing objection to the Deuteronomistic History hypothesis precisely denies the existence of any coherent, encompassing literary genre in these books, and views instead the Former Prophets as a random collection of texts of very different forms and origins. This specific — and much debated — issue will be the occasion to clarify the terms of the current debate and to elaborate in the following paper some proposals for a better and more appropriate understanding both of the form-critical approach and of the Deuteronomistic History.

## Two Major Problems

### How to Deal with Form Criticism?

There are as many definitions of the form-critical method as there are handbooks presenting the methods of historical-critical exegesis; hence it would be pointless to summarize them. It is enough to recall that the origins of the form-critical method are linked to the *religionsgeschichtliche Schule* (Gunkel, Gressmann).[1] Within the field of biblical studies, this approach can be understood as a reaction against the literary criticism à la Wellhausen that focused exclusively on the literary levels of a text, without investigating its social context of composition. The invention of *Formgeschichte* was of course tightly related to the discovery, in the middle of the nineteenth century, of an important amount of literature from Mesopotamia exhibiting strong similarities with the mythical texts of the Hebrew Bible. In addition, we should remember that Gunkel knew and appreciated the work of the Grimm brothers, who collected and classified German folktales and fairy tales. It is no surprise therefore that, for Gunkel, the Yahwist became the first "brother Grimm" of the OT: he was not an author, but a *collector*. The antipathy of Gunkel toward the concept of author had to do with the idea that most of the biblical texts actually derived from oral tradition. In his 1971 introduction to form criticism, Gene Tucker still made the following statement: "The first basic principle of form criticism is that most of the literature of the Old Testament had a long and often complicated oral prehistory."[2] This focus on oral tradition may be explained by the influence of romanticism and the quest for the very origins of biblical literature.

This is still manifest in Claus Westermann's commentary on the book of Genesis. Westermann is fully aware that the written texts of the patriarchal narratives cannot be older than the first millennium BCE. So he constantly resorts to oral tradition and oral patterns, such as "itineraries," "family stories," and so on, that, according to him, stem directly from what he calls "the time of the patriarchs." This is, in my view, an entirely apologetic and unjustified use of form criticism.

The problem is mainly related to the very notion of *Sitz im Leben*. The underlying presumption is that the identification of a form gives us the key to the recovery of the social setting from which it comes. Apart from the fact

---

1. Cf. H. Gunkel, *Genesis* (HAT I/1; Göttingen: Vandenhoeck & Ruprecht, 1901); H. Gressmann, *Mose und seine Zeit: Ein Kommentar zu den Mose-Sagen* (FRLANT 18; Göttingen: Vandenhoeck & Ruprecht, 1913).

2. G. M. Tucker, *Form Criticism of the Old Testament* (GBS; Philadelphia: Fortress, 1971), 6.

that this presumption is highly dubious, we do not have, in any case, a comprehensive sociological picture of "Israel," especially at the end of the Bronze Age and the beginning of the Iron Age. Hence the quest for the *Sitz im Leben* often produced circular arguments. In the 1960s and 1970s OT scholars invented, with the help of form criticism, an impressive number of festivals for almost every sanctuary. The supposed form of texts like Deut 26:5-9 or Joshua 24 led to the invention of covenant renewal festivals, which then became the setting for those "historical summaries." Today, we are of course much more cautious regarding such constructions. But does this mean that we should definitely give up the idea of the *Sitz im Leben*?

A last point should be mentioned. In his *Old Testament Exegesis*, O. H. Steck writes: "Form criticism not only treats small units, but also fundamentally treats collections and large literary complexes."[3] Nevertheless, the history of form-critical research shows that it was mainly devoted to the recovering of the smallest original units and the identification of their presumed origin in oral tradition. True, G. von Rad and M. Noth did address the form-critical problem of the Hexateuch and the Pentateuch, respectively, but even then they highlighted the oral tradition. For von Rad, the "little historical credo" (Deut 26:5-9) structuring the Hexateuch was inherited by the Yahwist from an old oral tradition.[4] According to Noth, the Pentateuch should be explained as a compilation of "larger units" (exodus, wilderness, conquest), each of them having its own oral origin.[5] Neither Noth nor von Rad ever raised the question of how one should deal with the Pentateuch or the Hexateuch *as a whole* from a form-critical point of view.

Nowadays, the fascination for the oral character of biblical literature is considerably diminishing in biblical scholarship. It has become quite clear that the concept of a steady oral tradition does not correspond to any historical reality, but is mostly an invention of OT scholars. As P. G. Kirkpatrick puts it, "oral tradition, far from preserving the sources of its past (whether they be entertainment or historical recollection, or both) constantly reinterprets that past in the light of the present."[6] In a more recent study, H. M. Wahl has

3. O. H. Steck, *Old Testament Exegesis: A Guide to Methodology* (SBLRBS 39; Atlanta: Scholars Press, 1998), 103.

4. G. von Rad, "The Form-Critical Problem of the Hexateuch," in *The Problem of the Hexateuch and Other Essays* (trans. E. A. Trueman Dicken; Edinburgh: Oliver & Boyd; New York: McGraw-Hill, 1966), 1-78.

5. M. Noth, *A History of Pentateuchal Traditions* (trans. B. W. Anderson; 1972; Scholars Press reprints and translation series 5; Atlanta: Scholars Press, 1981).

6. P. G. Kirkpatrick, *The Old Testament and Folklore Study* (JSOTSup 62; Sheffield: Sheffield Academic Press, 1988), 117.

shown that the writing down of oral traditions means transformation in form and content of the selected material.[7] We should therefore admit once and for all that "the jump into the world of living, oral communication in ancient Israel via form criticism is hardly possible any longer."[8]

Perhaps we should also return to the very beginnings of form criticism. Its starting point was the discovery of the parallels between biblical literature and documents from Mesopotamia (as well as Egypt and Greece). It is clear that this approach still remains basic to any study in the Hebrew Bible. In regard to the Deuteronomistic History, the comparison with written Near Eastern material could help to promote a better understanding of some structural forms and of the *Sitz in der Literatur,* if not the *Sitz im Leben.* But if we want to apply form criticism to such a comprehensive textual complex as the Deuteronomistic History, we need to address the preliminary problem of the very existence and coherence of the Deuteronomistic History.

## Is There a Deuteronomistic History at All?

Recently, the existence of a Deuteronomistic History running from Deuteronomy through 2 Kings has come under heavy attack. It should not be necessary to review all the criticisms raised against Noth's hypothesis, especially since some are more interested in postmodern deconstruction than in sane argument. Instead, I will concentrate on the studies by Westermann and E. A. Knauf, both of which attempt to question the coherence and the redactional unity of the Deuteronomistic History, but from very different perspectives and with different preoccupations.[9] Westermann's study is particularly interesting for our topic, since his argument against the Deuteronomistic History often resorts to form-critical observations.

---

7. H. M. Wahl, *Die Jakobserzählungen: Studien zu ihrer mündlichen Überlieferung, Verschriftung und Historizität* (BZAW 258; Berlin and New York: de Gruyter, 1997).

8. Steck, *Old Testament Exegesis,* 106.

9. C. Westermann, *Die Geschichtsbücher des Alten Testaments: Gab es ein deuteronomistisches Geschichtswerk?* (TB 87; Gütersloh: Kaiser, 1994); E. A. Knauf, "L''historiographie deutéronomiste' (DtrG) existe-t-elle?" in *Israël construit son histoire: L'historiographie deutéronomiste à la lumière des recherches récentes* (ed. A. de Pury, T. Römer, and J.-D. Macchi; MdB 34; Geneva: Labor et Fides, 1996), 409-18; ET: "Does 'Deuteronomistic Historiography' Exist?" in *Israel Constructs Its History: Deuteronomistic Historiography in Recent Research* (JSOTSup 306; Sheffield: Sheffield Academic Press, 2000), 388-98. Cf. also H. N. Rösel, *Von Josua bis Jojachin: Untersuchungen zu den deuteronomistischen Geschichtsbüchern des Alten Testaments* (VTSup 75; Leiden: Brill, 1999).

Taking up an older objection, Westermann first claims that the books inside the so-called Deuteronomistic History are so different that it is impossible to consider them as a coherent historical work. The circular conception characteristic of the time of the judges is in entire contradiction with that of the conquest story. The story in Joshua ends in 21:43-45 with the extermination of all Israel's enemies; during the era of the judges, however, Israel is continuously threatened by its neighbors. Hence Westermann claims that each book of the Former Prophets should be seen as stemming from a different social and historical context and undergoing a different process of composition.[10] According to him, the presence of small units like genealogies, itineraries, and notices, all of which would have been taken over from oral tradition without any changes, suggests that these texts stand very close to the events related.[11] But Westermann leaves entirely aside the question of how the transmission of these oral forms should be envisaged. His criteria to identify traditional, oral forms are also ambiguous and problematic. Hence it is rather surprising that he regards a text such as Josh 5:2-12 as a traditional "itinerary," since these verses convey a mix of Deuteronomistic and Priestly preoccupations. The death of the first generation in the wilderness, circumcision, and Passover have nothing to do with oral tradition; instead, this text must be understood as a postexilic literary creation.

Westermann's form-critical approach is therefore highly dubious. He is clearly less interested in explaining the process of formation and composition that gave to these books their "final," or present, shape, than in attempting to show that the gap between the texts (or the "small forms") and the (supposed) "historical" events to which they refer is minimal. When it comes to the question of the writing down of these stories, Westermann just observes: "There is no need for a special reason to explain the formation of the different historical books. It is enough to indicate the strong historical consciousness of the Israelite people."[12] If one had to accept such an argument, there would not be much need for historical exegesis of the Hebrew Bible.

One of Westermann's arguments is also taken over by Knauf, and it may deserve more consideration. He observes that, according to Deuteronomistic ideology, the exodus is the very beginning of Israel's history; therefore it would be surprising that the account of Israel's foundation did not begin

---

10. Westermann, *Geschichtsbücher*, 122.

11. Ibid., 81.

12. Ibid., 122. The German original reads: "Eines besonderen Motivs bedarf es für das Entstehen der einzelnen Geschichtsbücher nicht. Es genügt, auf das starke und lebendige Geschichtsbewusstsein des israelitischen Volkes hinzuweisen."

with that story. We will have to come back to this question later. Let us first examine the other arguments put forward by Knauf. He first points to the fact that the textual variants are much more important in the historical books than in the Torah. According to Knauf, this means that, contrary to the Pentateuch, there was no official version of these books until the third or second century BCE, which were edited and transmitted by different schools. Of course, the observation of the greater textual variance cannot be denied. But it may have another explanation: since the Pentateuch became the "canonical" document of Judaism from the fourth century BCE, its transmission was therefore necessarily much more controlled than that of the historical books.

Knauf also observes that the so-called Deuteronomistic History is never attested in the historical summaries or in the "historical" psalms, in contrast to the Pentateuch (e.g., Pss 74; 95), the Hexateuch (Pss 105; 114), or the "Primary History" covering the books from Genesis through Kings (e.g., Pss 78; 106; 136). If all these collections are documented in the Psalms, none mentions all the narrative traditions they contain, except for the late Psalm 105. So, for instance, apart from Psalm 105, in none of these Psalms do we find any allusion to the stories about the patriarchs. So it seems rather dubious that one might claim that these collections are firmly attested in the Psalms. Of course, some late texts try to summarize or even to "create" a Hexateuch (Josh 24) or a "Primary History" (Neh 9). But we also have, in my opinion, at least one summary of the Deuteronomistic History, which can be found in 2 Kgs 17:7-23. As almost everyone agrees, there can be little doubt that this text stems from the Deuteronomistic milieu. But it has often been overlooked that this commentary on the fall of Samaria hints at many important themes of the books from Deuteronomy through Kings. It is true that the text starts with the exodus tradition. But since no other theme from the Tetrateuch is alluded to, the opening verse may be taken as a summary of the book of Deuteronomy: "the people of Israel had sinned against YHWH their God, who had brought them up out of the land of Egypt . . . and they had feared other gods" (v. 7). The identification of YHWH as the God who led the people out of Egypt and the warning against other gods are two main themes of Deuteronomy.[13] Many of the sins enumerated in the following verses look back to the Deuteronomic law,[14] as does the mention of the *torah* and the *běrît* instructed to the fathers (vv. 13, 15). The mention of the driving out of the "nations" (v. 8) alludes to the book of Joshua. The forsaking of YHWH (v. 16) is the leitmotiv of the Deuteronomistic chapters in the book

---

13. See, e.g., Deut 5:6-7; 6:12-14; 29:14-18.
14. Cf., e.g., Deut 18:10-12 and 2 Kgs 17:17; Deut 12:2-3 and 2 Kgs 17:10.

of Judges.[15] The theme of the continuous sending of prophets (v. 13) starts in Judg 6:7-10 and continues with Samuel and all the prophets mentioned in the book of Kings. 2 Kgs 17:15: "they followed the nations that were around them" probably alludes to the wish for a king in 1 Samuel 8.[16] The cast images of two calves (2 Kgs 17:16) and the sins of Jeroboam (vv. 21-22) are a clear reference to 1 Kings 12. The passing of children through fire (2 Kgs 17:17) covers the time going from Ahaz (16:3) to Manasseh (21:6).[17] Finally, the comparison of Judah with Israel (17:19) alludes to the end of the southern kingdom in 2 Kings 24–25.

We may conclude, then, that 2 Kgs 17:7-23 presupposes or summarizes the *extent* of the Deuteronomistic History. It cannot be denied that inside the Deuteronomistic History we have different genres. But this does not exclude a certain unity of the whole work. Other arguments can be given in regard to this unity; but first we must briefly deal with the problem of the beginning of the Deuteronomistic History.

## Two Debated Issues

### Is There a Compositional Unity in Deuteronomy-Kings?

K. Schmid has recently reasserted that any comprehensive "history" including the books from Deuteronomy through 2 Kings had to start in Exodus. According to him, the original beginning of this history would be in Exodus 2, and its end in 2 Kgs 25:26.[18] This solution is attractive in that it solves the problem of the frequent allusions to the exodus in the Deuteronomistic texts. One may remember that already for Noth the beginning of the Deuteronomistic History did not seem very clear-cut; and Schmid is certainly right when he states that a "greater Deuteronomistic History" cannot start with Genesis, because of the different stylistic and ideological features of that book.[19] But if one adopts the idea that this "greater history" would always have included the books of Exodus and Numbers, other problems arise. How should we explain, for instance, the presence of texts like Deuteronomy 1–3, which recapitulate the events in

15. Judg 2:12, 13; 10:6, 10, 13.
16. Cf. 1 Sam 8:5 and 20: "So that we may also be like the other nations."
17. As well as the "host of heaven": Deut 4:19; 2 Kgs 21:3, 5; 23:4-5.
18. K. Schmid, *Erzväter und Exodus: Untersuchungen zur doppelten Begründung der Ursprünge Israels innerhalb der Geschichtsbücher des Alten Testaments* (WMANT 81; Neukirchen-Vluyn: Neukirchener Verlag, 1999), esp. 162-65.
19. Ibid., 56-102.

Exodus and Numbers? If Deuteronomy had always followed Exodus and Numbers, there would simply be no reason for Deuteronomy to open with a summary of the events reported in the previous books. On the other hand, the book of Deuteronomy is tightly linked to the following "historical books." The frequent allusions to the crossing of the Jordan make sense only if Deuteronomy and Joshua belong together.[20] The frequent allusions to the law about the king in Deut 17:14-15 prepare the various (Dtr) stories on the rise of kingship in 1 Samuel 8–12,[21] and the various Deuteronomistic layers of Deuteronomy 12 would be incomplete without 1 Kings 8 and 2 Kings 22–23. The formula of Deut 6:5 ("to love YHWH with all your heart, with all your soul, and with all your might") has only one exact parallel, in 2 Kgs 23:25.[22] One cannot doubt that the book found in 2 Kings 22 is the book of Deuteronomy. It is difficult to imagine that these cross-references are accidental.

In a forthcoming article, H. Roesel questions the existence of a comprehensive Deuteronomistic leitmotiv, which would link the books of Deuteronomy through Kings. I am convinced that such a leitmotiv does indeed exist. There are some features binding together Deuteronomy–Kings, which are almost entirely lacking in the Tetrateuch. This is the case of the אלהים אחרים, the "other gods." This expression is a Deuteronomistic standard occurring throughout the Deuteronomistic History, but which is attested only two or three times in the book of Exodus.[23] The theme of the worship of other gods and the rejection of YHWH runs through all the books from Deuteronomy through Kings, and offers a major explanation for the catastrophe of the exile and the destruction of both Israel and Judah.

The exile itself, the deportation out of the land given to Israel, is another "comprehensive leitmotiv" in the Deuteronomistic History. Except for

---

20. In the Tetrateuch allusions to the Jordan crossing are limited to Num 32:5, 21, 29; 33:51; 35:10. These texts are post-Dtr and post-Priestly and are probably due to a late Hexateuch redaction. This means that the linking of the book of Joshua to Deuteronomy was obviously not a preoccupation of the redactors who joined Deuteronomy to the Tetrateuch in order to form the Pentateuch, but was already present in the book of Deuteronomy *prior to the formation of the Pentateuch*.

21. See on this C. Nihan, "De la loi comme pré-texte: Tours et détours d'une allusion dans le débat exilique sur la monarchie en 1 Samuel 8–12," in *Intertextualités: La Bible en échos* (ed. D. Marguerat and A. Curtis; MdB 40; Geneva: Labor et Fides, 2000), 43-72.

22. Only in these two texts is מאד used as a substantive.

23. Exod 20:3 (= Deut 5:7); 23:13; 34:14 (singular). Outside the Dtr History the expression occurs 18 times in the Dtr parts of Jeremiah, once in Hosea (3:1), and in the Chronicler. Cf. T. Römer, *Israels Väter: Untersuchungen zur Väterthematik im Deuteronomium und in der deuteronomistischen Tradition* (OBO 99; Freiburg: Universitätsverlag; Göttingen: Vandenhoeck & Ruprecht, 1990), 85-87.

Lev 26:27-33, which is a very late (post-Dtr) text, there is no direct allusion to the exile in the Tetrateuch. Of course, a lot of the texts in this corpus may be understood in the light of the events of 597/587, for instance, Exodus 32, Numbers 13–14, and many more, but these texts never mention the exile explicitly. Only in the book of Deuteronomy is Israel's vanishing from the land clearly addressed (see, e.g., Deut 28:63-64). From there the announcement of the deportation occurs repeatedly in many of the "chapters of reflection," as Noth called them: Josh 23:13, 16; 1 Sam 12:15, 25; 1 Kgs 8:46-49; and 2 Kings 17. Related to this is the use of the root שׁמד, which is frequently attested in Deuteronomy and the Nebiim, but rare in the Tetrateuch.[24]

Deut 28:63 and 68 make the following announcements: "you shall be plucked off the land that you are entering to possess. . . . YHWH will bring you back in ships to Egypt by a route that I promised you would never see again." These threats are fulfilled at the end of the books of Kings: "So Judah was exiled out of its land. . . . Then all the people [who had not been deported to Babylonia] set out and went to Egypt" (2 Kgs 25:21, 26). The books from Deuteronomy through Kings are thus tightly bound, to the extent that *together* they explain why Israel and Judah could not escape from the fate that was announced by Moses from the very beginning.

There is also a form-critical argument for the unity of Deuteronomy–Kings. In that Deuteronomy is deliberately composed as a single and huge discourse of Moses at the end of his life, it provides the very pattern for the speeches and testaments in the remainder of the historical books (esp. Josh 23; 1 Sam 12; 1 Kgs 8).

True, the idea of a "greater Deuteronomistic History" is quite tempting. But the above arguments still make it plausible that its first, exilic, edition covered only the books from Deuteronomy through Kings. We may call this complex "crisis literature," because of the importance it gives to the explanation of the exile. But should we call it "historiography"?

## Is the "Deuteronomistic History" Historiography?

Until the 1970s, or even the 1980s, it was unproblematic to speak of biblical "historiography," and there was no doubt that such *Gattungen* as the Yahwist source, the Deuteronomistic History, and the Chronicler's Work were to be described as historiography. Since then, however, biblical scholarship has become engaged in a huge, passionate, and sometimes ideological debate about

---

24. In the Tetrateuch only in Gen 34:30 (niphal); Lev 26:30; Num 33:52.

the question of whether the Hebrew Bible may contain historiographical works. The discussion raises mainly the problem of the origins and definition of historiography. For if we adopt the Greek conception of *historia,* it seems indeed difficult to characterize such works as the Deuteronomistic History or the Chronicler's History as "historiography." According to Thucydides, a historian should use only reliable sources, avoid miraculous explanations based on divine interventions, and try to give objective descriptions of the facts that happened in the past.[25] In this respect it is quite appropriate to describe the Former Prophets as being still "mythical," since, for instance, narratives of divine intervention occur continuously in the Deuteronomistic History. Another difference between the biblical and the Greek histories concerns the conception of *authorship.* All the histories in the Hebrew Bible are anonymous works, which indicates that they have another function than the works of the Greek authors. In these histories the individuality and singularity of the narrator are not put forward; they are hidden, since the authors of the biblical stories endeavor to offer a gnomic vision of the past, that is, one that is beyond any alternative, critical interpretation.

So what should we call such a work as the Deuteronomistic History? Following J. Van Seters, who adopts the definition of the Dutch historian Huizinga, according to whom "History is the intellectual form in which a civilization renders account to itself of its past,"[26] it is possible to qualify the work of the Deuteronomist or the Chronicler as historiography. If, on the contrary, we wish to stress the differences between the histories in the Hebrew Bible and Greek or modern historiography, we should rather speak of a *narrative history,* by which is meant "the organization of material in a chronologically sequential order and the focusing of the content into a single coherent story, albeit with subplots."[27] There is in fact a clear sequential structure in the Deuteronomistic History: the foundation (Deuteronomy), the conquest (delimited by Josh 1 and 23), the time of the judges (delimited by Judg 2:6ff. and 1 Sam 12), the origins of the monarchy (delimited by 1 Sam 12 and 1 Kgs 8), the history of the two kingdoms (delimited by 1 Kgs 9 and 2 Kgs 17), and the history of Judah until its fall (with an "open end" in 2 Kgs 25). This is truly

---

25. Thucydides 1:21-22; C. F. Smith, trans., *Thucydides* (LCL; Cambridge: Harvard Univ. Press, 1956), 37-41.

26. Quoted in J. Van Seters, *In Search of History: History in the Ancient World and the Origin of Biblical History* (New Haven: Yale Univ. Press, 1983), 1.

27. L. Stone, "The Revival of Narrative: Reflections on a New Old History," *Past and Present* 85 (1979): 3. Quoted by H. M. Barstad, "History and the Hebrew Bible," in *Can a 'History of Israel' Be Written?* (ed. L. L. Grabbe; JSOTSup 245; Sheffield: Sheffield Academic Press, 1997), 54-55.

a history telling that constructs a chronology and creates its past.[28] The other biblical example for such a "narrative history" is the work of the Chronicler, which apparently tries to offer an alternative vision of Israel's history, with another sequential organization and a much more optimistic ideology.[29] Yet, if we may call the Deuteronomistic and Chronistic histories a "major genre," we also have to account for the fact that different forms and perspectives are included in the Deuteronomistic History.

## One Possible Solution: A Deuteronomistic Library

We cannot deal extensively with the *Sitze im Leben* of the different forms (and books) that are included in the Deuteronomistic History. To put it briefly, I would like to suggest that an important number of the forms we may distinguish do not have any oral origins but are imitations of Assyro-Babylonian literary conventions. The case is specially clear for the books of Deuteronomy and Joshua. The rhetoric of Deuteronomy has nothing to do with "Levitical sermons" or anything of that kind, but is taken over from the Assyrian vassal treaties; texts such as Deuteronomy 28 may have been directly copied from such treaties. The conquest stories in Joshua are also inspired from Assyro-Babylonian propaganda literature, as Van Seters and others have shown.[30] It might well be, as suggested by N. Lohfink,[31] that these two books were first published together as an anti-Assyrian propaganda literature under Josiah. The stories of Solomon also seem strongly influenced by Near Eastern literary patterns. The building of the temple is based on a common literary pattern,[32] and there was apparently a particular building genre in the ancient Near East, which was taken over by the Deuteronomists. The same may be said in the case of the story of the "book find-

---

28. See also Barstad, "History," 55.

29. See on this S. Japhet, "Postexilic Historiography: How and Why?" in *Israel Constructs Its History*, ed. de Pury, Römer, and Macchi, 144-73.

30. Van Seters, *In Search of History*, 330-31; see further K. L. Younger, *Ancient Conquest Accounts: A Study in Ancient Near Eastern and Biblical History Writing* (JSOTSup 98; Sheffield: JSOT Press, 1990).

31. N. Lohfink, "Kerygmata des Deuteronomistischen Geschichtswerks," in *Die Botschaft und die Boten* (Fest. H. W. Wolff; ed. J. Jeremias and L. Perlitt; Neukirchen-Vluyn: Neukirchener Verlag, 1981), 87-100.

32. Cf. V. A. Hurowitz, *I Have Built You an Exalted House: Temple Building in the Bible in Light of Mesopotamian and Northwest Semitic Writings* (JSOTSup 115; Sheffield: Sheffield Academic Press, 1992).

ing" in 2 Kings 22–23.[33] Finally, the framework running from 1 Kings 12 through 2 Kings 23 and structuring the accounts of the kings is borrowed from the royal Babylonian chronicles. This means that the "forms" and genres that inspired the first and the last books of the Deuteronomistic History come from well-attested Near Eastern literary patterns, taken over by the Deuteronomists. The situation is quite different for the books of Judges and Samuel, where the influence of the Deuteronomistic style is less obvious. In this case there are good reasons to think that the Deuteronomist took up older stories, while only slightly editing them. Thus there may have existed a "book of saviors" (the prototype of the present book of Judges),[34] a book of David's rise, and a book of the so-called succession narrative. Together with Deuteronomy–Joshua and the books of Kings, these books must have formed at first a loose collection, which was only later transformed into a coherent and well-structured work. We should probably assume therefore that some of the texts composing the Deuteronomistic History were already available *before* the creation of an encompassing historical work covering the time from Moses to the fall of Judah, but that such texts existed only as independent scrolls collected together in the same Deuteronomistic library. Where could we find such a library? The most probable solution in my eyes is the palace of Jerusalem under the reign of Josiah, especially if we assume that the origins of the Deuteronomistic movement should be located under the reign of Josiah — which means that most of these texts were used by the royal administration as political propaganda. During or after the exile, the scrolls of this library were more closely linked to each other by cross-references and the creation of an overarching structure, such as the Deuteronomistic discourses and the theme of the exile. Only then did these books become a Deuteronomistic *history,* trying to explain the present by constructing the past.

Have we solved the form-critical problem of the Deuteronomistic History? Probably not. But two results seem clear. First, there are enough arguments to maintain the redactional unity of Deuteronomy–Kings, which belong to the literary genre of "narrative history." Second, we should abandon some of our fantasies regarding form criticism. It may still be useful to identify literary genres, but we should definitely give up the idea of the existence of "pure forms," which would enable us to recover stable oral traditions. As

---

33. See, e.g., T. Römer, "Transformations in Deuteronomistic and Biblical Historiography: On 'Book-Finding' and Other Literary Strategies," *ZAW* 109 (1997): 1-11.

34. Cf. W. Richter, *Die Bearbeitungen des "Retterbuches" in der deuteronomischen Epoche* (BBB 21; Bonn: Hanstein, 1964).

we have seen, one of the basic impulses of form criticism was the discovery of Near Eastern literature, which paved the way for a better understanding of biblical texts. For the Deuteronomistic History, taking into account the Assyro-Babylonian parallels also gives us a few more insights into the *Sitz im Leben,* or should we say, the sociological and ideological contexts, of the Deuteronomistic party.

# Nehemiah 9 and the Problematic Concept of Context (*Sitz im Leben*)

BOB BECKING

## Introduction

In order to be part of a successful communication a text is molded after special forms. This basic and undeniable insight of form criticism holds for all kinds of texts, be they literary or religious, ancient or modern. Examples are easily found. A text starting with the sentence "Unfortunately we have to inform you . . ." is easily depicted as conveying an unpleasant message. It might refer to the fact that a book ordered is now out of stock, or it could be the opening sentence of a letter informing me that my application for a job has not been successful. In other words, the message unpleasant for the receiver is molded in standard and stereotypical language. Comparable remarks can be made for religious language. The phrase "O, eternal One, creator of all . . ." is easily depicted as the introduction to a prayer in which a devout person expresses his or her belief in a divine being that is seen as the ultimate ground of nature.

It is not my aim here to give a full display of the form-critical method. I would like to pay attention to one specific feature of this approach to texts. The informed reader has most probably detected various aspects of form criticism in my introductory lines. Next to the fact that texts are molded in forms, the following aspects have been hinted at:

1. A relationship exists between the form or *Gattung* of a text and the construction of words and phrases.
2. A text always functions in a certain context.

I will comment on both features. (1) A specific form is built up from elements that are specific or adequate to this form. A woe oracle, for instance, is almost always part of a prophecy of doom, and — the other side of the coin — an individual psalm of thanksgiving would usually contain a section that describes the distress a person had been in. (2) Texts function within a context, or as Gunkel suggested, texts are related to a *Sitz im Leben*.[1] Referring to texts that are contemporary with us can easily show this. A letter that informs me that my application for an interesting job has been refused functions in a specific social context that can be classified either as "being responsible for one's life by trying to get the best job available" or as "(un)employment." A religious text, for instance, beginning with the words "we are gathered here together . . ." reflects a ritual *Sitz im Leben*, a wedding or a funeral. We recognize these contexts quite easily for one clear reason: they are part of the symbolic universe we live in, or phrased otherwise, they are elements in the culture we were socialized to. The question that is pivotal to this contribution is: Would we recognize the contexts of texts from cultures at a distance, be it in time or space? I try to answer that question by discussing a text from the Hebrew Bible that was composed about twenty-four hundred years ago.

## A Few Remarks on the Book of Nehemiah

The book of Nehemiah, as it is now before us, relates the story of its main character. Nehemiah, a cupbearer in the Persian royal administration, is sent on a mission to the province Yehud — the territory of the former kingdom of Judah — to rebuild the ruined city of Jerusalem, especially the temple and the city walls. The book relates his deeds and doings: the completion of the temple, his measures on behalf of the poor, the reading of the Torah during the Festival of Booths, and Nehemiah's measures in the "mixed-marriage conflict." The present book might go back to the so-called Nehemiah memoir, a first-person report on the events. The book was probably composed in its final form during the fourth century BCE. Traditionally, Nehemiah has been construed as part of a greater work of history writing, the Chronistic History. This view has been questioned with quite convincing arguments. I am of the opinion that the book of Nehemiah should be treated as a text on its own and not as part of a "book" Ezra-Nehemiah.[2]

1. See H. Gunkel, "Die israelitische Literatur," in *Die orientalische Literaturen* (ed. P. Hinneberg; Leipzig: B. G. Teubner, 1925), 53-112.

2. On Nehemiah see H. G. M. Williamson, *Ezra and Nehemiah* (OTG; Sheffield: Sheffield Academic Press, 1987); T. C. Eskenazi, "Current Perspectives on Ezra-Nehemiah and the Persian Period," *CurBS* 1 (1993): 59-86; S. Japhet, "Composition and Chronology in the Book of Ezra-Nehemiah," in *Second Temple Studies: 2. Temple and Community in the Persian Period*

It is not the aim of this article to display in full all the details of the discussion of the emergence of the book of Nehemiah. I would like to concentrate on one textual unit within this book. In 9:1-5 it is related that on the twenty-fourth day of that same month[3] the Israelites were assembled with fasting, and with sackcloth, and with earth on them. They separated themselves from the "strangers," confessed their sins, and a prayer was uttered. After the prayer a covenant was concluded. The text of the prayer is in 9:6-37.[4]

## The *Gattung* of Nehemiah 9:6-37

I just classified Neh 9:6-37 as a prayer. The question, however, arises: What kind of prayer does this text contain? This issue has been discussed over the years and various proposals have been made. Gerhard von Rad suggested a proximity to the *Levitische Predigt*, a sermon rooted in the traditions of the Levites.[5] Nehemiah 9 has never been construed to be a sermon, but always as a prayer.[6] Mark Boda has argued that the text should be construed as a (com-

---

(ed. T. C. Eskenazi and K. H. Richards; JSOTSup 175; Sheffield: Sheffield Academic Press, 1994), 189-216; L. L. Grabbe, *Ezra-Nehemiah* (Old Testament Readings; London and New York: Routledge, 1998); R. D. Nelson, *The Historical Books* (Interpreting Biblical Texts: Nashville: Abingdon, 1998), 165-76.

3. The pronoun הזה, "in *this* month," suggests that the event took place a fortnight after the reading of the Torah by Ezra reported in Neh 8. This might be true for the narrative order — see T. C. Eskenazi, *In an Age of Prose: A Literary Approach to Ezra-Nehemiah* (SBLMS 36; Atlanta: Scholars Press, 1988), 100 — but I would not like to make claims on the historical level as regards this issue.

4. I do not construe Neh 9:5b as part of the prayer, pace, inter alia, Eskenazi, *In an Age of Prose*, 96; M. A. Throntveit, *Ezra-Nehemiah* (Interpretation; Louisville: John Knox, 1992), 102, but as a summons from part of a group of Levites to the Israelites to glorify YHWH; see also J. M. Myers, *Ezra, Nehemiah* (AB 14; Garden City, N.Y.: Doubleday, 1965), 158, 165-66; H. G. M. Williamson, *Ezra, Nehemiah* (WBC 16; Waco: Word, 1985), 303-4, 312; A. H. J. Gunneweg, *Nehemia* (KAT 19/2; Gütersloh: Mohn, 1987), 117-22; J. Becker, *Esra/Nehemia* (NEB 25; Würzburg: Echter, 1990), 92; Mark J. Boda, *Praying the Tradition: The Origin and Use of Tradition in Nehemiah 9* (BZAW 277; Berlin and New York: de Gruyter, 1999), esp. 25, 89-93.

5. G. von Rad, "Die levitische Predigt in den Büchern der Chronik," in *Festschrift für Otto Proksch* (Leipzig: Deichertsche und Hinrichs, 1934), 113-24; repr. in G. von Rad, *Gesammelte Studien zum Alten Testament* (TB 8; Munich: Kaiser, 1958), 249-61; ET: "The Levitical Sermon in I and II Chronicles," in *The Problem of the Hexateuch and Other Essays* (trans. E. W. Trueman Dicken; New York: McGraw-Hill, 1966), 267-80.

6. With the exception of C. R. Anderson, "The Formation of the Levitical Prayer in Nehemiah 9" (diss., Dallas Theological Seminary, 1987). See, e.g., Myers, *Ezra, Nehemiah*, 166-

munal) penitential prayer.[7] According to Boda, to be more precise, Nehemiah 9 stands in the tradition of penitential prayers that emerged after the fall of Jerusalem and that can be detected in other texts: Ezra 9; Nehemiah 1; Psalm 106; and Daniel 9. This is a set of texts that show some common elements. All of them are set in a, at least literary, context of discontinuity: the fall of the city of Jerusalem as a devastating calamity. They all reflect on the past and the role the ancestors of the prayers played in it, mostly assessed negatively as inadequate reactions to the love of God. Furthermore, the texts mentioned contain elements of penitence: the praying community feels sorry for the sins of the past and they confess that the doom they meet should be seen as the outcome of their guilt. Finally, these texts have a momentum of hope for reversal. These elements can easily be detected in the text of Nehemiah 9.

This *Gattung* of penitential prayer should be distinguished from the "communal lament," in which the representation of the past is more or less absent. This distinction should be connected to the traditio-historical background of the penitential prayer. Boda has noticed that in the penitential prayers the element of lament is silenced. He tries to explain this partial absence by relating the penitential prayers to the liturgical ritual of the *Rîb-Gerichtsdoxologie*. He especially points to Joshua 7, a text with considerable links to Ezra 9–10. In Joshua 7 the confession of sin is connected with the *Gerichtsdoxologie* and the element of lament is explicitly silence. In other words, this liturgical ritual supplies a context where people beyond the phase of lamentation are accepting their situation full of sorrow with an honest view on the past. Furthermore, an analysis of elements unique to the penitential prayers reveals that the texts are related not only to Deuteronomistic idiom and worldview, as is generally accepted, but also to texts with a priestly flavor. The penitential prayers, by implication, should not be seen as exilic

---

70: "Penitential prayer"; Williamson, *Ezra, Nehemiah*, 305-10: "Confession by the community and request for full restoration"; Gunneweg, *Nehemia*, 121-29; J. Blenkinsopp, *Ezra-Nehemiah* (OTL; Philadelphia: Westminster, 1988), 297-308: "Confessional prayer"; Eskenazi, *In an Age of Prose*, 96, 100: "(Communal) Prayer"; Becker, *Esra/Nehemia*, 93-97: "Bussgebet"; Throntveit, *Ezra-Nehemiah*, 102-6: "Sermon-Prayer of Confession"; H.-P. Mathys, *Dichter und Beter: Theologen aus spätalttestamentlicher Zeit* (OBO 132; Freiburg: Universitätsverlag; Göttingen: Vandenhoeck & Rupprecht, 1994), 67-68: "Gebet"; Grabbe, *Ezra-Nehemiah*, 55-56: "Prayer of Confession"; Nelson, *Historical Books*, 172-73: "Confessional prayer"; J. H. Newman, *Praying by the Book: The Scripturalization of Prayer in Second Temple Judaism* (SBLEJL 14; Atlanta: Scholars Press, 1999), 55-116: "Prayer."

7. Boda, *Praying the Tradition*, esp. 21-41; note that Boda has taken over some ideas of R. A. Werline, *Penitential Prayer in Second Temple Judaism: The Development of a Religious Institution* (SBLEJL 13; Atlanta: Scholars Press, 1998).

and postexilic descendants of the Deuteronomistic movement. They are nourished by various traditions.[8]

With these last remarks Boda is already anticipating his answer to the question of the *Sitz im Leben* of the penitential prayer. Before entering that discussion, I would like to remark that Boda's form-critical classification might be right. He presents his proposal in such a way that it can be controlled. The enumeration of a set of comparable texts makes clear that the *Gattung* proposed was an acknowledged mold to express religious ideas on doom and hope in a situation of despair. From the perspective of the program of this volume, it should be noted that the face of form criticism is changing here in that Boda is adding some sort of a historical depth-dimension to his argument, since he discusses in detail all the, I would say, intertextual relations and allusions of words and phrases in Nehemiah 9.[9] From his survey one can conclude that many of the words and phrases in the prayer could function in other literary contexts as well. This implies that the relation between a *Gattung* and its language is not always exclusive.

## The *Sitz im Leben* of Nehemiah 9:6-37

In the past various contexts for Nehemiah 9 have been proposed.[10] These proposals were, for obvious reasons, related to the ideas on the *Gattung* of the text. Boda strongly advocates the view that the *Sitz im Leben* of these penitential prayers should be associated with a kind of covenant ceremony that he construes for the Persian period.[11] This view is not his personal invention; he is, however, elaborating an idea that others have proposed.[12]

His proposal is based on his reading of several postexilic texts, such as Ezra 9–10; Nehemiah 5; 9–10, from which he detects the existence of a religious ceremony: a Persian period covenant ceremony.[13] This is apparently a ritual that can be classified as a crisis ritual, since it is not related to the annual festival cycle or to the human life cycle. In other words, the gathering of people for such a ceremony is not related to the rhythm of the agricultural

---

8. Boda, *Praying the Tradition*, 43-73.

9. Ibid., 89-187.

10. See, e.g., the chart in ibid., Appendix A, 198-202.

11. Ibid., 32-41.

12. See, e.g., F. Baumgärtel, "Zur Liturgie in der 'Sektenrolle' vom Toten Meer," *ZAW* 65 (1953): 263-65; Williamson, *Ezra, Nehemiah*, 275-76; Williamson, *Ezra and Nehemiah*, 43; Eskenazi, *In an Age of Prose*, 103-4; Throntveit, *Ezra-Nehemiah*, 95-96.

13. Boda, *Praying the Tradition*, 32-38.

year, nor is it provoked by events in a person's life (birth, circumcision, marriage, burial). The ritual is triggered by a devastating calamity in history and by the wish to cope with that calamity religiously. Elements of the ritual are: the reading of an ethical code, such as the Torah, a confession of sins in the past suggesting that the calamity was the result of human failure to live with the ethical code, the concluding of a covenant, and the taking of measures that must prevent a new calamity, such as the measures by Ezra with regard to mixed marriages.

A text functions in its context, or to phrase it differently: the comparison, or even confrontation, of the text with its context yields a meaning. According to Boda, the penitential prayer functioned as follows in the context of an early postexilic ritual: by reapplying the traditions of ancient Israel the accounts of the sinful past were settled so that the inhabitants of Yehud and Jerusalem, or at least the true Yahwists among them, were mentally ready for a new start in the framework of a new relationship.[14] In Boda's final interpretation the methodical approaches of intertextuality and form criticism coincide and support each other, leading to a significant reading of the text. Yet there is one issue that has to do with the — in my view — problematic concept of context. Before elaborating on this, I have to clarify that I am not challenging Boda's views as such. My problems are related to the form-critical approach in general, taking Boda's well-argued reading of Nehemiah 9 as an example.

## The Concept of *Sitz im Leben*

It is therefore necessary to have a closer look at the idea or concept of *Sitz im Leben*. Making a connection between a *Gattung* and a *Sitz im Leben* was the genius invention of Hermann Gunkel.[15] To understand Gunkel it is important to look at his *Sitz im Geschichte*. The form-critical approach is basically a countermovement to the slivering of the traditions and the fragmentation of the texts that were characteristic of the literary-critical method as elaborated by nineteenth-century scholars like Graf, Kuenen, and Wellhausen. Gunkel's fresh start was also intended as an appeal for what we now call the artistic beauty of the text. But contrary to current "new literary critics" who read the

---

14. Ibid., passim.

15. On Gunkel see W. Klatt, *Hermann Gunkel: Zu seiner Theologie der Religionsgeschichte und zur Entstehung der formgeschichtlichen Methode* (Göttingen: Vandenhoeck & Ruprecht, 1969); H. J. Kraus, *Geschichte der historisch-kritischen Erforschung des Alten Testaments* (2d ed.; Neukirchen-Vluyn: Neukirchener Verlag, 1969), 341-67.

texts of the Hebrew Bible preponderantly on a synchronic level, Gunkel construed the texts as expressions of the remote culture of ancient Israel. It should not be forgotten that Gunkel was motivated by the so-called religion-historical school, *religionsgeschichtliche Schule.* This approach aimed at a reconstruction of the history of ancient Israel not only at the level of main events, but also at the level of daily life. In other words, Gunkel's approach was connected to a more or less sociological perception of ancient Israel. It is in this connection that the concept of context should be understood.[16]

In Gunkel's view a text is related to a societal entity that informs us about the construction of daily life in ancient Israel. Gunkel and other form critics construe some sort of a double interaction between form and context: the form of a text informs us about the context, since a specific context generates specific forms. This double interaction is a vivid feature in the interpretation of the Psalms by Sigmund Mowinckel.[17] One can observe that many scholars who are applying the form-critical approach talk about the context of a form as of a real-life event that can easily be evoked by the use of a mixture of archeology, ancient Near Eastern texts, imagination, and common sense. It is exactly at this point that my criticism will start.

Let us return to Boda's proposal on the interpretation of Nehemiah 9. There are two ways in which I would like to challenge his remarks on the context of Nehemiah 9: (1) his interpretation of the available evidence; (2) the problematical character of a reconstructed *Sitz im Leben.*

## Critical Remarks on Boda's Proposal

Boda's proposal to determine the context of Neh 9:6-37 as an early postexilic covenant ceremony is mainly based on two features: (a) the comparison with texts like Ezra 9–10 and Neh 5:1-13; (b) the interpretation of the noun אמנה in Neh 10:1 as a synonym for ברית, meaning some sort of agreement or even covenant. Boda construes the narratives in Nehemiah 5 and Ezra 9–10 also as texts reflecting a covenant ceremony. He clearly makes a difference between preexilic ceremonies, as reflected in 2 Kings 23, and postexilic ceremonies, the main difference being that a text like 2 Kings 23 focused on moral conduct and

---

16. See Gunkel, "Die israelitische Literatur"; G. M. Tucker, *Form Criticism of the Old Testament* (GBS; Philadelphia: Fortress, 1973); K. Koch, *Was ist Formgeschichte? Methoden der Bibelexegese* (3d ed.; Neukirchen-Vluyn: Neukirchener Verlag, 1974), 34-48; J. Barton, *Reading the Old Testament: Method in Biblical Study* (2d ed.; London: Darton, Longman and Todd, 1996), 30-44.

17. S. Mowinckel, *Psalmenstudien* (6 vols.; 1921-24; repr. Amsterdam: Schippers, 1961).

general commitment of the Judeans in all dimensions of life (see esp. v. 3), while the relations on postexilic covenant ceremonies are restricted to a single aspect of morality: the care for the *personae miserae* in Nehemiah 5; and the mixed marriages in Ezra 9–10.[18] I do recognize that the three texts under consideration all reflect some sort of an occasional ceremony to solve problems in the organization of the postexilic community in and around Jerusalem, but I wonder if these ceremonies are not of too occasional a character to assume the existence of the possibility of gathering the community for specific occasions that was part of the social code of the Yahwistic group in postexilic Yehud. Or, phrased otherwise, could it also be mere coincidence that we find three examples of occasional ceremonies in the books of Ezra and Nehemiah?

Next to that I am wondering about what Boda would mean by "covenant" in this context. As is well known the Hebrew noun ברית is not easy to translate or understand. The word can denote the covenantal relationship in which the community with YHWH has been described throughout the Hebrew Bible. On the other hand, however, the word can refer to an agreement with or without obligations between individuals, groups, persons of different status in a group, and so on.[19] Within the three texts under consideration the noun ברית occurs as follows: in Nehemiah 5 the noun does not occur; in Neh 9:8 and 32 the noun refers to the relationship between YHWH and the people of Israel in the past; in Ezra 10:3 the noun occurs in the construction ברית כרת.[20] It should be noted that in Ezra 10:3 God is not the subject of the verb. Rather, the "we" group in the narrative functions as the subject. It is the religious leaders who are sealing an agreement with implications for the moral conduct of the Yahwists in the community. In other words, the ceremony is not specifically a covenant (renewal) ceremony, but should be interpreted as a political ritual to bind the community to a specific moral rule.

Boda construes the expression כרת אמנה in Neh 10:1 as a synonym of the expression כרת ברית. He acknowledges that this interpretation is disputable, but nevertheless he reads Neh 10:1 as an indication that after the penitential prayer a covenant was concluded by the religious leaders of the community.[21] Although many scholars have construed אמנה as a synonym of

18. Boda, *Praying the Tradition*, 35-36.

19. See, e.g., *DCH* 2:264-67.

20. On Neh 5 see Williamson, *Ezra, Nehemiah*, 231-46. On Ezra 10:3 and its context see, e.g., Williamson, *Ezra, Nehemiah*, esp. 150-51; B. Becking, "Continuity and Community: The Belief-System of the Book of Ezra," in *The Crisis of the Israelite Religion: Transformation of Religious Traditions in Exilic and Post-Exilic Times* (ed. B. Becking and M. C. A. Korpel; OTS 42; Leiden: Brill, 1999), 256-75.

21. Boda, *Praying the Tradition*, 32-34.

ברית, I am of the opinion that the noun אמנה refers to a "trustworthy regula-tion."[22] The use of a word specifically different from ברית is an indication that it might be the author's intention *not* to refer to a covenantal act.

In sum, in view of the fact that even Boda refers to the existence in the Hebrew Bible of penitential prayers that do not have their context in a specific ceremony,[23] we can safely surmise that penitential prayers — such as Nehe-miah 9 — were uttered on different occasions, sometimes in occasional cere-monies, sometimes in an unbound situation. It would therefore be better to assume that the *Sitz im Leben* of this genre is more psychological of character: prayers like this function in the context of a human being or a community that is wanting to settle accounts of the past in order to make a fresh start in life.

## *Sitz im Leben:* A Problematic Concept

Despite its roots in romanticism, the form-critical method, especially in its traditional form, is heavily influenced by nineteenth-century positivism. This implies that the contexts of the various forms in the Hebrew Bible have, mostly implicitly, been construed as real-time, reconstructible historical facts. From Gunkel to Klaus Koch — and beyond — the *Sitz im Leben* of a text has been presented as a touchable and knowable feature in the past that really was there.

Criticism has been uttered on the concept of the one-to-one relation so often applied in form criticism. Steck, among many others, refers to the fact that a specific genre can be used in its primary context, but can also be ap-plied in a secondary context.[24] The well-known mourning cry, introduced with the particle "Woe . . . ," has its original *Sitz im Leben* in the bewailing of a deceased, as can be inferred from 1 Kgs 13:30. Later this form was applied by the prophets in their descriptions of forthcoming doom for Israel and Judah, bewailing them beforehand as if they were deceased already.[25] This possibility

22. For the former see the outline in ibid., 33n42. For the latter see Williamson, *Ezra, Nehemiah,* 320; Gunneweg, *Nehemia,* 130-31; *DCH* 1:318. This meaning also suits in Neh 11:23, the other occurrence of the noun אמנה in the Hebrew Bible.

23. Boda, *Preaching the Tradition,* 38-40.

24. O. H. Steck, *Exegese des Alten Testaments: Leitfaden der Methodik* (12th ed.; Neukirchen-Vluyn: Neukirchener Verlag, 1989), 116-19.

25. See, e.g., W. Janzen, *Mourning Cry and Woe Oracle* (BZAW 125; Berlin: de Gruyter, 1972); D. R. Hillers, "*Hôy* and *Hôy*-Oracles: A Neglected Syntactic Aspect," in *The Word of the Lord Shall Go Forth* (FS D. N. Freedman; ed. C. L. Meyers and M. O'Connor; Winona Lake, Ind.: Eisenbrauns, 1983), 185-88; J. A. Wagenaar, *Judgment and Salvation: The Composition and Redaction of Micah 2–5* (VTSup 85; Leiden: Brill, 2001), 208-13.

of reapplying a form in a new context puts in mind the idea that the form used in Nehemiah 9 was originally at home in an individual ritual of confession of guilt, but was reapplied in the context of an occasional ceremony in postexilic times.

Postmodern — or better: postpositivistic — criticism of the idea of context is to be found for instance in a few remarks made by Rolf Knierim. He observes correctly that in the form-critical approach the social contexts form the "decisive generative forces for the emergence of generic texts."[26] But what do we know about these societal settings behind the texts? Knierim answers that question quite negatively. He simply states that we do not possess a comprehensive picture of society in ancient Israel.[27] Here the face of form criticism has turned completely pale. In his quite minimalistic approach, Knierim overlooks the character of historical "facts" and he misinterprets the kind of knowledge we have about the past.

What do we know about the past, how do we know that, and what is the status of our propositions about past events? These questions have been discussed the last twenty-five years or so especially in connection with questions like: Can a "history of ancient Israel" be written? What role would biblical and archeological evidence play in that writing?[28] I will not summarize that discussion — if that were possible — but only repeat my personal view.[29] A distinc-

26. R. Knierim, "Criticism of Literary Features, Form, Tradition, and Redaction," in *The Hebrew Bible and Its Modern Interpreters* (ed. D. A. Knight and G. M. Tucker; Philadelphia: Fortress; Chico, Calif.: Scholars Press, 1985), 123-65, esp. 144.

27. Ibid., 144.

28. An abundance of literature exists on questions like this. I mention here what I construe as the most important voices: B. Halpern, *The First Historian: The Hebrew Bible and History* (San Francisco: Harper & Row, 1988); E. A. Knauf, "From History to Interpretation," in *The Fabric of History: Text, Artifact and Israel's Past* (ed. D. V. Edelman; JSOTSup 127; Sheffield: Sheffield Academic Press, 1991), 26-64; P. R. Davies, *In Search of "Ancient Israel"* (JSOTSup 148; Sheffield: Sheffield Academic Press, 1992); I. W. Provan, "Ideologies, Literary and Critical: Reflections on Recent Writing on the History of Israel," *JBL* 114 (1995): 585-606; N. P. Lemche, *The Israelites in History and Tradition* (Louisville: Westminster John Knox, 1998); P. M. McNutt, *Reconstructing the Society of Ancient Israel* (Louisville: Westminster John Knox, 1999); T. L. Thompson, *The Mythic Past: Biblical Archaeology and the Origins of Biblical History* (London: Basic Books, 1999); W. G. Dever, *What Did the Biblical Writers Know and When Did They Know It?* (Grand Rapids and Cambridge, UK: Eerdmans, 2001).

29. See B. Becking, "Inscribed Seals as Historical Sources for 'Ancient Israel'? Jeremiah 40.7–41.15 *par exemple*," in *Can a "History of Israel" Be Written?* (ed. L. L. Grabbe; ESHM 1; JSOTSup 245; Sheffield: Sheffield Academic Press, 1997), 65-83; idem, "Ezra's Reenactment of the Exile," in *Leading Captivity Captive: The "Exile" as History and Tradition* (ed. L. L. Grabbe; ESHM 2; JSOTSup 278; Sheffield: Sheffield Academic Press, 1998), 40-61; idem, "Is de Hebreeuwse Bijbel een hellenistisch boek?" *NedTT* 54 (2000): 1-17.

tion should be made between two ideas: (1) the idea of history and (2) the idea of the past. "Past" refers to the period of time up to now. Given the irreversibility of time, it is impossible to enter the past. All we have are the relics of the past: the footsteps of humankind in a sea of time. "History" is a tentative narrative on the past. Any historian, ancient or modern, consciously selects and connects "events" from the past into a *narratio*. The historian, by profession, is responsible for the selection of the material and the connection made between various data. When history writing takes the form of a narrative it is an organization of the past and not a mere description of it.[30] In other words, any history is a proposal. Given the irreversibility of time, it is impossible to test a history. This does not imply a minimalistic or revisionistic position, since I would like to make a distinction between the narrative as a whole that cannot be verified, since it is the product of the mind of the historian, and the elements of the narrative, which can have the form of propositions on the past that can be checked against the existing evidence, texts, archival data, and results of archeological excavations.[31] When one is assessing a scholarly written history, all that can be asked for is internal consistency and evidence relatedness.

Let me return to the form-critical approach. A context, or *Sitz im Leben*, should be seen as a hypothesis on the past. In connecting evidence from the past, the form-critical scholar has made a representation of the past. In his mind he reenacted a piece of the past.[32] This implies that a *Sitz im Leben* is neither a mere description of social pattern from the past, as in the positivistic approach, nor a mere phantasm, as postmodern "historians" would like to have it. It is a proposal on the past, and I would like to treat it as a proposal. It should be noted that this status — being a historical proposal — makes the concept of context problematic.

## Text and Context: Between History and Hermeneutics

Reading a text — as a presentation of a form — in its context is an act of dating. What happens can be compared to the "lock-and-key" method used in

---

30. See, e.g., A. C. Danto, *Analytical Philosophy of History* (Cambridge: Cambridge Univ. Press, 1968); F. R. Ankersmit, *Narrative Logic: A Semantical Analysis of the Historian's Language* (The Hague: Mouton, 1983); Knauf, "From History to Interpretation"; H. M. Barstad, "History and the Hebrew Bible," in *Can a "History of Israel" Be Written?* ed. Grabbe, 37-64, esp. 54-60; Becking, "Inscribed Seals," 65-69.

31. See Ankersmit, *Narrative Logic*, 75-76.

32. On the concept of reenactment see R. G. Collingwood, *The Idea of History: Revised Edition with Lectures 1926-1928* (Oxford: Oxford Univ. Press, 1994).

dating (biblical) texts. A classic example of this method can be found in C. Hardmeier's monograph on the interpretation of 2 Kings 18–20.[33] The text, be it in an original form or in a final redaction, is construed as a key. The reconstructed history during which the text was written, or in which it received its final redaction, is to be seen as the lock. When lock and key fit, a date is found.

A few remarks need to be made:

1. There is the fallacy of circular arguing, especially when the key has been smoothed in a literary-critical way. As regards form criticism, circular reasoning has not always been avoided. One gets the impression sometimes that the *Sitz im Leben* has been invented for the text under consideration leading to some sort of a Baron von Münchhausen approach.

2. Another lock is always conceivable. Hardmeier dates 2 Kings 18–20* shortly before the exile, but a Maccabean date would also provide a nice interpretation. Since forms can function in a variety of contexts — as indicated above — a variety of possibilities is open.

3. Our knowledge of historical processes and patterns in ancient Isarel is not only debated but also limited. Any history of ancient Israel that goes beyond the enumeration of dates should be seen as a representation of the past in which the symbol system of the person who made this representation plays a role.[34] The lock in which the key is turned is not an objective entity but a proposal from the part of the historian. The same should be said about the context or *Sitz im Leben*. They do not form objective entities, but we are not left in the swamp of subjectivity. The more data we have for a certain period, the more we can reach an agreement.

Is reading a text in its context, for instance Nehemiah 9 in the context of an early postexilic covenant ceremony, a hermeneutical or a historical act?[35] That question cannot be answered in general, as I hope to have made clear in this essay. An answer to that question remains dependent on the character of

33. Chr. Hardmeier, *Prophetie im Streit vor dem Untergang Judas: Erzählkommunikative Studien zur Entstehungssituation der Jesaja- und Jeremiaerzählungen in II Reg 18–20 und Jer 37–40* (BZAW 187; Berlin and New York: de Gruyter, 1990).

34. See, e.g., Danto, *Analytical Philosophy;* Knauf, "From History to Interpretation."

35. The former is strongly suggested by W. G. Jeanrond, *Texts and Interpretation as Categories of Theological Thinking* (Dublin: Gill and MacMillan, 1988), 104-28; M. G. Brett, *Biblical Criticism in Crisis? The Impact of the Canonical Approach on Old Testament Studies* (Cambridge: Cambridge Univ. Press, 1991), 76-115. The latter is implied in Boda's view.

the evidence we have for a specific *Sitz im Leben*. That implies that as long as we do not have a fully controlled scholarly view on the social history of ancient Israel, the concept of context will be useful as well as problematic for interpreting texts from this remote culture.

# PART IV

# PROPHETIC LITERATURE

# The Basic Forms of Prophetic Literature

### DAVID L. PETERSEN

The title of this essay is, of course, a takeoff on a classic tome, Claus Wester-mann's *Grundformen prophetischer Rede,* translated into English as *Basic Forms of Prophetic Speech.*[1] This volume, originally published in 1960, sym-bolized the powerful influence of form criticism, as it had developed espe-cially in Germany, on North American biblical scholarship. For the purposes of this paper, I want to identify two elements prominent in that volume.

First, although Westermann had subjected the prophetic books and re-lated literature to a thoroughgoing analysis, the title of this book reflected a particular understanding of what prophets were about, namely, that they were primarily speakers. The book's title is *Basic Forms of Prophetic Speech,* not Basic Forms of Prophetic Literature. In this regard, it is interesting to note that, following Hans Wildberger, Westermann identified one type of litera-ture as the "prophetic account," even though it did not constitute a form of direct address. The bias was that prophets were essentially orators, and Westermann was obviously not alone in holding this position.

Second, Westermann identified several different modes of address. Nonetheless, he was willing to make a judgment that one, more than others, typified what the prophets were essentially about. Westermann thought that the announcement of judgment was by far the most prominent form of pro-phetic address. It was the *basic* form. There were, to be sure, variants of this form; he noted the woe oracle in particular. Then, further beyond the pale, were so-called borrowed speech forms, forms of discourse used in the society that the prophets took over for their own purposes. Westermann even speaks

---

1. C. Westermann, *Basic Forms of Prophetic Speech* (trans. H. C. White; Philadelphia: Westminster, 1967).

of these as "foreign forms," and of the ways they transmogrify that which the prophets presented as their primary message. These "foreign forms" included the legal procedure, the disputation, the parable, the lament, and the prophetic torah. These variants may reflect some elements of the announcement of judgment, but they have moved increasingly far from it. For the purposes of this paper, I omit discussion of what Westermann termed "the prophecy of salvation." So, even though Westermann spoke of basic forms, he focused on only one form, what has come to be known as the judgment oracle. Plurality within prophetic discourse was not part of his legacy.

In order to move the discussion forward, I argue that it is appropriate to speak about basic forms of prophetic literature. I maintain that the activity of Israel's prophets led to the formation of literary forms that naturally derive from the exercise of their prophetic roles. Since there were diverse prophetic roles, one should expect prophetic literature itself to be diverse. In this paper I identify five such roles and then describe the literature that grows out of their exercise. From a methodological perspective, this study integrates form-critical and social-world studies.

In an earlier study, I argued that the Hebrew Bible presents four role labels that reflect diverse forms of prophecy in ancient Israel.[2] The role labels are *ḥōzeh, rō'eh, nābî'*, and *'îš hā"ĕlōhîm*. The first two are normally translated "seer," the third, "prophet," and the fourth, "man of God." Although over time *nābî'* achieved primacy as the most prevalent term for prophet, these four role labels point to moments in Israel's history when not all intermediaries were known as *nĕbî'îm*; they point to situations in which not all intermediaries did the same thing; and they point to periods when intermediaries at the same time acted in different ways.

As a corollary, it is appropriate to think that differing kinds of prophetic activity normally resulted in different kinds of literature. As a result, I explore the four role labels mentioned above as something like Weberian ideal types. By using the notion of ideal types, I mean to suggest that one type of intermediary may be characterized by a certain kind of activity, but that behavior of another sort may be present as well. In addition, one kind of literature will be especially prominent as a reflection of one mode of prophetic behavior.

First then, the *rō'eh* or "seer." Though one may translate this Hebrew noun accurately with the word "seer," the use of this word in the Hebrew Bible suggests that the *rō'eh* exercised a role different from that of the *ḥōzeh*. One may view the *rō'eh* type prophet as akin to a diviner. If the term *rō'eh* refers to a kind of diviner, as 1 Sam 9:9 and 11 suggest, then we would expect a

---

2. D. Petersen, *The Roles of Israel's Prophets* (JSOTSup 17; Sheffield: JSOT Press, 1981).

certain sort of literature to reflect divinatory or prophetic consultative activity; it would be a chronicle of the divinatory process.

Such forms of intermediation involved overt social interaction. The intermediary has an audience, which itself takes the initiative in seeking information from the deity; Ezek 20:1 is a parade example: "certain elders of Israel came to consult the Lord, and sat down before me." Literature attesting to this form of prophecy will almost inevitably be written as a prose chronicle or narrative. That narrative may focus on the information garnered by divination, or it may report the process of social interaction itself, as is the case in 1 Samuel 9. Here the literature does more than simply present the request for a divinatory perspective; and it does more than preserve or record the utterance of the intermediary. The interaction of the intermediary with an audience, apart from the divinatory utterance, is itself part of the standard behavior of that prophet (as Jer 38:14-28 demonstrates).

Apart from the case of Samuel, who is called a rō'eh (1 Sam 9:9, 11), the Hebrew Bible includes other instances in which a prophet, not labeled rō'eh, performs this consultative role. Ezekiel 20 presents a scene in which the prophet, living in exile, received representatives from "the elders of Israel." They had come to "inquire from Yahweh." Yahweh speaks through the prophet, who responds to the elders, though in terms they had not anticipated.

Perhaps the most straightforward case of a prophet receiving a request for a divine oracle and then providing the expected response occurs in Zechariah 7–8. Again, representatives are sent. The citizenry of Bethel empowered legates to ask priests and prophets in Jerusalem, "Should I mourn and fast in the fifth month?" (Zech 7:3). The prophet responds: "The fast of the fourth month, and the fast of the fifth month, and the fast of the seventh, and the fast of the tenth, shall be to the house of Judah seasons of joy and gladness" (Zech 8:19). The prophet provides a wide-ranging negative answer to the emissaries: there are to be no more lamentations of that sort.

In these and other cases, prophetic literature derives from the interaction between the intermediary and those who want information from the deity. The deity's response, which is communicated by the prophet, is only one part of the larger literary complex. The prophet as diviner is clearly attested in one basic form of prophetic literature, the divinatory chronicle.

Second, ḥōzeh, also translated as "seer," figures prominently in several Judahite prophetic books (Amos 7:12; Isa 29:10; Mic 3:5-8). It is surely not coincidental that visions, ḥezyōnōt — or more precisely stated, vision reports — occur in these books. The vocabulary of visions is prominent even in the editorial formulas (Isa 1:1; 2:1; Hab 1:1).

For the purposes of this essay, it is sufficient to recognize that vision reports are often formulated in a stereotypical manner and normally written in prose. Moreover, there was a tradition in which a series of visions were reported (e.g., Amos's five visions, Ezekiel's four, and Zechariah's eight). Unlike the divinatory chronicle, these visions do not appear to derive from direct solicitation by an audience, though they may have resulted from intentional behavior by the intermediary (e.g., through incubation).

My contention involving the vision report is "stronger" than that of typical form-critical arguments. The vision report is often included in catalogues of *Gattungen* that a prophet might use to proclaim a message from the deity. It may be that some vision reports, such as Jer 1:11-15, represent rhetorical ploys. Nonetheless, it seems likely that the vision reports of Amos, Isaiah, Ezekiel, and Zechariah do indeed constitute reports of visionary or trancelike experiences. Hence one should think that Zechariah, in composing his vision reports, is not choosing one among several different literary forms in which to report his experiences and messages. One might think that Amos or Micah had selected what Westermann termed a "foreign" form to convey a message of admonition or judgment. But the vision report is a quite different matter. This literary form exists as a direct expression of the intermediary as visionary. From this perspective, the vision report is one of the basic forms of prophetic literature, attesting to one fundamental form of intermediation, that of visionary behavior.

Third, *nābî'*. The ideal type associated with this role label involves auditory perception and utterance by the prophet. Jeremiah's call narrative is salutary (Jer 1:4-10). According to this view, to be a prophet is to hear Yahweh's word or to have that word placed in one's mouth, and then to utter that word to others. Many Israelite and Judahite prophets, particularly after the schism that created those two nations (922 BCE) and before the defeat of Judah (587 BCE), acted in ways that allow us to understand them as *nĕbî'îm*.

Various types of utterance characterize this form of prophetic behavior. One may say that direct speech is a hallmark. These prophets were speakers, and their utterances were of two basic types: divine oracles, in which the deity speaks in the first person (e.g., Hos 11:1-7), and prophetic sayings, in which the prophet speaks in the first person and refers to Yahweh in the third person (e.g., Mic 3:5-8). Since admixtures of these two forms occur with some regularity, however, one should not construe them as fundamentally different in rhetorical force. Together, these two forms of discourse — divine oracle and prophetic speech — constitute a third basic form of prophetic literature.

Fourth, *'îš hā'ĕlōhîm* or "man of God" is used most frequently with reference to the prophets Elijah (1 Kgs 17:18) and Elisha (2 Kgs 6:6). They are "holy men," individuals who possess the power of the sacred. They function as inter-mediaries neither by speaking on behalf of the deity nor by "seeing into" the divine world. Rather, they themselves personify the world of the sacred in the profane, but without the ritual requirements of the priests, who occupy a simi-lar position on the boundary between the sacred and the profane.

Alexander Rofé has argued convincingly that the stories associated with these holy men form a special type of literature, which may be termed the leg-end.[3] In a classic form-critical argument, he observed that the *Sitz im Leben* of such stories is the telling of tales about the power of these people, often by circles of disciples (so 2 Kgs 8:4). Here, this type of prophetic literature, which focuses on these figures, has reportage as one of its hallmarks. These are nar-ratives written by someone other than the holy man; and these stories cele-brate his power. This literature deserves to be understood as prophetic litera-ture, since it attests to and derives from the behavior of the holy man, a role ancient Israelites deemed to be prophetic.

Fifth, the final element in this typology reflects individuals who bear no explicit title. Texts from ancient Mari attest such people who receive revela-tions through dreams. They were prophets, if you will, but that culture did not use its prophetic role labels to describe them. Similarly, I propose that at least one type of Hebrew Bible literature may derive from untitled intermedi-aries. We do not know the names or titles of those who wrote the speeches, stories, or comments embedded in the Deuteronomistic History. Some schol-ars think that these prophetic materials were a source or sources used by the Deuteronomistic Historian.[4] Other scholars contend that these materials were added to the Deuteronomistic History, as a prophetic redaction.[5]

Those individuals wrote from a perspective that valued highly the pro-phetic word. These authors testify to the power of individual prophets (e.g., 1 Kgs 12:15) or to the prophets in general (e.g., "his servants the prophets," 2 Kgs 24:2). We might label such authors as prophetic historians, people re-sponsible for the prophetic source or redaction evident in parts of the Deuteronomistic History. Moreover, we hear impressionistic echoes of such individuals in the Chronicler's History (1 Chr 29:29). These references allude to a style of intermediation in the form of history writing.

---

3. A. Rofé, "The Classification of the Prophetical Stories," *JBL* 89 (1970): 427-40.

4. For example, A. Campbell, *Of Prophets and Kings: A Late Ninth-Century Document (1 Samuel 1–2 Kings 10)* (CBQMS 17; Washington, D.C.: Catholic Biblical Association of America, 1986).

5. For example, W. Dietrich, *Prophetie und Geschichte: Eine redaktionsgeschichtliche Untersuchung zum deuteronomistischen Geschichtswerk* (FRLANT 108; Göttingen: Vanden-hoeck & Ruprecht, 1972).

Rofé has used the phrase "prophetic historiography" to describe some of this literature. It recounts events in the world of public affairs and the ways in which prophets are related to them. Such prophetic historiography attests that the prophet has a critical role to play in times of national crisis. 2 Kgs 18:13–19:37 offers a parade example according to which the narrator recounts Isaiah's interactions with Hezekiah during Sennacherib's assault on Jerusalem. Hezekiah prays, whereupon Yahweh provides a response through the prophet, proclaiming that the Neo-Assyrians will not defeat Jerusalem.

In conclusion, a brief review of basic prophetic roles and the literature typically associated with them demonstrates that one ought to expect diversity within the general category of "prophetic literature." Moreover, one may discern at least five basic forms of prophetic literature: divinatory chronicle, vision report, prophetic speech, legend, and prophetic historiography.[6] There is, of course, no simple correlation between prophets known by a particular role label and a certain form of literature. As a result, one may envision an individual prophet, for example, an Amos, both reporting visions and offering divine oracles. Similarly, Elijah may appear as both a holy man and a prophetic speaker. One prophet could engage in diverse forms of prophetic activity. As a result, prophetic books may include many forms of prophetic literature, for example, vision report and prophetic speech, as is the case in the book of Amos.

I began this discussion of form-critical work on prophetic literature by observing that Westermann had, like many before him, identified one primary form of prophetic discourse. However, I rejected a number of his claims. In so doing, I mounted an argument on behalf of true plurality within prophetic literature. Not all prophetic literature reflects prophetic speech. Here Westermann was not well served by the scholarly consensus of his day, namely, the conviction that prophets were primarily speakers. When we read what he wrote: "the prophetic books contain three major kinds of speeches: accounts, prophetic speeches, and utterances," we should immediately draw back and ask: Why should one construe accounts as speeches? Once we pose this question, and not only about narratives but also about legends and vision reports, we begin to create a fuller picture of what prophetic literature involves.

In addition, when we couple this form-critical and literary enterprise with a social-world approach to prophetic behavior in ancient Israel, we learn

---

6. I have argued elsewhere that symbolic action reports, commissioning reports, and prophetic biography are also important exemplars of prose prophetic literature (*The Prophetic Literature: An Introduction* [Louisville: Westminster John Knox, 2002]).

that there were diverse types of prophetic behavior. These led to the creation of certain basic forms of prophetic literature. Put quite simply, prophets did more than speak, and so prophetic literature involves more than prophetic speech. They divined, and so we have divination reports. They acted as holy men, so we have legends. They engaged in possession behavior, so we have vision reports. It is at this point that one of Westermann's contentions reappears as important, namely, that certain forms of prophetic discourse are truly the domain of Israel's prophets. To this extent, we may still speak of "basic forms," even though we should now think about the basic forms of prophetic literature, not just the basic forms of prophetic speech.

# The Prophetic Book:
# A Key Form of Prophetic Literature

EHUD BEN ZVI

## Introduction

This contribution addresses issues related to the genre of "prophetic book" and its sociohistorical background in postmonarchic Israel. I argue that the study of this genre and of its social setting is central for historical-critical studies of the prophetic books per se and for historical reconstructions of the society/ies within which and for which these books were written. Above all, this essay is to be construed as both a contribution to and a call for a new approach in the form-critical study of the prophetic books.[1]

Multiple references to oral genres such as oracles of salvation, lawsuit, prophetic announcements (of punishment, for instance), and the like can be found in form-critical studies of prophetic literature.[2] But references to the genre of "prophetic book" are few and tend to appear only in recent

---

1. To be sure, it has implications for all biblical books, but the study here focuses on prophetic books.

2. See "classical" works such as the commentaries of H. W. Wolff on prophetic books and cf. C. Westermann, *Basic Forms of Prophetic Speech* (trans. H. C. White; repr. Louisville: Westminster John Knox, 1991; original publication in German, 1964); idem, *Prophetic Oracles of Salvation in the Old Testament* (Louisville: Westminster John Knox, 1991; original publication in German, 1987). For lists of genres in prophetic books, see, e.g., M. A. Sweeney, *Isaiah 1–39* (FOTL 16; Grand Rapids: Eerdmans, 1996), 512-44; for "formulas" see 544-47; R. M. Hals, *Ezekiel* (FOTL 19; Grand Rapids: Eerdmans, 1989), 348-59; for "formulas" see 359-63; and M. H. Floyd, *Minor Prophets, Part 2* (FOTL 22; Grand Rapids: Eerdmans, 2000), 627-49; for "formulas" see 650-51.

---

An oral version of this essay was delivered at the 2001 meeting of the Canadian Society of Biblical Studies. I thank the participants in the session for their comments.

works.[3] Moreover, even when it is mentioned, the social product and socio-literary category of "prophetic book" rarely serves as the primary interpretive key for form- and historical-critical studies of the prophetic books of the Hebrew Bible.[4] Times are changing, however, as the prophetic-related contributions to the 2000 symposium on "The Changing Face of Form Criticism for the Twenty-First Century" seem to suggest.[5]

To be succinct, if we leave aside social and ideological preferences of "living" situations over "bookish" matters that have influenced past scholarship in the prophetic books, the fact remains that researchers never dealt directly with historical speakers, nor with flesh-and-blood prophets, nor with those who had the good or bad fortune to listen to them. Scholars were never privy to any direct oral communication that could have happened in ancient Israel. Rather they had and have access to written texts, and as far as it is relevant to this essay to a very particular type of written product, namely something that we may call (ancient) Israelite (or perhaps, biblical) prophetic books.[6] This being so, it seems reasonable to maintain that historically oriented research should pay much attention to the latter, and its form-critical and sociohistorical features.

---

3. For example, M. A. Sweeney, *Isaiah 1–39*, 532-33. One may notice Sweeney's statement that "research into the specific forms of the prophetic books is just beginning" (p. 532). Cf. idem, "A Form-Critical Rereading of Hosea," *JHS* 2 (1998): article 1, available at purl.org/JHS and at http://www.JHSonline.org.

4. One exception is E. Ben Zvi, *Micah* (FOTL 21B; Grand Rapids: Eerdmans, 2000).

5. The symposium was held as part of the annual meeting of the SBL, Nashville, Nov. 19-20, 2000. Revised versions of papers presented at this symposium are included in this volume.

6. The term "Israelite prophetic books" brings to the forefront that the books being discussed here were produced only within a particular ancient Near Eastern society that identified itself, theologically and ideologically, as Israel. The term "biblical prophetic books" brings to the forefront that these books eventually became part of the Hebrew Bible. Hereafter, I refer to "Israelite prophetic books" or simply "prophetic books." These terms are preferable to "biblical prophetic books" because the latter is anachronistic for a historical-critical study of these books. For other purposes, however, "biblical prophetic books" may well be the best designation (e.g., theological studies, studies of readings of these books among members of any particular community of faith that upholds or upheld a concept of "Bible").

As I expressed elsewhere, I am convinced that this Israel is, at least in the main, directly related to Jerusalemite-centered, Achaemenid Yehud, but the argument developed in this section is not dependent on the acceptance of this position.

## Defining Israelite Prophetic Books as a Particular Genre

To be sure, the category of "Israelite prophetic books" is a subcategory within that of "Israelite authoritative books." This being so, one has first to define the latter. To begin with, "authoritative books" is in itself a subset of "books." Thus the starting point must be the matter of what can be designated a "book" within the textual repertoire and produce of ancient Israel.[7]

A "book" is the full semantical equivalent of neither ספר nor מגלה in Biblical Hebrew. The former may refer to the material on which a text is written (e.g., Deut 17:18; cf. Isa 30:8 and notice the parallelism with לוח, "tablet") or to the written text, be it a letter (e.g., 2 Sam 11:14; 2 Kgs 10:7), a legal document, bill, or deed (e.g., Deut 24:1; Isa 50:1; Jer 32:16), a "historiographical" work (e.g., 2 Kgs 8:23 and passim in the "historical books," and see also Esth 10:2), a "historigraphical" work that contains accounts of prophetic visions (2 Chr 32:32), a "vision" per se (Nah 1:1), a list of descendants (e.g., Gen 5:1) or a particular genealogical list (e.g., Neh 7:5), or the instruction/torah of YHWH (e.g., Josh 1:8; Neh 8:3).[8] In addition, in Daniel the term ספר appears with a collective meaning, "letters" (in the sense akin to "learning" or "knowledge," or perhaps "arts and sciences" or "literature" in its most general meaning; see Dan 1:4, 17). The use of the term מגלה in the Hebrew Bible is more restricted. It points to "scroll," that is, the material that carries the writing, rather than the contents of the writing itself (e.g., Jer 36:27).[9] But the term "book" as it relates to the genre of "prophetic books" does point to the contents of the writing itself.[10] Further, there is not a necessary one-to-one relation between scrolls and "books." Scrolls may contain only one "book." This situation is helpful for archiving, retrieving, and even writing scrolls, given the size of many of the books. But some scrolls, even biblical scrolls, may contain more than one "book" (e.g., the twelve prophetic "books," or the Pentateuch, when skin-writing technology devel-

---

7. The concept being discussed here is by necessity historically dependent. See below.

8. See A. Hurvitz, "The Origins and Development of the Expression מגלת ספר: A Study in the History of Writing-Related Terminology in Biblical Times," in *Texts, Temples and Traditions: A Tribute to Menahem Haran* (ed. M. V. Fox, et al.; Winona Lake, Ind.: Eisenbrauns, 1996), 37*-46* (Hebrew section), esp. 37*-40*.

9. The expression מגלת ספר is another instance of a construct chain in which both nouns are at least partially synonymous. In post-Biblical Hebrew the word מגלה overtakes much of the semantic range of meaning of ספר. On these matters see Hurvitz, "Origins."

10. Cf. John Barton, "What Is a Book? Modern Exegesis and the Literary Conventions of Ancient Israel," in *Intertextuality in Ugarit and Israel* (ed. J. C. de Moor; OTS 40; Leiden: Brill, 1998), 1-14, esp. 2.

oped).[11] Conversely a "book" may be written in a number of scrolls, and particularly so if it is too large to be easily written in a papyrus scroll, or even a skin scroll.[12]

In sum, the concept of "book" should stand on its own, and not be confused — as sometimes happens — with Biblical Hebrew ספר, מגלה, or the English term "scroll." Needless to say, an ancient Israelite "book" is also not a codex or a Rabbinic Hebrew פינקס.[13] If so, how to define "book" as a written product of ancient Israelite society in general, and of its literati and those who supported them in particular?

I would propose the following definition of ancient Israelite "book" (hereafter, book): a self-contained written text that was produced within ancient Israel, and characterized by a clear beginning and conclusion, by a substantial level of textual coherence and of textually inscribed distinctiveness vis-à-vis other books, and that, accordingly, leads its intended and primary readers (and rereaders) to approach it in a manner that takes into account

11. See, e.g., "It is permissible to join the Torah and the Prophets in one scroll, so R. Judah; but the Sages say: The Torah and the Prophets must be written in separate scrolls. . . . Between a book of the Prophets and another, one should not leave the same empty space as between two books of the Torah" (tractate *Soferim* 3, Soncino edition). One may notice also that some scrolls at Qumran contain a number of different texts. For instance, 1QS (i.e., the Manual of Discipline/Rule of the Community), 1QSa (i.e., Rule of the Congregation), and 1QSb (i.e., Rule of Blessings) are all in one single scroll; 4Q448 includes both a portion of Ps 154 and a prayer for the welfare of King Jonathan (see E. Eshel, H. Eshel, and A. Yardeni, "A Qumran Composition Containing Part of Ps. 154 and a Prayer for the Welfare of King Jonathan and his Kingdom," *IEJ* 42 [1992]: 199-229). To be sure in these cases there is some connection between the documents included in the same scroll, but this does not amount to the creation of one single self-contained "book" or "work."

12. On size of scrolls and writing technology see M. Haran, "Book-Scrolls in Israel in Pre-Exilic Times," *JSS* 3 (1982): 161-73; idem, "Book-Scrolls at the Beginning of the Second Temple Period: The Transition from Papyrus to Skins," *HUCA* 54 (1983): 111-22; idem, "Book-Size and the Thematic Cycles in the Pentateuch," in *Die Hebräische Bibel und ihre zweifache Nachgeschichte: Festschrift für Rolf Rendtorff zum 65. Geburtstag* (ed. E. Blum, C. Macholz, and E. W. Stegemann; Neukirchen-Vluyn: Neukirchener Verlag, 1990), 165-75. On the practical, rather than theoretical, size limitations of skin scrolls, see also M. Bar Ilan, "From Scroll to Codex and Its Effect on Reading the Torah," *Sinai* 107 (1991): 242-54 (Hebrew); available in electronic format at http://faculty.biu.ac.il/~barilm/codex.html. To be sure, there were multitablet texts in the ancient Near East for centuries before the time of composition of the prophetic books, so the idea of one text written in more than one "material object" has a very long history in the area. On books, codices, scrolls, and membranae in the Roman period, see A. Millard, *Reading and Writing in the Time of Jesus* (Sheffield: Sheffield Academic Press, 2000), 61-83.

13. See M. Haran, "Codex, *Pinax* and Writing Slat," *Scripta Classica Israelica* 15 (1996): 212-22. See also Bar Ilan, "From Scroll to Codex," and bibliography mentioned there.

this distinctiveness.[14] An "authoritative book" is one that communicates an explicit or implicit claim for social and theological/ideological authoritativeness,[15] and was likely accepted as such by at least some substantial sector of the ancient readership and rereadership.[16]

I must stress that this definition does not restrict ancient Israelite books to any range of length or to any principle of composition. They may be short or long; they may be a compilation (e.g., the book of Psalms, Proverbs), a single and relatively short narrative tale (e.g., Ruth, Esther), or a lengthy work of ancient historiography (e.g., Chronicles). They may have undergone lengthy processes of composition or redaction, or none at all. They may even be written in one or two languages (Daniel, Ezra).

In addition, this definition does not restrict the genre of book to any particular mode of reading.[17] Nor does this definition assume that there should be one single type of internal coherence at work in every ancient Israelite book. For instance, there is a substantial difference between the type of literary coherence found in the book of Psalms and that in the book of Ruth; still both are ancient Israelite books.

14. Cf. Ben Zvi, *Micah*, 187.

15. Significantly, this holds true for those books that were included eventually in the Hebrew Bible and many that were not (e.g., Jubilees, Enoch, Temple Scroll). The basic difference between the two groups is not to be found in the presence or absence of claims to authoritativeness or any formal or genre marker, but on the level and range of the acceptance of the textually inscribed claims by different communities within Israel and through time.

The question of whether plainly nonauthoritative books were copied and passed from generation to generation in the early Second Temple period remains open, but significantly, none of them is extant, if they existed. Concerns about resources and the social location of the literati's writing may have been less conducive for the "success" and "reproduction" of social products such as highly literate texts that carry no claim for social authority. I discussed some of these matters in "Introduction: Writings, Speeches, and Prophetic Books — Setting an Agenda," in *Writings and Speech in Israelite and Ancient Near Eastern Prophecy* (ed. E. Ben Zvi and M. H. Floyd; SBLSymS 10; Atlanta: SBL, 2000), 1-29.

16. I cannot overemphasize that prophetic books were meant to be read, reread, meditated upon, again and again, to be read (and reread) to others who cannot read by themselves, and certainly not to be read once and then discarded. There are important implications to this seemingly simple observation. Books meant to be reread tend to show numerous instances of potential ambiguity, and lasting equivocality or polysemy at different levels. These features allow multiplicity of readings informing one another, and all together contributing to the rich tapestry of the text. These features are widely attested in the prophetic literature. See Ben Zvi, *Micah*, passim.

17. Such as sequential or nonsequential readings of the entire book, or separate readings of and meditations on literary subunits within the book, which is a practice that most likely took place — at least at times — in the case of Psalms and some portions of Proverbs.

This definition focuses rather on grounding features such as being an ancient Israelite text, and on the interaction between (a) textually inscribed markers that characterize each book and set it apart from other books in the religious and authoritative repertoire of the community; and (b) its primary readers, that is, the people who were supposed to read and study the book in its present form, the actual primary "social target" of this product.

Thus, for instance, the book of Psalms is set apart from Proverbs, despite the fact that both are Israelite compilations. Similarly, the book of Isaiah and the book of Jeremiah are clearly distinguishable, even if both are "prophetic books."[18] Significantly, this sense of distinctiveness applies to the book *as a whole* and *not* to a particular unit as separate from the book. To illustrate, the text of a psalm placed in the lips of the character David in 2 Samuel 22 (cf. Ps 18) does not affect the characterization of the book of Samuel as ancient historiography and surely does not make this book indistinguishable from the book of Psalms, even if they actually share most of the text of a literary subunit.[19]

It is worth stressing that this definition is not a universal one, but one that is deeply interrelated and valid within a particular society, in our case, ancient Israel.[20] The very definition of "prophetic book" as a text characterized by a clear beginning and a conclusion, by a substantial level of textual coherence and of textually inscribed distinctiveness vis-à-vis other prophetic books, and that, accordingly, leads its intended and primary readers (and rereaders) to approach it in a manner that takes into account this distinctiveness, is *by necessity* socially and historically dependent. It stresses the textually inscribed markers, the intended readership for whom these markers were created, and assumes that the primary readership was not too different from this intended readership.[21] But other readerships at different times may approach the book in a way that is governed by substantially different — and authoritative — interpretive keys.[22] So, for instance, they may read a short portion of a

---

18. See below.

19. Of course, the two literary subunits are an integral part of two different literary contexts and so, by necessity, they carry different meanings. See also, among others, 2 Chr 6:41-42 and Ps 132:8-10.

20. On these matters see below on the structure of prophetic books.

21. Cf. D. Kraemer, "The Intended Reader as a Key to Interpreting the Bavli," *Prooftexts* 13 (1993): 125-40.

22. One should note that primary readerships were also rereaderships. They read (and reread) the text at different times. So it is possible for these rereaderships to develop more than one reading. In other words, they could have reread at times a book in ways that were informed by but also additional to that suggested by the textually inscribed markers.

book in a way that is strongly informed by other pieces of what is considered "Scripture" within their circles rather than within its context in their "own" book. In fact, these readings have a very long history in both Judaism and Christianity.[23] Similarly, prophetic books or sections thereof may be read in different settings within the same society. Ritual readings, for instance, tend to create their own cadence, structure, and world of meaning. Literary conventions and theological or ideological uses of readings and books vary from time to time and from society to society.

"Israelite prophetic book" represents a subset within the genre of "authoritative Israelite book" that was already recognized in antiquity.[24] This subset consists of books that claim an association with a prophetic personage of the past (e.g., Isaiah, Jeremiah, Amos, Micah) and that are presented to their intended and primary readership as YHWH's word and, accordingly, as such books, claim to convey legitimate and authoritative knowledge about YHWH.[25] Each prophetic book is associated with a prophetic personage,[26] and *no* prophetic book is associated with more than one prophetic personage.

The repertoire of prophetic books reflects and creates a set of accepted prophets of the past with whom authoritative texts may be associated.[27] To be sure, theoretically many other prophetic books could have been added even to the present scroll of "The Twelve" had these books been included in the accepted repertoire of prophetic books. In fact, the scroll that contains the twelve books is still much shorter than the scrolls on which the books of Isaiah, Jeremiah, and Ezekiel were written.[28] The decision to include only a par-

---

23. See, e.g., midrash. On these matters cf. B. D. Sommer, "The Scroll of Isaiah as Jewish Scripture, or, Why Jews Don't Read Books," *SBLSP* (1996): 225-42; Barton, "What Is a Book?"

24. For example, Philo. See N. G. Cohen, "Earliest Evidence of the Haftarah Cycle for the Sabbaths between בתמוז יז and סוכות in Philo," *JJS* 48 (1997): 225-49, esp. 245-47.

25. See Ben Zvi, *Micah*, 187-88.

26. Whose image, to be sure, is construed by the book.

27. Needless to say, it also creates a tapestry of deeply interwoven accepted theological voices — all of them being a representation of YHWH's word — that inform one another and all together reflect and shape a multifaceted theological discourse.

28. See Haran, "Book-Size," 167-68. The scrolls containing the books of Isaiah, Jeremiah, and Ezekiel have, respectively, 16,933, 21,835, and 18,730 words; the one containing the twelve prophetic books has only 14,355 words. The combined number of words of *eight* of the twelve prophetic books (namely, Joel, Obadiah, Jonah, Nahum, Habakkuk, Zephaniah, Haggai, and Malachi) is only 5,317. In other words, even if eight additional prophetic books of equal average size would have been added to the scroll, it still would have been shorter than the one of Jeremiah. (Counting number of words is probably better than counting verses — as often done — for these purposes.) For the numbers see F. I. Andersen and A. D. Forbes,

ticular set of twelve prophetic books in the scroll — and perhaps even to compose and accept only fifteen "prophetic books" of this kind — points at a principle of controlled selection and required the existence of some social authority to include and exclude written texts (see the section below on social setting).[29] These considerations about social control should be taken into account in any study of the genre of the social product we call "prophetic book."[30] The same holds true regarding the fact that the composition of new prophetic books came to an end at some point in the Persian period.[31] Since that time, an additional feature was strongly attached to the genre of prophetic book, namely it is a genre in which no one can write, and accordingly one in which the number of books available is theologically or ideologically fixed "for eternity," as it were.[32]

## Structure of Prophetic Books and Related Matters

Prophetic books may vary in length. On the one side of the spectrum stands the book of Isaiah (16,933 words) and that of Jeremiah (21,835 words), on the other the book of Obadiah (291 words).[33] Three of these books were of such a

---

*The Vocabulary of the Old Testament* (Rome: Pontifical Biblical Institute Press, 1989); idem, "What Did the Scribes Count?" in D. N. Freedman, A. D. Forbes and F. I. Andersen, *Studies in Hebrew and Aramaic Orthography* (Biblical and Judaic Studies 2; Winona Lake, Ind.: Eisenbrauns, 1992), 297-318, esp. 309; and see also J. L. Crenshaw, *Joel* (AB; New York: Doubleday, 1995), 11-12.

29. The more so, if only fifteen prophetic books were produced to begin with. But such a claim cannot be proved, or disproved, for that matter. In any case, there are fifteen that were composed, read, reread, and studied by the late Achaemenid/early Hellenistic period. Although the number twelve "suits" the collection, other numbers may have suited as well (e.g., three, five, seven, seven plus one = eight, twenty-four, forty-nine). There is no strong reason to see the number twelve as the main cause that preempted the addition of prophetic books considered worthy of being included in the prophetic books' repertoire.

30. It is worth noting that despite the number of apocryphal works, none is actually an apocryphal prophetic book, i.e., there is no book that (a) resembles for instance the (biblical) books of Isaiah, Amos, or Zephaniah, and (b) is associated with a prophet not included among the fifteen. The reason for the lack of apocryphal prophetic books may be that this genre of representation of divine communication was replaced by others (e.g., apocalyptic works), but the matter is beyond the scope of this paper. On social control see also the section on primary social setting and bibliography mentioned there.

31. Or possibly, but in my opinion not so likely, in the early Hellenistic period.

32. One may compare this process to those that led to similar results in, for instance, the genre of "gospel."

33. See works mentioned in note 28.

length that they were written each in a single scroll; the twelve others, which were much shorter, were eventually written in one scroll, in a set series.[34] Still each one of these books was characterized as a free-standing book by their clearly separate beginnings, conclusions, and textually inscribed, marked differences in styles and word choices that create both a sense of coherence within the book and of separateness from other prophetic books (cf. Ezekiel with Isaiah). In fact, it is worth stressing that although at the very least the present form of most prophetic books goes back to similar groups of literati, these literati placed much effort on constructing a separate voice for each prophetic book, and to some extent for each "prophetic personage."[35] In other words, these writers and editors — who by themselves were readers too — did not confuse, or wish any intended or primary reader to confuse, for instance, Jeremiah with Haggai or Ezekiel. Moreover, the strong constraint to maintain the particular voice of each prophetic book (and indirectly, of each prophetic personage) was kept generation after generation, even when the book underwent further editions. Thus, for instance, those responsible for the MT additions of the book of Jeremiah phrased them in clear Jeremianic language.[36]

Prophetic books may vary in structure and in presentation. Only one of these fifteen is a narrative — although others may include short narrative sections. This "exceptional" book, Jonah, is the only member of a particular sub-

---

34. Practical reasons were probably the most important. See, among others, Bar Ilan, "From Scroll to Codex." To be sure, short texts were kept in individual scrolls due to liturgical considerations (e.g., "the Five Megillot"). It is possible that for ritual purposes, a haftarah scroll was used in antiquity. Cf. Cohen, "Earliest Evidence," 227. The only prophetic book among the Twelve that according to this logic should have been written in a scroll of itself was Jonah (and cf. *Num. Rab.* 18.21). But such a separate writing would have been unlikely, given the size of the other prophetic books (and contrast the situation with the five *megillot*).

35. I discussed these issues elsewhere; see E. Ben Zvi, "Looking at the Primary (Hi)story and the Prophetic Books as Literary/Theological Units within the Frame of the Early Second Temple Period: Some Considerations," *SJOT* 12 (1998): 26-43; idem, "Twelve Prophetic Books or 'The Twelve': A Few Preliminary Considerations," in *Forming Prophetic Literature: Essays on Isaiah and the Twelve in Honor of John D. W. Watts* (ed. P. House and J. W. Watts; JSOTSup 235; Sheffield: Sheffield Academic Press, 1996), 125-56.

36. It is noteworthy that even when sections of one prophetic book closely relate to sections of another, there is a substantial difference between the two texts that is consistent with the individual characterization of each prophetic book and character. I pointed to this phenomenon in a detailed analysis of Obadiah 1–7 and Jer 49:7-22 in *A Historical-Critical Study of the Book of Obadiah* (BZAW 242; Berlin and New York: de Gruyter, 1996), 99-114; cf. my previous comparative study of Zeph 3:3-4 and Ezek 22:25-29 in *A Historical-Critical Study of the Book of Zephaniah* (BZAW 198; Berlin and New York: de Gruyter, 1991), 190-206.

set within the category of prophetic books. It is a metaprophetic book, that is, a prophetic book that deals with or is even devoted to issues that are of relevance for the understanding of the messages of other prophetic books.[37]

Some of the prophetic books, but certainly not all, seem to include variations on a tripartite structure, namely readings in which the prophetic or divine voice is described as announcing (a) punishment against Israel, (b) punishment against nations other than Israel, and (c) salvation for Israel, or for both Israel and the nations.[38] Other prophetic books do not seem to follow this tripartite pattern, or any of its possible variations at all (e.g., Hosea, Jonah, Haggai). Perhaps more significant is that books that seem to follow a tripartite structure tend to show variations on this structure. These variations involve the order in which the three types of readings appear in the book,[39] rhetorical loops in which one (or two) of these types is repeated though with a very different slant (as in Zephaniah), and at times the explicit omission, though implicit inclusion, of one of these types.[40] The presence of so many variations creates by necessity structures that may be seen from different angles, including those that omit any reference to a tripartite structure. Indeed, at times the same book not only allows alternative structures — or alternative partial substructures — to be discerned (and to be subverted as well), but also seems to be written so as to encourage the intended, and likely the primary, readerships to develop a set of complementary rereadings of the book that inform one another, and each one is informed by one possible structure of the book.[41]

37. There are comments and sections in other prophetic books that can also be considered metaprophetic (e.g., Isa 55:7-11; Amos 7:12-15), but clearly there is no prophetic book that can be considered metaprophetic in its entirety. On this matter see E. Ben Zvi, *The Signs of Jonah* (JSOTSup 367; Sheffield: Sheffield Academic Press/Continuum, forthcoming 2003); idem, "Atypical Features, the Meta-prophetic Character of the Book of Jonah and Other Communicative Messages," paper delivered at the annual meeting of the Pacific Northwest AAR/SBL, Tacoma, WA, May 1999.

38. For recent criticism of the "tripartite structure," see M. A. Sweeney, *The Twelve Prophets* (Berit Olam; 2 vols.; Collegeville, Minn.: Glazier, 2000), 2:494; idem, "Zephaniah: A Paradigm for the Study of the Prophetic Books," *CurBS* 7 (1999): 119-45; idem, "A Form-Critical Reassessment of the Book of Zephaniah," *CBQ* 53 (1991): 388-408; and cf. the bibliography mentioned there and E. Ben Zvi, "Understanding the Message of the Tripartite Prophetic Books," *ResQ* 35 (1993): 93-100.

39. The more usual pattern is to follow the sequence mentioned above, but the text may follow a different order, because of a number of rhetorical reasons, including departure from common readers' expectations.

40. For example, the book of Obadiah, in which the announcement and fulfillment of punishment against Israel is implicitly presented as an event that has already happened in the world of the book and precedes the words of the speaker in Obad 1.

41. This feature is consistent with the fact that these books were meant to be read and

The only consistent structural elements in the prophetic books are: (a) introduction, (b) conclusion, and (c) the body of the book that consists of a series of "prophetic readings." The introduction of a prophetic book characterized it as such, identified it as a separate book that was directly associated with a particular prophetic figure from the past, and often — but not always — served to set the world of the book in a particular time within the construction of the past held by the intended and primary readers and rereaders. In many cases, either the introduction or often a portion of it likely served as a title of the book, and as such it construed a particular image of the book and of its character. Titles were also likely used as signifiers for the book in the discourse of the literati and as a retrieval tool.[42]

The conclusions not only set the boundaries of the prophetic books, but also conveyed a note of hope to the readers and rereaders of the book. Significantly, they tended to communicate also a sense of uniqueness to the entire book, just as the introductions did, but this time through their tendency to include markedly unique expressions (see, among others, Isa 66:24; Ezek 48:35; Hos 14:10 [Eng. 9]; Mic 7:20; Jonah 4:11; Mal 3:24 [Eng. 4:6]).[43]

The third and main element in all prophetic books is "prophetic readings." A book, that is, a written document or product, cannot contain anything but "writings," or better, "readings," that is, "writings meant to be read." Although the former term ("writings") brings to the forefront the work of the writer and the material aspect of the "product," the latter conveys a more pragmatic orientation that suits best the type of studies endeavored here. After all, written texts are activated in the imagination of their primary readers by the act of reading, and in the case of those who do not know how to read by the act of reading to them.

Elsewhere I defined "prophetic readings" as literary units within a prophetic book that show textually inscribed, discursive markers that were likely to suggest to its intended and primary readership that they were supposed —

---

reread. Indeed, such a multiplicity of rereading contributes to the community's ability to reread the book again and again.

42. It is likely that they served some archival needs. One may wonder whether these titles were somewhat reflected in the tags attached to the scroll in ancient libraries. Cf. M. Haran, "Archives, Libraries, and the Order of the Biblical Books," *JANES* 22 [= *Comparative Studies in Honor of Yochanan Muffs*] (1993): 51-61, esp. 60-61. See also G. M. Tucker, "Prophetic Superscriptions and the Growth of the Canon," in *Canon and Authority: Essays in Old Testament Religion and Theology* (ed. B. O. Long and G. W. Coats; Philadelphia: Fortress, 1977), 56-70.

43. These conclusions should not be confused with colophons. On this matter see Ben Zvi, *Micah*, 183-84, and bibliography.

or at least invited — to read and reread these sections as cohesive subunits within the frame of the prophetic book as a whole.[44] These are not simple readings, but "prophetic readings," that is, they claim for themselves the legitimacy and authority of a prophetic text, of YHWH's word. Given the success of these books, there is a strong likelihood that the primary readership or a significant portion of it resembled in many ways the intended readership of the book and approached it in a similar manner.[45]

A few observations follow from this definition. "Prophetic readings" can be of any size. They may stand separate or be organized into "sets of readings."[46] They may include one or more speakers, and may be written in either prose or poetry — though these categories are somewhat fluid.

Further, the term "readings" emphasizes the relation between perceived structures within a prophetic book (or any ancient authoritative Israelite book for that matter) and the social and historical location of the readership. Books can be read in many different ways, and so can subunits within them. Just as the category of "prophetic book" is socially and historically dependent, so is that of "prophetic reading."[47]

Just as important, this definition — and the related approach from which it stems — has strong implications regarding the level of polysemy in prophetic books. Since "prophetic reading" is the only genre present in the body of a prophetic book,[48] the entire body of the prophetic book is associated primarily with a single setting in life, namely, the reading of prophetic books by those able to read and reread them.[49] This unified setting allows for, and is fully consistent with, the presence of structurally multivalent verses or

44. See ibid., 188.

45. See ibid.

46. For example, Mic 4:1–5:14. See ibid., 88-141. I defined "set of prophetic readings" as a "cluster of closely related prophetic readings, usually around a certain topic" (ibid., 188).

47. Thus meaningful discussions of the "living" structure of a prophetic book, of its subdivisions into separate readings, and even of the genre of prophetic book have to be strongly qualified by an explicit reference to a particular time and society for which it holds valid. This chapter deals in its entirety with the genre of the ancient Israelite prophetic book from the perspective of its primary readership, as construed on the basis of (a) internal textual markers pointing to a particular intended readership, and (b) historical knowledge or likely reconstructions of the history of ancient Israel, particularly during the Achaemenid period. To be sure, other perspectives are just as worthwhile of study as the one discussed here. The choice made here does not reflect any hierarchical claim; it reflects only my personal area of expertise and interest.

48. A prophetic book may include also a "set of prophetic readings"; see above. But to state the obvious, a "set of prophetic readings" consists of "prophetic readings."

49. See below.

expressions, that is, short texts that are an integral part of more than one sub-unit (i.e., reading) in a prophetic book.[50]

To be sure, the rereadability of the book, as well as its textual cohesion, is strengthened by these short multivalent texts. But structural polysemy does not stop at this level. The intended and primary (re)readers of most (if not all) prophetic books are encouraged to read and reread these texts in a way that is informed by different possible structural outlines (or partial structural outlines), all of which can be substantiated at least in part by the presence of thematic and linguistic markers of cohesion.[51] Contrary to a previous tendency in research to choose the "best" of these outlines — and the subsequent division of the text into subunits — and accordingly disregard the others, the understanding of the structure in prophetic books advanced here points to a need to embrace a multiplicity of outlines. In books meant to be read and reread, the outlines are more likely to be complementary than alternative. To be sure, each of the textually marked outlines of a prophetic book led the intended and primary readership to different understandings of the text. But each of these readings informed the others, and by doing so, all together created a denser texture of meanings in the literati's community.[52]

That all subunits in a prophetic book are by necessity "prophetic readings" does not mean that all are the same, nor can such observation be taken as an attempt to forcefully homogenize prophetic literature.[53] It means only that these subunits share several features, such as being written subunits within a prophetic book meant to be read and reread. As texts to be read, reread, and read to, they are associated with particular social actions, participants, and settings, namely those that are required by the very act of reading. Surely, the first readership had to consist of literati able to read. There is no reason to confuse, however, their own reading and rereading of the text with

50. To mention an obvious case, the text of Mic 5:1 is an integral part of both 4:8–5:1 and 5:1-5. (More traditional form-critical studies tend to assign it to either one of them.)

51. To mention only one case, there are multiple possible outlines of the books of Zephaniah (cf. the outlines advanced in A. Berlin, *Zephaniah* [AB 25A; New York: Doubleday, 1994], 17-20; and Sweeney, *Twelve Prophets*, esp. 2:404, but see 2:494-524).

52. See the reference to multiple and complementary structures above. That one finds both textual markers that point to particular structures but also those that to some extent subvert them seems to suggest to the readership that no structure should be taken as the only acceptable one.

53. The case is analogous to the obvious true statement that all self-contained subunits in a newspaper are "newspaper readings." Yet there are substantial differences among them, and the same holds true even if one were to limit the "newspaper readings" to those that claim similar level of authority (e.g., "factual" news reports in "well-established" newspapers). See below.

their reading of the text — or portions of it — to the vast majority of the people in liturgical types of scenes that were controlled by the central authorities (cf. 2 Chr 17:7-9 and Neh 8, and implicitly in Deut 31:10-13).[54]

Whereas "prophetic readings" share their settings in the life of the community, they do deal with a large spectrum of diverse topics and do evoke a number of genres and situations in life.

There is no doubt that prophetic books asked their intended and primary readers and rereaders to construct images of living prophets of the past, and, to a certain extent at least, to identify themselves with the words of these prophets and with those of YHWH as they are communicated to them through the world of the book. Similarly, they were asked to identify with the Israel of the past and with the Israel of the future, as both were described and construed in these books.

Moreover, for these books to be successful — that is, accepted by the literati as authoritative literature and, therefore, studied, copied, and passed from generation to generation — the world of these books could not stand in a flagrant contradiction with the world of knowledge and the theological or ideological viewpoints shared by authorship and primary readership and rereadership.

From these observations it does not follow, however, that the world created and evoked in the book should be identical to the one that already exists in the world/s of knowledge. First, if one were to assume the latter, then new works would never be able to contribute substantially to the ongoing construction of worlds of knowledge, nor to any development in the images of the past shared by the community. Such static discursive and ideological worlds are extremely unlikely, if possible at all. Second, the prophetic books are not necessarily mimetical or historically oriented. In fact, books written to be read and reread again and again tend toward dehistoricization and generalization, so they could be read against more than one background.

The world of the past described in and construed by a prophetic book is likely to be pertinently consistent rather than mimetic with the construction of the past that was shared by the community and in which the characters of the book are set.[55] The term "pertinently consistent" here is meant to emphasize that a large spectrum of levels of constraint may be pertinent to a variety

---

54. Also cf. the later — but much earlier than medieval times — ritual readings from prophetic books as part of a haftarah cycle. See Cohen, "Earliest Evidence."

55. For instance, readers of the book of Micah are asked to recall their image of the monarchic period in general, and of the days of Jotham, Ahaz, and Hezekiah in particular, even if most of the readings tend to generalization and dehistoricization, as shown again and again in Ben Zvi, *Micah*.

of prophetic readings and prophetic books. Each case should be discussed on its own merits. Levels may vary from relatively strong constraints in some cases (e.g., Jer 39:1-10)[56] to relatively loose, but still present, constraints (e.g., Jonah). Constraints may affect some aspects of the text but not others; in addition, communities could hold diverse visions of their shared past. To illustrate, Zephaniah is described as a monarchic period prophet, but the construction of the time of Josiah advanced by the book is substantially different from that in the book of Kings, but similar to other constructions of the late monarchic past in prophetic literature.

To be sure, the reconstructions of the monarchic past of Judah shared by, for instance, a group of literati in Achaemenid Jerusalem do not and cannot mimic the most likely historical events and circumstances in monarchic Judah, as reconstructed by contemporaneous historical research. This being so, the most likely historical world of prophets, actual oral utterances, and the like are substantially removed, and at several different levels, from the world of the text of a prophetic book.[57] The latter is only as consistent as is pertinent to the unit, though never identical with some image of the past held by the primary authorship and readership. This image or these images are in turn merely representations of the past accepted by a particular group at a particular time, and the degree to which they may reflect the historical circumstances of the (imaged) past should be studied in each particular case, not assumed.

Of course, readings within a book could and did recall the rereaders' knowledge of textual genres other than "prophetic readings," and of situations in life that have nothing to do with reading a book, and should not be confused with that activity. In fact, it is often the case that "prophetic readings" required the intended and primary (re)readers to approach them in a way that is informed by such an external knowledge. There is nothing surprising about this feature. Any book — or written text, for that matter — must assume a certain world of knowledge of its readers without which no reading proficiency is attainable. No text is self-contained.[58]

There is no doubt that when the intended or primary readers read, for instance, a letter embedded in a book, or a reading that shows elements often

56. Certainly the text there could not have claimed that someone other than Nebuchadrezzar and Zedekiah played key roles in the narrative, nor that Jerusalem was not destroyed.

57. Cf. R. Linville, "On the Nature of Rethinking Prophetic Literature: Stirring a Neglected Stew (A Response to David L. Petersen)," *JHS* 2 (1999): article 3, available at purl.org/JHS and at http://www.JHSonline.org.

58. To state the obvious, even the most elementary written text in a language assumes at least a readership able to read that language.

associated with a court scene, they interpreted the world of the text in a way that was informed by what they thought was the social reality of the world in which the book is set, and that this view was shaped also by their own experiences and by their world of knowledge about, or construction of, their own time (i.e., in these examples, their experiences and knowledge of a court system and of how letters are written and used in their own times).[59]

Still it is important to stress that whereas a book may describe a letter, and whereas this description may be reminiscent of actual letters, a letter textually inscribed in a book is nothing but a particular representation of a letter within a textual world (e.g., 2 Chr 21:12-15). It is not an actual letter, just as reported speech in a text is not the same as spoken speech in actual social interaction.[60]

Written literary texts do not need to, and very infrequently do, advance a mimetic representation of a genre or social setting to bring it to the mind of the readers and rereaders. Texts may be evocative, but they are rarely fully mimetic. Indeed, given the rhetorical constraints of the world of the prophetic books, it is unlikely that mimesis was intended, not to mention realized in practice. Moreover, at times, typical speeches and scenes in a prophetic book are construed so as to fulfill the social expectations evoked by the text within the reading community, on the basis of their world of knowledge; but at times literary texts, including prophetic books, run counter to the expectations and associations created by even well-known literary genres. Defamiliarization of genres is a very familiar trope in the prophetic books.[61] Although defamiliarization implies the existence of something "familiar," it also makes the point that neither the genre of prophetic book nor that of prophetic readings carried strong mimetic constraints. Further, it suggests genre-competent intended and primary reader-

59. In other words, they probably tended to assume as a default option continuity between their own world and the world in which the text is set.

60. Cf. D. Tannen, "Introducing Constructed Dialogue in Greek and American Conversational and Literary Narrative," in *Direct and Indirect Speech* (ed. F. Coulams; Trends in Linguistics, Studies and Monographs 31; Berlin: Mouton de Gruyter, 1986), 311-32.

61. On this matter and taking the book of Micah as an example, see Ben Zvi, *Micah*, 26-27, 37-38, 47-50, 77-80, 149-51, 180-81 (cf. Mic 1:2-16; 2:1-5; 3:1-12; 6:1-8; 7:7-20). To some extent, traditional redactional, source, and form criticism attempt to refamiliarize defamiliarized texts, but creating new and now familiar texts out of the existing prophetic books. Irrespective of the critical strength of any of the textual reconstructions advanced by these approaches (see below), they do not deal in principle with the most obvious fact: defamiliarized texts did exist and no prophetic book asks or encourages its intended and primary readership to approach them in a way that refamiliarize them by means of these scholarly approaches. The book of Amos, to mention one, does not ask its readers to rediscover any "original book of Amos" but rather to approach the present book as a whole as "the book of Amos."

ships that were aware that prophetic books do not have to be mimetic and accordingly that construed their own expectations about what is written in the book, keeping that matter in mind. These genre-competent readerships expected familiarization as well as defamiliarization in these books. It is the tension between these two expectations that most likely informed their reading of these books, and contributed to their rhetorical appeal.

It is worth stressing that the fact that a genre is defamiliarized in a prophetic reading provides *no* reason to assume a redactional history that begins with a "perfectly familiar" unit that is defamiliarized by a later "redactor." Defamiliarization is above all a rhetorical device, and as such was understood by the intended audience. It is not a necessary marker of a complex redactional history, nor are there any textually inscribed markers that suggest that the intended or primary readership were supposed to understand it as such a marker.

To be sure, all these considerations raise serious concerns about the ability of the historian to reconstruct the life of the community within which one locates the primary readership on the basis of the surface claims of prophetic readings. These concerns are even stronger if the historian is to reconstruct the social life of actual societies associated with the society in which the world of the book is set.[62] Research should be continued in this area, but with

---

62. Keeping in mind all the obvious differences, a contemporary example might still be helpful: Representations of court practice in TV shows such as *Perry Mason, Ally McBeal, Law and Order,* or even TV commercials are not, do not have to be, and in fact cannot be full representations of present court procedures. Viewers with the most basic genre competence will easily recognize that this is the case. (Lawyers often comment about the difference between even the most "realistic" of these shows and the situation in actual life.) To be sure, should these shows remain available to a historian in the far future, she or he would be able to abstract some elements of court procedures on the basis of these shows. Moreover, any scholar at that time who would like to understand the implicit and explicit communicative messages conveyed by these cultural items to the intended historical viewership would have to take into account that the shows evoked in their viewers a set of images and connotations associated with court life. Yet these shows do play with these images, stress some aspects, overlook others, and even counter some common expectations. Moreover, most viewers are socialized to be "genre literate," so they understand that these images do not appear in the show for their own sake, as items separate from the show itself, but as part and parcel of a particular genre, such as a TV police/mystery show or a commercial. In other words, their understanding of the scene in the show that evokes the court scene in real life is construed in a manner that is strongly informed by their understanding of the genre within which the scene is presented.

Obviously, there are vast differences between TV shows or commercials and prophetic books. Yet an important point remains: those for whom the "text" — be it a TV show, a commercial or a prophetic book — is produced tend to understand it, and *its subunits,* in terms of the genre to which the text itself "belongs" and in terms of the usual constraints that relate

a clear awareness of the possibility of defamiliarization, and of the essential gap between evoked and actual situations. The recognition that subunits in a prophetic book can only be "prophetic readings" strongly contributes to this awareness, and so does the recognition that in many of these readings there is a clear tendency to dehistoricize the prophetic texts.[63]

## The Primary Social Setting of a Prophetic Book

Whereas everyone could, at least theoretically, speak, not everyone in ancient Israel was able to compose highly sophisticated works such as the prophetic books. In fact, only a small percentage of the population of ancient Israel were able to read literary works by themselves, and even less to compose them. If one focuses particularly on the Achaemenid period — which is the most likely time of composition of the prophetic books as they stand today — then there were very few people indeed who in each generation could compose these works or even directly read these works.[64]

Whatever images of social settings are created and referred to in the world of the book, the social location of the composition and the primary reading of the book is beyond dispute. Prophetic books were the direct product of a very small intellectual elite in society. Significantly, the same holds true for any other authoritative ancient Israelite book. There is nothing distinctive about prophetic books in this matter. Given the small size of this elite

---

to each genre, including constraints on the degree of required mimesis. This being so, the importance of the study of the genre of prophetic book comes to the fore.

63. In fact, despite the introductory verses, readers are often encouraged to contextualize (i.e., to approach the unit from a perspective that is informed by the other literary units in its textual vicinity) rather than to historicize their reading. Such a dehistoricizing process maximizes the identification of subsequent readers with the characters in the text, and allows all the affective elements with which this identification is associated. See, e.g., Ben Zvi, *Micah*, 43-45, 110-11, 128-30. Yet, at the same time, because of discursive reasons most prophetic books tend to be anchored in the monarchic past. See Ben Zvi, "What Is New in Yehud," forthcoming.

64. Only a few crucial points will be stressed here. I have dealt with some of these matters — and those related to "intention," see below — elsewhere. These issues require a full-size monograph treatment, which I plan to carry out in the relatively near future. In the meantime, see Ben Zvi, "Introduction," in *Writings and Speech*, ed. Ben Zvi and Floyd, 1-29, and bibliography cited there; Ben Zvi, *Micah*, 9-11; idem, "The Urban Center of Jerusalem and the Development of the Literature of the Hebrew Bible," in *Aspects of Urbanism in Antiquity* (ed. W. G. Aufrecht, N. A. Mirau, and S. W. Gauley; JSOTSup 244; Sheffield: Sheffield Academic Press, 1997), 194-209.

at any time, one must assume that at every single period, the primary reader-ship of all ancient Israelite authoritative books, at least during the Achaemenid and early Hellenistic periods, involved the same small social group of literati. The authorship of these authoritative books was located in the same social group, namely the bearers of high literacy. Authorship and primary readership were deeply interwoven at the social level.

Of course, form-critical and historical studies should still deal with the *images* of social settings that readings in a prophetic book may or do bring to mind in the primary readership (see below). But romantic ideas about charis-matic prophets and their disciples aside, the *primary* social location for the pro-duction and primary reception of prophetic books — and of the "prophetic readings" they are composed of — cannot be found anywhere but within a nar-row group of elite literati. This being said, social groups within a society do not exist in a vacuum. The world of knowledge and the worldview of high literati in Israel were surely influenced by those who were not — and likely the other way around — and yet they were probably substantially different.[65] Moreover, the existence and activities of such a group of literati, generation after generation, raise practical questions. Historical studies cannot avoid the matter of the allo-cation of social resources required to develop and maintain a cadre of bearers of high literacy and to support their work, as well as the justification for this allo-cation of social resources at least from the perspective of the center of power in Jerusalem that was able to allocate and control these resources.

The very authoritativeness claimed by the written products, that is, pro-phetic (and similar) books, along with the resources involved in creating and maintaining such a literary corpus, is consistent with — and perhaps even re-quires — an ideological or theological worldview according to which both the authoritative, highly literate writers/readers *and* above all their authoritative works belonged at the very least symbolically to the general societal sphere, to "all Israel."[66] The symbolic world, in turn, is not totally unrelated to the "actual

---

65. To some extent, one may compare the case with that of the Jewish sages in rabbinic times. They also composed written literature in a mostly illiterate society. See M. Bar-Ilan, "Illiteracy in the Land of Israel in the First Centuries c.e.," in *Essays in the Social Scientific Study of Judaism and Jewish Society* (ed. Simcha Fishbane, et al.; Hoboken: Ktav, 1992), 2:46-61. There are significant differences, however. For one there were fewer literati in Achaemenid Yehud than sages in rabbinic times, and above all, the social, historical, cultural and eco-nomic circumstances of Achaemenid Yehud are unlike those in Roman-times Palestine or Parthia (and, later, the Sassanid Empire). For a recent study on "who read and who wrote" in the late Second Temple period, see Millard, *Reading and Writing.*

66. Cf. Deut 31:10-13, among many other texts. But see also Hos 14:10 (Eng. 9). Authori-tative texts must be read and explained by the "correct" authorities. See below.

historical world." It is very unlikely that the main messages of the books the literati wrote, read, reread, and studied were meant to remain among themselves alone, and were not meant to affect society at large.[67] It is most reasonable to assume that at least portions of prophetic texts, that is, of texts that claim to communicate divine teachings, were read to and interpreted to a more general public; and given the claim for authoritativeness that the texts advance, that such public performances were likely to be controlled by the center of power in Jerusalem.[68] If this is the case, the interpretive authority of the literati was not as absolute as their roles of writers, direct readers, and brokers of the divine teachings and communications seem to imply.

Other constraints applied too. For instance, for the literati to be successful, their works as they were presented to the general society had to suit some of its expectations of what can constitute a divine teaching. In fact, in historical, rather than ideological, terms, their very role as brokers of what was considered divine teaching situates them by necessity as social intermediaries whose activity — both as writers and readers too — contributes to the cohesiveness of society and its sense of identity.[69]

It bears note that the recognition of a basically uniform social location for the authorship and primary readership of prophetic books does not lead to a uniform, intellectually deadening environment in form-critical studies, but rather to the blossoming of new horizons of research for these types of studies.

## Intention

The previous discussion has shown that the study of the social setting is deeply interrelated with that of the intention of the texts, that is, the roles that these texts were supposed to and most likely fulfilled within the society that

---

67. Needless to say, such a position would stand in diametrical opposition to claims advanced in many biblical texts, e.g., Deut 4:5-10; 31:10-13.

68. Cf. 2 Chr 17:7-9; Neh 8; Deut 31:10-13. Cf. Ben Zvi, "Analogical Thinking and Ancient Israelite Intellectual History: The Case for An 'Entropy Model' in the Study of Israelite Thought," forthcoming, which is a revised and enlarged version of "Entropy in Ancient Israel? And If So What?" paper presented at the 2001 meeting of the Pacific Northwest SBL. Cf. "The sword comes to the world for . . . those who teach Torah not in accordance with the accepted norm (ולא כהלכה)," *m. 'Abot* 5:9.

69. It bears mention that "restricted high literacy" and "general orality" were two interwoven phenomena in ancient Israel; they complemented and sustained each other. See Ben Zvi, "Introduction," in *Writings and Speech*, ed. Ben Zvi and Floyd.

created them.[70] These roles were multiple. The following represent an illustrative sample.

Within a mainly illiterate society, there was an iconic value to the authoritative texts that the literati wrote, which is exemplified in their role in the public sphere.[71] The materiality of the text served there as a signal of the presence and permanence of the divine guidance.

The contents (as opposed to the iconic value of the authoritative scroll) were, of course, considered YHWH's communications, that is, divine teachings. Above all, within the worldviews of the time, they served as an ideological or theological base for Israel's existence, for their "proper" behavior according to YHWH's will, and as a permanent link with the divine that was accessible to those who could read them, and through their intermediation to those who could not.

They also communicated and created a link to Israel's past — as they construed it — and explained that history in terms of the divine economy. Probably more importantly, they pointed at a trajectory set by the divine and to be fulfilled in the future. In doing so, they provided much comfort to Israel.[72]

Because of the reasons mentioned above, it is likely that the prophetic books or portions thereof were read aloud; that is, they were also "products" or raw material for "products" to be performed as it were, probably in ritual settings.

In all these roles, prophetic books — and other authoritative books — served important roles in building and defining community and identity. Significantly, to the best of my knowledge, no other society in the ancient Near East composed and included in its repertoire prophetic books like those that eventually ended up in the Hebrew Bible. In other words, even the genre of prophetic book by itself was an identity marker.[73]

Prophetic books also served functions within the world and life of the inner circle of their authorship and primary readership. These, along with other authoritative books, shaped and defined the social group directly in-

---

70. Of course, the intentions of the text are construed through its reading, which in the case of authoritative texts is interpersonal and communal. This being so, considerations regarding "intention" have to be strongly qualified by an explicit reference to a particular time and society for which they hold valid.

71. See, e.g., M. S. Jaffee, *Torah in the Mouth: Writing and Oral Tradition in Palestinian Judaism, 200 BCE–400 BCE* (Oxford: Oxford Univ. Press, 2001), 16; Ben Zvi, "Introduction," in *Writings and Speech*, ed. Ben Zvi and Floyd, 12-13; idem, "Analogical Thinking."

72. Cf. Sir 49:10.

73. Cf. midrash in Judaism, and gospel in Christianity. Incidentally, both were also unique literary genres.

volved in their composition, editing, reading, rereading, and study, and served to create their own image of themselves, as preservers and transmitters of the divine will and teaching.[74]

It is important to stress that all these roles applied to prophetic books and to other authoritative books in ancient Israel. There are differences, however. For instance, the general style and voice of these books set them apart from Psalms, pentateuchal, or "historical" books. These differences have bearing on the instructional intentions of these texts as perceived by their intended and primary readerships. Moreover, beyond the general similarities mentioned above, each prophetic book as a whole and, in fact, each individual reading within a book conveyed its own set of messages and images to these readerships. All the mentioned and general intentions of prophetic books in society do *not* replace the particular intentions of each text; rather, they serve as a frame from which the latter may be studied.

---

74. Elsewhere I dealt with the quasi-prophetic character of this self-perception. See Ben Zvi, "Introduction," in *Writings and Speech*, ed. Ben Zvi and Floyd, 13-14, and bibliography.

# Basic Trends in the Form-Critical
# Study of Prophetic Texts

## MICHAEL H. FLOYD

To discuss the current state of form criticism with respect to prophetic literature, we have to know not only what we mean by "form criticism" but also
what we mean by "prophetic literature." Form criticism has generally assumed modern historical criticism's definition of prophetic literature rather
than a traditional canonical definition. The category has thus been limited to
those biblical books that mostly consist of what appear to be prophetic
speeches. This rules out not only Jonah but also other books that Jews and
Christians have traditionally regarded as prophetic, including the historical
narrative that runs from Joshua through Kings, the Psalter, Daniel, and so on.
As we shall see, form criticism has now reached a point at which it needs to
reconsider its assumption about the extent of the prophetic corpus, as well as
its methods of analyzing the kind of literature that it has thus far thought to
be prophetic. I begin, however, with a review of analytical methods, and by
this route come back to the definition of prophetic literature.

As Hermann Gunkel (1862-1932) and other early form critics noticed,
many of the prophetic writings have rhetorical patterns *(Formensprache)* that
match narrative descriptions of oracular speeches made by prophets. Gunkel
thought that these rhetorical patterns were conventional generic forms
*(Gattungen)*, which typically functioned in the setting *(Sitz im Leben)* of prophetic oratory. From this observation he drew several conclusions: (1) Prophetic literature originated as prophetic speeches that got written down, perhaps after being transmitted orally for some time. (2) These transcribed
speeches were subsequently arranged and annotated by scribes, in a redactional
process that considerably distanced the production of the book from the
prophet himself. And (3) the core of originally oral material, spoken by the
prophet himself, could be retrieved from those parts of the text that showed the

prophetic rhetorical patterns in their most pristine forms. This original material then became the main source for a biographical account of the prophet's
career, and the secondary material was treated as evidence of how the prophet's
message for his own generation was reinterpreted for later generations.[1]

As form criticism was first practiced, it was more concerned with the
historical study of the prophets themselves than with the literary study of the
books named after them. It is this biographical goal that has proved elusive.
Using form-critical methods, scholars have not been able to reach much of a
consensus regarding the original core and subsequent redactional layers of
any prophetic book. In some cases results have converged enough to show
that the form-critical model remains a plausible explanation of how the
books in question came to be, but their development still cannot be traced
with any precision.[2] On the whole, then, the project has foundered. In order
for prophetic books to be read in terms of their historical development, the
original core of prophetic speeches must be more or less clearly identifiable,
and in view of the divergent results this no longer seems possible.

1. H. Gunkel, *Die israelitische Literatur* (1906; repr. Darmstadt: Wissenschaftliche
Buchgesellschaft, 1963), 28-38; idem, "Die Grundprobleme der israelitischen Literatur-
geschichte," in *Reden und Aufsätze* (Göttingen: Vandenhoeck & Ruprecht, 1913), 29-38; idem,
"The Prophets as Writers and Poets," in *Prophecy in Israel* (ed. D. L Petersen; trans. J. L.
Schaaf; IRT 10; Philadelphia: Fortress; London: SPCK, 1987), 22-73; trans. of "Die Propheten
als Schriftsteller und Dichter," in *Die großen Propheten* (ed. H. Schmidt; SAT II/2; Göttingen:
Vandenhoeck & Ruprecht, 1915), xxxvi-lxxii; idem, "The Israelite Prophecy from the Time of
Amos," in *Themes of Biblical Theology* (trans. R. A. Wilson; vol. 1 of *Twentieth Century Theol-
ogy in the Making*, ed. J. Pelikan; London: Collins/Fontana, 1969), 48-75; trans. of "Propheten:
II.B. Propheten Israels seit Amos," *RGG²* 4:1538-54. For the subsequent development of
Gunkel's views on the form criticism of prophetic literature, see C. Westermann, *Basic Forms
of Prophetic Speech* (trans. H. C. White; Philadelphia: Westminster, 1967); trans. of *Grundformen prophetischer Rede* (BEvT 31; Munich: Kaiser, 1960); K. Koch, *The Growth of the Biblical Tradition: The Form-Critical Method* (trans. S. M. Cupitt; New York: Scribner's Sons,
1969), 183-220; trans. of *Was ist Formgeschichte?* (Neukirchen-Vluyn: Neukirchener Verlag,
1964, 2d ed. 1967); W. E. March, "Prophecy," in *Old Testament Form Criticism* (ed. J. H. Hayes;
TUMSR 2; San Antonio: Trinity Univ. Press, 1974), 141-77; R. E. Clements, *One Hundred Years
of Old Testament Interpretation* (Philadelphia: Westminster, 1976), 51-75; G. M. Tucker,
"Prophecy and the Prophetic Literature," in *The Hebrew Bible and Its Modern Interpreters* (ed.
D. A. Knight and G. M. Tucker; Philadelphia: Fortress; Chico, Calif.: Scholars Press, 1985),
325-68; M. H. Floyd, "Prophecy and Writing in Hab 2,1-5," *ZAW* 105 (1993): 462-69; M. A.
Sweeney, *Isaiah 1–39; with an Introduction to Prophetic Literature* (FOTL 16; Grand Rapids:
Eerdmans, 1996), 1-30.

2. For example, this is particularly the case with respect to the study of Amos. See G. F.
Hasel, *Understanding the Book of Amos: Basic Issues in Current Interpretations* (Grand Rapids:
Baker, 1991), 91-99.

One alternative is to minimize the distinction between prophetic speaker and scribal redactor by rejecting form criticism's identification of the basic genres of prophetic speech. Under this approach, prophets are still considered speakers, but they were speakers whose remarks were shaped more by how they developed their topic than by how they followed conventions of oratorical form. Prophets made long, rambling speeches, the notes for which became the basis of the books named for them. These speeches now form extensive segments of text, which can be distinguished from one another by the coincidence of major topical and major rhetorical breaks. For all practical purposes, the prophets themselves can be regarded as the authors of the books named for them. Scribal redactors may have been involved, but their contribution was limited to the overall arrangement of speeches and the addition of minor annotations. The goal of the investigation is still essentially biographical; but now the bulk of the book — rather than a limited amount of supposedly original material — is to be read in terms of the prophet's life and times.[3]

This approach is problematic in two major respects. First, it simply ignores Gunkel's observation that the prophetic writings have rhetorical patterns resembling those in narrative descriptions of prophetic speech. This fact is hardly insignificant. Perhaps it needs an explanation different from the one that form criticism has thus far given it, but it deserves to be explained rather than ignored. Second, this approach trivializes the role of the scribal redactor. Even before the advent of form-critical methods, historical criticism showed that in most cases there was a major difference between any contribution possibly made by the prophet himself and the contribution made by later writers to the book bearing his name. In retrospect, the detailed theories along this line, based largely on source-critical methods, may now seem exaggerated; but the main claims have certainly withstood the test of time. Isaiah is the parade example of a prophetic book that has been reworked over a long period, in which any material that could possibly come from the prophet himself has been extensively augmented by material coming from later contributors. There is no reason to suppose that all other prophetic books match the extreme case of Isaiah, but there is also no reason to suppose that what is so obviously true of Isaiah is not to some extent true of other prophetic books as

---

3. Again, recent work on Amos provides a good indication of this trend. See, e.g., three major commentaries in English: J. H. Hayes, *Amos the Eighth-Century Prophet: His Times and His Preaching* (Nashville: Abingdon, 1988); F. I. Andersen and D. N. Freedman, *Amos* (AB 24A; New York: Doubleday, 1989); S. M. Paul, *Amos: A Critical Commentary on the Book of Amos* (Hermeneia; Minneapolis: Fortress, 1991).

well. For these reasons, the previously described alternative to the present impasse in form criticism seems to be a methodological dead end.

Another, more promising alternative is to raise the questions that form criticism has generally asked — the questions of genre and setting — but from a different starting point. Suppose we begin with what we think we know about prophetic literature as a result of the whole historical-critical enterprise, namely, that most of the books were produced at some chronological distance from the time of the prophets for whom they are named, perhaps as early as the exile but mostly in the postexilic period. Suppose we also begin with what we actually have, namely, the final form of the written text rather than some hypothetical collection of original prophetic speeches. What could we say on this basis about the genre and setting of prophetic literature?

Of course there is nothing very new about reading the final form of the text. We have learned to read synchronically from many of the disparate methodological camps that now comprise the fragmented field of biblical studies, ranging from canonical criticism to rhetorical criticism and reader-response criticism.[4] Studies of prophetic literature using such methods are on the increase. However, practitioners of these newer approaches seem generally uninterested in raising the question of genre systematically.[5] This is odd, particularly on the part of methods that define themselves in literary rather than historical terms, because genre is just as much a literary concern as it is a historical concern. I suspect that practitioners of literary methods tend to avoid the question of genre not for any good theoretical reasons but simply because it has been associated with form criticism's dubious project of reconstructing the original words of the prophets. They want to avoid anything that smacks of such historicism. In any case, and for whatever reason, practi-

---

4. J. F. A. Sawyer, "A Change of Emphasis in the Study of the Prophets," in *Israel's Prophetic Tradition: Essays in Honour of Peter A. Ackroyd* (ed. R. Coggins, A. Phillips, and M. Knibb; Cambridge: Cambridge Univ. Press, 1982), 233-49; F. E. Deist, "The Prophets: Are We Heading for a Paradigm Switch?" in *"The Place Is Too Small for Us": The Israelite Prophets in Recent Scholarship* (ed. R. P. Gordon; Winona Lake, Ind.: Eisenbrauns, 1995), 582-99.

5. This is certainly the case with the kind of canonical criticism pioneered by B. S. Childs ("The Canonical Shape of the Prophetic Literature," *Int* 32 [1978]: 46-68). More recently, reader-response approaches to prophecy, focused on the book of Isaiah, have similarly shown a lack of interest in the question of genre (e.g., E. W. Conrad, *Reading Isaiah* [OBT; Minneapolis: Fortress, 1991]; K. P. Darr, *Isaiah's Vision and the Family of God* [Literary Currents in Biblical Interpretation; Louisville: Westminster John Knox, 1994). See also the broader representation of literary approaches to Isaiah in R. F. Melugin and M. A. Sweeney, eds., *New Visions of Isaiah* (JSOTSup 214; Sheffield: Sheffield Academic Press, 1996), in which Sweeney is the only interpreter to consider the literary whole in terms of what might be called a genre category ("The Book of Isaiah as Prophetic Torah," 50-67).

tioners of synchronic methods that focus on the final form of the text are not giving the question of genre the attention it deserves, even from their own purely literary perspective.[6]

Similarly, although the newer critical methods make much of readers and their social location, they have not given systematic consideration to the sociology of reading in the ancient world — who could produce texts, who could read texts, the social settings in which texts were read, the methods by which texts were studied, the status of those who possessed texts, and so on. The synchronic approaches have tended to assume that although literacy may have been less common, the activity of reading in the ancient world was not very different from the activity of reading in our contemporary world, and that the phenomenology of reading can even serve as a kind of hermeneutical bridge from one context to the other. It is perhaps debatable whether this amounts to a theoretical inconsistency on the part of those who practice synchronic methods, but even from their own perspective the radically different sociology of ancient reading deserves greater scrutiny.[7]

To press the questions of the genre and setting of the final form of the text, rather than the genre and setting of original prophetic speeches, would be something of an innovation for form criticism itself, but one that is consistent with Gunkel's claims about the importance of these categories for the understanding of any ancient text — or any text, for that matter. Moreover, in this way form criticism might also contribute insights potentially useful

6. See, e.g., the two essays on genre in R. Cohen, ed., *The Future of Literary Theory* (New York and London: Routledge, 1989): "Literary Genres and Textual Genericity," by J.-M. Schaeffer (pp. 167-87), and "The Future of Genre Theory: Functions and Constructional Types," by A. Fowler (pp. 291-303). The death of genre analysis has been loudly proclaimed by some literary theorists, perhaps most notably F. Jameson (*The Political Unconscious: Narrative as a Socially Symbolic Act* [Ithaca, N.Y.: Cornell Univ. Press, 1981], esp. 136-45), but such obituaries seem premature. Although the article on "Genre" by F. Garber, et al., in *The New Princeton Encyclopedia of Poetry and Poetics* (Princeton: Princeton Univ. Press, 1993), agrees with Jameson that "g[enre] theory has been discredited by modern thinking about lit[erature]," it is also somewhat inconsistently forced to admit that "theorizing about g[enre] has not been so vigorous since the 16th c[entury]. The suggestiveness of the 20th c[entury]'s quite variegated work makes it a period of extraordinary achievement in the history of this stubborn, dubious, always controversial concept" (p. 458). Biblical criticism's shift from diachronic historical to synchronic literary methods does not in itself necessarily entail any diminished interest in genre analysis.

7. Issues related to the sociology of ancient reading are well surveyed by E. Ben Zvi, "Introduction: Writings, Speeches, and the Prophetic Books — Setting an Agenda," in *Writings and Speech in Israelite and Ancient Near Eastern Prophecy* (ed. E. Ben Zvi and M. H. Floyd; SBLSymS 10; Atlanta: SBL, 2000), 1-29.

to other synchronic approaches that would otherwise not want to be tainted by historical-critical methodology. Back in 1973 Rolf Knierim's essay, "Old Testament Form Criticism Reconsidered," paved the way for such a turn in scholarship, and the volumes on prophetic literature in the Forms of the Old Testament Literature series represent a step in this direction, particularly in attempting to deal with genre on the level of the text's final form.[8] On the whole, however, these studies have not given sustained consideration to the question of genre in relation to the setting of the text's final form. Not until now, that is, because the most recent volume in this series, Ehud Ben Zvi's study of Micah, presses the question of this prophetic book's setting very hard indeed, in a way that directly affects his conclusions regarding its genre.[9] I therefore focus on Ben Zvi's work as the most telling example of what I consider the most viable alternative in the form-critical study of prophetic literature.

Ben Zvi points out that, to the best of our knowledge, books like Micah were produced by the literati of Achaemenid Yehud who were probably concentrated in Jerusalem. He goes on to make several important observations about this group. First, given the small population that the city would have had, regardless of which estimates one may prefer, and given the small percentage of the population that was literate in ancient society, this group must have been very small, if not tiny. Second, given that in ancient society the ability to read, as well as the ability to write, was largely restricted to the literati, this small group must have produced such documents primarily for themselves to read. Third, if the contents of such documents were also intended for any wider audience — as they presumably were — this same group of literati would have also been the ones who mediated and interpreted their readings of the text to others in their society. Fourth, given the kinds of documents these literati produced, they must have been not only a cultural elite, but also a group with considerable religious and social authority.

If we judge from the case of Micah, these literati produced documents that claimed to be "the word of Yahweh." Although this "word of Yahweh" is attributed to someone named Micah, who is historically located "in the days of Kings Jotham, Ahaz, and Hezekiah of Judah," and whose prophecies are geographically associated with "Samaria and Jerusalem," very little of the

---

8. R. Knierim, "Old Testament Form Criticism Reconsidered," *Int* 27 (1973): 435-68; repr. in *Reading the Hebrew Bible for a New Millennium: Form, Concept, and Theological Perspective,* vol. 2, *Exegetical and Theological Studies* (ed. W. Kim, et al.; SAC; Harrisburg: Trinity Press International, 2000), 42-71.

9. E. Ben Zvi, *Micah* (FOTL 21B; Grand Rapids: Eerdmans, 2000).

book is explicitly related to any particular events in these times and places. There are occasional prospective references to the fall of the northern and southern kingdoms, which would have indeed come to pass by the time the book was written. The fulfillment of these particular prophecies serves as a warrant for taking the rest seriously. Much of the book, however, consists of social critiques that might be applicable at any time; and much of it concerns an ideal future that remains to be realized, not only with respect to Micah's time, but also with respect to the time of the author(s). There may well have been someone named Micah who prophesied in the eighth century, but this book is written about him, not by him. And its main concern is definitely not to describe this man's prophetic career. It is rather to enable the literati who produced the book to understand "the word of Yahweh" to them and their constituency, and to understand their own past, present, and future in light of this revelation. Micah is basically a character within the book they have created, who represents for the authors one typical aspect of their historical existence in relation to Yahweh. Ben Zvi simply calls such a document a "prophetic book," but he makes this common phrase a technical genre term defined as follows:

> A book that claims an association with a prophetic personage of the past and that is presented to its readership as YHWH's word. As such, the book claims to communicate legitimate and authoritative knowledge about YHWH. Those who were competent to read prophetic books, namely, the literati, constituted the primary readership of these books. These literati were the only group in society that had direct access to such books and the knowledge about YHWH that they claim to convey. These bearers of high literacy served as brokers of that divine knowledge to those who were unable to read by themselves (i.e., the overwhelming majority of the population). Prophetic books were not intended to be read only once, but to be read, reread, and meditated upon. It is to be stressed that [the superscription's designation of the book as "the word of YHWH"] signifies a book to be read, reread, and studied.[10]

This last point, that such texts are to be continually reread and meditatively studied, brings us to Ben Zvi's description of the way in which prophetic books are organized. The significance of Ben Zvi's observations can perhaps best be seen in light of Philip Davies's rather skeptical reaction to the currently fashionable holistic readings of prophetic books:

10. Ibid., 187-88.

Had [the authors of prophetic books] been creating literature for [scribal] study, they would presumably have provided more of a shape, by which I do not mean the kind of shape that ingenious modern literary and canonical critics and theologians can invent *post factum*. If someone intended any version of the book of Jeremiah to be consumed *as a whole,* as a single literary text, it would have been furnished with a structure and a point. But it has neither: it is rather the result of compilation, of a process of compositional accretion done without any intention of being "read" except by another copyist. . . . I am not saying that the contents were not intended to be read; only that they were not intended to be read as one reads a modern book, that is, as a whole, with the expectation of some overall shape, plot, or purpose. The obvious contrast with Hosea or Micah is Jonah; there is a text to be read as a whole.[11]

Davies sets up a continuum that extends, on the one end, from a document that is carefully composed to be read straight through to, on the other end, a document that is a more or less unorganized listing of textual data, into which scribes may look but through which they do not actually read. He suggests that prophetic books were designed to be read in a way that lies somewhere between these two extremes, and this is precisely where Ben Zvi's description of a prophetic book fits.

Ben Zvi observes that however sprawling a prophetic book like Micah may be, there are textual signals that mark off sections — explicit introductions and conclusions, repeated rhetorical patterns, shifts in thematic focus, and so on. Readers are thereby invited to treat these sections as cohesive reading units. Moreover, such signals can also show that some sections are grouped together, and that some sections are cross-referenced to one another even when they are not grouped together. Ben Zvi calls such sections of text "readings," and calls such groupings of them "sets." Prophetic readings and sets of prophetic readings are not necessarily interrelated in a tight linear sequence, but their overall arrangement is nevertheless important because it shows them to be "interwoven into the tapestry of the book in such a way that they inform each other."[12] Prophetic books are thus designed not to be read straight through from beginning to end, but to be read and reread section by section, and searched for their tapestry-like interconnections.

I do not take issue with Ben Zvi. On the contrary, I would affirm his

11. P. R. Davies, "The Audiences of Prophetic Scrolls: Some Suggestions," in *Prophets and Paradigms: Essays in Honor of Gene M. Tucker* (ed. S. B. Reid; JSOTSup 229; Sheffield: Sheffield Academic Press, 1996), 60.

12. Ben Zvi, *Micah,* 188.

conclusions as the inevitable starting point from which the form criticism of prophetic literature might now take its potentially most fruitful turn. If we press the question of genre on the level of the text's final form, and the question of its setting in terms of the sociology of mantic reading and writing in Achaemenid Yehud, Ben Zvi's work on Micah shows clearly the right direction in which to go. I would, however, press some points with implications for what the next steps might be.

First, with regard to genre, it is significant that Ben Zvi's definition of a prophetic book applies to much more than the books that have been recognized as prophetic literature by modern historical scholarship. Ben Zvi has defined a prophetic book as a text that has a prophetic figure from the past as its main character, identifies itself as a representation of the word of Yahweh, and claims to communicate authentic knowledge about Yahweh to its readership. This accurately describes books like Micah, in terms of which modern scholarship has defined the category of prophetic literature, but the same can also be said of Jonah, which modern scholarship has excluded from this category. Indeed, Ben Zvi's definition applies as much to the narrative books traditionally called "the Former Prophets" as it does to the oracular books included among "the Latter Prophets," and it could even include still other books that have traditionally been regarded as prophetic but not recognized as such by modern scholarship. The author of Micah makes this prophet from the past a character within the book he created, in such a way that the word of Yahweh itself also becomes, as it were, a speaking character within the book. Similarly, the author of what we have come to call the Deuteronomistic History not only recounts what prophets from the past have said in the name of Yahweh, but also makes the word of Yahweh itself a speaking character within the story.[13] In both cases the aim is to provide authoritative knowledge about Yahweh. Of course, these two authors represent these two types of characters and accomplish their common aim in very different ways, but before addressing these differences it is important to note the fundamental similarity, which Ben Zvi's definition of a prophetic book again allows us to appreciate.

Once we acknowledge the fundamental similarity, however, the need for further distinctions is immediately apparent. Micah and Samuel may both be prophetic books, but there is a big difference. In books like Micah oracular speech predominates, and narrative — if there is any — is subordinate to it. In books like Samuel it is just the opposite: narrative predominates and orac-

---

13. I have discussed the genre of "prophetic history" in M. H. Floyd, "The Nature of the Narrative and the Evidence of Redaction in Haggai," *VT* 65 (1995): 483-87.

ular speech is subordinate to it. On the one hand, Ben Zvi's definition of a prophetic book is of fundamental importance; on the other hand, it is so broad that it needs further differentiation to be of much practical use. This is readily evident when we compare books that modern scholarship has regarded as prophetic with those that it has excluded, but it is also evident when we compare books that modern scholarship has included within the prophetic corpus. For example, if we extend the categories that Ben Zvi has developed in his study of Micah to analyze Habakkuk, we could conclude only that it too is a prophetic book made up of various prophetic readings. This underscores the fundamental similarity between Micah and Habakkuk, but it does not really help us understand their obvious differences. These differences are not just incidental ones that emerge only on the level of the content of the sections of the book. They are factors to be reckoned with in describing the overall form of the text on the level of the book as a whole.[14]

If we take Ben Zvi's definition of a prophetic book as a starting point, it has far-reaching implications. If form criticism is really going to press the question of genre with regard to the final form of the text, we will need to do nothing less than redefine the corpus of prophetic literature itself, and at the same time develop categories for describing specific types of prophetic books.[15]

In order to distinguish different types of prophetic books, some attention has to be given to their constituent parts. Differences on the level of the book as a whole entail either different basic constituents or different combinations of the same basic constituents. On this subsidiary level of description, Ben Zvi's analysis of the text into prophetic readings (and sets of prophetic readings) has the same advantage and disadvantage as his definition of a prophetic book. On the one hand, his concept of prophetic reading is of fundamental importance because it shows how such books are designed to be read — as sections of text to be pored over, as we look for tapestry-like interconnections that are not necessarily in linear sequence. On the other hand this concept of prophetic reading is not in itself specific enough to capture what is really distinctive about the kind of prophetic book represented by Micah. When this kind of prophetic literature is compared with the kind represented by Jonah or the Deuteronomistic History, it is evident that some prophetic

14. For example, Habakkuk is a self-described *maśśāʾ* (1:1) and Micah is not, which means that their overall structural patterns are different. Compare Ben Zvi's description of Micah as a whole (*Micah*, 1-11) with the description of Habbakuk as a whole in M. H. Floyd, *Minor Prophets, Part 2* (FOTL 22; Grand Rapids: Eerdmans, 2000), 81-90. See further M. H. Floyd, "The מַשָּׂא as a Type of Prophetic Book," *JBL* 121 (2002): 401-22.

15. As in, e.g., Floyd, "*Maśśāʾ*."

literature is in fact designed to be read in a linear fashion — namely, the kind that is organized as narrative. It is further evident that the makeup of books like Micah fits Ben Zvi's description of a prophetic reading precisely because it consists of oracular speech without much, if any, narrative context. In order to distinguish specific types of prophetic books, we must take this fact into account and therefore identify the kinds and combinations of oracular speech that they are characteristically made of.

It is extremely important to add that this means going beyond Ben Zvi's definition of a prophetic reading, and not going back on it. With regard to the question of the genres of prophetic oracular literature we have come full circle, back to Gunkel's observation that the rhetorical patterns of prophetic texts like Micah match those found in narrated descriptions of speeches made by prophets. However, this fact cannot now engender any renewed quests for the historical Micahs and their original words. It must instead provoke us to ask why the prophetic writers who authored books like Micah often chose to address their readers with the same rhetorical conventions used by speaking prophets to address their hearers. We must not lose sight of the fact that the sections of prophetic books are, in the final analysis, prophetic readings and not prophetic speeches. However, we must also address the fact that even though they are prophetic readings and not prophetic speeches, they nevertheless continue to use the conventional rhetorical patterns that are characteristic of prophetic speeches — as Ben Zvi's own analysis shows again and again. It is this very fact that enables the text to be read in the nonlinear, recursive fashion so aptly described by Ben Zvi.

If form criticism of prophetic literature takes the kind of turn that I have just outlined in dialogue with Ben Zvi, pressing more radically the question of the genres of prophetic literature as such, we will be more starkly confronted with the question of the setting in which prophetic literature was produced. Form criticism has tended to emphasize the setting of prophetic speech rather than the setting of prophetic literature, because information about the former lent itself more readily to the historical-critical project of reconstructing the biographies of the great prophets. The latter has been addressed only as a kind of afterthought, through simplistic references to "schools" and "redactors" as the kinds of agents that would be self-evidently involved in literary production of any kind. Little consideration has been given to the particularities of producing such a distinctive kind of literature in an ancient social context under the historical conditions in which postexilic Jews found themselves. But if we follow Ben Zvi's lead, in order to understand the nature of prophetic literature we will have to attend to setting in this sense.

Several basic aspects of the social and historical context in which the prophetic literature was produced, which Ben Zvi has identified, have already been mentioned.[16] In addition, he has explored two major implications of the role that the tiny scribal elite assumed, as authoritative mediators of divine knowledge to the recently reformed Yehudite community. First, they supported the ideological project of giving divine legitimation to the Persian colonial government established in Jerusalem by the returning exiles. This is evident in the motif of a restored and about-to-be glorified Jerusalem that is prominent — albeit to varying extents and in different ways — in all the prophetic books. Second, the same scribal elite produced a corpus of prophetic books in which there is considerable theological and literary diversity. Ben Zvi argues that in view of the very few scribes that Yehudite society could have sustained and the limited resources at their disposal, this diversity can no longer be attributed to various different circles of literati engaged in theological debates and partisan conflicts. It is rather the result of a policy pursued by one and the same small scribal group, to rework various still extant preexilic documents whose perspectives were more or less compatible with their own ideological project. By cultivating such diversity in theological and literary discourse, they demonstrated all the more convincingly their continuity with preexilic traditions.[17]

The corpus of prophetic literature produced by the postexilic literati certainly claimed to be an authoritative expression of "the word of Yahweh" to the Jewish community, and these literati presumably held the kind of social position that would allow them to make such a claim. These and other such observations made by Ben Zvi, noted above, have considerably advanced the discussion of prophetic literature's setting. For example, it must now be acknowledged that the writers of the prophetic books were not mere "redactors," that is, not just inert transcribers of oracles spoken by others. They were rhetorically skilled writers who selected and reinterpreted older prophetic traditions so as to express their own prophetic mind and voice. By their production and promulgation of prophetic texts, they were making a power play. But what kind of power play?

The bold strokes with which Ben Zvi has sketched the setting of prophetic literature provide a helpful starting point for the discussion of this question, but some of the more specific aspects of his description are debatable. He argues that the writers of prophetic books were attempting to create

16. See pp. 302-4 above.

17. E. Ben Zvi, "The Urban Center of Jerusalem and the Development of the Literature of the Hebrew Bible," in *Urbanism in Antiquity: From Mesopotamia to Crete* (ed. W. E. Aufrecht, N. A. Mirau, and S. W. Gauley; JSOTSup 244; Sheffield: Sheffield Academic Press, 1997), 204-6.

for themselves a kind of monopoly on divine knowledge: Prophetic books "contributed to the construction of a world in which YHWH's word is a written text to which only the literati have *direct* access. . . . In that world the literati turn into mediators between YHWH, the patron and as such the provider of knowledge, and Israel, the client who needs that knowledge to maintain its ways and to fulfill its obligations to the patron."[18] In line with this general view of the literati's aims, Ben Zvi holds that with their prophetic texts they were trying to discredit the authenticity of prophecy in other forms, that the production of prophetic literature in Yehud would have precluded the production of similarly authoritative prophetic literature elsewhere, that those who wrote Yehudite prophetic literature thereby asserted the right to be the exclusive interpreters of what they had written, and so on. Of course these and similar claims began to be made as a more or less canonical corpus of prophetic literature developed. They certainly presuppose the existence of prophetic writing. The question is whether the very phenomenon of prophetic writing in itself necessarily entails such views, so that they can be imputed a priori to the writers of the prophetic books, or whether such views emerged subsequently within the debate about how such literature should be interpreted. This remains to be seen, and the nature of the prophetic scribal power play needs further discussion. Two areas of investigation would particularly improve our understanding of what was at stake in their production of prophetic literature.

First, it would help to know more about the relationship between the Yehudite literati and the Persian imperial administration. Jon Berquist has recently argued that the scribes who performed the empire's archival tasks were also the ones who wrote the incipient collection of Jewish canonical Scriptures. This is certainly plausible, because any text-producing group would probably have needed some kind of patronage, and the imperial bureaucracy would have been a very likely source. For the present, however, descriptions of the official dimension of the scribal role in the Persian period remain largely speculative.[19]

Second, it would also help to know more about how the Yehudite literati viewed themselves in relation to Jewish communities of the Diaspora. Even if the Yehudite literati enjoyed some measure of official power in Yehud itself, they would not have wielded any jurisdictional influence over their

18. Ben Zvi, *Micah*, 11.

19. J. L. Berquist, "Wisdom and Scribes in Persian Yehud" (paper presented at the annual meeting of the SBL, Nashville, Nov. 21, 2000). Berquist describes the social location of scribes in Achaemenid Yehud on the basis of indirect reflections of the scribal role in wisdom literature. He extends his generalizations to cover the production of law and history, as well as wisdom, but does not mention prophetic literature.

coreligionists elsewhere. They may have been able to force their view of Jerusalem's theological centrality on their local political constituency, but wider acceptance of this view — which eventually did win out over the alternatives even among Jews outside Yehud — could have come about only through effective persuasion. Similarly, if the Yehudite literati intended that the texts they wrote would remain in Yehud itself, they could have aspired to control the interpretation as well as the production of those texts. If they intended for these texts to reach the wider Jewish community, however, they could not have entertained such aspirations. In other places textual interpretation would have been limited to similar groups of literati, since they were the only ones who could read. But the Yehudite scribal establishment would not have been able to control directly how scribal groups elsewhere interpreted its texts. I cannot consider here the extent to which the intended audience of Second Temple literature encompasses the Diaspora as well as Yehud. It must suffice to point out that there are texts clearly intended to show the theological centrality of Jerusalem for those who remain in exile, as well as for those who return and those who have lived there all along.[20]

Depending on the outcome of these and other such investigations, the power play of the Yehudite prophetic scribes may be understood in different ways. They clearly understood themselves as speaking for Yahweh, and they clearly voiced divine approval of the Persian colonial administration to which they were somehow related. It is one thing to imagine them as cultural imperialists, imposing their view by a virtual threat of force on those under local political control. It is quite another thing to imagine them as organic intellectuals, persuasively winning widespread approval of their controversial viewpoint among a theologically diverse and geographically scattered minority group. An accurate characterization of the Yehudite literati probably lies somewhere between these two stereotypical extremes.

Form criticism is only now beginning to consider questions of genre and setting with regard to prophetic literature itself, as opposed to prophetic speech. The results are thus far tentative and incomplete, but even such results show the enduring importance of form-critical concerns for our understanding of prophetic literature. The shift from a primarily historical to a primarily literary orientation does not do away with the questions of genre and setting. To grasp the meaning of prophetic literature these questions will still have to be asked, even if form criticism itself loses its identity as a distinct subdiscipline of biblical studies.

---

20. For example, Zech 5:5-11. See M. H. Floyd, "The Evil in the Ephah: Reading Zechariah 5:5-11 in Its Literary Context," *CBQ* 58 (1996): 51-68.

# Toward Form Criticism as an Explication of Human Life: Divine Speech as a Form of Self-Transcendence

## MARTIN J. BUSS

Form criticism has often been described as a kind of historical criticism. A simple statement like this is not very meaningful, for the terms "form criticism" and "historical criticism" can both be used in a variety of ways. I will show that "form criticism," as I understand it, is not a subdivision of "historical criticism" if that is understood as being interested primarily in the particularity of a text. Yet it is indeed a subdivision of "historical criticism" if this is understood as an "explication of human life" that recognizes particularity but does not limit itself to this aspect.

To see the difference between these conceptions, it is best to begin with a sketch of how this issue developed in modern and postmodern times. I have given a detailed account of this earlier[1] and so will present here only some of the highlights of that development.

"Historical criticism" as a procedure that focused primarily on the particularity of a text became prominent from the end of the Middle Ages on. During that time an interest in particularity increased in large parts of Europe, especially in England, Italy, the Netherlands, Germany, and France, and in countries contiguous with these.[2] The interest in particularity played a role in at least four contrasts: (1) between human individuals; (2) between groups, such as "nations" and "religions"; (3) between time periods, with their respective cultures; and (4) between "facts" and "values," for "facts" were thought to be particular and have no intrinsic connection with anything else. In philoso-

---

1. *Biblical Form Criticism in Its Context* (JSOTSup 274; Sheffield: Sheffield Academic Press, 1999).

2. Prominent early figures were William of Ockham (14th century CE) in England and Lorenzo Valla (15th century) in Italy.

phy such an outlook was known as "nominalism," for it held that all general terms and all terms for relations are human constructions — "names" — while in reality itself there are only particulars.

The particularist outlook gradually became more pervasive until the nineteenth century, although it was never held in pure form. (In fact, it is not certain that pure nominalism is viable in a nonskeptical form.) It was a feature of what is commonly called "modernity." The whole complex was closely associated with the rise of the middle class, which favored individualism, and led to such phenomena as republican forms of government and capitalism.

This "modern" development can be clearly seen in biblical studies in the rise of particularist historical criticism. During the sixteenth and seventeenth centuries, there was an interest in the differences between individual authors, with their characteristic styles and emphases. Detailed attention was also given to the fact that manuscripts and translations of the biblical text differed from one another, as well as to numerous concrete matters, such as the design of Solomon's temple. In the eighteenth and nineteenth centuries, the interest in differences brought about a veritable revolution in the picture of the historical development of biblical writings. The revolution was aided by an important aspect of individualism, namely, that individuals were permitted and indeed encouraged to think for themselves and to submit the authorities of their groups to critical evaluation.

The relativization of the authority of the Bible had definite social, economic, and political implications. Specifically, republican forms of government probably drew some inspiration from the Bible (which is to a considerable extent skeptical of kings), but they also moved well beyond biblical politics. Capitalism built on Christian, especially Calvinist, skepticism about human generosity, but it gained even more from a downgrading of the authority of the Bible, such as of the tenth commandment, which prohibited "coveting" and thus condemned an accumulation of property, which happens, of course, also in noncapitalist societies (cf. Isa 5:8; Mic 2:2).

Most biblical scholars did hold the Bible in high regard in certain respects. However, the particularist distinction between "fact" and "value," useful as it might be in supporting accurate ("objective") investigation, created difficulty for approaching biblical literature as a source of inspiration. A division of labor was created, at least in theory. Historical scholarship was to focus on particular facts, while evaluative questions — including the continuing relevance of a text — were assigned to "theology" or to some similar kind of reflection. That was true especially in Protestantism, which was deeply indebted to nominalism. From the point of view of societal change, there was an advantage in the distinction between "fact" and "value," for it meant that the recognition of a certain situation in the past did not automatically imply approval of it. Yet the distinction also meant that, when historical criticism is pursued with only this in mind, it is meaningless.

At the end of the nineteenth century, a social and intellectual reorientation took place. This reorientation was based in large part on a recognition that modernity (including capitalism) had created major problems in addition to providing features that continued to be valued. Specifically, the new ethos rejected a one-sided interest in particularity. This meant (1) that individualism was balanced by social concern, (2) that international and interreligious connections were established (although this development had a rocky path), (3) that more appreciation was again expressed toward past phenomena, in the recognition that current conditions by no means represented unadulterated "progress," and (4) that "facts" and "values" are not distinct or, in any case, not separate.

Gunkel's work in biblical criticism was very much part of this postmodern reorientation, as the following considerations show: (1) He balanced an individualistic approach with attention to genres. (2) His vision extended beyond Israel to worldwide phenomena. (3) Although he did not automatically accept the authority of biblical texts, his treatment of them had a personal, enthusiastic character that is rare in writings that are addressed to biblical specialists. (4) He saw intrinsic connections between phenomena and did not envision merely discrete facts. Accordingly, Gunkel's program was directed against what he called "historical criticism," by which he meant the particularist version of it. He did favor what he called "history," which recognizes particularity but not only that.

Gunkel's students and admirers, however, followed his path only to a limited extent. In Hebrew Bible studies, comparative visions were indeed strongly present, at first, in works by Jahnow, Baumgartner, Wendel, Mowinckel and other Scandinavian scholars, and later in writings by Westermann. However, most of the rest of scholarship (including that of von Rad) lacked this dimension.

The more narrowly focused kind of form criticism did recognize the importance of the community. One can call its outlook "group-particularism." Commonality was recognized but only within Israel or within the Christian community. This pattern had an unfortunate political parallel in National Socialism, which arose from the same general orientation: a social interest, together with skepticism toward cooperative internationalism. To be sure, during the twentieth century biblically oriented group-particularists did not engage in violent behavior toward others, as had happened in Christianity previously. Thus the parallel with National Socialism was only partial.

In terms of scholarship, a problematic step was taken by followers of Gunkel, when — in line with Gunkel in this respect — they attempted to reconstruct oral traditions presumed to lie behind the text on the basis of assumptions that oral forms were shorter and more regular in their use of genres than were written texts. This created the impression that form criticism represents a branch of particularist criticism, one that deals with the oral phase of a text's history. The problem with this interpretation was that reconstruction along this line violated standard procedures of historical criticism, specifically by making those unwarranted assumptions.

During the 1960s the recognition that this kind of form criticism was highly questionable became widespread. Thus there emerged a version of form criticism that focused primarily or even entirely on the synchronic structure of texts, such as in my analysis of the book of Hosea, in a theoretical presentation by Gene Tucker,[3] and in the series, The Forms of the Old Testament Literature. These analyses were not strongly "historical," in the sense of "diachronic"; but, other than my own, they were primarily particularist. That is, although genres were observed — so that individualism was muted — generic patterns were considered only within the boundaries of Israel. It is true, contributors to the series may well have been influenced implicitly by a knowledge of other traditions, but there is no explicit acknowledgment of such a perspective.[4]

In fact, at that time, many theologians and biblical scholars in the United States (especially Protestants) held that the Bible is relevant only for members of specific religious traditions — Jews and Christians — and the studies that followed this group-particularist line often addressed only members of such a tradition. What was done in such studies — whether they were called "form-critical" or not — has indeed often been helpful as a contribution to scholarship and to religious inspiration. Nevertheless, they failed to deal with many significant issues, not only since they ignored other groups but also since they made limited use of the human sciences, such as psychol-

---

3. I used the term "synchronic" for this, although without rejecting diachronic views altogether (Martin J. Buss, *The Prophetic Word of Hosea: A Morphological Study* [BZAW 111; Berlin: Töpelmann, 1969], 2); Gene M. Tucker, *Form Criticism of the Old Testament* (GBS; Philadelphia: Fortress, 1971).

4. For instance, Sweeney is one who is quite aware of Buddhism, as I know from conversation; he has even published a comparative study of the rise of kingship in Israel and Japan (Marvin A. Sweeney, *The Origins of Kingship in Israel and Japan: A Comparative Analysis* [Occasional Papers 22; Claremont, Calif.: Institute for Antiquity and Christianity, 1995]). However, such knowledge has made no overt impact on his commentary on Isaiah 1–39 (Marvin A. Sweeney, *Isaiah 1–39* [FOTL 16; Grand Rapids: Eerdmans, 1996]), as far as I can see. Will he go further in this direction in the future?

ogy and anthropology. A radicalization of nominalism at the end of the twentieth century could support this orientation.

Offered herewith is an alternative, which does not stand in competition
with these ways, but which represents another path that is little traveled. It can
utilize insights reached by particularist procedure, although the detailed problems with which historical criticism deals often do not need to be solved before
one can proceed in the way proposed. For instance, it may not be important to
know how much of the book of Hosea was produced in the eighth century BCE.

For this alternative, a definition of "form criticism" can be presented on
the basis of Gunkel's characterizations of a genre. Gunkel employed as criteria
for identifying a genre the following three features: (1) a certain life situation,
(2) a characteristic content (both thoughts and moods), and (3) a typical linguistic form. Gunkel assumed that these aspects are tightly connected on an
oral level. This assumption must be rejected. However, one can define "form
criticism" as *a procedure that gives simultaneous attention to human life processes (social and psychological), to human thoughts and feelings, and to linguistic formulations. It explores how these relate to one another, not indeed rigidly,
but also not in a way that is altogether arbitrary.*

In looking for such interrelations, this project is contrary to a so-called
postliberal theology, which holds that only verbal form, not experience, is relevant for faith. To be sure, there is no necessary connection between verbal
form and thought content or experience. Yet certain associations of linguistic
form and human life have a ring of appropriateness.

The procedure thus offered is "historical" in the sense that it deals with
data of the past and in the sense that it recognizes that particular structures of
human life vary. But it does not consider particularity to be more important
than generality, nor does it examine past phenomena as objects of curiosity.
Rather, it looks to those data in order to see what they furnish as a challenge
to one's own life. It does so by using scholarly procedures, such as sociology,
psychology, and the general history of culture, including religion. It is thus an
"explication of human life."

The suggested procedure has a certain similarity with informal approaches to the Bible. However, it differs from them in that it uses the scholarly ways mentioned. It uses them in the belief that "facts" (including the
findings of scholarship) are not separate from "values" (or matters of faith
and ethics) but that there is, rather, a reciprocal relation between them.

I will attempt to give an example of form criticism in this key. Since very
little has been done along this line, the attempt must be regarded as strictly
exploratory. Only when several investigators have put their hands to this —
building on and correcting one another — can one speak of a truly disciplin-

ary move. I hope that a project of this sort will become just as much a going concern (which includes contestation!) as, say, the archeology of the Levant. Just as archeology involves a number of disciplines, so does the path projected here, although the disciplines are in part different: the history of religions, psychology, sociology, rhetorical/poetic analysis, philosophy, theology. Not everyone needs to be equally engaged with all of the aspects mentioned, but when this is a more-or-less cooperative endeavor, the various angles can be explored by different persons. Furthermore, it is not necessary that one always makes a somewhat detailed reference to another religious tradition or to a specific psychological or philosophical work that is relevant. The mere fact that one is aware of such matters can make a difference.

Specifically, the focus of the present essay will be on the linguistic form of divine speech. (Incidentally, Gunkel did not think that the linguistic aspect of a genre is its most important one, but he did think that the linguistic side is often the easiest one with which to begin an analysis, presumably since it is the side that is most immediately available in the text.) Expressions placed in the mouth of God constitute a very large part of the Hebrew Bible. It is, then, appropriate to ask why that is so.

A hint concerning the significance of divine speech is given by the fact that the style is highly correlated with a certain kind of content. This correlation can be determined by a fairly ordinary literary analysis, in conjunction with reflection.

Thus one can observe that the content associated with divine speech is one that often deals with ultimate questions, especially with Origin and End. Origin and End are ultimates in a dynamic structure. The Origin covered in the Pentateuch — where divine speech is prominent — concerns the origin of the world as a whole, the origin of Israel and of its various subgroups, the origin of the sanctity of certain geographical locations, and the basis of a moral/legal/ritual order. The End is an important theme in prophetic literature, where divine speech is also very prominent. When the End is positive, it is always presented as an action of God, not as something humanly deserved or brought about.

In contrast, divine speech is almost entirely absent from wisdom literature (Proverbs, Job, and Qohelet). Certain exceptions to this rule appear in Prov 1:20-33; 8:4-36; 9:4-6, 11, where personified Wisdom (an aspect of God) speaks in an abstract way (with little or no concrete directions),[5] and in Job

---

5. A certain specificity does appear in Prov 8:13 (which refers to pride, arrogance, and perverted speech), as well as in 9:7-9, 12, if these items are indeed part of the speech of personified Wisdom, and not (as appears to be the case) an application of it.

38–41, where God presents a basically negative answer, which indicates that human knowledge is limited and that humanity is not God's only concern. These divine speeches in Proverbs and Job serve the important purpose of indicating that the content of wisdom literature is not independent of the ultimate category of creation. However, the specific instructions and reflections presented in the wisdom books in the form of human speech all deal with finite or penultimate matters, such as success in work, in the family, and in politics. Furthermore, wisdom literature has moderate standards, which a person might actually fulfill. Thus it can refer to persons who are "righteous," who fulfill those standards for the most part. The righteous can expect good consequences, although, as Job and Qohelet observed, they do not always or even regularly obtain them.

To be sure, finite matters appear not only in wisdom literature but also in the Pentateuch and in the Prophets. Indeed, in the Hebrew Bible there is not a definite division between ultimate and more limited issues; on the contrary, they are intertwined. Nevertheless, the point in the present context is that the literary form of divine speech is closely associated with ultimacy.

One can now ask, Why should there be this connection? Possible answers lie in the area of psychology. One answer that suggests itself is that the form of divine speech expresses, on the human side, receptivity toward a reality greater than oneself. This receptivity is not just passivity, simply doing nothing, but "hearing" (without this, there would be no need to refer to God's speaking). Hearing involves a semi-active process, in which one imaginatively takes up the position of the speaker to whom one gives attention. That is a kind of self-transcendence.

Indeed, a major feature of human life is to take up imaginatively a position outside one's own specific location. Piaget called this "decentering." He did not intend that term to refer to the absence of any center but rather to the process in which some imaginary center that lies outside oneself is chosen, such as when one considers a physical object and imagines how it appears from a position where one is not standing now. When this process refers back to one's own actual being, it is called "reflexivity." That is what creates selfhood. Only if one can look at oneself — something that one can do only if one adopts a stance outside oneself — can one be said to have a "self." In other words, selfhood and self-transcendence belong together.

One aspect of self-transcendence is being absorbed by a reality outside oneself for its own sake. This form is ecstatic, deeply enjoyable — at least at the moment when it occurs (sometimes it leads to an action that later gives one physical pain). It is thus not self-abnegating in the sense of being directly hurtful to oneself. At the same time, there are reasons to think that selfhood, which includes self-transcendence, is made possible only in a social context, in which one has received the look of another person with whom one in some way identifies. Selfhood is then inherently social.

Human beings are not merely reflexive; they are also reflective. They realize that, for a "true" view of things (if there is one), one needs to identify with a reference point beyond oneself. In biblical religion such a reference point is called "God."

Philosophers have dealt with this issue, so that one can attempt to make contact with their efforts. It is commonly said in philosophy that it is impossible to take up a "God's-eye view," since it is too comprehensive. Although this statement is correct, it fails to make a distinction between what one can actually do and what one can do imaginatively, as an approximation. Actually taking up God's position is impossible. One can, however, ask, How may this appear to God (or, in other words, in a large view)? Such a question is crucial for biblically based religions, as well as for others. Indeed, a question of this sort — which can be worded nontheistically — is important for overcoming self-centeredness. (Even an acknowledgment of one's own location is a form of self-transcendence, if it indicates a readiness to consider other perspectives.)

A serious problem, to be sure, arises when one thinks that the imaginative identification is also an actual identification, that one really knows God's point of view. This problem leads some philosophers (and others) to say that one should not adopt a religious position at all. Human beings, however, probably always take up some sort of ultimate position — such as Marxism, Nietzscheanism, or agnosticism — even if they do not call that position "divine." Indeed, from my readings it appears that Marxists and many others seem to be even more self-assured and critical of others than is the average religious person. If that is true, the reason may be that they have no good way to distinguish their own position from a more comprehensive one, which is beyond their ken. (The book of Job furnishes an example of such a distinction within the Hebrew Bible.) But perhaps religious and nonreligious persons are equal in their self-assurance. In any case, a desire to see things from a comprehensive point of view does not in itself imply dogmatism.

In biblically based religions, God has usually been thought of as maximally knowledgeable. A view along this line may already have been present in the Hebrew Bible. It is true that omniscience (which is, in any case, a problematic concept) is not attributed there to God, but God is thought to have greater knowledge than any human individual does. A practical implication of this view is that ethics should take account of maximal knowledge, that is, of as much as is possible under any given circumstance.[6] A single person's knowledge will be highly limited, but the total knowledge available to those to whom one looks for guidance (such as academic, religious, or political figures) should ideally be as full as possible. To put this in practical terms: no reasonably complex position can be "true" in an absolute sense, but "truth" — including "moral truth" — can be increasingly approximated as one adds relevant information and approaches the matter from as many angles as possible. (Even Nietzsche said this,[7] although he is well known for denying "truth" in an absolute sense.) One aspect of the significance of divine speech, which expresses a perspective larger than that of any human individual, then, lies in a call to be open to maximal knowledge.

For this purpose, it is necessary to explicate what can be meant by "knowledge." In my experience (is this not true for everyone?), when I encounter another being, I often have a sense that this other lays a claim on me, that it "speaks" to me. Levinas gave eloquent expression of this sense when he spoke of the "face" of the other, looking at one or (as he preferred to say) "speaking" to one.[8] Before him, Buber had spoken of how even in nonhuman objects "we are aware of a breath from the eternal *Thou*."[9] A "cold" form of knowledge — such as is standard for nominalism — of course, does not include such sensitivity, but that restriction is due to a deliberate decision to draw a line between knowledge and ethics. In contrast, a scientific knowledge that includes listening has been set forth more recently; one version of it has been described as a feminist way, although not as one limited to women.[10]

Does the Hebrew Bible support the kind of knowledge that involves sympathetic hearing? The answer appears to be yes, but one has to make an important qualification. The Hebrew Bible describes the "cry" or "call" (ṣʿq or qrʾ) of one who is oppressed, poor, or otherwise suffering, not as a voice that reaches a human hearer directly, but rather as one that comes to God's hearing.[11] Someone who listens *with* God will be affected by such a voice. One can

6. This is the opposite of John Rawls's position, which favors a political system based on minimal knowledge of specific matters.

7. Friedrich Nietzsche, *Werke* (ed. G. Colli and M. Montinari; 8 vols.; Berlin: de Gruyter, 1967-77), VI/II, 383.

8. Emmanuel Levinas, *Ethics and Infinity* (Pittsburgh: Duquesne Univ. Press, 1985), 87.

9. Martin Buber, *I and Thou* (New York: Scribner's Sons, 1937), 6-8, 101.

10. Evelyn Fox Keller, *Reflections on Gender and Science* (New Haven: Yale Univ. Press, 1992), 138, 164, 165.

11. For example, Exod 22:22; Judg 4:3; Isa 5:7 (probably not just directed to God); 19:20; Ps 9:13 (Eng. 12); 77:2 (Eng. 1); 120:1; Job 34:28.

regard such a process as being implicit in the biblical care for the poor and the oppressed.

Of course, the question can be raised whether it would not be better if the call of the sufferer would reach the human hearer directly, instead of indirectly via God, but one must remember that the human world (and, I think, also the nonhuman one) is full of calls for attention, which would completely overwhelm an individual hearer if they are not mediated somehow.[12] Thus one must differ from Levinas, who held (if I understand him correctly) that an infinite, or at least a superior, call comes directly from the human other. Instead of treating the neighbor's claim as absolute, as Levinas apparently did, it may be appropriate to channel that claim via God, who has a wide view, which means that each individual's claim is relativized. Obviously, a danger in doing so is that attention to God (such as in ritual) becomes a substitute for attention to the other. This is indeed a perennial problem in religion; it underlies the criticism of the major prophets against a kind of religion in which such a substitution takes place.

These brief reflections point to the association of a linguistic form (divine speech) with a certain context (ultimacy) and with certain structures of human life (self-transcendence and receptivity). One can go further in examining the details of this structure. On the individual level, for instance, one can seek to determine how prophetic ecstasy embodies transcendence or how a claim to be in an ecstatic condition affects a prophet's ability to give direction and express criticism. On the social side, one can show how "listening to the other" is a very important social operation. One can discuss the ways in which the Israelite community (reified for a moment) made room for certain specialists that handle different aspects of divine speech — especially priests and prophets. One can also explore how such specialists have taken advantage of their position to the apparent detriment of others and how they have been manipulated by kings for their own purposes, just as nowadays religious and academic professionals pursue their own interests and are open to being manipulated by others. Such examinations will show that life is complex. Some of these considerations have, in fact, already been pursued by scholars.

However, I want to go on to an important question. Is the self-transcendence that is exhibited in the form of divine speech peculiar to Israel, or has it also operated elsewhere?

A look at Buddhism will quickly show that self-transcendence is not pe-

---

12. Jainism calls on people to be sensitive to all pain, including that of the physical world. Not surprisingly, then, it includes the ultimate ideal of starving to death. This ideal is usually projected for a future incarnation; thus the present response can be moderate.

culiarly Israelite, but it will also indicate that religious traditions are not identical with one another, either in verbal expression or in the human processes they embody.[13] Of course, both the Hebrew Bible and the very far-flung Buddhist literature exhibit significant internal differences. Yet it is possible to point to some of the features characteristic of each.

One of the central tenets of Buddhism is the denial of a substantive "self." Buddhism holds that what we think of as a person is actually a collection of constantly changing phenomena and, further, that the constellation that will go tomorrow under a name with the initials, say, "M.B.," will not be the same as the constellation that goes under that same name now. Aside from the very reasonable observational arguments that Buddhism can present to support this view, one can ask for its motivation. A basic motivation seems to be a desire to undercut self-attachment, which is the basis of most of our worries and strains. If, for instance, the future "M.B." is different from the present "M.B.," why should the present "M.B." be concerned about that entity more than about another being whose initials might be, say, "R.F."? This principle would apply also to family members. Why should "M.B." be more concerned about "A.B.," with the same family name, than about "A.G.," who belongs to another family? It should be clear from these questions that the avoidance of suffering that Buddhism seeks through reducing or eliminating worry and disappointment is integrally related to ethics, as that is stated in the Four Noble Truths.[14]

What is happening here is a version of self-transcendence (which is connected with reflexivity). It takes place without a personified center, "God," with whom one can identify in imagination. Nonreligious thinkers believe, of course, that one can operate without such a center; they thus use Piaget's term "decentering" in the sense of one's having no center. Buddhism has taken an interesting intermediate position. In one sense it denies that there is a solid Reality around which the rest is positioned, for it sees everything as dependently interrelated and relative. Yet "nirvana," the very absence of solid reality or a recognition of such absence, becomes a luminous condition, which furnishes an orientation. Just how nirvana is related to everyday reality (with a lower-case *r*) is a question that is answered differently by different Buddhist groups.

---

13. The reference to Jainism made earlier (n. 12) also shows that self-transcendence is not peculiar to Israel.

14. The Four Noble Truths are (briefly): (1) suffering is pervasive, (2) the cause of suffering is craving, (3) a cessation of suffering is possible through abandoning craving, (4) cessation comes specifically through right understanding, right aspiration, right speech, right conduct, right livelihood, right endeavor, right awareness, right consciousness (cf. Sangharakshita, *Vision and Transformation* [Birmingham: Windhorse, 1999]).

It is now possible to ask whether the difference in conception between Israelite and Buddhist thought has a practical effect. One difference may be that Buddhism is less "active" in some sense, more peaceful, it seems. But one needs to avoid a simple stereotype in this regard.

One can wonder, of course, whether or how Buddhism experiences a call to attention similar to that expressed in the Hebrew Bible. This question has two positive answers. One is on the theoretical verbal level. On this level one can observe that Buddhist literature speaks of "hearing the *dharma* (true orientation)." Furthermore, Buddhism has a verbal expression for sympathetic attention, namely, "compassion."

The other relevant answer is on the level of nonverbal experience. Both research and informal experience have shown that a common form of Buddhist meditation heightens receptive attention to phenomena. The reason for this condition is as follows: An active, goal-oriented state of mind reduces attention to phenomena that are not relevant to the goal being pursued; if goal orientation is reduced in meditation, more phenomena come into one's perception — without one's seeking them. Something like this meditative state, with its receptive attention to other beings, may also take place in biblically based experiences when they are oriented toward divine assurances or promises in such a way that reliance on human exertion is reduced.

There is thus considerable correspondence between the Israelite structure expressed in the linguistic form of divine speech on the one hand, and the Buddhist theme and experience of nirvana on the other. (Incidentally, on the behavioral level, Buddhism rejects caste distinctions; this may constitute another parallel with biblical literature.) Yet there are also differences, which may even lead to mutual illumination and enrichment.

It should be noted that the structures outlined are rather ideal. In practice, most forms of Buddhism moderate the denial of selfhood through the idea of reincarnation. Specifically, most Buddhists hold that, even though there is no substantive entity that continues in this life and beyond, a given interconnected bundle of properties to which we assign a certain name is expected to stand in continuity with a future bundle, which survives death through being reincarnated. The progress of such a bundle (which can be enhanced by moral behavior) is a concern for most Buddhists. In fact, from an observer's point of view, it is doubtful that a Buddhist society would be able to continue otherwise. After all, a definite amount of self-concern — including a concern for one's family — is necessary for human survival. The central problem for society is how to balance such limited self-concern with a concern for others. Similarly, in the Hebrew Bible, the "wisdom" books of Proverbs and Qohelet are more moderate in their ethics than the major prophets are. Furthermore, in the third division of the Jewish canon there are other books with a strongly humanistic character, including three books in which women play major roles (Ruth, Esther, Song of Songs), indicating that women were not thought of as especially passive or receptive.

Such considerations raise issues of sociology. In order to function, any society requires a certain amount of prosocial rather than individualistic behavior. On the human level, self-transcendence is one way in which such behavior is supported. That does not mean that selfhood is no more than a means toward survival. On the contrary, self-transcendence, like much of culture, sometimes appears to exceed the amount that is needed for group survival in a way that can be welcomed. For instance, it is by no means certain that listening to music by Bach will enhance individual or group survival (although that possibility has been suggested). Similarly, a concern for weak members of a society may in many cases not contribute to group survival. However — as is well known in evolutionary theory — for the survival of an entity, it is not necessary that each of its processes contribute to that end as long as the overall pattern is able to continue in some way. In fact, self-transcendence can be explained not just sociologically, but philosophically, by observing that without such a process we would not be talking about reality.[15]

Another sociological issue concerns the factors that led to the emergence of Israelite faith and Buddhism almost simultaneously. I have dealt with this issue elsewhere briefly[16] and will not repeat that here, except to say that when looking for the potential relevance of biblical texts for the present, one must keep in mind differences in social arrangements between then and now. Both biblically based religions and Buddhism have, in fact, already undergone considerable change, probably in response to social developments. Yet the reflection that one is not oneself the center of the universe seems to be of continuing relevance.

Has this analysis sharpened our understanding of the Hebrew Bible? Perhaps so, but probably something more important has happened. Our focus has turned away from looking at the biblical text as either a curiosity or an arbitrary authority and has moved instead toward a clarification of issues that are significant for our own existence, although room has been left for vari-

---

15. There are, to be sure, philosophers who deny both self-transcendence and the possibility of speaking about reality.

16. "Hosea as a Canonical Problem," in *Prophets and Paradigms* (Fest. Gene Tucker; ed. S. Reid; JSOTSup 229; Sheffield: Sheffield Academic Press, 1996), 87-88.

ability. This is an "explication of human life," one that involves not only the past but also the present writer and, I hope, the reader. If this explication gives attention to verbal patterns, it can be called "form criticism." The example given here is an exploratory effort in this direction.

# Rhetorical Criticism and Beyond
# in Second Isaiah

## PATRICIA K. TULL

When I received the invitation to address the changing face of form criticism, I was puzzled at first. As Amos might have said, I am not a form critic, nor the son of a form critic. But since the conversation involves the relationship of form criticism to other methodologies, I gather that I was invited as an interloper from the synchronic borderlands.

I came to biblical studies from very much the other side of critical method. What James Muilenburg announced in 1968 as a new method beyond form criticism, called "rhetorical criticism," was similar to what I grew up on in university departments of literature, during the reign of New Criticism.[1] I was trained first to tune in to a text itself, and not to the world behind it. Yet the authors we read, Blake, Eliot, Thomas Mann, steeped as they were in cultural history and literary citation, begged for broader readings than New Criticism allowed. So upon encountering diachronic methods later in seminary, I anachronistically experienced them as something new, something energizing, something "beyond New Criticism," so to speak. I entered seminary and discovered historical criticism just as biblical scholarship was discovering literary methods. That is why I am fascinated by Muilenburg — it seemed to me I saw him at the border crossing, passing in the other direction.

Lately I have been pondering the theoretical and unfortunately all too practical problems of teaching exegetical method. Exegesis in general, like form criticism, gets tangled in the complex relationships of the typical and the unique, the Platonic ideal and its earthly manifestations. To divide exegesis by methodological steps is necessary heuristically, but the reality is always

---

1. This SBL presidential address was published as James Muilenburg, "Form Criticism and Beyond," *JBL* 88 (1969): 1-18.

messy. Questions overlap in some places, leave gaps in others, and they do not evenly fit real passages. I have a student, a former lieutenant colonel, who asked me recently for a template, a form to fill out, a one-size-fits-all for exegetical method, the Platonic mold into which each individual text can be poured. I told her there is no such thing, that all I can do after presenting general methods is to guide her through exegesis of Genesis 4, Psalm 19, and Daniel 7, and hope that instance after instance of the individual and unique will gradually build a template in her mind that is sufficiently fixed to resist vagueness but sufficiently flexible to be useful.

Such tension between the typical and the unique finds striking analogies in the theoretical wrestlings of form critics. It seems to be one of the larger recurring themes. Rolf Knierim pondered it in his 1973 article, "Old Testament Form Criticism Reconsidered," in which he pointed out that we possess typicalities of texts only in individual manifestations: "It is entirely possible to identify a text-type behind an individual text. . . . But if this is only a partial influence on the text, one could completely misunderstand the meaning of the text as a whole."[2] Knierim proposed setting up a framework within which form-critical tools could be applied more flexibly and variably, becoming subservient to the factors that dominate texts, rather than dominating them. Admittedly, that enterprise would be complex and uncertain. He explored the new typologies he thought must be studied to fit form criticism more closely to real texts.

Muilenburg also struggled with this question, but sought resolution in other ways. Though his work coincided with the golden age of form criticism in the mid-twentieth century, and he called himself a form critic throughout his career, still, by the time he delivered his SBL presidential address in 1968, he noted "a sense that the method has outrun its course."[3] He suggested the necessity of venturing "beyond the confines of form criticism into an inquiry into other literary features"[4] and he called that "beyond," rhetorical criticism.

This tension between the typical and the unique has come to represent somewhat of a fault line between form critics and rhetorical critics. Insofar as form critics sort texts into generic categories, they lay hold of a very real aspect of texts, that is, their defining relationship to other texts. But insofar as they submerge a text's uniqueness, they risk ignoring where a text stands *in relation to* the genres it inhabits. Rhetorical criticism takes equal and opposite risks. Insofar as rhetorical critics focus on a unique text, analyzing its own internal

2. Knierim, "Old Testament Form Criticism Reconsidered," *Int* 27 (1973): 458.
3. Muilenburg, "Form Criticism," 4.
4. Ibid.

logic and rhetorical patterning, they risk ignoring the role of other texts both in this text's shaping by authors and in its comprehension by readers.

I cannot with any confidence suggest how this tension ought to be addressed within form criticism. The work of Marvin Sweeney and others who interweave form criticism with other disciplines seems to provide helpful clues. What I can with more confidence speak to is the resolution toward form criticism within rhetorical criticism.

I will broadly trace these issues by taking a swift romp through various interpreters' comments on Second Isaiah. This will be a whirlwind tour, approximating the depth and scope of the five-European-countries-in-four-and-a-half-days trip. I chose Second Isaiah for several reasons: First, because though it is replete with good form-critically recognizable material, it has long been known to raise substantial problems for form criticism. Second, because it was the locus in which Muilenburg developed his ideas about rhetorical criticism. Third, because it was also the literature in which I came to see how very much rhetorical criticism relies on form criticism.

I will focus on one small segment of text, with the hope that it is representative enough to suggest more than can be said in this brief article. It is Isa 51:9-10:

> Awake, awake, put on strength,
>     arm of YHWH.
> Awake as in days of old,
>     generations long ago.
> Are you not the crusher of Rahab,
>     the piercer of the dragon?
> Are you not the one drying the sea,
>     the waters of the great deep,
> the one making the depths of the sea a road
>     for the redeemed to pass?

Because of Second Isaiah's propensity to reutilize and combine forms, form critics tend to disagree on its genre classifications. There has been general agreement, however, on this segment, that it reflects psalmic communal laments, especially in the following elements: the invocation calling upon God to awaken, the reminder of the past when God acted powerfully, and the specific references to cosmic battle and exodus.

Joachim Begrich and Claus Westermann, each in his own generation, offered highly influential form-critical studies of Second Isaiah.[5] Both had

---

5. Joachim Begrich, *Studien zu Deuterojesaja* (Munich: Kaiser, 1963); Claus Westermann, *Isaiah 40–66* (trans. D. M. G. Stalker; OTL; Philadelphia: Westminster, 1969).

trouble visualizing what was going on with this particular text, and each resorted in different ways to creating rather odd stories of its origin. Begrich viewed these words as an actual lament by the prophet, voicing his own doubt-filled questions and betraying his own uncertainty. The response in vv. 12-16 Begrich called the divine granting of a petition in the form of a priestly oracle of salvation.[6]

Such a claim raises situational questions. In what sense did Begrich mean this? Did he envision the prophet, who otherwise boldly reassured Zion of God's comfort, having a sudden attack of existential angst? If so, who delivered this oracle of salvation to the prophet? The relationships between original setting and prophetic portrayal, between actuality and dramatization, between the spoken and the written, became muddied at this point. Because the *form* originated in lament discourse, Begrich saw the *passage* as originating as an actual lament.

Westermann, who was much indebted to Begrich, posed the origin of these words in the prophet's experience as well. For him also these verses came into being as an actual lament — but not by the prophet. Rather they were, as he confidently put it, "word for word without change, the beginning of a community lament" in actual use by the prophet's audience.[7] Westermann posited what follows in vv. 12-16 as a divine answer delivered by the prophet.

The insight that Begrich and Westermann shared is this passage's generic origin in communal lament and priestly salvation oracle. But their explanations of how the forms jumped the fence from liturgy to prophetic discourse differ dramatically. For Begrich it was the prophet who lamented and was answered by God; for Westermann it was the exiles who lamented and were answered by (God through) the prophet. In both scenarios the dialogue originated as an actual event experienced on the stage of the prophet's life.

Muilenburg's 1956 commentary represents a transition point in form-critical study of Second Isaiah, displaying many elements of the methodology he would later name "rhetorical criticism."[8] Long before his time, scholars had recognized that form criticism suits Second Isaiah only uneasily. Already in 1914 Hugo Gressmann noted that traditional forms underwent alterations when used by Second Isaiah.[9] A steady stream of form critics, including Begrich, had suggested that the use of genre in Second Isaiah was somehow

---

6. Begrich, *Studien zu Deuterojesaja,* 167.

7. Westermann, *Isaiah 40–66,* 240.

8. James Muilenburg, "Isaiah 40–66," *IB* 5:381-773.

9. Hugo Gressmann, "Die literarische Analyse Deuterojesajas," *ZAW* 34 (1914): 254-97.

imitative or adaptive. It remained for Muilenburg to posit that the work is better understood as a creative composition than as a record of oral sayings.

Muilenburg's beginning point was the dramatic poetry for which he saw the prophet masterfully responsible. He did not even attempt to trace this passage back to a spoken event. What Begrich and Westermann saw as reflections of actual dialogue Muilenburg saw as drama staged in the prophet's imagination. As such, this passage was for him an eschatological interlude between *literary* strophes, an apostrophe *in the form of* a lament. According to Muilenburg, the poet had just portrayed God as repeatedly assuring imminent salvation. Now "the prophet breaks out in a fervent invocation of God's conquering arm . . . a passionate cry that the salvation may come now."[10] This is followed by the prophet's portrayal of God's immediate, emphatic, and rhetorically masterful reply.

Muilenburg introduced dramatic shifts in understanding this passage and others like it. Second Isaiah was not a written transcription of exchanges between the prophet and God or the prophet and other people. The prophet was not a character on the stage in the way that Isaiah or Jeremiah was, exchanging words with Ahaz or with God. Rather, the prophet's imagination itself *was* the stage, a very large stage, upon which God, Zion, Cyrus, Daughter Babylon, the nations, the servant, and even the ends of the earth all interacted.

Muilenburg's descriptions of Second Isaiah's aesthetic force and beauty called attention to many aspects of the book crying out for acknowledgment. As Richard Clifford has argued, however, this focus led Muilenburg to divorce the text from its contexts, and to overlook its relationship to historical events. Rhetorical criticism in the Muilenburg style has often verged on an aesthetic formalism that loses sight of rhetorical environment.

Clifford's own rhetorical-critical work retained Muilenburg's view of Second Isaiah as dramatic poetry created in the prophet's imagination.[11] But Clifford never lost track of the world of historical events. He posited the prophet not as a lyric poet but as an orator, a rhetorician whose aim was not to write pleasing poetry, but rather to persuade the audience to return to Jerusalem. Like Yehoshua Gitay in his work on Isaiah 40–48, Clifford concentrated on the language not for its own sake, but as a vehicle for pragmatic persuasion.[12]

10. Muilenburg, "Isaiah 40–66," 595-96.

11. Richard J. Clifford, *Fair Spoken and Persuading: An Interpretation of Second Isaiah* (New York: Paulist Press, 1984).

12. Yehoshua Gitay, *Prophecy and Persuasion: A Study of Isaiah 40–48* (Bonn: Linguistica Biblica, 1981).

Clifford too called attention to the similarity of Isa 51:9-10 to communal lament psalms and their shared elements: allusions to the exodus, vivid descriptions of the present afflictions, and pleas for divine intervention. Then he pointed out that the psalmic laments do not within themselves contain a fourth, vitally important element, the priestly oracle in response to the lamenting community. However, he said, "all four elements of the national lament show up in our passage" — the pleas for assistance and the allusions to the past occur in the address to God's arm in vv. 9-10.[13] Significantly, not only the priestly response but also the depiction of afflictions is transferred to the divine answer. Like Muilenburg, Clifford drew attention to repetition and dramatic sequencing. Moving beyond Muilenburg, Clifford analyzed the redistribution of forms and genres into a new literary whole, and attended continually to their persuasive purposes. In Clifford's work the typical became a baseline for understanding more clearly the individual and the unique.

My own work on the passage is best characterized, like Clifford's, as rhetorical.[14] I focused on a particular rhetorical trope that had been noted in passing but not studied: the prophet's appeal to societal memory, and reshaping of memories in order to persuade. Though memory is not a trope easy to get at form-critically, it is a recurring motif in Second Isaiah's message. From start to finish, Isaiah 40–55 remembers, and re-collects, elements of Jerusalem's past, constructing a picture for the audience's present that bids to persuade them of the inherent unity between then and now. Second Isaiah does not simply assume the past, but asserts it:

> Remember the former things of old,
> for I am God, and there is no other,
>    God, and there is none like me,
> telling from the beginning the end,
>    and from ancient times things not yet done,
> saying, "My purpose will stand,
>    and I will do all that I wish." (Isa 46:9-10)

Even when the prophet says to forget, it is a paradoxical imperative. Reminding his contemporaries that their God is the one who makes a way in the sea, a path in the mighty waters, the prophet says, "do not remember the things of old. . . . I am doing a new thing: I will make a way in the *desert,* and in the *wilderness,* rivers" (43:18-19). In other words the new divine action the

---

13. Clifford, *Fair Spoken,* 170.

14. Patricia Tull Willey, *Remember the Former Things: The Recollection of Previous Texts in Second Isaiah* (SBLDS 161; Atlanta: Scholars Press, 1997).

prophet asserts is only the old one rearranged for new circumstances. The book is filled with such tensions between continuity and discontinuity, remembrance and revision.

Second Isaiah's trope of memory relies heavily on recollecting themes, forms, and even phrasing that the audience will recognize. Such an appeal to memory matters rhetorically. Words, cadences, and forms of discourse that an audience already knows evoke memories, rich with associations. Second Isaiah taps into Judah's imaginative matrix of shared text, shared memories of how the universe has been verbally constructed. In singing old tunes in new settings, Second Isaiah enables contemporary events as constructed by the prophet's understanding to assume the garments of historical and even cultic significance. At the same time, the prophet takes the opportunity to recast older motifs, to adapt them to present necessities.

It was in examining what might have been familiar to the prophet's contemporaries that form criticism became essential for me. As many have noted, Second Isaiah makes liberal use of psalms and psalmic forms. Most if not all of these are psalms that form critics have viewed in connection with the cult of Jerusalem's first temple: the communal laments lying behind these verses in Isaiah 51 all mourn national disasters, and at least two of them are thought to be specifically connected with the destruction of the temple and with the loss of the Davidic kingship.[15] Other parts of the book echo enthronement psalms, royal psalms, and royal Zion hymns. Though they reflect different genres, all these psalms converge on one motif: Jerusalem's security. What is more, they all do so by recalling, in one way or another, the myth of the divine battle with the primordial elements of the sea.

The language of Isa 51:9-10 is richly endowed with associations with communal laments, such as Psalms 44, 74, 77, and 89, as well as a psalm that is often overlooked by commentators because it is not a lament, Psalm 93, which describes God as being clothed in majesty and girded with strength, enthroned from of old and dominating over the forces of the raging seas. Reuse of such psalmic language focuses exilic alienation into a particular, familiar, liturgical construction. It frames the question in such a way that when the answer comes, when in chap. 52 the prophet suggests that the exiles depart from Babylon and participate in God's return to Zion, this notion may be viewed not as some preacher's dangerous idealism, but as God's own answer to long-spoken prayers, God's purpose from ancient times.

Common to the psalms behind it, but missing from Isaiah 51, are repeated references to God's reign as king. This element — which would have

---

15. For a fuller discussion of the use of psalms in Isa 51:9-10 see ibid., 144-51.

been anticipated by audiences familiar with the motif — is deferred both by the lament and by the oracle of salvation that follows it. Instead, the divine answer is framed as a steady stream of acknowledgments, responses to plaintive laments, many of them pointedly expressed in the book of Lamentations. Only after this — after God claims to be Zion's comforter, promises reversals of all she has suffered, and bids *her* to awake and to arise from the dust — only after all this is the deferred element of the Jerusalem psalms voiced:

> How beautiful upon the mountains
>   are the feet of a messenger,
> a proclaimer of peace, a messenger of good,
>   a proclaimer of salvation,
> one who says to Zion, your God reigns! (Isa 52:7)

Much more remembrance is going on in this brief passage than I can discuss here. What I want to highlight at this point is the importance for rhetorical criticism of paying attention to the use of the familiar for innovative purposes. The drama that Muilenburg envisioned on the stage of the prophet's imagination is probably not a direct reflection, as Westermann thought, of specific events in the prophet's world, but it certainly reflects the dialogical reality of questions being asked about the future of the exilic community. This particular prophet's framing of those questions claims authority both by its appeal to tradition and by its creative adaptation to present circumstance.

To study a matter such as this without maintaining the tension between form criticism and rhetorical criticism would be impossible, since both the typical and the unique must be heeded. One of the challenges to rhetorical criticism is that texts do not bear their meanings in isolation, but in relation to prior discourse. At the same time, one of the challenges to form criticism is that the prophetic and psalmic forms never stood still, never became perfectly cataloguable monuments of speech, but were always in motion, always transmuting into new patterns, jumping from genre to genre, combining into larger complexes of "mixed types" and intricately woven rhetoric.

This tension between conventional forms and their always shifting expressions applies not only to the Bible we study but to our methods themselves. When we talk about the changing face of form criticism, we are not talking about a methodology that ever had a fixed point from which it is now changing, but rather a grouping of ideas, presuppositions, and methods that have evolved and shifted from the beginning moment on. Each scholar not only reflects a genre of exegetical analysis; we also introduce unique, individual twists that bend and often reshape the genre in which we profess to work. Fortunately, just as we do not have to find the one prototypical tree to know we are in a forest, we also do not have to find the one pure definition of method to know we are doing exegesis.

# Zechariah's Debate with Isaiah

## MARVIN A. SWEENEY

### I

The last several decades have seen tremendous methodological change in the modern critical study of the prophetic books.[1] For much of the late-nineteenth and twentieth centuries, scholars employed a variety of diachronic tools, such as form- and redaction-critical analysis, that frequently resulted in a fragmented reading of the prophetic books. Books such as Isaiah were divided into several parts that were considered as if they were indepen-

---

1. For discussion of the contemporary study of the prophetic literature, see Joseph Blenkinsopp, *A History of Prophecy in Israel* (rev. ed.; Louisville: Westminster John Knox, 1996); Marvin A. Sweeney, "Formation and Form in Prophetic Literature," in *Old Testament Interpretation: Past, Present, and Future. Essays in Honor of Gene M. Tucker* (ed. J. L. Mays, D. L. Petersen, and K. H. Richards; Nashville: Abingdon, 1995), 113-26; idem, *Isaiah 1–39; with an Introduction to Prophetic Literature* (FOTL 16; Grand Rapids and Cambridge: Eerdmans, 1996), esp. 1-30; idem, "The Latter Prophets (Isaiah, Jeremiah, Ezekiel)," in *The Hebrew Bible Today: An Introduction to Critical Issues* (ed. S. L. McKenzie and M. P. Graham; Louisville: Westminster John Knox, 1998), 69-94; David L. Petersen, "The Book of the Twelve/The Minor Prophets (Hosea, Joel, Amos, Obadiah, Jonah, Micah, Nahum, Habakkuk, Zephaniah, Haggai, Zechariah, Malachi)," in *Hebrew Bible Today*, ed. McKenzie and Graham, 95-126. For discussion of exegetical methodology in the broader field of biblical studies, see Steven L. McKenzie and Stephen R. Haynes, eds., *To Each Its Own Meaning: An Introduction to Biblical Criticisms and Their Application* (rev. ed.; Louisville: Westminster John Knox, 1999); John Barton, *Reading the Old Testament: Method in Biblical Study* (rev. ed.; Louisville: Westminster John Knox, 1996); Robert Morgan with John Barton, *Biblical Interpretation* (Oxford Bible Series; Oxford: Oxford Univ. Press, 1988); Douglas A. Knight and Gene M. Tucker, eds., *The Hebrew Bible and Its Modern Interpreters* (Philadelphia: Fortress; Chico, Calif.: Scholars Press, 1985).

dent prophetic books, based on the view that the segments of the book presented the works of different prophets who lived in different historical periods. Likewise, individual oracles would be singled out as "authentic," resulting in the dismissal of much material as the theologically irrelevant works of later redactors or tradents who misunderstood the words of the prophets and corrupted their meaning. But scholars are increasingly turning to synchronic literary reading strategies that consider the literary form, perspectives, and intertextual relationships of an entire prophetic book. Frequently, the perspectives of traditional interpreters play an important role in such discussion. This, of course, does not entail a naive rejection of earlier diachronic methods, but it often provides an opportunity for both synchronic and diachronic perspectives to be employed together. The book of Isaiah, for example, has benefited immensely from such study, resulting in a much richer interpretation that takes seriously both the form and formation of the entire Isaian corpus.[2]

It is with these considerations in mind that I here reexamine several aspects of the book of Zechariah. Three fundamental reasons underlie the choice of Zechariah. First, like Isaiah, Zechariah is generally divided into a First, Second, and Third Zechariah with little consideration as to how the component parts of the book relate to one another within the whole.[3] Second, traditional Jewish interpretation of Zechariah, including Targum Jona-

---

2. See Marvin A. Sweeney, "The Book of Isaiah in Recent Research," *CurBS* 1 (1993): 141-62; idem, "Reevaluating Isaiah 1–39 in Recent Critical Research," *CurBS* 4 (1996): 79-113; Uwe Becker, "Jesajaforschung (Jes. 1–39)," *TRu* 64 (1999): 1-37.

3. For discussion of research on Zechariah, see Brevard S. Childs, *An Introduction to the Old Testament as Scripture* (Philadelphia: Fortress, 1979), 472-87; Wilhelm Rudolph, *Haggai — Sacharja 1–8 — Sacharja 9–14 — Maleachi* (KAT XIII/4; Gütersloh: Mohn, 1976); David L. Petersen, *Haggai and Zechariah 1–8: A Commentary* (OTL; Philadelphia: Westminster, 1984); R. J. Coggins, *Haggai, Zechariah, Malachi* (OTG; Sheffield: Sheffield Academic Press, 1987); Carol L. Meyers and Eric M. Meyers, *Haggai; Zechariah 1–8* (AB 25B; Garden City, N.Y.: Doubleday, 1987); Samuel Amsler, André LaCocque, and René Vuilleumier, *Aggée, Zacharie, Malachie* (CAT XI/C; Geneva: Labor et Fides, 1988); Carol L. Meyers and Eric M. Meyers, *Zechariah 9–14* (AB 25C; New York: Doubleday, 1993); Henning Graf Reventlow, *Die Propheten Haggai, Sacharja und Maleachi* (ATD 25/2; Göttingen: Vandenhoeck & Ruprecht, 1993); Paul L. Redditt, *Haggai, Zechariah, Malachi* (NCB; Grand Rapids: Eerdmans, 1993); David L. Petersen, *Zechariah 9–14 and Malachi: A Commentary* (OTL; Louisville: Westminster John Knox, 1995); Robert Hanhart, *Sacharja* (BKAT XIV/7:1-8; Neukirchen-Vluyn: Neukirchener Verlag, 1999); Edgar W. Conrad, *Zechariah* (Readings; Sheffield: Sheffield Academic Press, 1999); Michael H. Floyd, *The Minor Prophets, Part 2* (FOTL 22; Grand Rapids and Cambridge: Eerdmans, 2000), 301-558; Marvin A. Sweeney, *The Twelve Prophets* (2 vols.; Berit Olam; Collegeville, Minn.: Liturgical Press, 2000), 2:559-709.

than,[4] the Babylonian Talmud, and the commentaries of Rashi (R. Solomon ben Isaac, 1040-1105), [5] Abraham Ibn Ezra (1089-1164),[6] and Radak (R. David Kimhi, 1160-1235),[7] indicates the identification of the prophet Zechariah ben Berechiah ben Iddo with one of the two men commissioned by the prophet Isaiah ben Amoz to witness the naming and significance of his son Maher-shalal-hash-baz. Third, the extensive intertextual citations and allusions in Zechariah point to a special interest in the book of Isaiah on the part of Zechariah.

Consideration of each of these factors points to a concern within the book of Zechariah to present the prophet as an authentic witness to the prophecy of Isaiah. Specifically, it presents Zechariah's prophecy as a challenge to and ultimate fulfillment of the earlier work of Isaiah; whereas Isaiah viewed the rise of the Persian Empire and Cyrus as an act of G-d that called upon Jews to cooperate with the Persian authorities, Zechariah maintains that the building of the temple points to the overthrow of the Persian Empire as divine sovereignty from Jerusalem is to be established over all the nations.

## II

The current consensus in modern critical research holds that the book of Zechariah comprises two and possibly three major components, each of which constitutes the work of a different prophet.[8] Thus Zechariah 1–8 is gen-

4. For a critical edition of Targum Jonathan to the Prophets, see Alexander Sperber, *The Bible in Aramaic*, part III, *The Latter Prophets According to Targum Jonathan* (Leiden: Brill, 1962).

5. For the commentaries of Rashi on the Prophets, see standard editions of *Mikra'ot Gedolot* on the prophets. Discussion of Rashi appears in Aaron Rothkoff, et al., "Rashi," *EncJud* 13:1558-65.

6. For the commentary of Ibn Ezra on Isaiah, see many editions of *Mikra'ot Gedolot*, although it is frequently printed at the end of the book. A critical edition appears in M. Friedländer, *Commentary of Ibn Ezra on Isaiah* (2 vols.; 1873; New York: Philipp Feldheim, n.d.). For discussion of Ibn Ezra, see Stanley Abramovitch and Naphtali Ben-Menahem, "Ibn Ezra, Abraham," *EncJud* 8:1163-70.

7. For the commentaries of Radak on the prophets, see standard editions of *Mikra'ot Gedolot*. A critical edition of Radak's commentary on Isaiah 1–39 appears in Louis Finkelstein, *The Commentary of David Kimhi on Isaiah* (Columbia University Oriental Studies 19; New York: Columbia Univ. Press, 1926). Discussion of Radak appears in Frank Talmage, "Kimhi, David," *EncJud* 10:1001-1004; Frank Talmage, *David Kimhi: The Man and His Commentaries* (Cambridge and London: Harvard Univ. Press, 1975).

8. For bibliography, see the works cited in n. 3 above.

erally held to represent the work of the late-sixth-century prophet Zechariah, who prophesied in support of the building of the Second Temple. The primary basis for this conclusion is the appearance of the prophet's first-person accounts of his eight visions in which he relates various images pertaining to the significance of the building of the temple. Zechariah 9–11/12–14 is generally held to represent the work of a second, much later writer from the early Hellenistic period, who presented an apocalyptic vision of the return of the Messiah to Jerusalem and the overthrow of past leadership. The primary bases for this assertion are the formally distinct character of this material, which begins with the superscription מַשָּׂא, its apocalyptic content, and the explicit mention of the Greeks as part of its portrayal of the king's return. Zechariah 12–14 is sometimes considered to be an even later work of a third Zechariah based on its own מַשָּׂא superscription and its overall portrayal of cosmic war against the nations that ultimately results in their worship of God at Zion during the Festival of Sukkot.

Nevertheless, there is ample reason to contest the assertion that Zechariah 1–8; 9–14 or 9–11; 12–14 constitutes the literary structure of the book.[9] The fundamental reason for such a challenge is that the current consensus is based on redaction-critical considerations that are designed to identify and to isolate early or original literary units, but that do not address the question as to how those units might work together to create a rhetorically coherent text that is designed to communicate with its reading or listening audience.[10] Consideration of such features provides the basis for a very different view of the book's literary structure.

Indeed, the book begins not with a superscription but with a narrative statement that provides the chronological setting from which the entire book is to be read: "In the eighth month, in the second year of Darius, the word of YHWH was unto Zechariah ben Berechiah ben Iddo the prophet, saying. . . ." The following material in vv. 2-6 then relates YHWH's words to the prophet in which YHWH expresses past anger at earlier generations and how those generations responded to the call to return to YHWH and follow YHWH's ways. This material therefore serves as a dated introduction to the book be-

---

9. See now Conrad, *Zechariah*, 11-44; Sweeney, *Twelve Prophets*, esp. 561-67.

10. For discussion of rhetorical criticism and its role in assessing the interrelationship between text and audience, see Phyllis Trible, *Rhetorical Criticism: Context, Method, and the Book of Jonah* (GBS; Minneapolis: Fortress, 1994); Patricia K. Tull, "Rhetorical Criticism and Intertextuality," in *To Each Its Own Meaning*, ed. McKenzie and Haynes, 156-80. For discussion of the impact of such considerations on form-critical methodology, see Marvin A. Sweeney, "Form Criticism," in *To Each Its Own Meaning*, ed. McKenzie and Haynes, 58-89; Ehud Ben Zvi, *Micah* (FOTL 21B; Grand Rapids and Cambridge: Eerdmans, 2000).

cause it commissions the prophet to call upon the present generation to do the same thing, that is, return to YHWH and carry out YHWH's purposes in relation to the construction of the new temple.

Two additional narrative date formulas like that of Zech 1:1 appear in 1:7 and 7:1. Insofar as their dates proceed from the initial date of 1:1 and provide the context for the material that follows in each instance, they appear to signal the beginnings of two further blocks of material that together constitute the body of the book of Zechariah.

The first appears in 1:7, "On the twenty-fourth day of the eleventh month — it was the month of Shebat — of the second year of Darius, the word of YHWH was unto Zechariah ben Berechiah ben Iddo the prophet, saying. . . ." The balance of the text in 1:7–6:15 then presents the prophet's autobiographical account of the eight visions in which an angelic guide explains to him the significance of the various images that relate to the reconstruction of the temple, including the divine horses (1:7-17); the four horns (2:1-4); the city with a wall of fire (2:5-17); the ordination of Joshua ben Jehozadak as high priest (3:1-10); the menorah and two olive shoots (4:1-14); the flying scroll (5:1-4); the woman in the ephah (5:5-11); and the four chariots proclaiming the "branch," Joshua ben Jehozadak (6:1-15).

The second appears in 7:1, and it is syntactically related to the formula in 1:7 by the initial ויהי: "And it came to pass in the fourth year of Darius the king, that the word of YHWH was unto Zechariah on the fourth day of the ninth month, in Kislev. . . ." The narrative then relates a question posed to YHWH/Zechariah concerning the propriety of continued mourning for the loss of the temple. Following the posing of the question in vv. 1-3, the prophet's answers to the question then appear in a series of sections beginning in 7:4, each of which is introduced by a version of the formula, "and the word of YHWH was unto me/Zechariah, saying." The first in 7:4-7 relates the prophet's contention that YHWH did not request the fast. The second in 7:8-14 calls for righteous action on the part of the people. The third in 8:1-17 conveys the message of past prophets who likewise called for righteous action. The fourth in 8:18-23 portrays YHWH's call for rejoicing, not fasting, as the nations will come to Zion to join Jews now that the new temple is about to be established.

Although most scholars consider Zechariah 7–8 to be a self-contained unit, one must ask about the function of the following material in Zechariah 9–11/12–14 insofar as it too is concerned with nations that will come to Zion. Although these chapters are formally distinct and may well have been composed at different times and for different purposes than Zechariah 7–8, they play an important role in the present form of the book by providing a detailed portrayal as to how the scenario of the nations' coming to Jerusalem to join Jews will take place. Thus Zechariah 9–11 provides a detailed description of the righteous king's approach to Jerusalem and the overthrow of the worthless shepherds who have governed the people and prevented the full restoration of the nation from exile. Zechariah 12–14 then relates the warfare that will emanate from the holy center in Jerusalem as first Israel and then the nations are defeated and brought under YHWH's sovereignty, culminating in the worship of YHWH at Sukkot as all the nations join Israel in recognizing YHWH's sovereignty over all creation. It would seem then that the narrative statement in 7:1 establishing the chronology of the question concerning fasting posed to Zechariah and the prophet's answer introduces not only Zechariah 7–8, but Zechariah 9–14, insofar as Zechariah 9–14 provides the bulk of the prophet's answer as to how YHWH's call for rejoicing at the establishment of the temple will actually be realized throughout all of creation.

Thus the overall structure of the book is designed to call on the people to return to YHWH by relating the significance of the restoration of the temple. The introductory instruction of the book in 1:1-6 relates the basic theme that the people should adhere to YHWH's expectations. The balance of the book in 1:7–14:21 then provides the rationale why they should do so. Zechariah 1:7–6:15 relates the prophet's visions that point to the ultimate significance of the building of the temple that will result in the crowning of Joshua ben Jehozadak as the "branch" or YHWH's righteous ruler. Zechariah 7–14 then relates YHWH's calls for rejoicing at the full completion of the temple when the righteous king has been established, the worthless shepherds overthrown, and the nations join Israel at Jerusalem to acknowledge YHWH's worldwide sovereignty at Sukkot.

## III

Having established the literary and thematic coherence of the book on synchronic grounds, it is now necessary to consider the identity of the prophet to whom the book is attributed. The introductory chronological statements in both 1:1 and 1:7 identify the prophet as Zechariah ben Berechiah ben Iddo. This would not provide cause for special notice were it not for the fact that the narrative historical accounts of the restoration of the temple in Ezra-Nehemiah identify the prophet not as Zechariah ben Berechiah ben Iddo, but simply as Zechariah bar Iddo (Ezra 5:1; 6:14).[11] The discrepancy in

---

11. Cf. Neh 12:16, which indicates that Zechariah is part of the Iddo clan or "house of the father."

names is frequently noted but rarely examined closely, as most scholars are willing to accept the evidence of Neh 12:16 that Zechariah is clearly a descendant of Iddo. Insofar as the designation "ben/bar Iddo" could indicate either that Zechariah is the son of Iddo or his grandson, the matter is not considered to be overly important to contemporary scholars.

Nevertheless, it is noteworthy that the first two elements of the name Zechariah ben Berechiah (ben Iddo) do correspond very closely to the name of one of the men chosen by the prophet Isaiah ben Amoz to witness to the birth of his son Maher-shalal-hash-baz as a sign or symbol for the coming invasion of Israel by the Assyrian empire. According to Isa 8:1-4, Isaiah selected Uriah the priest and Zechariah ben Yeberechyahu to serve as "reliable witnesses" for the writing of the tablet on which the name Maher-shalal-hash-baz was inscribed. Indeed, the name Yeberechyahu *(yĕberekyāhû)* in Isa 8:2 is a minor linguistic variant of the name Berechiah of Zech 1:1, 7 *(berekyâ)*.

Although most modern scholars would correctly maintain that Isaiah and Zechariah refer to two entirely different figures who were separated historically by some three centuries, ancient and medieval sources and commentators have noted their correspondence and have drawn some conclusions as to the identity of the two figures. Thus Targum Jonathan renders YHWH's statement to the prophet in Isa 8:2, "and call to witness before me as reliable witnesses the curses that I spoke for the future in the prophecy of Uriah the priest, and behold, they have come; also all the comfort that I spoke for the future in the prophecy of Zechariah bar Yeberechyah, I am about to bring it back." The reference to the curses in the prophecy of Uriah the priest refers to the prophet Uriah mentioned in Jer 26:20-23 who was executed by King Jehoiakim for speaking against the city of Jerusalem in the late-sixth/early-fifth century BCE. The reference to the comfort of Zechariah bar Yeberechyah refers to the scenario of restoration articulated by the prophet Zechariah ben Berechiah ben Iddo in the book of Zechariah.

The Babylonian Talmud likewise equates the two faithful witnesses mentioned in Isa 8:2 with the later prophets Uriah and Zechariah ben Berechiah ben Iddo. A baraita in *b. Mak.* 24 relates that R. Gamaliel, R. Eleazar ben Azariah, R. Joshua, and R. Akiba went to Jerusalem. When they came to Zophim, the present-day site of Hebrew University that overlooks the old city of Jerusalem, they rent their garments and wept as they saw a fox emerge from the ruined site of the holy of holies following the Roman destruction of the temple. R. Akiba, however, expressed joy. When his colleagues asked him to explain, Akiba cited Isa 8:2, in which God instructs Isaiah to summon two faithful witnesses, Uriah and Zechariah ben Yeberechyahu. Akiba states that there is no other connection between the two than to show that the words of Zechariah are conditioned by the words of Uriah; that is, in order for Zechariah's scenario of restoration to take place, Uriah's scenario of destruction must first be realized. In the perspective of the Talmud, Isaiah's witness refers to the prophet Zechariah.

Rashi makes these identifications clear in his commentary on Isa 8:2 in which he points specifically to the identification of Isaiah's Uriah the priest with the prophet Uriah ben Shemaiah from Kiriath-jearim in Jeremiah 26 and to the identification of Isaiah's Zechariah ben Yeberechiah with the book of Zechariah's purported subject, Zechariah ben Berechiah ben Iddo from the second year of Darius. To support his claim for the latter, Rashi cites Zech 8:4, "again, old men and old women will sit in the streets of Jerusalem," as a representation of the comforts that Zechariah would speak concerning the future. Rashi further asserts that Uriah serves as a sign for Zechariah in that Zechariah's prophecies of comfort presuppose the judgments or curses previously spoken by Uriah and realized in the form of the Babylonian destruction of Jerusalem. In this respect he draws on the Talmud's statement that the fulfillment of the prophecy of restoration by Zechariah is conditioned upon the fulfillment of the prophecy of destruction by Uriah. Again, Rashi presupposes the equation of the Isaian Zechariah with the later prophet Zechariah.

R. Abraham Ibn Ezra also draws upon this understanding in his commentary on Isa 8:2. He does not relate the equation in detail, but simply states that Uriah was then the high priest, that Zechariah was a great human being, and that the statements of the sages concerning the prophecies of Uriah and Zechariah are well known. His statement that Uriah was then the high priest explains why the priest Uriah in Isa 8:2 and the prophet Uriah in Jer 26:20-23 should be considered as the same man. His reference to the sages of course refers to the above-cited talmudic tradition in *b. Mak.* 24. His reference to Zechariah as a great human being is somewhat enigmatic with respect to chronology, but it does indicate that Ibn Ezra views Isaiah's Zechariah and the prophet of the book of Zechariah as one and the same person.

Radak builds on Rashi's position with a much more extensive commentary on Isa 8:2. He likewise notes the identification of Isaiah's Uriah the priest and Zechariah ben Yeberechyahu with Jeremiah's Uriah ben Shemaiah and Zechariah ben Berechiah ben Iddo with much the same phraseology and citations as Rashi and Ibn Ezra, but he adds references to Isaiah's later commands to "bind up the testimony and seal the Torah among my teachings" in Isa 8:16 so that they might be read and realized in the future. He states that although Uriah and Zechariah were from the time of Isaiah, the talmudic sages (i.e., *b. Mak.* 24) certify that in fact they spoke at different times as indicated by the later witnesses to their prophecy in the books of Jeremiah and Zechariah. Indeed, it is striking that Radak wrestles with the chronological implications of this claim. He states in the introduction to his commentary on Isaiah that God sent other prophets in the days of Isaiah, including Amos, Zechariah, and Hosea. He also states in his commentary on Zech 1:1 that "the term 'prophet' (נביא) refers to Zechariah, apparently a reference to his earlier equation of the Isaian figure with the prophet Zechariah, and his statement that "it is possible that Iddo was also a prophet" links Zechariah's (grand)father Iddo to the author of the words of Iddo mentioned in reference to the reign of Rehoboam in 2 Chr 12:15. Certainly, the figures of Rehoboam, Isaiah, and Zechariah span a period of some four hundred years, and scholars have long recognized Radak's tendency to compress time in his understanding of historical events — he was after all fundamentally a grammarian, philosopher, and exegete, not a historian.[12] Nevertheless, Radak's placement of the prophecy of Zechariah's (grand)father Iddo in the days of Rehoboam and the writing of Zechariah's prophecy in the days of Isaiah allows him to construct a temporal sequence that reinforces the notion that Zechariah's (and Uriah's) prophecy is well known prior to its realization in the Second Temple period. Again, the Isaian Zechariah ben Yeberechyahu and the prophet Zechariah ben Berechiah ben Iddo are one and the same person in Radak's view.

Although one can hardly conclude on historical grounds that Isaiah's Zechariah ben Yeberechyahu and the prophet Zechariah ben Berechiah ben Iddo were the same person, the recognition of some relationship between the two figures in Targum Jonathan, the Babylonian Talmud, and in the commentaries of Rashi, Ibn Ezra, and Radak is noteworthy. Given the extensive use of the book of Isaiah in Zechariah, it would appear that the rendering of the prophet's name as Zechariah ben Berechiah ben Iddo, in contrast to Zechariah ben/bar Iddo in Ezra 5:1 and 6:14, may have been a deliberate attempt by the author of Zechariah to equate the prophet with the Isaian figure.[13]

---

12. See, e.g., Talmage, *David Kimhi*, 115, who points to Radak's understanding of the chronology of Judg 18–21 that requires him to follow midrashic tradition in concluding that Phineas was three hundred years old.

13. A similar conflation of figures from two very different historical periods appears in LXX 3 Kgdms 12:240, in which the prophet Shemaiah the Enlamite *(Samaian ton Enlami)* delivers the dynastic oracle to Jeroboam ben Nebat. Shemaiah thereby replaces Ahijah the Shilonite who delivers the oracle to Jeroboam in MT 1 Kgs 11:29-39 and LXX 3 Kgdms 11:29-39. Most interpreters assume that Shemaiah is the same prophet who tells Rehoboam not to go to battle against Jeroboam in 1 Kgs 12:22-24, but the name *Samaion ton Enlami* apparently transliterates *šĕma'yāhû hannehĕlāmî*, "Shemaiah the Nehelamite," the false prophet mentioned in Jeremiah's letter to the exiles (Jer 29:24-29). The so-called LXX B account of 3 Kgdms 12:24a-z thereby attributes Jeroboam's dynastic oracle to a false prophet, which undermines his claims to the throne of northern Israel (cf. Zipora Talshir, *The Alternative Story: 3 Kingdoms 12:24a-z* [Jerusalem Biblical Studies 6; Jerusalem: Simor, 1993], 105).

## IV

Scholars have long noted that the book of Zechariah makes extensive use of earlier biblical tradition from both the Pentateuch and the Prophets. Indeed, the Prophets are well represented in the introduction to the book that refers to the attempts by the former prophets to convince the people to return to YHWH. One might also note Zechariah's citation of Jeremiah's prophecies in Jer 25:11 and 29:10 that the Babylonian exile would last for some seventy years, and the references to Zerubbabel or Joshua ben Jehozadak as the "branch" (Zech 3:8; 6:12), reflecting earlier statements in Jer 23:5 and 33:15 that refer to the future righteous Davidic monarch as the "branch." The prophets are also well represented throughout Zechariah 7–14,[14] and the prophet Isaiah is particularly well represented in these chapters to the extent that some early modern critics even argued that Zechariah 9–14 represented the earlier work of Isaiah or at least that of the Isaian figure Zechariah ben Yeberechyahu.[15] Although this hypothesis can hardly be accepted, it is apparent that Zechariah 7–14 indicates a major interest in the prophets and especially in the Isaian tradition.

Zechariah's interest in Isaiah appears in chaps. 7–8, which relate the question concerning the need for continued mourning for the loss of the temple now that it is to be rebuilt. After questioning whether the requirement for mourning was indeed authorized by YHWH, the narrative in 7:4-7 reports Zechariah's initial answer that the time for rejoicing has come instead, and that such rejoicing was authorized by the former prophets. Zech 7:8-14 reiterates the rationale for punishment as the people refused to listen to the former prophets. Zech 8:1-17 then relates a number of quotations from and allusions to the words of various prophets, including Jeremiah, Haggai, and especially Isaiah, who appears to be the source for the statements of YHWH's zeal for Zion (Zech 8:1-2; Isa 9:6 [Eng. 7]); that Jerusalem will once again be called a righteous city (Zech 8:3; Isa 1:21-26); that old men and old women will once

14. In addition to the commentaries cited above, see also W. A. M. Beuken, *Haggai-Sacharja 1–8: Studien zur Überlieferungsgeschichte der frühnachexilischen Prophetie* (SSN 10; Assen: Van Gorcum, 1967); Albert Petitjean, *Les Oracles du Proto-Zacharie* (EBib; Paris: Gabalda; Louvain: Éditions Imprimerie Orientaliste, 1969); R. A. Mason, "The Use of Earlier Biblical Material in Zech 9–14 (A Study in Inner-Biblical Exegesis)" (Ph.D. diss., Univ. of London, 1973); K. Larkin, *The Eschatology of Second Zechariah: A Study of the Formation of a Mantological Wisdom Anthology* (CBET 6; Kampen: Kok Pharos, 1994); Nicholas Ho Fai Tai, *Prophetie als Schriftauslegung in Sacharja 9–14: Traditions- und kompositionsgeschichtliche Studien* (Calwer theologische Monographien 17; Stuttgart: Calwer, 1996).

15. See Y. M. Grintz, "Zechariah," *EncJud* 16:953-58, esp. 958, which ascribes this conjecture to Berthold as early as 1814.

again sit in the streets of Jerusalem (Zech 8:4-5; cf. Isa 65:20); the references to the remnant of the people (of Israel) who will witness restoration (Zech 8:6; cf. vv. 11-12); the bringing of a deliverer from the east (Zech 8:7-8; Isa 41:2; 41:25); the references to new growth in the land (Zech 8:12; Isa 1:29-31; 6:11-13; 11:1-16; 37:30-32; 40:1-11; 41:17-20; etc.); and so on.

The culmination of this interest in the early words of comfort by the prophets — and especially by Isaiah — appears in Zech 8:19-23, which relates the interest of the nations in coming to Zion to seek YHWH and to join with Jews because they have heard that YHWH is with them (cf. Isa 7:14). The language and imagery of this passage draw heavily on the idyllic image of the nations streaming to Jerusalem to seek YHWH with the result that they will turn their swords into plowshares and their spears into pruning hooks so that they will learn war no more. This vision has a prominent place at the outset of the book of Isaiah in 2:2-4, but it is noteworthy that the Zecharian citations of the passage do not correspond to the Isaian version, but to the version in Mic 4:1-5. This is particularly noteworthy in that the Mican version of this passage introduces a sequence in Micah 4–5 in which the nations will first oppress and exile Israel, and then Israel under the leadership of its new righteous Davidic monarch will attack, defeat, and subjugate the nations, resulting in the idyllic scenario articulated in 4:1-5. This stands in striking contrast to the Isaian version of the passage, which presupposes that Israel will join the nations in seeking YHWH and that both the nations and Israel will share in punishment from YHWH as they are purified and prepared for the idyllic vision of Isa 2:2-4.[16]

It is also striking that the scenario by which this idyllic situation is achieved in Zechariah 9–14 draws heavily on Isaian texts and imagery. Ultimately, its portrayal of Jerusalem's and Israel's combat against the nations prior to their submission to YHWH corresponds to the Mican scenario by which world peace is achieved, not to the Isaian version that posits mutual punishment from YHWH for both Israel and the nations. This suggests that the Zecharian scenario by which YHWH's worldwide sovereignty is recognized is deliberately intended to differ from that articulated by Isaiah. In effect, Zechariah engages in debate with Isaiah and differs concerning the means by which YHWH's sovereignty is established and recognized throughout the world. Instead of positing the scenario of mutual punishment from YHWH for both Israel and the nations as articulated in Isaiah, Zechariah follows Micah's scenario of combat between Israel and the nations that results ultimately in world peace.

16. For discussion of these perspectives, see Marvin A. Sweeney, "Micah's Debate with Isaiah," *JSOT* 93 (2001): 111-24. See also idem, *Isaiah 1–39*; idem, *Twelve Prophets*, ad loc.

The use of Isaian imagery appears already in the portrayal of the righteous king's approach to Jerusalem in Zechariah 9. Although many maintain that the reference to Greece in Zech 9:13 indicates that the chapter depicts Alexander the Great's approach to Jerusalem, the itinerary varies from that of Alexander and corresponds much more closely to the itinerary of the Assyrian kings mentioned in Isa 10:5-34 and Isaiah 36.[17] Indeed, this itinerary provides an important part of the basis for those who would claim that elements of Zechariah 9–14 are to be dated to the time of Isaiah. It is noteworthy that in the Isaian itineraries the route from Aram through Phoenicia and Philistia was a route by which Israel was conquered and subjugated to the Assyrians; the route in Zechariah becomes the route by which the righteous king approaches Jerusalem to redeem it from the oppression of enemy nations.

Isaian imagery continues to play a major role in Zechariah 10–11, which relates YHWH's calls for the removal of the shepherds who rule the people. After stating that the people wander like sheep for lack of a shepherd, Zechariah states the intention to punish the leaders so that the people of Judah and Joseph will be strengthened. The scenario continues with YHWH's signaling for the restoration of the exiled people from Assyria and Egypt; this of course employs the imagery of Isaiah 11, which envisions the restoration of Israel's and Judah's exiles at the time when a righteous Davidic monarch will ascend to the throne. It concludes with a symbolic act by the prophet, who dismisses three shepherds in the temple and dons the implements of a worthless shepherd to symbolize the incompetent leadership of the people. Most scholars presuppose that this material criticizes the Jewish leadership of the people in the postexilic period, but several observations are in order: (1) the use of Isaiah 11 in this passage points to the restoration of righteous Davidic rule; (2) the term "shepherd" in Isaiah never denotes a Jewish monarch, but it is employed in reference to the Persian king Cyrus ("my shepherd," Isa 44:28), who is also designated as YHWH's messiah and temple builder in Isa 44:28;

17. Alexander marched along the southern coast of Asia Minor and defeated the Persians at Issus, located at the point where the eastern Mediterranean coast turns to the south. He reportedly sent an expedition to Damascus, but led the bulk of his army south along the Mediterranean coast into Phoenicia (see Martin Hengel, "The Political and Social History of Palestine from Alexander to Antiochus III [333-187 B.C.E.]," in *CHJ*, vol. 2, *The Hellenistic Age* [ed. W. D. Davies and L. Finkelstein; Cambridge: Cambridge Univ. Press, 1989], 35-78, esp. 35-45). By contrast, Zech 9 indicates an itinerary that begins in northern Syria, i.e., Hadrach, Damascus, and Hamath, which corresponds generally to the Isaian depiction of the routes taken by the Assyrian kings in their invasions of the land of Israel (see Isa 10:5-34; 36:13-21). When read in relation to the return of the righteous king in Zech 9:9-10, the itinerary suggests the route by which the new Davidic king would return to Jerusalem from exile in Mesopotamia.

45:1; and (3) the symbolic dismissal of three shepherds likely refers to the failure of the first three Persian monarchs, Cyrus, Cambyses, and Darius, to bring about YHWH's plans for world peace as articulated in Isaiah. The concluding curse against the worthless shepherd in Zech 11:17, that a sword may strike his arm and that his right eye may become dim, apparently takes up Isaian references to YHWH's grasping the right hand of the "shepherd" Cyrus in Isa 45:1 and statements that YHWH's servant is a dim wick that will not be quenched (Isa 42:3-4). It would appear that Zechariah 10–11 disputes Isaiah's contention that YHWH's messiah Cyrus, and indeed the Persian kings at large, would bring about the restoration of the people and the city of Jerusalem as the center for YHWH's worldwide sovereignty.

Finally, Zechariah 12–14 lays out the scenario of combat against the nations that will take place on the day of YHWH. Indeed, the "day of YHWH" is one of the most prominent motifs of the book of Isaiah; following the idyllic picture in which Israel is invited to join the nations who seek YHWH at Zion in Isa 2:2-5, Isa 2:6-21 describes a scenario of worldwide judgment in which YHWH will punish all who are arrogant on the day of YHWH. The motif appears at several key points afterward (e.g., Isa 13; 34; etc.), and the constant references to "that day" in the first part of the book demonstrate its pervasive role. But whereas Isaiah envisions a cooperative effort in which YHWH's Torah and justice will go out to the nations who will then return the exiles of Israel and Judah to Jerusalem, Zechariah 12–14 envisions a scenario in which Judah and Jerusalem will engage in combat against the nations of the world that threaten them, most notably against the shepherd associated with YHWH, until Judah and the house of David are purified and the nations acknowledge YHWH's sovereignty by worshiping at the temple at Sukkot. At that point the book of Zechariah closes with the assertion that Jerusalem and Judah will then constitute the holy center of the world.

Again, Zechariah challenges Isaiah's assertion that YHWH's purposes are to be accomplished through the rule of the Persian monarchs. Instead, the book envisions a scenario in which foreign rule is overthrown, and Judah and Jerusalem are purified to serve as the holy center for YHWH's worldwide sovereignty.

## V

In conclusion, it appears that a synchronic reading of the book, coupled with the observation made by the Targum, Talmud, Rashi, Ibn Ezra, and Radak that Zechariah ben Berechiah ben Iddo is to be associated with the Isaian figure Zechariah ben Yeberechyahu, points to a deliberate attempt by the author of the book of Zechariah to challenge or debate key elements of Isaiah's vision for the establishment of YHWH's sovereignty throughout the world. Whereas Isaiah envisions a cooperative effort between the nations and Israel in which the Persian king, Cyrus, will act as YHWH's messiah and temple builder, the book of Zechariah envisions the overthrow of foreign rule and the reinstitution of a purified Judah and house of David as a result of the reestablishment of the temple in Jerusalem. This of course points to debate within Judaism, particularly within the prophetic tradition, during the early Persian period concerning the significance of the temple's restoration and the continuity of foreign rule. Whereas parties centered on the Isaian tradition, such as Ezra and Nehemiah, would have advocated submission to and cooperation with the ruling Persian authorities as the appropriate means to realize YHWH's sovereignty in the world, other parties centered on the Mican and Zecharian traditions, such as Haggai and perhaps Zerubbabel, would have looked forward to the overthrow of Persian rule as the final step prior to the establishment of YHWH's sovereignty on earth.[18]

## The Book of Zechariah

*Structure Analysis*

18. Earlier versions of this paper were presented at the annual meeting of the Association for Jewish Studies, Chicago, Dec. 19-21, 1999; the Claremont Bible Lectures, Claremont School of Theology, Claremont, CA, March 27-28, 2000; the Methodist Theological Seminary, Seoul, May 17, 2000; and the University of Pretoria, July 20, 2000. I would like to thank Prof. Marc Brettler, Association for Jewish Studies Program Chair in Bible; Associate Dean Karen Dalton, Claremont School of Theology; Prof. Tai-il Wang, Methodist Theological Seminary, Seoul; and Prof. Jan G. Van Der Watt, University of Pretoria, for their efforts in making these presentations possible. In addition, I would like to thank Ehud Ben Zvi for his pointers in reading medieval Hebrew texts.